COMPUTERS AND DATA PROCESSING: Introduction with *BASIC*

COMPUTERS AND DATA PROCESSING: Introduction with BASIC

THIRD EDITION

KEITH CARVER
Sacramento City College

JOHN WILEY & SONS
New York   Chichester
Brisbane   Toronto   Singapore

Production Supervisor	Jan M. Lavin
Manuscript Editor	Susan Giniger
Cover Photography	Stephen Green-Armytage.
Technical Art	Blaise Zito Associates, Inc.

Library of Congress Cataloging in Publication Data

Carver, D. K.
    Computers and data processing.

    Rev. ed. of: Introduction to business data processing.
2nd ed. © 1979.
    Includes index.
    1.   Electronic data processing.   2.   Business—Data
processing.   3.   Basic Computer program language)
I.   Title.

QA76.C3619   1983   001.64   82-15956

ISBN 0-471-09834-5

Printed in the United States of America

10 9 8 7 6 5 4 3 2 1

To my wife June, who did all the typing and most of the suffering through this book.

PREFACE

This edition of *Computers and Data Processing: Introduction with BASIC*, 3rd ed. is significantly different from its predecessor, *Introduction to Business Data Processing*, 2nd ed. As the title implies, the text recognizes that computers are no longer just the tool of business and industry. The age of the computer is rapidly becoming the "age of the microcomputer." The chances are very good that many of you already own your own computer, or certainly have access to one.

Over the years we have seen a steady increase in the level of sophistication, the computer "savvy," so to speak, of our beginning students. More of you have had access to computers prior to coming into class. This fact brings us to one of the difficulties with any beginning-level book: How do you make it suitable for both the absolute beginner and the student who has his or her own personal computer? How do you orient a text toward the student who will take only the beginning course and the student for whom this is merely the first step in a long line of courses in computers? This edition is designed to satisfy both these needs.

The key word that can be applied to the text is "exposure"—to the ideas, terminology, and methods of a science that has captured the imagination of the world. It contains the basic information that you need to be truly "computer literate" in today's society. Chapter 1, Computers and Society, describes the place of computers in our society; what it means to be computer literate; what effect automation can have on you; and what you can expect from increased computer use in our world.

Chapter 2, Data Processing in Perspective, puts the use of the computer into historical perspective. Chapter 3, Computers and the DP Cycle, describes the basic elements of a computer system and, in general, how they work. This is done early in the text so that you will observe computers in use in places and situations that you had not noticed before.

Chapter 4, Data Entry Methods, takes you to where it all begins—the entry of data into the computer. By the end of this chapter you should be able to recognize that this is where automation originates. The next two chapters—Chapter 5, The Central Processing Unit, and Chapter 6, More About the Central Processing Unit—show how the computer works internally. The point to be gained here is that this is the general way in which all computers work, whether large or small.

Chapter 7, Computer Input and Output, acquaints you with both the traditional and the newer, more sophisticated forms that are available today. Computer inputs and outputs are going through turbulent times in which each new method is improved upon so rapidly that today's technology is soon outdated. The advent of talking calculators, computers that listen, color video screens and color drawings in three dimensions are just a few examples.

Chapter 8, Auxiliary Storage Media, and Chapter 9, File Access Methods, discuss topics which, although more familiar, are still an integral and exciting area of computer use. Dynamic changes are going on in storage technology—changes that will affect you more directly than you can imagine. We are living in a time when our desire for data of all kinds has grown into an obsession. But we must have someplace to store all this data and methods to access it, otherwise all our efforts to collect and catalog it will have been wasted.

In Chapter 10, Computer Software, we explore the software or programs that make the computer do our bidding. How do you write a program? Chapter 11, Problem Solving with the Computer, takes you through the step-by-step process. In this chapter you will learn that programmers work by careful analysis of a problem and great attention to detail.

Chapter 12, BASIC Programming—Part I, and Chapter 13, BASIC Programming—Part II, introduce you to actual programming using the BASIC language. These two chapters amount to a complete text in BASIC themselves. There should be no need to buy a BASIC textbook as a supplement. As these two chapters explain, the BASIC language has not been standardized. This means that when you work on your own personal computer you might have to make some changes to the program, but they will be minor. Whenever you get the chance, try running the programs shown in the book, make your own variations, or try to work out the 45 BASIC problems to be solved on the Computer which are located at the end of each of these two chapters.

In Chapter 14, Small Computer Systems, you take a look at the world of small computers with its falling prices, increased capabilities, and rising speeds. Are you interested in buying your own microcomputer? Appendix B, Buying a Microcomputer, outlines some of the questions to ask yourself and the salesperson *before* you buy. In addition, this appendix briefly profiles three of the most popular microcomputers: Radio Shack, IBM, and Apple. Chapter 15, Data Communications, is a look at an area which in recent years has become difficult to distinguish from data processing.

Chapter 16, Data Base Systems, deals with a topic that we have heard so much about: data banks. Here you will get a glimpse of what these are, and why business, industry, and the government are setting up systems that can access massive amounts of data.

Chapter 17, Office Automation, is particularly important because business is finally realizing that word processing and data processing are remarkably similar—that they are two sides of the same coin. This awareness is evidenced not only in the large computer systems but in the microcomputers that can process words and data with equal ease.

Chapter 18, Systems Considerations, is directed toward management and its feeling for and use of data processing methods and facilities.

Support materials that accompany the text include an Instructor's Manual, a Student Workbook, transparencies, Slides and Slide Manual, Tests Book, and a computerized version of the Tests.

I want to express my thanks to the many users whose comments and suggestions contributed to this new edition. I especially want to thank the following reviewers for the greatly appreciated suggestions and refinements during the developmental stage of this text: Dr. David Whitney, San Francisco State University, Professor Gregory G. Hardesty, Sullivan Junior College of Business; Professor Jerry Kinard, Southeastern Louisiana University; Professor Richard Manthei, Joliet Junior College, and Professor Elvin H. "Al" Campbell, Golden West College, who also prepared the Student Workbook.

Keith Carver

CONTENTS

COMPUTERS AND DATA PROCESSING: Introduction with BASIC

CHAPTER 1 COMPUTERS IN SOCIETY

LEARNING OBJECTIVES

Upon completion of the chapter you should understand the following:

How technology has grown in recent years; the driving forces behind this phenomenom.

The impact of the technology of automation upon you individually and upon society as a whole.

The compelling need for computer literacy.

What effect automation may have upon individual privacy and what can be done about it.

The extent and nature of the problem of computer crime and what can be done about it.

What the career fields are within the data processing industry and the tasks that will be expected of you.

The current and prospective growth of information technology is the most important development society has experienced since the automobile, the cotton gin and the steam engine.

Infosystems, January 1980

CHAPTER CONTENTS

THE GROWTH OF TECHNOLOGY

Anthony J. Weiner, a noted futurist, wrote about "Computers and the Future of America" and said

The computer revolution is the most advertized revolution in world history. Yet one of the funny things about it is that we probably still underestimate its impact.[1]

What is most interesting about that statement is that it was made in 1977. Looking back from today's position we can see that Weiner was exactly right. Despite all our best guesses about the future effect of computers upon our lives, we are still underestimating its impact. It would seem that the word "revolution" was well chosen. Visible evidence of the changes are all around us. For example, today approximately one half of the U.S. labor force is engaged in some aspect of the information industry. Over 90% of business-related jobs involve direct or indirect contact with a computer.

The rate of change in computer technology is so fast that it dwarfs one's imagination. Consider some of these points.

If the same proportional increase in speed and decrease in price had taken place in the transportation industry over the same period (1950 to 1980) a coast to coast flight would now cost about two cents and take less than a second.[2]

microelectronics → branch of electronics that deals w/
the miniaturization of electronic circuits & components.
quantum → elemental unit of energy.
mammoth → immense, vast, great size.

COMPUTERS IN SOCIETY **3**

(Courtesy Infosystems)

- SEE THE COMPUTER
- SEE THE BIG COMPUTER
- SEE THE BIG FAST COMPUTER

"This looks like a pretty fundamental course!"

© INFOSYSTEMS

Another way of putting it is that in 1957, according to one report, the *total* power of all the computers in the United States was about 10 million instructions per second. By 1982, that figure could be exceeded by a *single* large-scale computer.[3]

Microelectronics have been the driving force behind this quantum technological leap. Today's microcomputer (a topic to be covered in a later chapter) that costs $100 has approximately the same computing capability of a mammoth computer that cost one million dollars in 1950. Of course, you, the reader, can sit back and say "That is all very well, but surely things will have to slow down—technology can't always progress at this rate." You are right, this growth rate could slow down, but all the evidence indicates that, if anything, this rate of change will *increase*, not decrease.

But now the important question is, How do you and I—how do all of us—deal with this change? We live in a computerized society and, whether we like it or not, it is going to become more and more computerized. Let's take a look at what this can mean to us—how all this change will affect us.

pervasive → spread to every part of

THE IMPACT ON SOCIETY

Part of the reason that the impact of computers on society is so great is the fact that computers are getting smaller, cheaper, faster, and more reliable. Already they are an indispensable way of life. They are all pervasive; i.e., they have filtered into almost every aspect of our lives, and the only safe assumption is that they will continue to do so at an even greater rate in the future.

In 1951, about 30 years ago, the first general-purpose computer was installed by the Bureau of Census. This time period corresponds to the life maturation cycle of today's adults. Thus, one whole generation of Americans has been raised in a computer environment. The psychological impact of this fact is of enormous importance because ever-increasing numbers of us are thinking in terms of computers.

How are we using computers? A better question would be to ask how are we *not* using them. Through technology we have been able to put all the functioning parts of a computer onto a single silicon chip that is smaller than a thumbnail. When this chip and its related components are installed in your car's carburetion system, you have what we call a "smart" or "intelligent" device (Figures 1.1 and 1.2).

This same technology has given us "smart" sewing machines where the press of a button determines the stitch pattern that will be sewn; low-price computer video games; hand-held devices that play chess with us (and may win more often than not); electronic typewriters that correct spelling mistakes before reproducing the letter—the list is endless.

For example, Figure 1.3 shows an electronic flash subassembly for a Eastman Kodak camera. The device is equipped with a light-sensitive integrated-circuit chip and preprogrammed intelligence. It automat-

FIGURE 1.1
Computer on a chip.

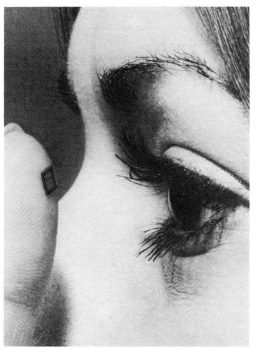

FIGURE 1.2
Computerized engine control.

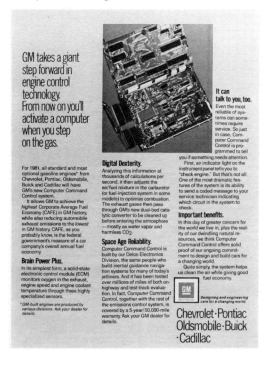

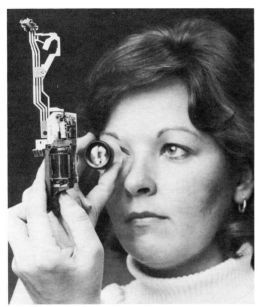

FIGURE 1.3
"Intelligent" camera element.

ically monitors lighting conditions, decides whether a flash is needed, and supplies the light. In effect, you have a computerized camera.

But the list does not stop there, as the technology is being extended into an amazing number of areas. For example, witness the incredible boom in the sales of electronic games, particularly during the Christmas season. Not only do these games (chess, checkers, video games, etc.) seriously challenge, and often beat the user, but many of them have the capability of voice output. The latter feature will be discussed in detail later in the text; still, these games defy our imaginative powers. Ten years ago, who would have thought that computer-driven games would be sold for under $10 today?

A spin-off of the games will be with us soon—automobiles that contain sensor-triggered computerized speech units that will verbally alert the driver to potential problems such as a low fuel condition, low oil pressure, incorrect battery charging rate, etc.

The top-of-the-line computer games use your home television as an output device for the system. Mattel's Intelligent Television System offers a variety of preprogrammed packages that include math games, sports, logical judgment, and even family financial planning. Then, too, some of these new intelligent devices outgrew their game status when manufacturers realized that users were becoming more aware of computer capabilities. Tandy-Radio Shack's TRS-80 programmable color computer offers true computing power through a keyboard computer that connects to your television set (Figure 1.4).

FIGURE 1.4
TRS-80 color computer.

Probably the first encounter most of us have had with computers is through our interactions with large corporations and the way they process data. Banks, department stores, grocery stores, the telephone company, utility companies, etc., all use computers to transact business on the spot, that is, as it occurs. As a matter of fact, once these firms have gone into automation, it is highly unlikely that they will ever revert back to the "good old days" of the precomputer society. Instead, they will continue to make more and more use of this electronic tool.

But a newer, and perhaps greater, revolution is on its way: It's the second part of the computer revolution brought about by the merger of computer and communications technology. We are a nation that is dominated by information. Industry has an overwhelming need to acquire and disseminate information to widely dispersed locations. A later chapter will show how the methods and hardware of both data processing and communications have been integrated into a combination that will be the way of the 1980s.

Remote data processing using small typewriterlike terminal devices will mean that more and more of us—businesses and individuals alike—will have access to the power of the computer. Through networks of terrestrial and satellite communication stations, data processing capability will be available almost everywhere. For example, a concept called Viewdata or Videotext is underway right now in France and parts of the United States. It ties together the local telephone, your TV set, and the computer. By dialing a local number you can have pages of data displayed on the screen. The ultimate goal of the operation in France is to eliminate the annual expense of printing telephone books for every home. Of course, information retrieval through this system is not limited to the telephone book: the system offers the potential of delivering customized information into the home and office. An extension of the French Videotext is Teletel Videotext Service which has begun on a trial basis. For the price of a single call, the user can call up and see video information on a variety of services such as news reports, restaurant reservations, airline and railroad tickets, stock quotations, etc.

Many applications are heir apparent to this new and powerful force. In fact, almost all areas of society have urgent needs that can be addressed by the combined computer/communications technology. But a question must be asked. Have we, as a society, outstripped our own ability to assimilate this new technology and all its implications? If you aren't already aware of it, computer technology can be a double-edged sword. What will be the effects of automation? If knowledge of computers is necessary to "survive," how do I acquire literacy in data processing? What about personal privacy in an impersonal world? Who controls access to computer data? How secure is that data from accidental or deliberate tampering or destruction?

AUTOMATION AND YOU

To the average person, data processing is sometimes discouraging in its complexity, often frightening in its power, and occasionally rewarding in its results. Most people know that data processing affects them, but they are not yet completely sure it is a good thing. Typically, someone will remember the few times something went wrong with their "computerized bills" rather than the hundreds or thousands of times the operation worked correctly. Then, too, the average person is concerned about rapidly becoming more and more involved with data processing, and he or she is not sure they approve of that either.

For some, the sheer frustration of having to deal with a highly automated society has brought out some bizarre instances of human behavior. In California, a sheriff shot a computer for uncontrollably spewing forth arrest records. A Minneapolis citizen took exception to a computer's actions by pouring honey into the terminals, and a New York computer was attacked by a screwdriver-wielding malcontent. Professor Sanford Weinberg of St. Joseph's University has been doing research since 1979 on Cyberphiliacs (those who are compulsive computer programmers). For some, the phobia keeps workers from functioning at their best and may cause the classic symptoms of "nausea, sweaty palms and high blood pressure. One of the major causes of the phobia is the feeling that you have lost control."[4] Both the University of Minnesota and the Massachusetts Institute of Technology are now training managers to cope with employees who can't handle computer stress.

IN URBAN PLANNING COURSE STUDENTS TAKE REINS OF CPU-RESIDENT 'CITY'
By Deborah Wise
CW Staff

LOS ANGELES—Apex City, population 250,000, is run by 150 University of Southern California (USC) students who make policy decisions, plan budgets, provide services and monitor their results over a five-year-period—all in the course of one semester.

The city exists in the university computer. Those students who enroll in "Public Administration 220—Simulated Policy Making in Urban Systems: Theory and Practice" assume the roles of the city's decision makers and try to govern Apex City.

The program, now used in more than 100 colleges in the U.S. and seven foreign countries, was developed in 1974 by researchers at the University of Michigan and USC. The data base was established by combining several environmental and urban planning prediction models which were then enlarged over the years to create a comprehensive information base on which a city's governmental decisions could be based.

"They linked these models so as to demonstrate their cross-impact effect," explained Dick McGinty, executive director of USC's Center for Multidisciplinary Educational Exercises (Comex) and a class instructor.

Strategies as Input

At the beginning of the semester, the students assume roles as politicians, urban planners, environmentalists, journalists or members of different interest groups. They attend lectures on various policy theories and then devise their own strategies for Apex City. The instructors input these strategies into the computer at the end of class. Each class session represents one year in the life of the city.

Like all new technologies that have a direct effect on society in general, automation is seen as both a curse and a blessing. On the one hand, it promotes increased production, cuts down on waste, and raises our standard of living. On the other hand, some people feel automation is dehumanizing the social process in a number of ways and that it results in a higher rate of unemployment. The truth lies somewhere between these extremes.

In the 1950s there were serious cries that widespread unemployment

At the beginning of the next class, the computer generates a printout newspaper called *Metro-Apex News* that reports the impacts of the previous year's policies.

For example, if the budget was cut, there may be a headline in the paper to the effect that crime rates have risen because of the decrease in number of police. Through the process, students become aware of the tertiary effect of their policy decisions as well as such immediate impacts as financial crises, McGinty said.

This method of practical application of theoretical principles has proved successful at USC, he maintained, noting that students become more involved in the class when they can actually influence the direction of the city's administration.

Civics Course

"The course is a basic and valuable civics course that teaches students how to become effective citizens and public administrators by producing hands-on experiences," McGinty said.

Government agencies such as the Department of Trade and the Department of Defense have used the simulation program to test prospective policies. However, McGinty said its use in the classroom is intended less for formulating predictions than for getting the students involved in running a city.

The program was written in Fortran and runs on IBM 360 mainframes, but it can be adapted to other systems, according to McGinty. In addition, it can be used in various configurations for different classes. At Cornell University, for example, students themselves put the information into the computer and vary the programs.

would result from the application of electronic computers to routine clerical tasks. Of course, machine processing of data had been going on since the turn of the century, but the awesome speed and power of this new device reawakened the fears of the past. At the time, these fears had some validity because computer usage was aimed directly at the routine clerical tasks that were easy to automate. Even at the clerical level, very few people were "fired" because of the installation of computer systems. In most instances it was a case of "not hiring" rather than firing.

According to a 1980 Department of Labor study, fear of job losses due to automation have simply not been borne out by the figures. Employment of clerical workers during the 1960–1980 period increased about 85%. The report conceded that automation in *some* industries has eliminated jobs and forced workers to upgrade their skills. But the number of people required to manage, operate, program, service, and handle the input to and output from computer systems was far beyond anyone's imagination at the time. In effect, we created a whole new industry with an almost insatiable need for new workers.

Why is the demand so great? Part of the reason lies in the fact that "the introduction of computers made possible work that was previously impractical, because it would have been too costly and would have taken too long by precomputer technology."[5]

Another part of this demand can be attributed to our population boom of the 1950s and early 1960s coupled with our desire for a higher and higher standard of living. According to Alvin Toffler, author of *Future Shock* and *The Third Wave*, this change is worldwide. He says that the new civilization that is growing out of the existing social and technological society will stress, among other things, decentralization over collectivization and smallness over bigness. This, in turn, is increasing the need for improved communication among the newly formed fragments of the new society. To Toffler, this explains the explosive growth in the popularity of computer technology.

But where does this leave you? What if you are one of those who is threatened by automation? What is the answer? Perhaps the first line of defense is to follow the old adage that says "If you can't beat them, join them." In other words, retrain yourself to fit into our information society. Inevitably, the jobs "lost" to this new technology will be replaced by jobs that require workers with greater skills than before.

One interesting facet of this new technology is that, in a way, it feeds on itself. By that we mean that the technology can be used as a tool to train those who will have to deal with it most directly. As shown in an article in *Computerworld* newsmagazine, students at the University of Southern California can attend an environmental and urban planning course that uses the power of the computer to simulate various courses of action. They assume various roles in the policy-making process and devise various strategies to run Apex City—a city that exists solely inside the computer.

One interesting change has already come about because of this shift to a new society—satellite offices and the growth of "cottage" information industries. The integration of computer and communication technologies will encourage decentralization and the development of small local offices. To the firm the benefits are a reduction in the amount of expensive downtown office space and a happier working staff that does not have to face the traditional rush-hour commuting traffic. This trend is continuing to the point where more and more people are asking for computer terminals at home as a normal job benefit. We are seeing

©INFOSYSTEMS

"That's carrying automation a little too far!"

the rapid use of the number of part-time clerical/information-type jobs performed at home terminals linked to the corporate computer system. This change to a different work style offers unique opportunities to the handicapped who cannot travel to the job but can perform satisfactorily in the home environment.

COMPUTER LITERACY

According to many sources, we, the general public, are facing a national crisis—an illiteracy that threatens the future growth of the United States. At least, those are the views of Dr. Arthur Leuhrmann, Associate Director of the University of California Lawrence Hall of Science. He says:

Computers provide a powerful new tool for thinking about and solving real-world problems. Almost any job anyone could imagine can be done better and faster with the help of computers, and people who know how to use them have a tremendous advantage over those who don't.[6]

Yet, despite the critical importance of computer literacy, the general public knows practically nothing about the capabilities and workings of computer systems. To Leuhrmann, the ignorance of data processing is similar to the problems that followed the invention of the printing press in the 1400s. The full implication of this technological development remained unappreciated for nearly four centuries. Part of the crisis, he believes, can be solved by establishing formal computer education programs in the public schools. The National Council of Teachers of Mathematics goes on to say that schools should take advantage of the power of calculators and computers at all grade levels and that computer literacy should be a part of the education of every student. In today's society the ability to use and understand computers is as basic as reading, writing, and arithmetic (Figure 1.5).

An indication of what the future may hold in this area is indicated by what is happening in Minnesota. The Minnesota Educational Computer Consortium (MECC) connects more than 90% of the state's educational institutions to a central computer at the University of Minnesota. Although most students work on a class project basis, they are receiving instruction in the basics of computer systems. A 1979 survey of eleventh grade students showed that 56% had had hands-on experience with the system via remote terminal devices and that 35% had written at least one computer program. In Philadelphia, more than 75,000 students are served by another computer system and for them, proof of computer literacy is required for graduation from high school.

In a public library in Menlo Park, California, there are four desktop computers that can be used without any fee. They are part of a program to acquaint people with computers. Fifteen minutes of instruction teaches the people how to turn it on and off, insert a cassette tape, load a program, and respond to computer actions. The teaching assistant is 12 years old and well-qualified to hold this job. On weekends the kids line up to get their names on a sign-up book and there have been as many as 15 people waiting to use one of the machines. Mostly the users play various computer games, but games are an important learning

FIGURE 1.5
Computer on the job.

methodology in that they teach quick response, strategies, and mathematical abilities.

Although adults may have some misgivings about computers, children and the younger generation do not seem to share that problem. If anything, they revel in the technology rather than fear it. In 1979, Computer Camp ran its first summer camp for boys and girls between the ages of 10 and 15. During the two-week sessions, each participant engages in the usual camp activities of horseback riding, swimming, and tennis plus computer operations and programming. The camp provides one computer for every two campers, although many of the campers bring their own computers. The mornings are devoted to programming and computer applications and the afternoons are left open for other activities, but most campgoers prefer to spend a good amount of their free time working on advanced computer projects.

Just what is a computer? What is its makeup? How does it function? What kind of work can I do with it? All these are legitimate questions and will be answered in the following chapters. However, you probably already know the basic functions of a computer. It is an electronic device that accepts the input of data, processes it according to a predetermined pattern (a computer program) and outputs the results either for immediate use (printing) or future use by some method of storage. The physical components of a system are called *hardware* as opposed to programs, which are called *software.*

PRIVACY IN THE COMPUTER AGE

The right of privacy is the hallmark of a free society and now that right is coming under attack from a source that could never have been visualized by our founders. The very aspect of computers that makes them such a useful tool for society is the same quality that threatens our most precious right. Computers operate most effectively on large, homogeneous masses of data called *data banks* or *data bases*. Without computers, the government as we know it today would cease to function because computers are highly efficient processors of information. For example, in 1977 the Treasury Department issued 610 million checks at a cost of 2 cents per check compared to 18 cents to do the job manually.

Since the efficiency of a computer system tends to increase (and costs decrease) as the system grows larger, there is a natural tendency to gravitate toward larger and larger data banks. And, the most cost-effective way to do this is by tying together many computer systems into a network of data banks. Thus, the users do not have to generate each piece of information that is needed but can simply tie into the data bank that is developed by another agency. Theoretically, a participating agency could gain access to records stored in any of the data banks. Obviously, the potential for abuse is not only there but is exceedingly tempting.

At this point some questions need to be asked. What happens if this data falls into the wrong hands? Exactly what kind of data on individuals can be stored? By whom can this data be stored? Who is responsible for its accuracy? Who authorizes access to it? Who prevents unauthorized access?

Some years ago, the General Services Administration proposed putting together a computer network called FEDNET that would include virtually every modern computer in the government. The project was abandoned when the public and Congress reacted adversely to the announcement. Similar projects developed by other government agencies have been opposed as threats to privacy and a violation of civil liberties.

How extensive are these data banks? According to *U.S. News and World Report* (April 10, 1978):

Some 3.9 billion records on individuals now are stored in the personal-data systems of 97 federal agencies, according to reports filed under the Privacy Act of 1974. Most of the records are available at the touch of a button and, in combination with records of other agencies, can produce a full picture of the financial, medical, political and personal life of almost any American.[7]

Who maintains these data banks? According to the 1978 article these were the main federal government data banks. Note that this does not include the data stored by the individual states or by private business firms such as banks, insurance companies, etc.

THE MAIN DATA BANKS

Department of Health, Education and Welfare: 693 data systems with 1.3 billion personal records including marital, financial, health and other information on recipients of Social Security, social services, medicaid, medicare and welfare benefits.

Treasury Department: 910 data systems with 853 million records that include files on taxpayers, foreign travelers, persons deemed by the Secret Service to be potentially harmful to the President, and dealers in alcohol, firearms and explosives.

Justice Department: 175 data systems with 181 million records including information on criminals and criminal suspects, aliens, persons linked to organized crime, securities-laws violators and "individuals who relate in any manner to official FBI investigations."

Defense Department: 2,219 data systems with 321 million records pertaining to service personnel and persons investigated for such things as employment, security or criminal activity.

Department of Transportation: 263 data systems with 25 million records including information on pilots, aircraft and boat owners, and all motorists whose licenses have been withdrawn, suspended or revoked by any state.

Department of Commerce: 95 data systems with 447 million records, primarily Census Bureau data, but including files on minority businessmen, merchant seamen and others.

Department of Housing and Urban Development: 58 data systems with 27.2 million records including data on applicants for housing assistance and federally guaranteed home loans.

Veterans Administration: 52 data systems with 156 million records, mostly on veterans and dependents now receiving benefits or who got them in the past.

Department of Labor: 97 data systems with 23 million records, many involving people in federally financed work and job-training programs.

Civil Service: 14 data systems with 103 million records, mostly dealing with government employees or applicants for government jobs.

Before you panic, however, let's take a look at the other side of these large computer networks. First, just because a large data bank exists, you cannot automatically assume that the information is being abused. Under the regulations of the Privacy Act, Congress has attempted to keep track of how much personal information the various government agencies are entering into the data banks. Every agency must file an annual report of how many computers it has and how many personal records are stored in them. Second, the Freedom of Information Act gives you the right to inspect, copy, correct, or amend much of the personal information contained in most government data banks. The same act provided for the cofidentiality of personal records and identifying data. The agency must determine that no violation of privacy will result from the release of personal information to a third party.

But there are other kinds of data banks as well. Consider the network that links data banks containing information about available tissue for cornea transplants. Set up by Emory University, it ties together 18 eye banks which handle about 60% of the transplant tissue in the United States.

The National Driver Register is another interesting use of a computer data bank. Its files contain information on any person whose driving license has been withdrawn because of drunk driving or an involvement in a fatal accident. Prior to the establishment of this system, a person whose license had been revoked could simply go to a neighboring state to acquire a new one.

You are urged not to lose sight of the fact that data banks existed long before computers. Manila file folders and 3-by-5 cards have been our main storage media for years. When computers are introduced into the mix, they function simply as a new form of storage and as a device by which specific records can be retrieved quickly.

A final note on privacy. There is a growing body of thought that, in order to take advantage of the benefits of technology, the concept of privacy may have to be reevaluated or adjusted. If we are increasingly required to divulge more and more private information and if it becomes increasingly difficult to keep this data private, then perhaps we will change our ideas of the social value of certain kinds of information. Man is a very adaptable creature and may make this change gradually as we move further and further into the age of information.

But Americans are not the only people concerned about privacy and the access to information. "Trans-border data flow" is a term we are beginning to see and hear more frequently. Data (or information—the two terms are used interchangeably here) in the form of words and numbers, tends to flow beyond arbitrarily drawn land boundaries. Because the United States has led the world in computer technology, the flow of information has been from foreign countries into America. In the past this was of no great concern, but now other nations are awakening to the realization that information is a source of both wealth and power. They now realize that this inflow has resulted in enormous financial gain to our economy, and they are taking steps to rectify what might be called a "balance of information" deficit.

Most other nations have very strict privacy laws, while the United States does not. The approach being taken by many nations is that firms in their countries will not be allowed to transmit data to another country that has less strict privacy laws. In Canada, for example, the Foreign Investment Review Board prevented a large U.S. telecommunications firm from increasing its ownership percentage of a subsidiary unless the company agreed to perform the data processing tasks in Canada, rather than transferring them across the border into the United States.

Concern over the matter has been so great that the issue is being negotiated within the Organization for Economic Cooperation and Development (OECD) right now. No one knows how much all this

Color videoscreen showing graphic art.

Computers in use in the arts and sciences

Computer-generated representation of chemical structure.

Computer art at the Pompidou Centre in Paris, France.

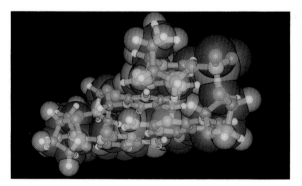

Music generated through the computer being displayed on the video screen.

Control room of automated plant.

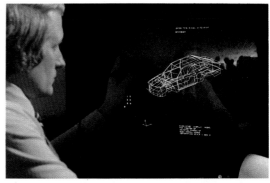

Computer Aided Design (CAD) at Ford Motor Company.

(At right) Computer-controlled cutting and sizing of lumber in a sawmill.

Computers in manufacturing

(Below) Microprocessor-controlled robot welders at the General Motors assembly plant in Lordstown, Ohio.

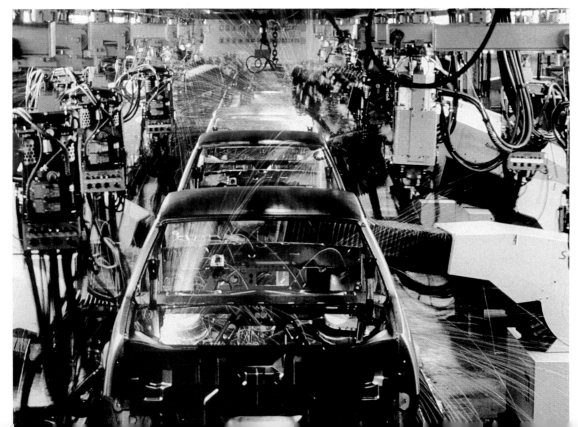

Learning to play better tennis through the computer.

Performance profile of high jumper.

Computers at use in sports

Computer simulation of high jumper's action.

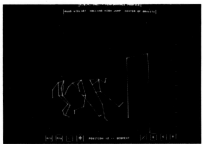

Bowling scores shown on video screen.

Computer simulation of aircraft design characteristics.

Computers at use in space

(Below) Air war technicians orchestrate a mock battle using control consoles and light sticks.

Mission Control Center, Houston, Texas.

Air traffic controller at work.

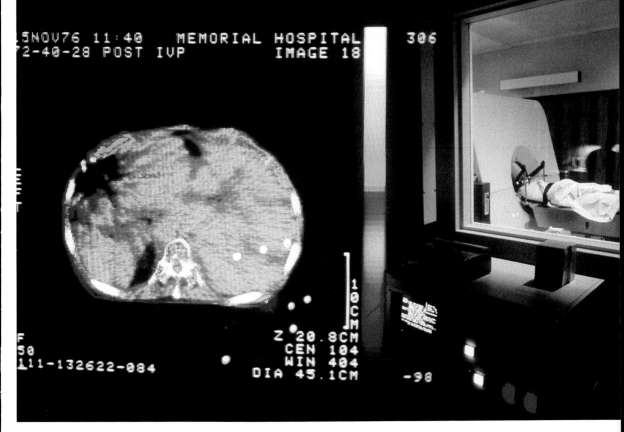

Computer-aided tomography—CAT scans at Sloan-Kettering Hospital.

Computerized blood-pool scan.

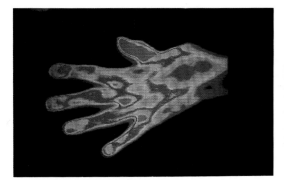

Computer-controlled sensing devices look for hot spots that indicate the presence of arthritis.

Computers and medicine

Transistorized "bionic" arm.

Children at a computer camp where they play and learn.

Preschool graphics for young learners.

Kids Love Computers!

(At left) Special educational system for retarded children.

More than one child can learn at the same time.

Word processing via computers.

Computers in the home and office

(At left) Microprocessor-controlled home appliances.

Everyone is using a computer now!

(Above) Apple II computer with color video graphics and communications capability.

Controlling lasers for manufacturing.

At the supermarket.

(At left) In shopping centers.

Computers are everywhere

At the stock market.

information is worth, but one estimate is that 80% of the world's traffic in data either originates or terminates in the United States.

SECURITY AND COMPUTER CRIME

Security is a companion to privacy and the term refers to two aspects of stored data: abuse of the data by those authorized to have access to it; and physical security in the sense of preventing destruction of or tampering with the data records. Unfortunately, remote data processing via communications links offers unique opportunities to criminals to tap into the data files of banks, insurance companies, and even the government itself.

Donn Parker, perhaps the nation's leading expert in the area of computer crime, feels that the losses through sophisticated crime will increase dramatically during the next decade. He points out that "the average haul in a computer-assisted bank fraud is $450,000, compared to $19,000 netted by manual laboring embezzler. Whenever new changes are introduced into computer technology, new opportunities immediately arise for abuses."

To meet this problem, computer security must grow along with computer technology. The problem is that the increasing complexity of computer systems and the trend toward data processing that is distributed at remote locations has put security enforcement at a severe disadvantage. Usually, the most vulnerable spot in a computer system is the actual transmission medium (a topic covered in a later chapter). For example, microwave transmission, which carries over 70% of the U.S. telephone traffic, is easily tapped. Satellite transmission is even easier to access so that encryption or coding of vital data is the only reasonable answer.

No computer system is 100% secure. In most cases, unauthorized use of the computer comes from employees who want to use the system to play various games. After that it often becomes a matter of a mental challenge to see if they can gain access to a data file that has been denied to them. In one sense, these are not true computer "crimes," although the ethics of such activities are highly questionable and can often lead to dismissal from the firm.

A U.S. Navy research team used ordinary telephones to gain access to the data bank of a computer system that had been sold to the Navy as inpenetrable. A General Accounting Office team was able to enter a "secure" Social Security facility and walk off with computer tapes containing the names and addresses of 1.1 million beneficiaries. In another case, a clerk entered fictitious food stamp claims into a computer-based welfare system and made off with $90,000 worth of stamps before being caught.

As the last example indicates, computer crime does not require extensive knowledge of computers in order to be successful. A resourceful bank teller who had a knowledge of only his own terminal in the bank was able to embezzle over $1.5 million over a period of three years. The only reason he was caught was that he was arrested during a raid on a bookie operation.

One of the major difficulties with computer crime is it is very difficult to ascertain its extent. Frequently, a company that discovers a computer-related crime is extremely reluctant to report the crime. The reason for this, of course, is that they fear the loss of public confidence and trust more than they do the loss of dollars. A second part of the problem is that there are very few laws on the books that deal specifically with computer-related crime. The laws are beginning to be developed but may be difficult to enforce unless more cooperation is forthcoming from business firms.

Another dimension to the problem is that accounting auditors and law enforcement personnel have, at best, minimal training in computer crime capabilities. The FBI recently set up a four-week course to teach its agents the rudiments of computer operations and investigative methods to deal with this type of crime. They needed to know how to investigate it, how computer fraud differs from other crimes, where the evidence is, and how to handle the evidence.

Physical security is a little easier to handle because you can isolate the equipment in special rooms and generally restrict access as well as making the usual arrangements for standby power, fire protection, and the like. Computers are beginning to become popular terrorist targets in Europe, so these protective measures are likely to be more strictly enforced in the future. For example, New York City just issued a 108-page manual covering security standards for its 20 major data processing centers.

CAREERS IN DATA PROCESSING

In some ways the nature of the data processing (DP) industry has been seriously misunderstood by the general public that often thinks of it as a robotlike, impersonal activity. Unfortunately, those who work on the fringes of DP activity frequently tend to perpetuate this impersonalism. For example, surely some of you who are reading this sentence have at one time or another had something go wrong with the customer billing process—a charge item is recorded twice or for the wrong amount or a payment is not recorded at all. When you complain to an account clerk or someone who is only remotely involved in data processing the classic response to your question of "What happened?" is "Sorry, the computer made an error!"

Most people who give any thought to this response would realize that it is a face-saving, semihumorous way to take care of a potentially embarrassing situation. A more accurate response would be that somebody—a person, a live, breathing human being made the error by entering the data incorrectly, posting it to the wrong account, or missing the transaction entirely, etc. All of this, however, is not to say that the computer *hardware* (such as printers, storage devices, circuit chips, etc.) cannot malfunction. It does, and to a degree that often infuriates operating personnel, but built-in safeguards do a fairly effective job of preventing hardware mistakes from continuing through the system.

So, a far more likely source of the error is in the people-related data processing activities. In general terms we could include those who prepare data for entry into the computer's system, programmers who make the computer perform very specific tasks, and operators who physically run the machines. Programmers are particularly involved with *software,* a broad term that includes computer programs and all the allied forms and supporting paperwork that goes into program preparation. (A later chapter will cover this development process in detail.)

Since data processing requires so many people we can begin to identify job titles and career paths for those of you who may be seriously interested in this area. A 1980 survey by National Personnel Associates, a network of technical and managerial recruitment firms, listed computer personnel at the top of 103 other occupations. Number one was computer programmers, followed by computer systems analysts, and then by electronic circuit design engineers. The reason for the surge of interest in data processing was attributed to the explosive use of small computers in almost all aspects of our lives.

In 1972 the General Services Administration of the federal government listed 10 job categories in data processing. A 1980 survey by *Datamation* magazine showed 55 job titles broken into 12 broad areas.

1. *Corporate Staff* (4 titles): Includes the top executive for all data processing and is responsible for DP advanced financial and personnel planning; usually coordinates DP activities with other corporate departments.
2. *Division or Department Staff* (4 titles): Approximately parallel to the corporate staff titles but at a lower level and with less overall influence on company policy. In both areas the term MIS (for Management Information Systems) may be included in the job titles.
3. *Systems Analysis* (5 titles): The range of titles covers from manager to trainee in this area. The systems analyst works with users to define data processing projects in terms of equipment capability, and formulates the best computer solution. The trainee position is usually filled by someone who has had prior DP experience and yet will spend much time learning the analysis process before actually producing any solutions to large or complex problems.
4. *Application Programming* (6 titles): Again, ranging from manager to trainee and team librarian, this group is responsible for the development of effective, efficient, well-documented programs. The applications programmer takes the task outline as prepared by the systems analyst and translates it into a program of coded

instructions used by the computer. The trainee at this level usually works at small tasks under the direct supervision of a more experienced programmer.

5. *System Analysis/Programmer* (5 titles): This job area is a combination of the System Analysis and the Application Programming areas just covered and reflects the fact that job titles and functions contained therein are not standardized. A common title in this area is Systems Analyst/Programmer, which can cover a very wide range of tasks. The title also reflects the fact that one person often may be responsible for broad problem analysis, solution design, and program formulation.

6. *Operating Systems Programming* (6 titles): Often called systems software programming, this group works with computer operating systems, which are extremely complex and sophisticated computer programs that allow applications programs to function efficiently.

7. *Data Base Administration* (2 titles): As this is a relatively new job area, these people have the function of analyzing the company's computerized information requirements and coordinating the collection, storage, and organization of data.

8. *Data Communications/Telecommunications* (3 titles): This group is responsible for the design of data communications networks, traffic analysis, installation and operation of data links, and providing for data communications software.

9. *Computer Operations* (8 titles): The eight titles here cover a wide range from manager to trainee, librarian, and postprocessing clerk. In general, the group is responsible for the operation of computers, job scheduling, and monitoring of operational efficiency. The senior computer operator operates the system console and is responsible for all operations during a shift period. The trainee often is assigned to mount magnetic storage media, such as disk or tape and working printers and other peripheral equipment.

10. *Production Control* (4 titles): The primary task of this area is that of setting up and scheduling jobs for processing by the operators.

11. *Data Entry* (4 titles): As the title indicates, this group performs the data entry and verification functions.

12. *Other Positions* (4 titles): This catchall area has one interesting job title that may ultimately emerge as a separate area of its own: Word Processing Operator. A later chapter will cover the operations and techniques of this rapidly emerging technology.

You may have noticed that the list covers jobs in data processing departments in private firms and government agencies but that it omits many other segments of the industry.

1. DP sales people, at both the retail and industrial levels.
2. Jobs in the manufacturing of computers and all related subassembly items.

3. Maintenance and technical personnel at all levels.
4. Free-lance data entry operators, programmers, consultants, educators, etc.

SUMMARY OF IMPORTANT POINTS

☐ Technology is entering a period of growth that is unparalleled in history. Every indication is that tomorrow's advances will significantly dwarf those made yesterday.

☐ Advances in the microelectronic industry have been the driving force behind this revolution. Today, all the functioning parts of a computer can be placed on a single electronic chip smaller than a thumbnail.

☐ The microelectronic chip has permitted the fabrication of a whole host of consumer and industry "smart" or "intelligent" devices, including games, calculators, etc.

☐ The combination of computer and communication technology has resulted in the rapid dissemination of information to remote locations through vast computer networks.

☐ Automation is a two-way street that provides us with better service at a cheaper price, but which requires users who know how to work with the new wave of technology.

☐ Very likely, the outcome of this revolution will be in the form of restructured social priorities and job concepts.

☐ Unfortunately, the general public is not well informed about computers and information technology and, in many cases, evidences outright hostility. Literacy in computer operations is seen as a necessity for survival of the next decade. Furthermore, education for computer literacy must begin in the lowest levels of our schools.

☐ Privacy is a major concern in this new era. The growth of large data banks coupled with communication network capability has resulted in monumental amounts of information available at the touch of a button. How this information will be used and who has access to it are questions that will be increasingly important as we get further and further into the 1980s.

☐ Security goes hand-in-hand with privacy. Physical security is concerned with the protection of the computer facilities and making certain that the data is not stolen, tampered with, or destroyed.

☐ Computer crime is a particularly troublesome area because it is difficult to detect and because of the reluctance of many firms to report this type of theft. Data transmission facilities often are the most vulnerable part of computer systems.

☐ A computer is an electronic device that accepts the input of data, processes it according to a predetermined pattern, and outputs the results. A computer system consists of input and output devices, the central processing unit (CPU), and auxiliary storage capability.

☐ Data processing is an intensely people-oriented activity that requires workers in all its phases, including management, programming, system analysis, data entry, word processing, communications, and electronic design and fabrication.

GLOSSARY OF TERMS

Hardware—the physical parts of a computer system such as printers, videoscreen devices, circuit chips, etc.

Input—the general term used to describe the act of entering data into a DP system, or the data being entered.

Information—data which is of use to management, as opposed to raw data which has not been worked upon (manipulated).

Output—the general term describing data or information leaving a DP system. Output data may be sent to the printer, to auxiliary storage, or to other devices.

Software—In a narrow definition, software is the computer program that causes a computer to perform a particular task. If a broad definition is used, software can include almost all tasks and operations that are not specifically hardware related.

THOUGHT QUESTIONS

1. How has automation directly affected you and the way you live? If you can't think of any direct effects on you, perhaps you can come up with examples of how automation has affected people you know.
2. The chapter discussed various types of "smart" devices. Name other consumer devices that you think will be produced in the future. What "smart" items would you like to see developed?
3. Has anyone in your family been displaced or put out of work by automation? If so, how was it handled? Did that person have an opportunity to "grow" into a new job that required a knowledge of automation?
4. How do you feel about data banks? Do you consider them to be a menace to your privacy?

5. How would you control the access to data banks? Who should have access?
6. What should be the minimum background for a person to be computer "literate?"
7. Should the theft of money via computers be treated the same as other forms of robbery?
8. Suppose that in a school situation you not only do your class problems on the machine but play computer games as well. Does the time you spend playing games constitute robbery? Explain your answer.
9. As an extension of the previous question, suppose that you also use the computer to print a mailing list for your boss. Assuming that the school forbids such activities, does that constitute robbery? Explain your answer.

CHAPTER 2
DATA
PROCESSING IN
PERSPECTIVE

LEARNING OBJECTIVES
Upon completion of the chapter you should understand the following:

The origin of early data processing methods.

The importance of the work done by Charles Babbage in the analytical engine.

The historical need for data processing methods and how the needs were met by punched-card DP.

How technology led us to the modern state of computer design and fabrication.

The terms related to computer speed.

The nature and makeup of the data processing industry.

CHAPTER CONTENTS

Chapter 1 dealt with computers and their effect on society. Emphasis was placed on the explosive growth of technology—growth that is so rapid that it is difficult for DP professionals to keep up with the latest advances. But it hasn't always been this way. Historically the changes were slow in evolving and a brief look at some of the more important events will help to place modern data processing in better perspective.

EARLY PROCESSING METHODS

Certainly you are aware that the processing of data is not anything mysterious. The peoples of the world have used an astounding number of devices over thousands of years in an effort to handle or manipulate data easily. One of the earliest devices, the abacus (Figure 2.1), may still be the most commonly used device in the world today. Thus, the foundation for the development of the computer was laid over many centuries. The first successful mechanical adding machine was invented in 1642 by an 18-year-old French genius, Blaise Pascal, who built it to help his father do accounting work. Later, a young German mathematician, Gottfried von Leibnitz, developed a mechanical device that was capable of addition, multiplication, division, and the extraction of square roots. Over the years a series of improved calculating devices were built, but the first radical change came in the early 1800s.

FIGURE 2.1
Abacus data processing device.

CHARLES BABBAGE
AND HIS ENGINES

In 1812 an English mathematician from Cambridge University, Charles Babbage, conceived the idea of a steam-powered calculating machine which he called "difference engine." It was to be capable of calculating logarithmic and astronomical tables to six places of accuracy. A model of his special-purpose calculator (Figure 2.2) was demonstrated in 1822 and it was well enough received that the British government granted Babbage money to continue the project. Work proceeded slowly, partly because machinists could not produce parts to the required tolerances and partly because Babbage expanded the scope of the machine to 20 places of accuracy. Perhaps even more important, however, was his idea for a totally new and different type of calculator—one that could handle any type of mathematical computation.

His new idea led him further away from the original difference engine until the British government finally withdrew its financial support. As a matter of fact, the difference engine was never completed in his life-time, although it was finished by others in later years.

Babbage devoted his time, his life, and his fortune to this new project, called the "analytical engine." He continued with the new project but, unfortunately, had little tolerance of those who could not match his intelligence or vision, so he was seldom in the good graces of those who could help him. He left many drawings of his machine and years later his son succeeded in building part of the arithmetic unit. The analytical engine was to be composed of:

FIGURE 2.2
Part of Babbage's difference engine.

1. Input in the form of punched cards, an idea borrowed from the principles of the Jacquard loom.
2. A "store" where arithmetic values could be housed.
3. A "mill" or arithmetic unit to perform calculations.
4. A control section to work on internally stored instructions.
5. Automatic output of answers.

The new ideas contained in Babbage's analytical engine set him apart from his mathematical predecessors. All his ideas are contained in the modern computer and, because of this, we can justifiably give him the title of "Father of the Computer." It should be mentioned that Babbage's companion, Lady Lovelace, has the distinction of being the world's first programmer, as she actually wrote mathematical programs for his analytical engine.

It is doubtful that his analytical engine would have functioned even if he had not had difficulty in communicating with the influential people of his time. The state of the art of manufacturing was simply not capable of performing to the exactness required by Babbage. More than anything else, Charles Babbage had the great misfortune to be born nearly a hundred years too early. Babbage died in 1871 having completed only a few parts of his marvelous engine.

Another English mathematician, George Boole, made a major contribution to the computer industry in 1854, but his ideas, much like Babbage's, had to wait for a century until they were really appreciated. In that year he published "The Laws of Thought," a treatise wherein he transformed pure logic into symbolic notation. His mathematics, called Boolean algebra, enabled computer designers a hundred years later to design efficient and complex electrical circuits with relative ease.

PUNCHED-CARD DATA PROCESSING

After the time of Babbage, new and better versions of mechanical calculators and printing devices were developed, but no single invention was capable of handling data on a large scale until 1890.

The old saying that "necessity is the mother of invention" seems to be borne out by the example of the punched card. You are probably aware that the U.S. Constitution requires that a census be taken every 10 years. In 1880, as they had done in the past, enumerators went out across the country, took the census, and wrote their findings on sheets of paper. The figures were tallied by hand with the final result that it took approximately 7½ years (through 1887) to finish a census of some 50 million people. From the known growth rate it could be easily calculated that the 1890 census would not be finished in time for the 1900 census, etc. To overcome this problem the bureau sought the aid of Dr. Herman Hollerith, a noted statistician of the time (Figure 2.3).

Dr. Hollerith had already been experimenting with mechanical methods of counting and tabulating, and he proposed the idea of having the enumerators code and hand punch the information into long paper strips. In the field this task turned out to be awkward and the strips were replaced by cards, each with a capacity of 240 hand-punched holes. The idea of holes punched in cards to represent information to a mechanical device was not new. It had been put into practical operation many years earlier by a Frenchman, Joseph Marie Jacquard, for the weaving of repetitive patterns into cloth. Jacquard's idea revolutionized the weaving industry, but its use in data processing lay dormant until put into practice nearly a hundred years later by Dr. Hollerith.

FIGURE 2.3
Herman Hollerith.

When the punched cards were returned to the Bureau of the Census, they were run through the Hollerith tabulating machine. Each card was placed manually in a holding mechanism in such a way that an electrical circuit was completed wherever a hole was detected. The completion of the circuit activated a dial-type counter on the face of the machine so that the tabulations could be read visually. Obviously, this was a great improvement over the old system; the 1890 census of over 60 million people was completed in only 2½ years (Figure 2.4).

With the success of his method, Dr. Hollerith expanded and improved the equipment. He left the Bureau of the Census and applied his punched-card method to the railroad, insurance, and manufacturing industries. In 1896 he formed the Tabulating Machine Company to market his machines and methods, both of which became quite popular in the eastern states. Dr. Hollerith left the company shortly after the turn of the century, but the company continued to develop new equipment. By 1914 there were four basic punched-card machines in operation:

1. A keypunch, for punching holes in cards.
2. A hand-operated gangpunch for punching repetitive data into a deck of cards simultaneously.
3. A gravity-fed vertical sorter for arranging cards into selected groups.
4. A tabulating machine for summing the data from punched cards.

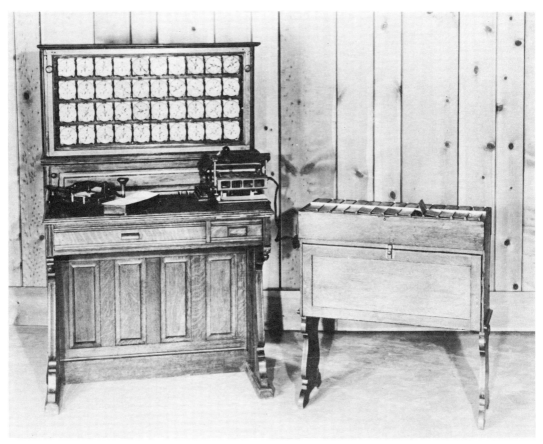

FIGURE 2.4
Herman Hollerith tabulating machine.

The firm expanded by various mergers to become Computing-Tabulating-Record Company and finally, in 1924, to be known as International Business Machines Corporation (IBM). Over the years the format of the punched card changed until it reached the present standard capacity of 960 holes per card. With each decade came improvements in the machinery, and along with these improvements came greatly increased speeds and reduced manual handling.

Perhaps the single biggest undertaking for punched-card equipment during these early years was the installation of the Social Security System in the 1930s. The initial operation called for setting up accounts for 30 million people, and the success of this system virtually assured the acceptance of punched-card processing methods. Although punched-card data processing has all but disappeared, it was the dominant method from 1930 to the early 1960s, when computers began to be used extensively. However, there are still many who remember the plugboards that had to be wired to make a particular machine do a job

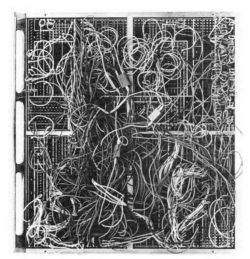

FIGURE 2.5
Wired plugboard for punched card accounting machine.

(Figure 2.5). Figure 2.6 shows an electric accounting machine that was used in the early 1930s. Note the boxlike unit in the front of the machine that holds the plugboard unit.

DATA PROCESSING ENTERS THE MODERN AGE

Punched-card data processing lasted for nearly 70 years (1890 through the 1950s) as the major method for processing masses of data. From the time of Babbage until the late 1930s there was no machine designed that could match the complexity of the analytical engine. Then a series of large, electromechanical calculators/computers began to be developed. These experimental machines served as a proving ground for design theories, and most were used to do ballistics calculations during World War II. Each new computer ushered in new technology so that by 1945 we were very close to building a modern computer.

In the late 1930s, Dr. John V. Atanasoff of Iowa State College conceived the idea that electronics, particularly the electron tube, could be used in the construction of a computer. Dr. John Mauchly and J.P. Eckert at the University of Pennsylvania Moore School of Electrical Engineering incorporated these ideas in the building of ENIAC (Electronic Numerical Integrator and Calculator), which was originally intended as a special-purpose machine to calculate ballistic firing tables, but ended up being a general-purpose device. ENIAC was completed in 1946 and

FIGURE 2.6
Punched card accounting machine—1933.

earned the distinction of being the world's first electronic computer.
The machine itself was huge—it had over 18,000 vacuum tubes, weighed
30 tons, and could perform about 300 calculations per second. With the
exception of the input of data and the output of answers, data was
stored and manipulated electronically. All prior electromechanical
machines were doomed to obsolescence by the speed of ENIAC (Figure
2.7).

A major step forward in the history of computers was made possible
by the theories postulated by a mathematician, Dr. John von Neumann,
in 1946. His ideas established the fundamentals of the computer design,
including the basic idea that the program directing the actions of the
computer should be housed within the computer itself. In today's
terminology this is known as the *stored program concept*. Prior to the
"von Neumann concept," programs were built directly into the ma-

FIGURE 2.7
ENIAC computer in operation.

chine, which meant that each change of programs required many hours of detailed work rewiring the machine. It was also von Neumann who demonstrated that computers could be used for business purposes, an idea that was almost unthinkable at the time. From his ideas came EDVAC (Electronic Discrete Variable Automatic Computer), built at the University of Pennsylvania. It was the first computer capable of doing nonscientific work.

The *New York Times* stated on the death of Dr. von Neumann early in 1957: "He was recognized as the world's leader in the development and construction of the high speed computing machines . . . that have made possible the solution of problems that would otherwise require many lifetimes to solve."

By now computers began appearing regularly. Perhaps the most important of these was one started by a corporation founded by Mauchly and Eckert. The Bureau of Census again was interested in a computer to do its tabulations and contracted with Mauchly and Eckert for the work. Their company was acquired by the Remington-Rand Corporation, which delivered UNIVAC (Universal Automatic Computer) to the bureau in 1951. In comparison to ENIAC it could perform about 1000 calculations per second. UNIVAC was then produced on a modified assembly-line basis and has the distinction of being the world's first commercially produced computer. Thus, more than a century passed from the time of Charles Babbage and his radically new idea of an analytical engine to the advent of UNIVAC (Figure 2.8).

We constantly hear that we have entered the age of the computer, yet we must realize that until 1951, there was only a handful of computers in the world and each of these was produced on a one-of-a-kind experimental basis. The computer age only started, really, with the second half of this century; and yet today the computer, in a 30-plus year period, has had an enormous impact on the way we live.

FIGURE 2.8
UNIVAC I computer showing racks of vacuum tubes.

COMPUTER GENERATIONS

In DP terminology we speak of computers in terms of the generation to which a particular machine belongs. As you would suspect, all the computers named so far are of the first generation. Machines of this era were physically large, inflexible in operations, and somewhat difficult to keep running. The major reason for the difficulties was that these machines used a great many vacuum tubes, which generated large amounts of heat, which in turn forced the builders to install bulky cooling systems. Another point of irritation was that a tube would often not fail completely, but would work at something less than full capacity. This would then cause inaccurate results.

The speeds of first-generation equipment varied over a wide range. Some machines could perform about 10 additions per second, which

FIGURE 2.9
First, second, and third generation computer components.

FIGURE 2.10
IBM first-generation computer.

represented a considerable improvement over the punched-card equipment speed of roughly one addition per second. EDVAC was listed as performing an add operation in a few one-thousandths of a second—more commonly referred to as a *millisecond*.

Second-generation computers were characterized by a considerable reduction in physical size, increased reliability, and greater speed. The major contribution to all this came from the transistor, which replaced the vacuum tube and eliminated much of the heat and difficulty in air conditioning (Figure 2.9). Speeds increased across the board as, one by one, the individual operations began to fall into the *microsecond* (one-millionth of a second) range. More and more firms entered the market and the resulting competition acted as a driving force to the industry as a whole. Faster, better, and more specialized input/output (I/O) equipment became available to go along with the new techniques developed by both the manufacturers and the users. Figure 2.10 shows an IBM first-generation computer.

Third-generation equipment entered the DP scene in the mid-1960s. Greater speeds again became possible with improved technology and special manufacturing techniques. That which was experimental in the second generation became commonplace in the third. To the user, there was a more important change between the second and third generation: *modularity*. Modularity can best be explained by making reference to second-generation equipment. In the second generation, users acquired equipment based on, among other things, the maximum use of data processing they could foresee for their company. In many, if not most cases, the business executive underestimated company needs and quickly found that the equipment would not do the job envisioned. The only alternative was to get rid of the old equipment and "trade up" the computer line. Unfortunately, to change from one computer to another—even to another computer from the same company—meant fantastic expense in retraining personnel and rewriting programs. Most third-generation computers, however, were modular in design so that the user could get increased speed and capability by adding hardware modules to a basic unit.

Speeds in the third generation were in terms of fewer and fewer microseconds, until some reached the nanosecond (one-billionth of a second) level. A nanosecond is a difficult concept to grasp, but perhaps it can be illustrated by thinking of this. It takes light a little more than one second to travel from the earth to the moon, but light can only move about 12 inches in a nanosecond. Captain Grace Hopper, a legend in data processing, likes to end her lectures by handing out "nanoseconds" to the audience—wires cut into 12-inch lengths. Figure 2.11 shows a third-generation chip used in IBM computers.

Third generation is behind us now, even though many third-generation machines are still in use. Many people feel that fourth-generation computer systems came in during the mid-1970s with the

FIGURE 2.11

Third-generation circuit chip.

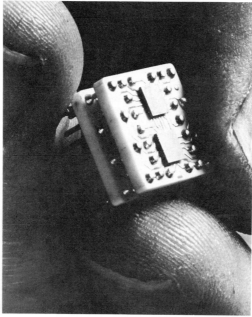

FIRST LARGE-SCALE COMPUTER, ENIAC, TURNS 35 YEARS OLD
By Lois Paul
CW Staff

PHILADELPHIA—Although there was no ice cream and cake, a birthday was celebrated here this week as Eniac (Electronic Numerical Integrator and Computer), the world's first large-scale computer, turned 35.

Eniac was built for the Army during World War II at the Moore School of the University of Pennsylvania School of Engineering and Applied Science. It weighed 30 tons, took up 15,000 sq ft of space and cost $400,000 to build in 1945. Its 18,000 vacuum tubes consumed 150 kilowatts and it could do 5,000 calculations per second.

One of the two men credited with its creation, J. Presper Eckert Jr., described Eniac in a recent interview as "the equivalent to a simple Radio Shack computer of the type that sells for $500."

However, during the celebration of Eniac's anniversary this week, University of Pennsylvania students proved that even a Radio Shack Corp. TRS-80 can beat the old veteran. Using sections of the original Eniac and a TRS-80, the students ran a program to square all integers from one to 10,000. Eniac suffered a crushing defeat, completing the task in six seconds to the TRS-80's one-third of a second.

Eckert, who at 61 is a vice-president of Sperry Univac in suburban Montgomery County, built Eniac with Dr. John Mauchly, who was a physicist at Ursinus College when they met. With the nation at war, Mauchly suggested in 1942 that research be conducted on an electronic computer.

Needing a device to speed calculations required to improve the accuracy of artillery, the Army Ballistics Research Laboratory in Aberdeen, Md., approved the project in 1943. Three years later, Eckert and Mauchly completed Eniac and it was moved to Aberdeen and used there for about two years.

Eckert and Mauchly formed Eckert-Mauchly Computer Corp., which was bought in 1950 by Remington Rand. This later became the Sperry Univac division of Sperry Corp. Eckert said that he and Mauchly each made about $250,000 in selling their company to Remington Rand. Mauchly died in 1980.

As for Eniac, which was once an electronic marvel and remains a historic landmark, most of it has been stored in the Smithsonian Institution, out of sight, for more than a quarter of a century.

introduction of microprocessors (see Chapter 14) that were fabricated with large-scale integration (LSI) of electronic circuits. Fifth-generation may already be here in the form of VSLI (Very Large-Scale Integration) that can place an extraordinary amount of circuitry in an extremely small area (Figure 2.12). The obvious advantage to packing so much circuitry into a small area is that it cuts down significantly on the time it takes electricity to travel between the elements in the system.

Computer speeds are rapidly approaching the *picosecond* level, i.e., one-trillionth of a second. Using different terminology, we often speak of computer speed in terms of MIPS (millions of instructions per second) that a computer can execute. Today, most of the medium-scale machines operate in the 2-to-15 MIPS range. More important, though, is that with the increase in speed came an additional increase in machine capability. For example, modern computers can perform several tasks concurrently, and this has greatly increased the ability of the system to handle larger work loads. Fourth-generation computers continued the trend of the second generation toward more, better, and faster I/O and peripheral equipment, and more versatile programming languages. There is some discussion of what the next computer generation will be. Many feel that the new generation of computer systems will not be hardware oriented at all: Instead, a new type of sophisticated software or mass storage devices might herald the change.

OVERVIEW: THE DATA PROCESSING INDUSTRY

The size of the data processing industry, either in terms of units of equipment or dollar sales, is always a point of conjecture. Although it would seem to be a simple task to accumulate sales figures, the problem is one of semantics and definitions. Traditionally, the "mainframers," that is, those firms that produce the large, complete computer systems have been at the heart of the industry. IBM, Honeywell, Burroughs, Control Data Corporation (CDC), National Cash Register (NCR), UN-IVAC, and Digital Equipment Corporation (DEC) are generally conceded to be the sales leaders.

However, the rapid decline in hardware price coupled with an awareness of the need for computer data processing has made profound changes in the marketplace. The popularity of the small desktop home and business computers produced by Tandy Corporation (Radio Shack), Apple Computers, IBM, Atari, and Commodore (PET) have forced the manufacturers of large computer systems to reconsider their market strategy. Even those manufacturers that have concentrated their efforts on the mid-size computers have been affected by this trend. In 1977, *Computerworld* magazine reported that the number of computers

FIGURE 2.12
Circuit chip photographed against a dime.

installed had gone from some 50 systems in 1953 to 175,000 in 1976 and would reach 500,000 in 1980. And yet, in 1980 Tandy Corporation alone reported sales of approximately 200,000 of their computers.

As mentioned earlier, some of the reasons for the continuing growth of sales in the United States is the trend toward simplification of complex user applications, the steadily decreasing cost of electronic hardware items, and the growing use of computers to offset the rising cost of labor. A medium-size one-of-a-kind computer that cost nearly $3 million in 1953 dropped to one-eighth of that ($380,000) in 1976. In 1981 a comparable system costs approximately $100,000 to $150,000. Note, too, that these are actual dollar figures and are not adjusted for economic conditions. It is worth noting that the major decrease in computer costs has taken place in the electronic components with only a slight decrease in the cost of mechanical devices such as printers. Even so, total system prices are expected to continue their decline.

Another large segment of the industry is comprised of firms that do not manufacture CPUs but concentrate on peripheral equipment, such as terminals, printers, and various auxiliary storage devices. From there the circle widens to include manufacturers of hardware subcomponents, communications and transmission equipment, paper and forms, microfilm and graphic supplies, service bureaus, software houses, and DP management services.

SUMMARY OF IMPORTANT POINTS

☐ Two examples of mechanical calculators were those developed by the Frenchman, Blaise Pascal, and the German, Gottfried von Leibnitz, in the 1600s.

☐ In the 1820s, Charles Babbage, an English mathematician, first worked on what he called a "difference engine," which was an advanced mechanical calculator.

☐ Babbage later envisioned a machine, called the "analytical engine," which would be capable of performing a wide range of mathematical functions under program control.

☐ Neither of his machines were completed in his lifetime, but his ideas encompassed all the basic parts of a modern computer. Babbage planned for
Card input.
A place for the storage of arithmetic values.
An arithmetic unit to do calculations.
A control section to work on internally stored instruction.
Automatic output of answers.

☐ Punched-card data processing was mainly the idea of Dr. Herman Hollerith, who used his method and machines to process data for the Bureau of Census in 1890.

☐ Punched-card systems were dominant until the late 1950s when computer systems began to be installed in increasing numbers. Today, complete punched-card installations are all but gone.

☐ ENIAC, the world's first all electronic computer, was completed in 1946 by John Mauchly and J.P. Eckert.

☐ In 1951 Mauchly and Eckert at the Remington-Rand Corporation built UNIVAC, which is recorded as being the first commercially built computer.

☐ The term "generation" is often used to distinguish the time period in which a particular computer was built.

☐ First-generation computers were slow and inefficient by any modern standards, and featured electron-tube technology.

☐ Second-generation machines were built with transistors that greatly reduced the power and air-conditioning requirements of the devices of the previous generation.

☐ Third-generation machines use a wide range of manufacturing and design technology to produce large-scale integration (LSI) of internal circuitry. This has made it possible to place an entire central processing unit on a single electronic chip.

□   Third-generation machines also introduced the idea of modularity—that the capability of a computer system could be expanded by adding modules of hardware as needed.

□   Fourth-generation computers took advantage of very large-scale integration (VLSI) fabrication techniques that compressed electronic circuitry into smaller and smaller chips.

□   Computer operational speeds have increased from the millisecond level (one-thousandth of a second) to the picosecond level (one-trillionth of a second).

Millisecond	one-thousandth of a second
Microsecond	one-millionth of a second
Nanosecond	one-billionth of a second
Picosecond	one-trillionth of a second

□   The data processing industry is in a period of radical change that has been brought on by the incredible demand for small desktop computers for both home and industry.

□   Today, the power of a giant computer of the 1960s can be had in a minicomputer that may cost one-tenth of the price of its predecessor. The trend is toward the production of cheaper, faster, more reliable, and more versatile computers.

GLOSSARY OF TERMS

Atanasoff, John V.—a computer pioneer who first conceived the idea of an electronic computer.

Analytical engine—the name given to a theoretical computer envisioned by Charles Babbage in the early 1800s.

Babbage, Charles—an English mathematician, sometimes called the "Father of the Computer" because of his pioneering work on his difference engine and analytical engine.

Difference engine—the name given to an advanced calculator designed by Charles Babbage.

Eckert, J.P., Jr.—a codeveloper of the ENIAC computer at the University of Pennsylvania.

EDVAC—an advanced computer that followed ENIAC; built at the University of Pennsylvania (Electronic Discrete Variable Automatic Computer).

ENIAC—the world's first electronic computer (Electronic Numerical Integrator and Calculator).

Generation—a differentiation of the ages to which computer equipment belongs. Considerable controversy exists as to what generation we are currently in. Depending upon your definition we are at least into fourth-generation and possibly into fifth-generation.

Hollerith, Dr. Herman—a famous statistician and developer of the first punched-card equipment. His name is still associated with various aspects of modern DP.

Keypunch—a machine much like a typewriter, for punching holes in cards.

Mauchly, Dr. John—a codeveloper of the ENIAC computer at the University of Pennsylvania.

Microsecond—one-millionth of a second.

Millisecond—one-thousandth of a second.

Modularity—the concept of designing computers in "building block" format to promote efficient and economical upgrading of the equipment.

Nanosecond—one-billionth of a second.

Picosecond—one-trillionth of a second.

Sorter—machine used for placing punched cards into predetermined groupings.

Tabulating machine—A punched-card machine capable of adding numbers from cards and printing a total.

UNIVAC—a division of the Sperry-Rand Corporation (formerly Remington-Rand) and also the name given to the first commercially produced computer.

Von Neuman, Dr. John—the famous mathematician who formulated the "von Neumann" concept that the program to direct the action of the computer could be stored internally within the computer.

THOUGHT QUESTIONS

1. From what was discussed in the chapter, do you think that a firm that started with punched-card equipment would have an easy time in switching to computer data processing? Would experience with punched-card operations in any way prepare the company for entry into the computer world?

2. What is the state of the computer industry today? What firms are its leaders? What company or brand names are you familiar with?

3. In what specific areas of data processing do you think the greatest future change will come. On-the-job use of computers; school use; home use; etc.?

4. What is the importance of computer speed? Isn't the computer fast enough already? Why are designers trying to make faster machines?

CHAPTER 3 COMPUTERS AND THE DP CYCLE

LEARNING OBJECTIVES

Upon completion of the chapter you should understand the following:

The components of a computer system and how they relate to each other.

How a computer is used and the general nature of the input, processing, and output functions of a computer system.

The seven steps in the processing cycle and how they relate to business operations:

Collecting the data.

Converting data to machine-acceptable form.

Verifying the data.

Transmitting data from one place to another.

Manipulating or processing the data.

Storing the data for future use.

Outputting the data.

CHAPTER CONTENTS

Many people have pointed out that the development of industrial technology mainly enhanced man's physical capabilities while computer technology has enhanced man's mental processes. Charles P. Lecht, author of "Waves of Change" put it very succinctly by saying, "What the lever was to the body, the computer system is to the mind."[1]

So we are participating in a second industrial revolution in which we are mechanizing intellectual activity rather than physical activity. Just what kind of machine can do these things? It is time to take a closer look at the makeup of a computer system.

ELEMENTS OF
A COMPUTER SYSTEM

Immediately we run into a problem because a computer is not all that easy to define. Generally, a computer is an electronic device that accepts the input of data, processes the data according to a predetermined pattern, and outputs the results. In the early days of computing we might have added the point that the machine is "programmed" and this alone was sufficient to differentiate it from any type of calculator. Today, of course, we have "programmable" calculators, some of which have input and output devices—a point that makes the definition of terms a bit difficult. Obviously a computer DP system implies that a computer is at the heart of the complex. What is not so obvious, however, is that computer systems can take an almost infinite variety of forms. We can illustrate the general structure of any computer system by means of the schematic shown in Figure 3.1.

Data and the programs that will work on the data initially enter a computer system through some type of input unit such as a typewriter terminal or reading device that handles the familiar punched card. The "computer" itself is more accurately called the central processing unit,

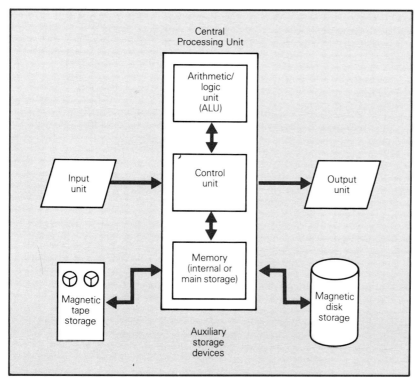

FIGURE 3.1
Components of a computer system.

or CPU, and consists of three major parts: the control unit; the arithmetic/logic unit (ALU); and, memory. As the name implies, memory is the place in which we hold or store both the computer program and the data that is currently being worked upon.

The computer program is executed or acted upon by the control unit, which controls and coordinates the system hardware as directed by the individual instructions contained in the program. In order to process some of these instructions the control unit may have to make use of another part of the central processing unit—the arithmetic/logic unit, which performs calculating and logical decision-making activities.

The results of the computation steps are likely to be answers of the type with which we are familiar—bills, paychecks, reports, shipping documents, etc. In most cases, these answers are transmitted to an output device such as a printer. It may be, however, that we wish to store some of the raw data and/or the processed answers for use at a later date. Due to the size limitations of memory the data will be written onto (or stored onto) auxiliary storage devices such as magnetic tape or magnetic disks. Later, when this data is needed, it will be read into memory for further processing or transmitted to an output device as before.

Although this is a simplified overview of a computer several points are worth noting now.

1. Manipulation or processing of data takes place in the CPU memory and arithmetic/logic areas, not in auxiliary storage.
2. Memory itself is limited in capacity and is deceptively small. Memory is usually spoken of as being capable of storing thousands of characters (a single letter or a single digit are each a character). Many good small- to medium-scale computer systems operate quite well on 32,000 to 256,000 characters of memory. With the continuing drop in memory prices, however, more and more computers are getting memories of 1 million or more characters.
3. The word "memory" is not really a good one because it implies the idea of storage of data. Data is not really "stored" in memory. A record of data such as a single charge sale transaction is brought into memory to be processed, not to be stored. Generally, this record remains in memory only long enough to be manipulated and is then replaced by another data record. Its "memory life" is perhaps only a fraction of a second.
4. As opposed to memory, auxiliary storage is spoken of in terms of millions, billions, and even trillions of characters. Since most storage media such as magnetic tape and disks consist of small, replaceable units, storage is virtually unlimited.
5. Computers are programmed. A program is defined by the Computer Software Copyright Act as "a set of statements or instructions to be used directly or indirectly in a computer in order to bring about a certain result."

Of course, none of these ideas should be very startling because humans operate in a manner very similar to computers. Our inputs are in the form of sight, smell, touch, etc., and our brain is the central processing unit that drives the system. We have a limited amount of memory, but still far more than any computer ever built, and we can use it in complex ways that technology has not yet been able to duplicate.

Our output is likely to be in the form of speech or writing and we are "programmed" by our contacts with society—our parents, friends, school, church, etc. We even use auxiliary storage in the form of records, tapes, file folders, and books to store masses of information that are not contained in our memory but which can be retrieved fairly quickly. Fortunately, humans have a unique ability called the creative thought process that allows them to do things no computer could ever do, no matter how complex. Thus, when you look at a computer system it may be well to recognize that its components are remarkably like those that you use all the time.

Another point to consider is that size has nothing to do with the makeup of a computer system. The fact that the CPU may be physically small for one application and much larger for another application is of

FIGURE 3.2
Small-scale computer system.

little importance. What is important is the fact that every computer system must contain the components shown in Figure 3.1. An example of a small-scale system in which the components are marked for visual reference is shown in Figure 3.2.

The next illustration (Figure 3.3) shows the similar components of a medium-scale computer system. In normal practice, one of the input/output terminal units will be designated for sole use by the operator to control the action of the entire computer system; on small systems, however, this activity may be handled by the operator/ programmer from a terminal that can also be used for regular input and output.

Before leaving this section, one further point concerning computers must be discussed. Computers can be described in a variety of ways; but perhaps the most basic breakdown is in terms of the kind of data they handle. In this text, when we use the term computers we are speaking of *digital* computers (i.e., those that work with information in the form

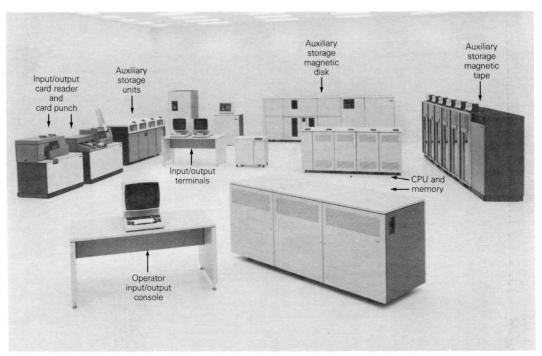

FIGURE 3.3
IBM 4341 medium-scale computer system.

of numbers or letters with which you are familiar) as opposed to *analog* computers, which work with a continuous stream of physical data coming from sensing devices that may monitor pressure, voltage, or heat

"It was a good trade! They got Eddie Felton, The Mark 17 computer and a hundred dollars worth of software . . . We got the soft drink machine."

readings. Analog computers are usually found in specialized industries, such as petroleum manufacturing, steel making, or paper making, and they are generally used to regulate a specific manufacturing process. Also, computers of this type are usually not available on a mass-market basis, since they must be built to do specific jobs. Scientific operations are particularly dependent upon sensory data that requires processing by an analog computer. Analog devices are usually faster than their digital counterparts, but they generally lack the precision of the digital computer and data often is not stored for future use.

USING THE COMPUTER: AN EXAMPLE

Now that you know about the components of a computer system, let's see how all the parts work together to accomplish a specific task. In our example we consider what happens during processing of a payroll operation. In setting up the example we will have to make certain assumptions as outlined below.

1. Payroll data on each employee has been gathered, entered into the computer system, and stored on disk auxiliary storage. The individual data records would contain information such as name, address, social security number, date of birth, telephone number, number of dependents, special deductions, working classification, hourly pay rate, etc. Note that one vital piece of data is missing: the number of hours worked during the previous pay period.

2. The company pays employees weekly and has a payroll program (written by a company application programmer) that is also stored upon a disk. Since this program is used frequently, it is kept on a disk for quick reference and use.

3. The number of hours worked each week is recorded by the employee's supervisor and turned into the payroll office every Friday. The payroll program is run the following Monday and paychecks are distributed the next day.

4. The time sheets become the "source" of the data on each employee and somehow this data must get into the computer system before any processing can take place. The following chapter will go into detail about data entry methods, but for now, since punched cards are such a visible form of data we will assume that the time sheets (source documents) are given to a keypunch operator who punches the hours worked and employee identifying data into cards. (The next chapter will show that there are faster and better ways to do this.) This part of the operation is shown in Figure 3.4.

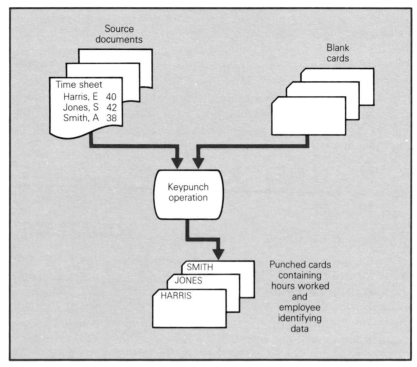

FIGURE 3.4
Source data punched into cards.

On Monday morning the program run that will result in the production of employee paychecks is started. The process is as follows.

1. The operator, working at the system console unit, will cause a copy of the payroll program to be read from disk into memory. This action is relatively simple since every stored program is identified by a specific name or number. The operation is analogous to going to the library to get a specific book from the shelves. In addition, the operator will place the punched cards in the hopper of the card reader. At this point a schematic of the system would show the following arrangement (Figure 3.5).

2. The operator, still working that console, now instructs the control unit to execute the payroll program. The program itself consists of a series of very precise, orderly instructions that, in total, "does" payroll. More specifically, the payroll program will read in the *first* record of weekly payroll data from the card reader. Note that the card is moved into the card reader where its contents are read and transferred electronically to memory. The card then passes through the reader to the output stacker. The program will then find the matching record of employee "permanent" data and read

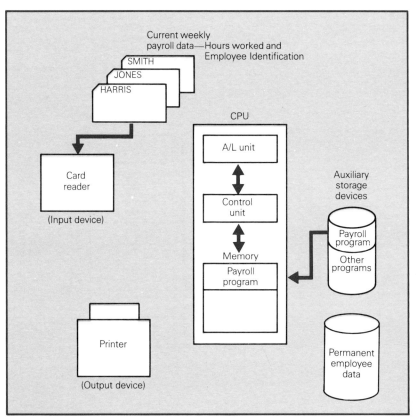

FIGURE 3.5
Payroll example—step 1.

it in from disk. Figure 3.6 illustrates the state of the computer
system at this point.

3. Next, the program will process the payroll data in accordance with
the instruction in the payroll program. Since arithmetic operations
are involved, the control unit will make use of the arithmetic/logic
unit when necessary. Answers or results of computation will be
derived from this internal processing step and output to the printer
(paychecks) and auxiliary storage (for later use in employee tax
form preparation, federal and state reports, etc.) (Figure 3.7).

At this point we have processed one record of data and produced one
paycheck. The program will have been written so that it will continue
to read and process employee records again and again, but only one
at a time, until all the incoming card records have been processed.
Therefore, steps 1 to 3 will be repeated for employee Jones, then Smith,
and so on. Note that the data pertaining to a single employee is only in
memory for a short time, perhaps a small fraction of a second, before it

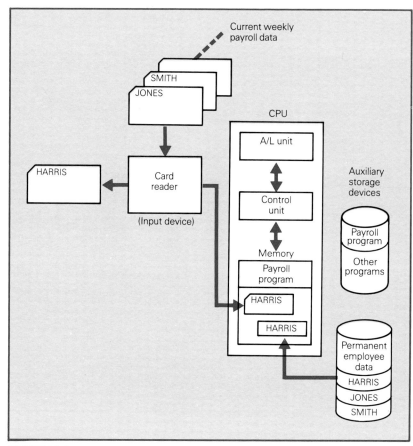

FIGURE 3.6
Payroll example—step 2.

is replaced with new incoming data. This should further illustrate that computer memory is not a place of permanent storage. Sometimes it is called "primary storage" as opposed to auxiliary storage, which is also known as "secondary storage." In reality, memory is a place of action rather than a place of storage. Finally, when the payroll program is finished, the operator will read into memory another program, perhaps one to do inventory processing or customer billing. Figures 3.8–3.10 show the computer in various uses.

THE PROCESSING CYCLE

The diagram shown in Figure 3.1 was exactly that—a diagram of a typical computer system. In that diagram we did not concern ourselves with the brand of hardware, the size of the system, or the use to which it was being applied. What we are concerned about is that the

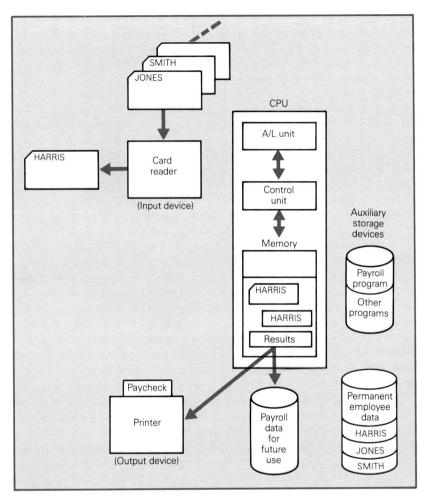

FIGURE 3.7
Payroll example—step 3.

processing of data always involves a general series of steps known as the processing cycle. Each computer installation does not necessarily perform every one of the seven functions listed below. They will plan to do only those functions that are pertinent to a specific job and a single computer program might encompass all seven of the steps or it may be concerned with only a single step.

In total, the seven functions are a logical, orderly progression of steps that must be performed to achieve a specific goal, such as the automation of customer billing or inventory accounting. The job of determining what steps to perform and the depth of such performance is the task of the systems analyst and/or programming manager.

1. *Collect the pertinent data.* Obviously, the key word here is the term "pertinent." Collecting too much data or unneeded data is just as wasteful as collecting too little. Typically, data will be in the

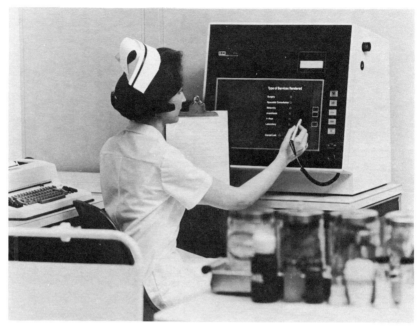

FIGURE 3.8
Computer at use in a hospital.

form of sales receipts, credit memos, purchase orders, bills of lading, written reports, dictated letters, etc. The data now becomes the input to the system.

2. *Convert the data to machine-acceptable form.* The conversion of data to machine-acceptable form is not as easy a task as it might appear. In order to get efficient and accurate conversion, it is first necessary to do a large amount of planning. One of the primary rules of data processing is that, if at all possible, data should be converted only once. The conversion process usually involves a great deal of human effort and frequently is the major bottleneck to the further handling of the data. Historically, keypunching or the punching of data into cards has been the primary method of data conversion and, for this reason, was used in the example. Today, more and more key entry methods use something other than cards as the input/storage media. Video screen input and OCR (optical character recognition), another input technique, offer some interesting possibilities that will be discussed later in the textbook.

3. *Verify the data.* Verification of data can be done as a separate function or it can be included at the time of conversion. Our problem here is one of making sure that the data is correct prior to its entry into the main stream of the system. The term GIGO—now somewhat dated, standing for garbage in, garbage out—is still appropriate. What point is there in processing incorrect data at fan-

FIGURE 3.9
Computer used in a business.

tastic speeds if the answer is certain to be garbage? No machine yet devised can take incorrect information and make it correct. Our example assumed that the incoming card data were correct, but this is not always an assumption you can make.

4. *Transmit the data.* In many installations data transmission may not be pertinent and could therefore be skipped. Frequently, however, data is captured at a location that is remote from the place of processing and some sort of transmission must take place. A later section will be devoted to data transmission, the equipment used, and examples of systems where transmission is necessary. Traditionally, we have only thought of transmitting records of data such as those concerning inventory or payroll transactions. Recently, however, we have seen the need to transmit reports, letters, memos, etc., along with numeric data.

5. *Manipulate the data.* The term manipulate has the same meaning for data processing as it does in ordinary usage. Remember that

FIGURE 3.10
Computer at use in engineering.

data in its raw state is of doubtful value. It is only after it has been manipulated or processed (sorted into a particular order, totaled, etc.) in some way that it becomes "information." As stated before, information, not data, is the lifeblood of the business; it is upon information that managers make their decision, and this information may be in either numerical or alphabetic form. (Since the distinction between the terms is not always made, we shall use the words interchangeably in this text.)

6. *Store the data.* In some cases, data is not used immediately. In other cases, it is used for its immediate value and also stored for future reference. If this is so, then it must be stored in such a way that it can be referenced when needed. This function is, as are many things in data processing, far easier said than done. Complex

WORLD'S BIGGEST DP CENTER

This is just a minute part of what is claimed to be the world's largest data-processing facility, which is operated by McDonnell Douglas Automation Co. (McAuto) in St. Louis. The $70-million building covers over 18 acres. The computer equipment covers 3 acres, and is worth $133 million, almost twice as much as the building.

Thousands of commercial clients are served by the center, which also handles dp operations for parts of McDonnell Douglas Corp. of St. Louis, which owns McAuto. The extent of the center's hardware and software defies summarization. There are 13 large computers from IBM and Control Data. Most of the IBMs are 3033s, which are arranged in clusters. They run under the MVS operating system, and are supported by a pool of 90 IBM 3400 series tape drives and 530 IBM 3330 and 3350 disk drives. Over 2,000 employees work at the center. (Source: Reprinted from *Computer Decisions,* April 1981, p. 16A, Copyright 1981, Hayden Publishing Company. Photo courtesy of McDonnell Douglas Automation Company.)

information storage and retrieval operations are performed on vast data bases (structured data in storage) and are among the newest techniques available to management.

7.   *Output the data.* After the data has been manipulated and put into meaningful groups, it must be communicated to management for use in the company's activities. In most cases, these outputs from the system take the form of printed reports to managers, bills or letters sent to customers, paychecks to employees, etc. In a highly automated situation, much of the output from one program is very likely to become input to another program.

SUMMARY OF IMPORTANT POINTS

☐   As opposed to the development of industrial technology, which enhanced human physical capabilities, microelectronics extend human mental capabilities.

☐   Any computer system, whether large or small, consists of the following components.
The CPU, or central processing unit, which controls the action of the system.
Memory, where data is actually manipulated.
Auxiliary storage such as magnetic tape or disks, where data is stored for future use.

☐   The CPU is comprised of three major components.
An arithmetic/logic unit for calculating and logical decision making.
A control unit that has the job of control and coordination of the system hardware.
Memory that holds both the program currently being executed and data upon which the program works.

☐   Data is manipulated only within the central processing unit, not on auxiliary storage.

☐   A program is defined as a "set of statements or instructions to be used directly or indirectly in a computer in order to bring about a certain result."

☐   Digital computers, as the term indicates, work with data in the form of digits or alphabetic characters.

☐   Analog computers work with data in nondigital form, such as temperature readings, pressure indications, etc.

☐   Generally, all programs follow the same basic pattern as follows.

The program is brought into memory and executed by operator action.
Records of data are read into memory from input or auxiliary storage devices by program direction.
Characteristically, a program works on one record of data until that record is completely processed, then another record is processed.

☐ The processing cycle consists of the following.
Collecting the data.
Converting the data to machine-acceptable form.
Verifying the data for accuracy.
Transmitting the data from one point to another (not always required).
Manipulating the data.
Storing the data.
Outputting the data.

GLOSSARY OF TERMS

Analog computer—a specialized computer that handles data coming from sensing devices rather than data in digital form. It is usually used in special scientific applications or as a process-control device.

Arithmetic/logic unit—a part of the central processing unit in which calculations and logical decision making are performed.

Auxiliary storage—a place for the long-term storage of data. Storage of this type usually is on magnetic media, such as magnetic tape or disks, and has the capability of storing millions or even billions of characters. (Also known as secondary storage.)

Central processing unit (CPU)—the electronic device that controls all other parts of the computer system.

Control unit—the electronic part of the central processing unit that, under program direction, coordinates the action of the system hardware.

Data conversion—the act of changing data from one form to another form. For example, source data often has to be converted to a machine-readable format before computer processing can take place.

Digital computer—a general-purpose computer that handles data in numerical or digital form.

GIGO—the term standing for garbage in, gar-

bage out. It simply means that if incorrect data is fed into the system, incorrect answers will result.

Magnetic disk storage—storage units using a flat circular plate with a magnetic surface on which data can be stored.

Magnetic tape storage—storage units using thin, plastic tape on which data is stored magnetically.

Manipulating (data)—the act of working on data to put it into a form that has greater meaning to the user.

Memory—that part of the central processing unit that is used to temporarily hold the program that is being executed and the data upon which the program works.

Program—a set of statements or instructions to be used directly or indirectly in a computer in order to bring about a certain result.

Processing cycle—seven steps:
Collecting the data.
Converting the data to machine-acceptable form.
Verifying the data.
Transmitting the data.
Manipulating the data.
Storing the data.
Outputting the data.

THOUGHT QUESTIONS

1. How is it possible for both very large and very small computers to be made up of the same basic internal elements? What difference would there be between these elements on a small and a large computer?

2. The chapter outlined the steps involved in using a computer for a payroll application. Follow the same process for a customer billing application in which you start with balance owed file, a new charge amount file and a payments file, all of which are on auxiliary disk storage. Assume that a customer billing program has been written and is also stored on a disk.

3. In what ways can the order of steps in the processing be changed? Make up an example illustrating why you would want to change the order.

4. Historically, accounting systems have been the first areas to be automated. Why? Is this the place you would start if you were automating a business?

CHAPTER 4
DATA ENTRY
METHODS

LEARNING OBJECTIVES
Upon completion of the chapter you should understand the following:

The unit record concept as applied to the standard punched card.

How numeric, alphabetic, and special characters are represented in a punched card.

The use of source documents for the origination of data and how records of data are broken into individual fields of data.

The nature and use of key data entry and the trend away from cards.

What intelligent terminals are and how they are used in the entry process.

Various alternatives to key data entry and the conditions under which they can be used successfully.

Retail point-of-sale systems.

Optical character recognition and how it is used.

Voice data entry.

CHAPTER CONTENTS

As this chapter will show, there are many of ways of entering data into a computer system. The punched card has long been the traditional form of data entry even though faster and better methods have been available for many years. Part of the reason for the slow entrance of other methods is that the early computers were heavily oriented around punched-card techniques. As recently as June 1980, *Infosystems* reported that the punched card was still the primary means of entering data. Since then enormous changes, mostly brought on by the rapid decline in the price of electronic components, have occurred. However, cards are a good starting place since it is very likely that you have seen or handled a punched card at one time or another.

PUNCHED CARDS:
THE UNIT RECORD CONCEPT

As explained in the chapter on the history of data processing, the punched card has been in use a long time. The card might also be called a unit record card because this is exactly the function it performs. The unit record principle rests on several ideas.

1. All the information concerning a particular business event or transaction can be contained in a single card. As an example, all the details (data) of registering at school would be punched into a single card and this becomes a single or unit record of data.
2. The second basic premise of the unit record principle is that once this data has been captured in a card, repeated processing or manipulation of the data can take place at machine speed. The data can then be moved, processed, and rearranged in endless ways.

This matter of machine speed is worthy of further discussion at this point, particularly in relation to the passage of data through the DP system. Machines can operate on data at a tremendous speed if, and only if, the data is in machine-acceptable form. Converting data into this form has long been one of the major bottlenecks of the DP industry. Throughout the chapter some of the methods that have been devised to overcome this problem are shown. For many years, however, the punched card was the main medium employed to bridge this gap between man and machine.

Currently there are two major types of punched cards in use: the card using the coding structure designed by Dr. Hollerith and a special smaller card originally designed for use in the IBM System 3 computer (96-column card).

THE STANDARD PUNCHED CARD

By now the punched card (sometimes called an "IBM" card) has become a familiar sight to all of us. We even joke about the classic warning not to "staple, spindle, fold, or mutilate." We also take for granted its multitude of uses: When punched, it serves as a storage place for data; it is used as a vehicle for the entry or exit of data; it is sometimes used as a basic business form for accounting purposes.

The basic card, which is capable of holding 80 characters of information, is shown in Figure 4.1. Note that the top edge is called the "12-edge" and the bottom edge is the "9-edge" of the card. These terms are important since cards are described as entering various machines 9-edge first or 12-edge first. Also note that the card is divided into 80 vertical columns numbered 1 through 80. Horizontally along the length of the card are 12 rows in which punches can be made. (The basic punched card does not have any printing for the 12 and 11 rows.)

CARD CODES

Data is represented by means of one, two, or three punches in a single card column. The various punching positions in the card (rows) are divided into two groups—digit punching and zone punching. Rows 0 (zero) through 9 are known as the *digit* punches and rows 12, 11, and zero are *zone* punches. The 0 (zero) row, as you can see, serves a

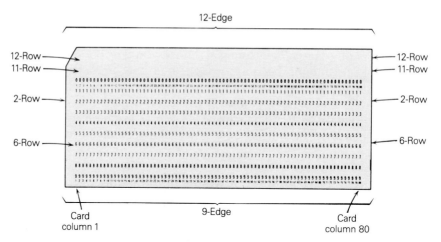

FIGURE 4.1
Card format.

double function: when we record the digit 0, it is a digit punch; but when we record alphabetic or special characters the zero is part of the zone punching.

Numeric data is represented by a single punch in a given card column. For example, if we want to store the value 7 in a card column 23, we simply punch a hole in row 7 of that column. To store the two-digit value 65 in a card, we would punch a 6 and a 5 in two adjacent card columns.

The punched-card format requires that alphabetic data be repre-sented by two punches in the same card column: a zone punch (12, 11, or 0) and a digit punch (1 through 9). The characters A through I consist of a 12 zone punch and one of the digit punches 1 through 9; J through R are made by an 11 zone punch and one of the digit punches 1 through 9; and S through Z are made with a 0 zone punch and one of the digits 2 through 9. (Note that since there are only 26 alphabetic characters, the last group, consisting of eight letters, starts with the digit "2".)

Letter	Zone Punch	Digit Punch
A through I	12	1 through 9
J through R	11	1 through 9
S through Z	0	2 through 9

Just as with numeric data, alphabetic data, such as names, can be punched in consecutive card columns anywhere in the card. Figure 4.2 shows the zone and digit punching rows and how the characters are made up from the various punching combinations. The illustration also shows a few of the special characters that can be made with the Hollerith code. They follow no set rule although most of them are made up of three punches per card column.

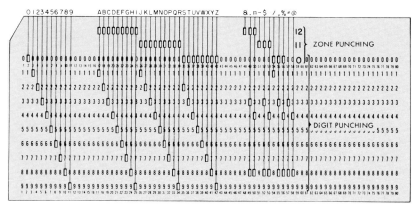

FIGURE 4.2
Punched-card coding structure.

SOURCE DOCUMENTS AND FIELDS OF DATA

Where does data come from? The origins are almost endless but the one with which we are familiar involves some type of source document, usually a piece of paper. In some cases, you are the originator in that you fill out a document, as in the case of a bank deposit form or a magazine subscription request. In some cases the record of data originates from a source document that is filled out by someone else at the time of data origination. For example, a speeding ticket is filled out by a highway patrol officer or a doctor fills out a medical report form or a medical prescription tag. These are just a few ways in which data originate and you can certainly think of other formats that you have seen and/or used.

Collecting data is not a trivial problem. The task of designing a document to collect data is actually quite difficult. The trick is to gather only the data items that are needed and to exclude the data which is available but which is not needed. As a matter of fact, too much data is worse than useless for two reasons. First, it wastes the time of the person doing the collecting. And second, too much data tend to obscure the vital data that is required.

Each individual data item on a source document is called a field of data. A data record is always comprised of at least one, but usually several fields of data. Thus, a magazine subscription form that you might have filled out would probably contain the following fields.

Field	Location in Record (Card Columns)
Last name	1–12
First name	13–23
Street address	24–40
City	41–55
State	56–57

Field	Location in Record (Card Columns)
Postal ZIP code	58–67
Date	68–73
Length of subscription	74–75
Amount paid	76–80

The key point to understand now is that a large amount of time, energy, and thought goes into the design of a source document that is used to collect data. The format is standardized right down to the number of characters that can appear in each field. Thus, when the source document is turned over to a keypunch (or "data entry") operator, the operator always knows the field name, its length, its position within the data record, and whether it can contain numeric, alphabetic, or mixed data. With cards, data fields are indicated by vertical lines separating the card columns, and frequently they are further differentiated by printing on the card itself. Figure 4.3 shows a card on which we have recorded information according to this format.

The data from the cards is entered into the computer system by a card reader unit that senses the holes, and translates the patterns of holes into electronic impulses that are sent to memory. After being read, the cards exit from the internal part of the card reader and go into a stacker.

KEY TO STORAGE SYSTEMS

As mentioned earlier, data can be converted to machine form in many ways. However, data entry of any type does not "just" happen. The entire operation is set up by the firm after, and only after, a number of preliminary steps have been completed. Management determines what outputs it needs (reports, checks, etc.) and, from these outputs,

FIGURE 4.3
Fields within a record.

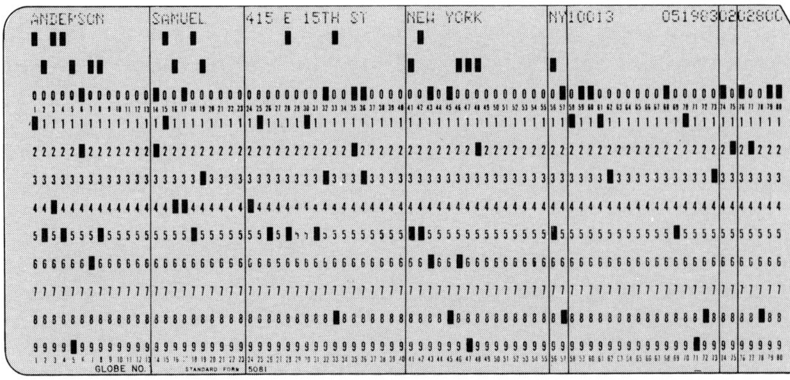

specialists in business systems work back through the operation to determine what source data is required for a specific job. Once the inputs are known, the next task is to arrange for the collection of source data (sales slips, bills, shipping documents, etc.) and to specify the format of the data fields within the record. From this point on the operation becomes a periodic process of entering data according to the predetermined format specifications.

Historically, the keypunch (or more correctly, a card-punch machine) has been the most commonly used device for data entry. Keypunching is a process in which raw data is put into an intermediate medium (cards) for subsequent entry into the computer system. As you probably know, use of this method is declining in favor of newer devices that either enter data directly into the computer or onto a faster, more versatile storage medium. For years the workhorse of the punched-card era was the IBM 029 Cardpunch (Figure 4.4).

Various surveys have shown that from 30 to 50% of a computer system's expense goes for data preparation. With costs in this range it is no wonder that a multitude of alternatives to the traditional punched-card method are available. Today, the problem is one of how to choose the best method from all that are available. Even attempting to categorize these methods is risky, as their functions frequently overlap one another.

Video-screen, cathode-ray-tube (CRT) devices have replaced the keypunch as the dominant form of data entry. The operator keystrokes from a source document and the information enters a buffer or temporary storage area within the unit and is displayed upon the screen. Verification is accomplished by visual inspection of the contents of the

"MURDER, EH? I'M IN FOR BENDING,
FOLDING AND MUTILATING,
COMPUTER CARDS."

FIGURE 4.4
IBM 029 cardpunch machine.

screen. Keyboard controls allow the operator to backspace and rekey over the error until satisfied that the data is correct. A visible marker or pointer light, called a *cursor,* shows the operator the spot where the next data character will be entered. When it appears that the data is correct, a special key causes transfer of the data to the main computer system.

The benefits from such systems are impressive when compared to card data entry—a throughput rate increase of 20 to 40%. Five major advantages to this method are as follows.

1. The data disks and tapes containing the keyed data can be handled at magnetic tape and disk speeds rather than at slower card-reader speeds.
2. Faster keystroking is possible because the operator does not have to wait for all the card positioning and handling that is common to the keypunch.
3. Greater accuracy is inherent with the input technique.
4. Freedom from the 80-character record format used with cards. This

point is particularly important because once you change from cards to a magnetic storage medium you can create and store data records of almost any size.
5. Communications capability on some systems.

In terms of complexity, the next higher level of data entry hardware would be a stand-alone terminal that has tape cassette or diskette storage. Virtually all key-to-storage devices use some type of memory (called a buffer) for temporarily storing data before it is written onto the storage medium.

MULTISTATION SYSTEMS

A more sophisticated form of key data entry is the multistation system such as is shown in Figure 4.5. In the systems illustrated, data is keyed onto individual diskettes by each operator. The dual-data station, designed for centralized, high-production data entry, is used by two operators concurrently, each keying to a separate diskette. The single-operator unit operates as a decentralized, stand-alone data entry work station.

The computer contains the logic circuitry and temporary storage areas (buffers) that are necessary to control data entry from multiple work stations. Systems of this type can control up to 64 terminals although 4 to 16 terminals are more common. The disk contains input

FIGURE 4.5

Multistation data entry system.

formatting information, a program library, and serves as a storage area for key input data.

Printers are often used with multistation disk systems to provide hard copy printout of batches of data, error reports, and operator statistics as compiled on each operator during entry procedures. A supervisory station may be used for regular data entry or to check on disk and format status, keystation status, etc.

INTELLIGENT TERMINALS

The terminal entry devices discussed in the previous section can be classed as "dumb" terminals in that they have no internal computational power of their own. However, some data entry terminals are very sophisticated and are known as "intelligent" terminals. Terminals of this type actually contain a small central processing unit and are programmable. They not only accept entry data but process it according to a stored set of instructions. Individual keys on the keyboard (called "soft" keys) can be programmed to perform tasks that are common to a particular application.

It is the sophistication of this type of device that permits the operator to use a more free form of data entry. The computer can perform a variety of editing and verifying operations on the incoming data. Typically the system can:

1. Prevent keying errors by blocking the use of certain keys (alphabetic keys when numeric data is being entered).
2. Generate repetitive fields to eliminate keying.
3. Reformat data fields into different order. Data formats for various jobs are stored in memory and the correct one recalled as needed.
4. Store the data.
5. Output data upon request either to a CRT screen or, in some cases, to a printer.
6. Provide for data insertion and correction.

One major benefit of video terminals is a general decrease in the number of errors, in comparison to standard keypunching, because of the visual method of verification. A second benefit is the increased input speed, as the operator does not have to wait for card positioning, which is common to the keypunch unit.

Another capability of some of the "intelligent" terminals is forms overlay. The programmer/operator can actually create (by using a special program on that machine) a business form, such as an invoice or inventory document, that will appear on the screen (Figure 4.6). The entry operators can then key directly into predesignated areas on the form.

In addition to acting as stand-alone data entry devices, "smart" terminals can act as preprocessors to take some of the processing burden off the main or host computer. They partially process the

FIGURE 4.6
"Intelligent" data entry terminals.

incoming data before it reaches the main computer system. Here, the terminal may check the input data for validity, length of fields, etc., before releasing it to its own auxiliary storage or to the central processing unit. Figure 4.7 shows a terminal that uses a quarter-inch cassette magnetic tape for the storage of data records. Cassettes have the advantage of being easily mailed from regional offices, warehouses, and the like, if communication capability is not present in the system. The computer into which the data will be entered usually does not accept cassette tapes directly. Instead, the tapes are inserted into an off-line device called a *pooler* which records the information on full-size magnetic tape reels. Cassettes generally hold over 100,000 characters of information, which means that eight hours of data entry can be stored on a single cassette.

ALTERNATIVES TO KEY DATA ENTRY

Much of the data used by businesses today is actually recorded twice. Often, the initial source data is recorded on some type of document (bill of sale, credit memo), but this data is not in machine-acceptable form. The second recording operation takes place when the data from the source document is translated into machine-acceptable format

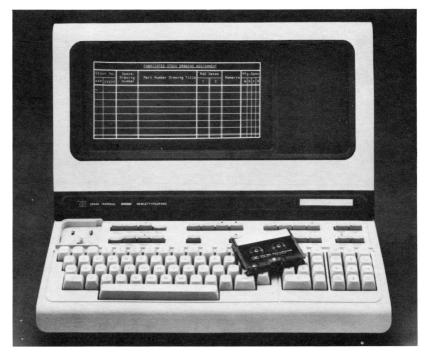

FIGURE 4.7
Data entry terminal with cassette storage and forms overlay.

during the key entry process. As you know, keying has as its main disadvantage the fact that the speed and accuracy of the process is limited by the human factor. Over the years the data processing industry has tried many methods to get around this problem. Some of these methods may be familiar to you, but let's take a closer look at alternate methods of capturing and entering data.

POINT-OF-SALE SYSTEMS (POS)
Electronic point-of-sales (POS) systems first originated in the early 1950s, but only in the last 5 to 10 years have they gained general acceptance by retailers. In 1975 it was estimated that over 50% of all cash registers in the country had been converted to some form of POS.

Depending upon the application, point-of-sales terminals perform several functions.

1. *Operator Guidance.* Keyboards have been designed to include a 10-key grouping for numeric data in special function keys that operate in a predetermined sequence to lead the clerk through the entry process.
2. *Data Collection.* Data is collected via key entry or optical scanning and is ultimately entered into the main computer system.

3. *Computations.* Small computers (microprocessors) are built into the terminals that perform item extensions, tax calculations, totals and subtotals, amounts tendered, and change offered.
4. *Communications.* Data collected in Step 2 is sent to the host computer immediately or captured on magnetic tape cassettes or some auxiliary storage media.
5. *Output.* Output may take the form of visual display, printed receipts for customers, internal documents, or all of the above.
6. *Inventory Control.* Perhaps the single most important attribute of POS systems is that they provide accurate inventory control. This aspect is extremely important when you consider that an average department store may stock over 1 million separate items, while a supermarket may have over 10,000 items on hand.
7. *Credit Authorization.* Instant credit authorization is particularly critical in some retail businesses. For those applications, a direct, or *on-line* connection between the terminal and the main computer is necessary.

Point-of-sales systems can be divided into two broad categories: general retail merchandise systems and supermarket systems. Retail merchandise systems, such as those found in Sears and Penneys, are characterized by the need for credit authorization and product identification capability. Terminals of this type often are programmable and therefore applicable over a wide range of uses. The retailer simply fills out forms describing details of the store operation and the functions needed on each terminal. The terminal manufacturer programs the information into a tape cassette that is either loaded directly into the terminal or into a minicomputer to which many terminals are linked. This approach allows the system to handle such diverse operations as electronic funds transfer and receiving and marking functions.

Typically, terminals of this type cost $3000 to $5000 and may be fitted with a variety of options, including a "light wand" reader. Merchandise information is read by passing the wand over the face of the price tag. A special color bar code on the price label indicates the brand, size, and price to the system (Figure 4.8).

Of the two general types of POS systems, supermarket systems have been lagging behind, even though the technology is currently available. The major block to the widespread usage of supermarket systems is acceptance by both the retailer and the customer. In turn, this acceptance hinges upon the use of a special identifying code for supermarket products.

The food industry, after a lengthy and intensive search, came up with a special coding system to mark the majority of items in food stores—the Universal Product Code (UPC). The 10-digit code (see Figure 4.9) is optically readable and uses the first five digits to identify the individual manufacturer. The second set of five digits identify the product by name and size.

FIGURE 4.8
Point-of-sale cash register terminal.

At the checkout stand the code is read by a wand as described above or by moving the item in front of a fixed scanner. The scanner reads the thickness of and the distance between the lines to determine the coded values. For example, a one is coded as shown.

FIGURE 4.9
Universal product code.

A seven is coded as indicated.

The resulting product code is fed to the computer, where the price is retrieved from storage. The price is then sent back to the terminal display unit and printed on the customer cash register tape.

Advantages of the system include 15% faster checkout time; fewer POS registers compared to regular cash registers; quick and accurate inventory control; and labor reduction. However, the single most controversial issue has not been fully resolved. Retailers want to eliminate individual price marking, which would mean a substantial savings in labor. Consumer groups, on the other hand, are fighting to continue the traditional unit marking. Local legislation will probably decide the matter in the form of a compromise to shelf pricing. The retailer then must decide whether the other benefits are worth the cost of a POS system.

Finally, a last note on data entry systems. With the advent of portable data entry devices, retail stores have an ideal inventory and ordering tool. In the late evening hours, after the store is closed, a clerk can survey the shelf stock and optically read or key in information on those items that need to be reordered. Battery-powered units of this type usually record the data on cassette tapes or on special memory packs (Figure 4.10).

FIGURE 4.10
Portable recorder in an inventory application.

OPTICAL DATA RECOGNITION

Optical recognition of data has long been a dream of DP systems designers mainly because of its potential speed advantage. In theory, the idea is very basic and follows the same pattern of data representation that we have seen throughout the text. Data (letters, digits, etc.) is represented by black marks, while the lack of data is indicated by the absence of a mark. However, the problem is not as simple as it sounds; the trick is to get the unit to recognize specific characters from a whole host of possible symbols. Generally, these and other problems have been solved, yet the ultimate problem of trying to read handwritten data still remains. How do optical readers work? As shown in Figure 4.11, light is focused on the document and is reflected back to the photocells. The optical reader detects a mark because of a gross difference in the amount of light reflected back from a mark or a no-mark. (A dark area on the paper will obviously absorb more light than will the absence of a mark.)

Optical Mark Reading. As the name optical mark reader implies, the equipment is capable of reading marks as opposed to actual alphabetic or numeric characters. Originally, optical mark readers were used almost exclusively in the scoring of tests (Figure 4.12), but today they are also used in data entry systems for the collection of payroll, inventory,

FIGURE 4.11
Optical data recognition.

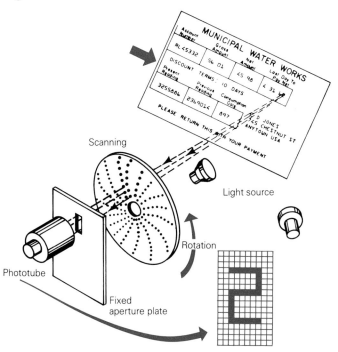

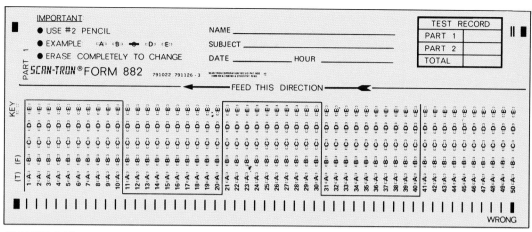

FIGURE 4.12
Optical mark test scoring sheet.

and production information. The interpretation of the mark is determined by reference to a particular point on the paper, a timing mark(s)
which usually appears on the edge of the page. One advantage of the
mark reader is that marks can be made with a regular No. 2 lead pencil
and clean erasures are permitted. Optical *character* recognition (OCR)
equipment, on the other hand, uses many more complex and expensive methods for the recognition of alphabetic and numeric characters.

The bar-code readers used in the retail trade for point-of-sale data
collection also fall into the general category of mark readers. Actually,
a wide variety of bar and mark coding schemes have been developed
for special applications.

Optical Character Recognition (OCR). Optical character recognition
is a form of input in which data that is understandable to humans is
converted into a computer-acceptable form. OCR has been part of
electronic data processing for over 25 years but has yet to gain wide
acceptance. Part of the reason for this is that the early machines were
very expensive, awkward to use, and operated with a high document
reject rate—over 15%. Much of the early trouble came because these
units had to be able to read hundreds of type fonts (a full assortment of
one size and style of printing type). Over the years, the OCR manufacturers and the major users have worked to adopt standard fonts.
The result was a font called OCR-A, which was developed by the
Business Equipment Manufacturers Association (BEMA) and adopted
by the American National Standards Institute (ANSI). A second font,
called the Farrington 7B, may be more familiar to many of you because
it is used primarily with credit cards utilizing embossed or raised
characters. Print quality degrades rapidly with cards of this type, which
makes optical reading a problem the more the card is handled (Figure
4.13).

FONT NAME	CHARACTER SETS
OCR A NRMA	0123456789 ACDMNPRUXY.″/$>
OCR-A subset (A)	0123456789 |YJH
OCR-A subset (B)	0123456789 $.+-
OCR B	0123456789 .-$

FIGURE 4.13
Optically readable characters.

Some of the document scanning devices are complete systems by themselves. Figure 4.14 shows an OCR document reader that can read a wide range of document sizes and formats. In addition, the scanned material can be stored internally or sent to the computer, sorted into pockets, or output to a line printer.

Because of the sophisticated electronics available in the resident minicomputer, most OCR devices have a "clipped character" feature that enables the system to read correctly as long as 80% of the character is present. Almost all document scanners have ways of notifying the operator when a field cannot be read. These "can't reads" are displayed to the operator for immediate on-line correction.

Readers of this type have been used quite successfully in *turn-around* situations where partially completed, machine-readable documents are sent to customers for completion and return. Additionally, many document readers are capable of reading hand-marked information along with the printed OCR characters. These two capabilities have made it possible for business firms to handle large volumes of documents economically (Figure 4.15).

The break-even point at which an OCR operation becomes economically feasible will vary with each type of operation. Some very successful uses of OCR document readers include the following.

1. Utility turn-around billing just described.
2. Airline recording of ticket/coupon information.
3. Hospital billing information.
4. Credit card processing.

Some document readers can read hand-printed numeric data. Figure 4.16 shows "constrained" handprint that must be printed (carefully) if the system is to read it successfully. The reading is done by a curve-tracing optical reader that seeks out and follows the hand-printed

FIGURE 4.14
Optical document reader.

numeric character in an attempt to recognize a valid pattern. For small operations, it is possible to utilize individual OCR wand devices that read character by character as the unit is moved across the document (Figure 4.17).

HANDPRINT DATA ENTRY

One of the newest methods of data entry appears to be the same as the constrained handprint that was shown in previous illustration. The main difference, however, is that the printed material is not read

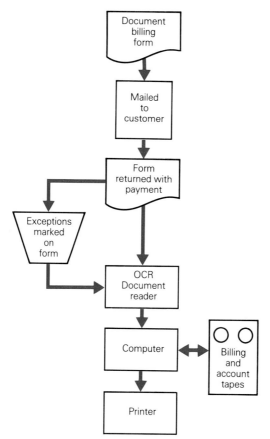

FIGURE 4.15
OCR turnaround billing system.

optically. The document is placed on a pressure-sensitive writing surface where every stroke of the pen or pencil is translated into electrical signals and sent to the computer system. Wrong characters can be corrected by writing over the original character. The computer then examines the way in which the character was formed and relates that to the patterns of all the characters stored in its memory. As the

FIGURE 4.16
Handprinted characters.

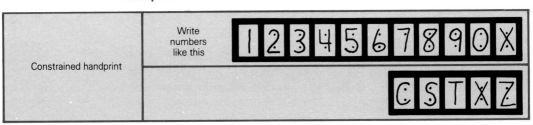

FIGURE 4.17
Hand-held optical reader.

character is recognized, it is displayed upon a one-line screen to provide a visual verification to the user.

Systems of this type are particularly applicable to random entry types of jobs such as the preparation of insurance policies or claims, and telephone order processing. Another advantage of handprint data entry is that it can be used quickly and easily by untrained personnel, particularly those who might be intimidated by a video screen terminal.

An even more interesting feature of the unit is that signatures of authorized users can be digitized and stored in memory. In special banking applications the digitized signature can be compared against a newly written signature before allowing certain types of monetary transfers or withdrawals.

VOICE DATA ENTRY

One of the most promising forms of source data entry is directly via voice. Continental Can Company is using this method to improve its

THE GREAT DATA FAMINE
Art Buchwald
Washington Post
September 28, 1969

One of the major problems we face in the 1970s is that so many computers will be built in the next decade that there will be a shortage of data to feed them.

Prof. Heinrich Applebaum, director of the Computer Proliferation Center at Grogbottom, has voiced concern about the crisis and has urged a crash program to produce enough data to get our computers through the seventies.

"We didn't realize," the professor told me, "that computers would absorb so much information in such a fast period of time. But if our figures are correct, every last bit of data in the world will have been fed into a machine by Jan. 12, 1984, and an information famine will follow, which could spread across the world."

"It sounds serious," I said.

"It is serious," he replied. "Man has created his own monster. He never realized when he invented the computer that there would not be enough statistics to feed it. Even now, there are some computers starving to death because there is no information to put into them. At the same time, the birth rate of computers is increasing by thirty percent a year. Barring some sort of worldwide holocaust, we may soon have to find data for 30,000,000 computers with new ones being born every day."

"You make it sound so frightening."

"It is frightening," Prof. Applebaum said. "The new generation of computers is more sophisticated than the older generation, and the computers will refuse to remain idle just because there is nothing to compute, analyze, or calculate. Left to their own devices, the Lord only knows what they will do."

quality-control operations in its Chicago Metals operation. The input unit consists of a small microphone headset connected via wire or a wireless transmitter to a speech-recognition terminal where the words are analyzed and identified by the computer.

When the operator is first assigned to the voice data entry terminal, the speech-recognition system must be "trained" to recognize an individual voice by having the person repeat each word 10 times. The system can handle up to 200 words, but 30 to 50 is more common. Since

"Is there any solution, professor?"

"New sources of data must be found. The Government must expand, and involved studies must be thought up to make use of the computers' talents. The scientific community, instead of trying to solve problems with computers, must work on finding problems for the computers to solve."

"Even if the scientists really don't want the answer?"

"Naturally. The scientific community invented the computer. Now it must find ways of feeding it. I do not want to be an alarmist, but I can see the day coming when millions of computers will be fighting for the same small piece of data, like savages."

"Is there any hope that the government will wake up to the data famine in time?"

"We have a program ready to go as soon as the bureaucrats in Washington give us the word. We are recommending that no computer can be plugged in more than three hours a day."

"We are also asking the government for $50 billion to set up data manufacturing plants all over the country. This data, mixed with soy beans, could feed hundreds of thousands of computer families for months."

"And finally we are advocating a birth control program for computers. By forcing a computer to swallow a small bit of erroneous information, we could make it sterile forever, and it would be impossible for it to reproduce any more of its kind."

"Would you advocate abortions for computers?" I asked Applebaum.

"Only if the Vatican's computer gives us its blessing."

the system learns the specific voice characteristics of each user, dialects, accents, or foreign language can be recognized. Day-to-day voice changes, such as are caused by colds, generally do not cause any special problems.

In addition to the microphone, each operator has a small alphanumeric display device that verifies acceptance of the words. If an error is detected, the operator says "erase" and reenters the correct term. If the data on the display is correct, it is acknowledged with

FIGURE 4.18
Audio processing.

"OK" and continues on. "In another use, some of the new Wang office computer systems have been designed to process audio data as well as data in traditional form (see Figure 4.18)."

SUMMARY OF
IMPORTANT POINTS

☐ The storage of data in cards rests on the unit record principle in which all the information concerning a single transaction is contained in one card.

☐ The standard punched card has a limitation of 80 characters formed in 80 vertical card columns.

☐ Zone punches are made in the 12, 11, and 0 rows. The digit punches are the 0 through 9 rows when numeric data is being entered. When alphabetic data is entered the digit portion is punched in rows 1 through 9.

☐ Numeric data is entered by a single punch in a card column. Alphabetic data is entered by a combination of a zone and a digit punch in the same card column. Special characters are usually formed with three punches per card column.

☐ A record of data is comprised of at least one but usually several fields of data, such as customer name, address, and amount of purchase.

☐ Verifying is an extremely important operation in the data entry process because the computer is incapable of correcting data entry errors.

☐ Key to storage systems offer an array of combinations involving stand-alone systems or multistation configurations. Storage media can take the form of regular magnetic tape reels, cassette tapes, diskettes, or disk auxiliary storage.

☐ In most cases, the systems depend upon the use of intelligent or programmable data entry terminals. Small computers within the units perform many of the functions previously relegated to keypunch operators. Consequently, we have intelligent systems that provide extensive editing, error checking, and reformatting of input data.

☐ Point-of-sales and optical reading were presented as alternatives to the key entry process.

☐ Various source-data-acquisition systems have been used to capture data at its point of origin.

☐ Inventory control was, and still is, the most important feature of most source-data-acquisition systems. Point-of-sale systems were described with a reminder that the retail food supermarkets have not yet fully adopted POS, even though their Universal Product Code is ready and workable.

☐ Optical data recognition devices have been around for many years, but only recently have they begun to be used in any significant quantity.

GLOSSARY OF TERMS

Buffer—a small amount of memory in some terminals where data is held temporarily for editing, formatting, or similar functions.

Data field—the column or consecutive columns used to store a particular piece of information.

Digit punch—any of the punches made in the 0 or 1 through 9 rows of the Hollerith card. The 1 through 9 digit punches are combined with the zone punches to make alphabetic characters.

Font—a full assortment of one size and style of printing type.

Hollerith card—the name given to the punched-card developed by Dr. Herman Hollerith. It is also commonly known as an IBM card.

Intelligent terminal—any input/output device that is programmable. To be "intelligent," a terminal must have some type of central processing unit in addition to memory or storage capability.

Keypunching—in data processing, the manual act of reading information from a source document and punching it into a card by means of keystrokes.

96-column card—a smaller punched card designed for use with the IBM System 3 computer.

Optical data recognition—the general term to describe any form of optical recognition of data. Included in the ODR are optical mark readers (such as used in test scoring), document readers, and specialized readers for specific industry usage.

Optical mark reader—an optical recognition device that is limited to the reading of marks instead of characters.

Pooler—a device for consolidating and/or converting key entry data into a form acceptable to the main computer. Typically, cassette tapes are converted to standard tape form.

Turn-around document—a machine-readable document produced by the computer and used in a billing process. The form is sent to the customer for completion and then becomes a direct input document to the system.

Unit record—the term applied to punched-card equipment because it uses a card that is a complete record itself.

Verifying—the act of checking the original keyed data to see if it is correct.

Zone punch—a punch in the 12, 11, or 0 row of the Hollerith card. The zone punches are usually combined with the digit punches to make alphabetic characters.

THOUGHT QUESTIONS

1. Why has there been a reluctance by many businesses to drop the punched-card entry method in favor of direct keyed entry?
2. List some of the data-input verification functions that could be performed by an intelligent terminal. Be specific and show some examples of the kinds of errors that could be caught here before they go into the main computer.
3. Discuss a situation that you have seen that involves some form of optical data recognition. What do you perceive as its drawbacks? Its advantages?
4. Have you seen any applications of voice data entry? Other than the application described in the text, where else do you think it could be used?
5. How much money should a company be willing to spend to verify data?
6. How accurate should data be? Is it necessary to always have 100% accuracy? At what point is data sufficiently accurate to be processed successfully?
7. Think of some examples in which a high degree of accuracy is necessary as opposed to otheE applications in which computer verification is not as important.

CHAPTER 5
THE CENTRAL PROCESSING UNIT: INTERNAL STORAGE

LEARNING OBJECTIVES

Upon completion of the chapter you should understand the following:

The makeup of computer memory and the nature of several memory devices, including core, semiconductor, and bubble memory.

That data is stored in memory as a series of switching elements turned on or off.

The need for and use of virtual storage methods.

That many memory devices are in the experimental stage, but that the gap between experimental and practical can be very large.

How a circuit chip is made.

How data fields are represented in memory.

That most modern computer systems represent data internally in one of two 8-bit formats: EBCDIC or ASCII.

CHAPTER CONTENTS

The previous chapter showed you some of the devices and methods used to enter data into a computer system.

More accurately, data is entered into *memory,* which is also called *internal* or *primary storage*. What we need to find out now is what memory is and how it is used. The following chapter will cover the other two parts of the central processing unit, the control unit and the arithmetic logic unit.

COMPUTER MEMORY

Computer memory differs from auxiliary storage (magnetic tape or disk, mentioned earlier), sometimes called secondary storage, in several ways.

1. *Speed.* Obviously the term speed is relative but it generally means the amount of time it takes to *access,* i.e., "get to" or retrieve a character. Computer memory speed is expressed in terms of microseconds or nanoseconds (one-millionth or one-billionth of a second), while auxiliary storage operates at the millisecond level (one-thousandth of a second). The faster, newer computers have memory cycle times of 100 nanoseconds or less—a time measurement that is difficult to comprehend. Another way of expressing this speed is to say that it takes 100-billionths of a second to go into memory and retrieve a stored character. The term "character," by

the way, refers to a single symbol, such as a digit or a letter of the alphabet.

2. *Storage capacity.* Capacity is another relative term, but the amount of memory within a machine is typically expressed in thousands of characters. Actually to the question of how much main storage a system has, the answer is normally given by using the letter K, which means thousands. (Technically, K is equal to 1024, which means that a 64K machine actually has 65,536 characters of storage.) Thus, a computer that contains 64,000 characters of memory would be described as a 64K machine. In recent years the price of memory has dropped so drastically that many of the latest computers have a memory size of 1 to 4 million bytes. (One "megabyte," or 1 Mbytes of memory.)

    Auxiliary storage, on the other hand, is more frequently expressed in terms of millions of characters of storage. Some auxiliary storage devices, such as disk and tape, can store several hundred million characters each. Special mass storage devices, however, can store trillions of characters.

3. *Use.* One of the major differences between the two kinds of storage is in the way they are used. Memory is used to store information that is *currently* being worked upon. A key point here is that data can only be worked upon (i.e., manipulated) within the central processing unit. This means that the first step is to bring data into memory either through the data entry process discussed previously or from auxiliary storage (magnetic tape and disk). For example, customer charge and payment records will be held in auxiliary storage. When a customer makes a payment on account, the data record is read in from auxiliary storage (i.e., brought into memory), updated or changed in some way, and then placed back into auxiliary storage. In this particular case, the updated customer information not only will be stored on an auxiliary storage device but most likely some sort of printed output or visual record of the transaction will be prepared.

4. *Addressability.* Each storage position in memory is addressable by the programmer. By this we mean that the programmer can cause the computer to go directly to the desired storage position and perform a specific operation. In all cases, however, the data record must be brought into internal (or main) memory prior to being operated upon. With magnetic tape storage, for example, the storage medium simply has to be searched in order to find a particular piece of data. Data records on magnetic disk are directly addressable and offer a considerable increase in speed. (The makeup and use of auxiliary storage will be discussed in detail in a later chapter.)

5. *Cost.* Although the price of memory has decreased dramatically in the last 10 years, in terms of cost per character, computer memory is far more expensive than auxiliary storage. Therefore, most computer systems employ a small amount of memory and large quantities of inexpensive auxiliary storage.

MAGNETIC CORE MEMORY

For a period of nearly 20 years, virtually all computers used magnetic core for main memory. Today there are few, if any, new computers being manufactured with this type of memory. Still, core was so common in the past that the term core has become synonymous with memory.

The term core is particularly descriptive because each core is a very small iron "doughnut" with a hole in the center. The standard 18-mm (millimeter) core is slightly larger than the size of the period at the end of this sentence, and yet it has three or four wires strung through the 10-mm hole in the center. Made from special metallic compounds that permit rapid magnetization, the cores are charged electrically to hold data in a simple ON–OFF or *binary* form. Each core is really a switch that is either ON (one) or OFF (zero) according to the direction in which the magnetism flows, as shown in the following illustration:

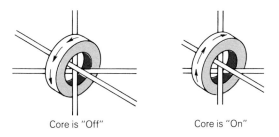

Core is "Off"   Core is "On"

These cores or switches operate exactly the same way your typical house light switch works—the lights are either on or off. Early in the history of computer development, designers found the binary ON–OFF method to be an efficient, fast, cheap, and reliable way to represent data internally. Each switching element, such as the cores just depicted, is known as a *bit*, which is an abbreviated form of the term "binary digit." All by itself, a single core or binary element is not too useful, but when they are strung together in combinations of four or more bits, they can represent or store a single character.

Figure 5.1 shows how an actual piece of data is stored in core memory. Notice that the configuration requires eight switching elements (cores) in a particular ON or OFF configuration to store a single character. The illustration also shows how a string of bits becomes synonymous with a memory location.

Even though core machines are rapidly disappearing, this brief discussion has been given because the term is still used and apparently will be for quite some time. In addition, a core diagram is an excellent way for you to visualize the idea of a single, addressable position of memory.

SEMICONDUCTOR MEMORY

In the 1970s improved manufacturing methods and new technological developments combined to lower the price of semiconductor memory devices below that of core. Core then began to be replaced by the

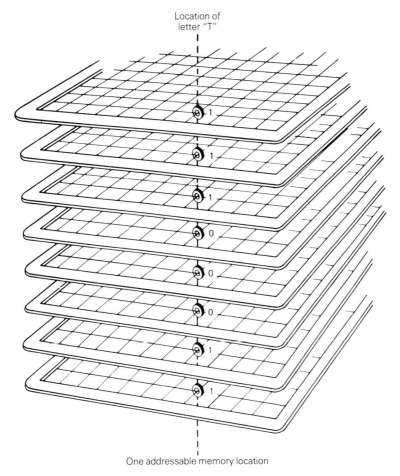

FIGURE 5.1
Core memory showing the storage of a single character.

cheaper and faster semiconductor chips. The term refers to the fact that the device acts as a gate (or a light switch) and either allows electricity to flow through (the ON state) or breaks the flow of energy (OFF state).

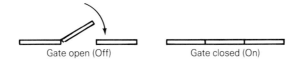

The microscopic-size circuits are etched onto silicon chips that become the building blocks that form the components of the central processing unit. A magnified view of a silicon semiconductor chip is shown in Figure 5.2. This chip is about one-twentieth of an inch square and holds 64K *bits* or 8000 characters. Chips are already being

FIGURE 5.2
Fire ant alongside 64K-bit memory chip.

produced that hold eight times as much, about 500K bits of information. As the size of these circuit elements decreases so do the power requirements and the access times. Semiconductor memories have one major drawback in that they are *volatile*. In core memory, the individual cores are magnetized either on or off and stay that way even if power is lost. Semiconductor memory does not magnetize anything, so it is dependent upon an uninterruptible power supply.

In discussing computer memory, three other terms need to be mentioned. Both semiconductor memory and core memory are said to be *random access,* meaning the user can access any storage position in the same amount of time. Semiconductors all have this capability and are often called *RAM* chips (random access memory).

In contrast to RAMs, we have *ROM,* which stands for *read-only memory.* Some semiconductor chips are made in such a way that they can be randomly read, yet the information contained there can never be altered. Finally, there is *PROM* or *programmable read-only memory.* These are ROM chips whose contents can be changed by prolonged application of ultraviolet light and then rewritten electronically (Figure 5.3). However, PROMs cannot be altered by the programmer. The use of ROMs and PROMs will be shown in a later chapter on microprocessors.

BUBBLE MEMORY

Although bubble memory is one of the newer storage techniques, scientists at Bell Laboratories were working on such devices in the

FIGURE 5.3
Ultraviolet light focused on a PROM chip.

1960s. Chips of garnet or synthetic ferrite are coated with a thin layer of magnetic film that can be magnetized to form minute negatively charged regions (bubbles) in positively charged strata. In keeping with the binary nature of computer electronic components, the presence of a bubble represents a binary one, while the absence of a bubble is a binary zero. Electrical charges are used to control the generation, storage, detection, and movement of the bubbles to a precise degree even though they are only one-millionth of an inch (micron) wide.

One of the advantages of bubble memory is that, unlike semiconductor memory, bubble memory is nonvolatile; that is, loss of electric power does not destroy or alter the values that are stored. In the late 1970s and early 1980s there was a great deal of excitement and hope for the future of this technology. After some initial successes, however, attempts to improve access time and to increase storage capacity were disappointing, particularly in competition with other memory devices. Despite this, bubble devices do have some specific uses where their light weight, dependability, low power consumption, and ruggedness make them ideal for use in hostile or difficult environments. For example, some manufacturing environments present extremes of dirt, dust, or shock, and bubble memory is ideally suited for these uses. One of its first applications was in portable terminals, but so far its major use has been in the telephone industry, where bubble memory is used to store the recorded messages that we often hear. Figure 5.4 shows a 256K bubble memory chip photographed against a magnified portion of the chip's circuitry.

FIGURE 5.4
Bubble memory chip.

VIRTUAL STORAGE

As mentioned earlier in the textbook, computers of the 1960s and early 1970s commonly had memory capacity in the range of 32K to 256K characters. Users often wanted more memory, but the cost was too high at that time. In the 1970s we saw a dramatic decrease in the price of memory so that 1 and 2 million byte memories became more common on large computer systems. Despite these increases, new computer applications made even greater demands on memory and virtual storage or virtual memory was devised as a solution to the problem.

The problem that virtual storage solved has been around for a long time, the problem faced by the programmer of not having enough physical memory for a program. One solution involved the expenditure of considerable effort to devise exotic and often tricky ways to reduce the number of lines of code in the program. A second and burdensome approach was that of segmentation in which the needed segment of the program was in memory being executed, while those segments that were not needed at that moment were stored out on disk. When the first segment completed, 'the next segment was brought into memory and executed. Note that in this method the second segment was overlayed on top of the previous segment (Figure 5.5). A variation on this method involved keeping the main program in memory and bringing in smaller segments as needed.

Although virtual storage is dependent upon the physical hardware of memory and disk storage, it is really a software concept. On virtual

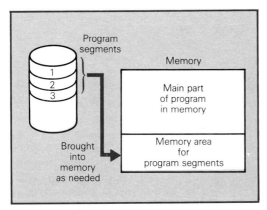

FIGURE 5.5
Virtual storage concept.

storage machines, the computer system software *automatically* takes care of the program segmentation chores. The net effect is that the programmer can ignore the limitations of memory and program without worrying about program segments. A second advantage is that the system software is likely to do a better job of making efficient use of memory than could the programmer. Virtual storage software is extremely sophisticated and, in turn, makes its own demands upon the facilities of the system. In some cases, the system is not capable of handling the swapping chores efficiently and spends more time looking for and swapping segments than it does in actual processing. When this occurs, the system is said to be "thrashing," much like a non-swimmer that has been thrown into a lake.

MEMORY: THE FUTURE

At this point, the most likely future successor to semiconductor and bubble technology will be the Josephson junction which offers the potential speed of one nanosecond (one-billionth of a second). Today, most high-speed computers operate in the range of 30 to 50 nanoseconds. One limiting factor in computer cycle time is the distance that electricity can travel along a wire in a given amount of time. In 1 nanosecond, for example, an electric impulse can travel about 12 inches along a wire. To speed up computer operations, one approach has been that of placing the components closer together. The fastest computer today, the Cray-II, has done exactly that and the designers have achieved a cycle time of approximately 12 nanoseconds. The limiting factor, however, has been one of trying to find ways to dissipate the heat generated within the closely packed components.

The Josephson junction or electronic gate is a logical solution, since the unit is a superconducting device that operates at cryogenic temperatures; that is, within a few degrees of absolute zero. It generates little heat and is the fastest switch known. It can change states (from on to off) in approximately 6 picoseconds or 6 one-trillionths of a second. Since the maximum speed of the central processing unit is determined by the time it takes a switch to change states, the potential of the Josephson junction is enormous. In addition, these switches can also store information so they can be used in both memory and the control unit.

Millions of dollars and a great many years of research have been devoted to the device and its use in computers. Fortunately, building Josephson chips may not be too great a task, as fabrication techniques probably will follow established semiconductor technology. Who needs machines with this speed? Even at today's speeds, computers are not fast enough to do even a reasonably good job on complicated tasks such as weather prediction. Westinghouse just purchased a Cray computer because they felt they needed additional computing power for their engineers and scientists involved in the design of high-technology equipment, such as nuclear reactors, steam turbine generators, solar energy, and the like (Figure 5.6). Beyond that, Japan announced in

FIGURE 5.6
CRAY-1 computer at the National Center for Atmospheric Research.

1982 that the government would help back a long-range plan to produce a superfast computer—perhaps a hundred times faster than those that exist today—by the year 1990.

DATA FIELDS IN MEMORY

Earlier in the chapter you saw how a single character was stored by means of a series of bits (binary switches) turned on or off. Depending upon the particular programming language used, the programmer can manipulate a single character stored in memory. And in some cases, it is even possible to work at the bit level; i.e., to manipulate a single bit within a character. However, the normal process is to work with entire fields of data.

When data was shown in a punched card it was in the form of data fields such as employee number, employee name, and hours worked. The process is exactly the same for data entered from a video screen input device or from auxiliary storage units. In addition, it makes no difference whether memory is actually comprised of core, semiconductor chips, or bubbles, as the representation of data is still in the form of a series of bits turned on or off.

An important point to understand here is that whoever is working with the data *knows* precisely the nature and order of the fields that make up the records being handled. For example, the programmer knows that the fields within each record appear in the following order.

Customer Identification Number
Customer Name
Date of Transaction
Amount of Purchase

In addition, the programmer knows that the identification number field is numeric and 9 digits long; that the name field is alphabetic and 20 characters long, etc.

When the data record enters memory, it will go into consecutive memory positions, as shown in Figure 5.9.

Note that, as shown in the diagram, our 80-column card record was read into memory as 80 characters, some of which are numeric, while others are alphabetic. The card's-worth of data occupies 80 positions of memory, but the computer is incapable of "knowing" where one field begins and another one ends. Instead, the programmer must tell the system where a field starts and stops and the kind of data it contains. It is the programmer's responsibility to manipulate the fields properly within memory.

MAKING A CIRCUIT CHIP

Ingenious electronic engineering coupled with some of the cleanest work processes imaginable are the keys to the production of integrated circuit chips. The process starts with an order from a customer for a chip to perform a specific function. The proposed chip gets its start on an electronic "breadboard" made up of old-fashioned transistors, diodes, etc., on which the circuitry design can be tested. Before computers became part of the design phase, the complex circuits were formed as a series of interconnected lines that resemble an immensely detailed street map. The large-scale design was then digitized point by point for entry into the computer to begin the shrinking process. Digitizing of the drawing is done by technicians who use a magnifying eyepiece to follow each line of the electronic maze. In turn, the eyepiece is attached to a computer that records every movement along the path that the technician follows. In this sense, the act of digitizing is much the same as providing map coordinates for particular geographic locations.

An integrated circuit is even more complex than most people realize because a chip is actually composed of many layers of material. Each layer, of course, requires a different drawing, and as more and more devices get packed into a chip, the cost increases dramatically. Today, the complex drawing process is being replaced with specialized artwork and sophisticated computer-aided design (CAD) tools. According to one industry spokesperson, "Before CAD, a 100,000 transistor chip would have taken 60 man-years to lay out and another 60 man-years to debug."

After the design specifications have been entered into the system, the computer is used to control an electron-beam exposure system. This is a lithography process in which the intense electron beam etches the structure of the chip on chemically treated glass. The finished glass plates then become the stencils or "masks" used for the next part of the fabrication process.

In the meantime, much like baking cookies, the production department bakes trays of silicon wafers whose electrical behavior can be altered by the addition of minute quantities of photosensitive and acid-resistant chemicals. Then, the glass masks or stencils are used to bombard the wafers with ultraviolet light that alters the chemical nature of selected areas on the chip.

Testing the chip (Figure 5.7) is done by computer-controlled devices and a reject rate of 50% is not uncommon. To alleviate the high reject rate, more and more chips are being designed with redundant or extra circuits. Then, if one part of the chip is faulty, the extra set of circuits can perform the same function. Finally, the individual chips are sawn out, wired to electric leads, and mounted in holding cases. After all that work, a chip with over 10,000 circuit gates or elements may cost less than $25.

FIGURE 5.7
Testing a chip on a wafer.

How precise are some of these manufacturing techniques? Consider this: A human hair is about 100 microns wide (a micron is a millionth of an inch). Very large-scale-integration (VLSI) manufacturing involves fabrication of circuit parts that are only 3 microns wide! Work is already underway on circuit elements that will be 1 micron in width. Figure 5.8 depicts a display of computer circuitry in the Boston Museum of Science.

FIGURE 5.8
Computer display at Boston Museum of Science.

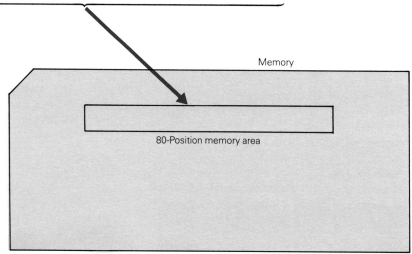

FIGURE 5.9
Data fields entering memory.

DATA REPRESENTATION

Earlier in the text we pointed out that data entering into a computer is converted into a format or code that the system can understand. Since the computer is an electronic device, it is perfectly suited to a binary code, i.e., a code that consists of the presence or absence of an electrical pulse. Actually, this concept should not be that new to you since the Hollerith card code discussed in Chapter 4 was really an ON–OFF configuration. For example, a value of 6 was represented by the presence of a punch in the 6 row. Another way of looking at the card coding structure is to think of it as an arbitrary arrangement of symbols that are always in one of two states—on or off—which is the equivalent of the presence or absence of an electrical signal. Alphabetic characters were a little more complex because the coding involved two punches per card column. However, by looking at a card it should be easy to see that each alphabetic character is still a binary arrangement of holes–no-holes.

Most people are familiar with the decimal system, and it would be extremely inconvenient for us to try to read or understand data in any other form, yet the computer cannot operate internally in decimal form. To get around this operational difference between man and machine, the computer:

1. Accepts information in decimal form.
2. Changes the data into binary.
3. Does the calculations in binary.
4. When the results are to be printed, the system changes the format and outputs the answers in decimal form.

It would be nice at this point to be able to dismiss the topic of data representation on the basis that the user really does not need to know about the internal workings of the machine. However, with more and more personal or small computers appearing on the market, the chances are becoming greater that you will be dealing directly with the machine. The details of numbering systems are covered in the Appendix, but let's take a brief look at data representation.

Earlier in this chapter we mentioned that most machines use a series of at least 4 bits to code or store a single character in memory. Second-generation machines generally used a 6-bit structure, but modern systems use one of two 8-bit arrangements: EBCDIC (extended binary coded decimal interchange code: ebb-sa-dick) or ASCII (American standard code for information interchange: ask-key).

The EBCDIC structure is common to IBM machines and is often called "byte." Actually, the term is in such common usage that the response to the question, "How much memory does your machine have?" is often made in terms of bytes, even if the machine does not actually have the EBCDIC byte storage format (Figure 5.10). The ASCII code also uses 8 bits, but represents the symbols with a different coding structure (Figure 5.11).

SUMMARY OF
IMPORTANT POINTS

☐ Computer memory differs from auxiliary storage in several ways.
   Memory is faster than auxiliary storage.
   Auxiliary storage is larger.

Alphabetic Character	EBCDIC 8-Bit Coding	
	Zone	Digit
A	1100	0001
B	1100	0010
C	1100	0011
D	1100	0100
E	1100	0101
F	1100	0110
G	1100	0111
H	1100	1000
I	1100	1001
J	1101	0001
K	1101	0010
L	1101	0011
M	1101	0100
N	1101	0101
O	1101	0110
P	1101	0111
Q	1101	1000
R	1101	1001
S	1110	0010
T	1110	0011
U	1110	0100
V	1110	0101
W	1110	0110
X	1110	0111
Y	1110	1000
Z	1110	1001

Numeric Character	EBCDIC 8-Bit Coding	
	Sign	Digit
0	1111	0000
1	1111	0001
2	1111	0010
3	1111	0011
4	1111	0100
5	1111	0101
6	1111	0110
7	1111	0111
8	1111	1000
9	1111	1001

FIGURE 5.10
EBCDIC coding structure.

FIGURE 5.11
ASCII coding structure.

Character	Code	Character	Code	Character	Code
A	01000001	P	01010000	0	00110000
B	01000010	Q	01010001	1	00110001
C	01000011	R	01010010	2	00110010
D	01000100	S	01010011	3	00110011
E	01000101	T	01010100	4	00110100
F	01000110	U	01010101	5	00110101
G	01000111	V	01010110	6	00110110
H	01001000	W	01010111	7	00110111
I	01001001	X	01011000	8	00111000
J	01001010	Y	01011001	9	00111001
K	01001011	Z	01011010		
L	01001100				
M	01001101				
N	01001110				
O	01001111				

Memory is not really a place of storage, but is where processing action goes on.

Memory positions are individually addressable, while auxiliary storage is either not addressable or is addressable in terms of records rather than characters of data.

In terms of cost per character or per storage position, memory is more expensive than auxiliary storage.

☐ Core was the dominant form of memory until the 1970s, when it was replaced by semiconductor chips.

☐ There are various forms of memory chips.
RAM—random access memory.
ROM—read-only memory.
PROM—programmable read-only memory.

☐ One of the latest memory devices is bubble memory. These are circuit chips made in such a way that the presence or absence of tiny magnetic bubbles can signify a one or zero binary condition.

☐ Virtual storage is a hardware/software concept that gives the programmer the appearance of having an unlimited amount of computer memory in which to work. The system does this by breaking a large program into segments or pages and bringing them into memory whenever needed.

☐ Data fields in memory are made up of a series of contiguous memory locations and it is the responsibility of the programmer to see that these fields are handled correctly during input, processing, or output.

GLOSSARY OF TERMS

Access time—the time it takes to retrieve data from a storage device or to move it from memory to the control unit.

Addressability—the characteristic of certain storage devices in which each storage area or location has a unique address. This address is then usable by the programmer to access the information stored at that location.

ASCII—an international binary code used for interchange or communication of information between machines.

Bit—Binary digit. A single binary position that can exist in only one of two states: ON (1) or OFF (0).

Bubble memory—a memory method that uses areas of negative charges in positive strata to represent binary 1 and 0.

Byte—the term applied to one storage position in many modern computers. A byte is actually comprised of a string of eight binary digits and is common to most IBM systems. See EBCDIC.

Core memory—a form of storage in which information is represented by the magnetization of small iron cores.

Core plane—a grid of wires upon which small iron cores are strung. A series of core planes are stacked to make up main memory.

EBCDIC—extended binary coded decimal interchange code. See byte.

PROM—programmable read-only memory. Memory chips that normally can only be read, not written upon. However, the application of ultraviolet light can erase the contents of PROM so that it can be rewritten.

RAM—random access memory. Memory whose contents can be read and/or written upon.

ROM—read-only memory. Memory circuitry that can only be read and which cannot be written upon.

Virtual storage—a hardware/software technique that allows the programmer to write programs that are larger than main memory. The system automatically breaks the program into pages and brings the pages into memory when required.

Volatility—the term used in reference to whether a memory chip loses its contents when power is turned off.

THOUGHT QUESTIONS

1. How can the Hollerith card coding structure be thought of as an ON–OFF arrangement or binary coding structure?
2. Why doesn't the internal operation of a computer system take place in decimal form?
3. What do you think will happen if the programmer incorrectly "tells" the computer the size of a data field?
4. How can you preserve data in volatile memory if power is lost?
5. What happens to the data that is stored in nonvolatile memory when the electric power is turned off.
6. What kind of information might be contained in ROM?

CHAPTER 6
MORE ABOUT THE CENTRAL PROCESSING UNIT

LEARNING OBJECTIVES

Upon completion of the chapter you should understand the following:

How the control unit performs its job of maintaining overall control of the computer system.

What firmware is and how it is used.

The general nature of registers and how they are used.

The composition of computer instructions and how instructions are processed by the control unit.

The way in which the arithmetic/logic unit works.

The nature of computer logic.

The steps in the execution of a simple program.

The use of parity checking by computer systems to verify the correct coding of a character within memory.

CHAPTER CONTENTS

Now that you know what memory is, the next area of concern is what to do with the data once it is in memory. In broad terms, the answer is quite simple: By means of a program, we manipulate the data so as to solve the particular problem we are working upon.

What do we mean by the term "manipulate" the data? Well, in the simplest case, little or no manipulation may be involved. If, for example, we wished only to *read* in the card record, as shown in the previous chapter, and then *write* the record of data onto auxiliary storage (tape or disk), then no manipulation would be necessary.

On the other hand, even the simplest payroll problem is likely to involve multiplication of hours worked by the rate of pay; the calculation of deductions; and the subtraction of deductions, to come up with a net pay amount. Even simple programs that do not involve arithmetic computation usually require that fields be moved or repositioned to make for better looking printed output. Virtually all programs, however, require the services of all three parts of the central processing unit: memory, the control unit, and the arithmetic/logic unit.

THE CONTROL UNIT

Memory and its operation were covered earlier and now we wish to concentrate our attention on another part of the central processing unit—the control unit. In terms of physical makeup, the control unit (and the arithmetic/logic unit) consist of miniaturized integrated-circuit chips that usually are mounted on small (8 × 5 inch) plug-in boards.

The general function of the control unit is to supervise and coordinate all operations of the computer. Some of its specific activities are to:

1. Recognize instructions (as opposed to data).
2. Execute specific instructions from a set of available instructions.
3. Alter or change (as directed by the program) the sequence in which the instructions are executed.
4. Provide for the transfer of data to and from memory and the arithmetic unit.
5. Provide temporary storage for answers or partial results that are generated during arithmetic operations.
6. Coordinate input/output operations.
7. Provide precise timing for the entire operation by means of an electronic clock.

In performing its functions, both the control unit and the arithmetic/logic unit make use of *registers*. A register is nothing more than a small amount of memory (often two to eight positions) that functions as a temporary storage area during control and/or arithmetic/logic operations. For example, the *accumulator* is a register that is used to store temporarily data that is being manipulated by the arithmetic/logic unit. The *program counter* register stores the memory address of the next instruction to be executed by the control unit. The *instruction* register contains the instruction that is currently being executed by the control unit. The *address* register holds the address or location of a value stored in memory.

In general, then, the control unit is a *hardware* device that fetches an instruction from memory, translates it into specific electronic signals, and routes these signals to other electronic components (such as the arithmetic/logic unit) according to extremely precise timing. It may appear that the hardware activities just discussed are fairly clearcut. However, in actual practice the distinction between hardware and software is not quite so clear. Instead, other techniques and devices have been developed that fall somewhere in between.

For example, if the circuitry of the control unit is permanent or "hardwired," it means that the system must be programmed with the exact set of instructions for which it was designed. Thus, the electronic architecture of the chip determines the nature of the language understood by the computer. On the surface it would seem that this is no disadvantage at all. However, as the users "grow" with their machine, often they become aware of needs and uses that were not anticipated originally. Frequently, software is already available for these needs but written for a type of computer other than that owned by the business firm. Converting the programs to fit your machine is usually too expensive and the ideal situation would be to have your machine be able to accept programs written for another computer.

Most of the larger, modern computers get around this problem by providing some capability for changing the basic way in which the control unit itself functions. Some systems provide this system flexibility by means of special read-only-memory (ROM) circuitry. When called into action, this circuitry, in effect, changes the nature or operating characteristics of the machine. Because of this circuitry, the user is able to *emulate,* or run, programs written for one machine on another, different computer. In this case, the emulator circuitry is a hardware part of the control unit.

Another way to provide emulation capability is by means of *firmware.* Figure 6.1 shows firmware from a floppy disk being loaded into a computer. The firmware, or special system software, consists of a series of *microinstructions,* each of which causes execution of an

FIGURE 6.1
Firmware being loaded into the control unit via flexible disk.

extremely basic, simple processing function. (Hence the term microcode or microinstructions as opposed to regular instructions.) The term firmware is appropriate because usually it is only the manufacturer that can provide this level of programming. Microprogramming, as you may well have already guessed, is very difficult to write because it requires a detailed knowledge of the design and circuitry of the computer.

COMPUTER INSTRUCTIONS

Computer instructions may be of a variety of types, *but* each instruction causes one specific action to take place. An instruction to "Read a card from the card reader" would, upon being executed, cause the data from a card to be entered into a particular area of memory. Computer instructions are divided into two basic parts: an *operation code* and *operand(s)*.

1. *Operation code.* An operation code is an alphabetic or numeric character(s) that causes the computer to perform a specific operation. For example, an "op code" of 13 might be interpreted by the hardware circuitry to mean "move data within memory." The code itself is very likely to be different with each machine and involves considerable remembering on the part of the programmer working with such codes. You will appreciate the above statement when you realize that a large computer might have up to 500 individual operation codes in its instruction set. (Actually, this isn't quite as bad as it sounds, as there may be only 40 or 50 commonly used codes. These you would learn fairly quickly and the others could be looked up in a manual when needed.)
2. *Operand(s).* An operand(s) usually refers to the location of data that is to be worked upon. Data may be located in main memory or in registers, as discussed earlier. Most computers have either one or two operands, and the number of operands serves as a rough indication of the power of the system. A typical two-operand instruction using data stored in registers is shown here:

Op Code	1st Operand	2nd Operand
21	7	4

This instruction may mean: Add (operation code 21) the contents of register 4 (second operand) to the contents of register 7 (first operand). (The presumption made here is that the programmer previously had placed specific data into registers 4 and 7.)

Computers with only one operand in the instruction format usually make use of a special register called an accumulator, which was discussed earlier. The instruction 4602386, for example, would

RESEARCHERS TRYING TO GROW BIOCIRCUITS
By Tim Scannell
CW Staff

UNIVERSITY, Miss.—Imagine a computer circuit that has a physical dimension of roughly a millionth of a meter.

Now imagine a similar circuit that is 500 times smaller but every bit as functional. Sound far-fetched?

Not to a group of scientists and researchers across the country who have discovered that molecules and even bacteria can be manipulated and grown in a laboratory to produce computer circuits. In theory, their research would result in replacing the billions of molecules that presently make up a silicon chip with a single home-grown atom. These atoms could then be grouped together to build a pint-size computer that is more powerful than today's most sophisticated supercomputers.

Although the biotechnology field is far from crowded, a number of major firms and the U.S. government have already jumped on the research bandwagon. IBM began preliminary work on molecular electronics as early as 1975. And at least one firm has sprouted that is totally dedicated to applying genetics and biology to the design of molecular-level microcircuits.

However, there are problems that make the first functional "test tube" computer more a product of science fiction than of science fact. This is because a great deal of present-day molecular experimentation is a "hit or miss" proposition where setbacks and dead ends are familiar friends, according to Robert M. Metzger, an associate professor of chemistry at the University of Mississippi.

actually mean "add (op code 46) the field beginning in memory position 02386 location to that which is already in the accumulator." In this type of operation the answer is developed by the addition circuitry and then placed in the accumulator.

The execution of a computer instruction is actually a complicated process that is performed by hundreds of internal circuits. As mentioned earlier, most of this circuitry is hardwired, but in some cases the work is done by emulator circuits residing in firmware or read-only memory.

All computer operations take place in fixed intervals of time as measured by an electronic clock. A set number of timed impulses make up what is known as a *machine cycle*. A machine cycle, then, is the period of time in which the computer can perform a specific machine operation. Each instruction that is executed is comprised of a

"There is no guarantee that once we make it, the molecule will behave the way we want it to," Metzger commented. "It's the luck of the organic chemist."

Metzger, along with Dr. Charles Panetta, is presently experimenting with different chemicals and chemical compounds in an attempt to produce a synthetic current-carrying molecule. The molecules can be constructed as either electron donors or electron acceptors.

Once the molecules are built, donors and acceptors will be separated by layers of thin metal, according to Metzger. To produce the on-off bit modes of a traditional computer, electrons will be switched from one molecule to another via a chemically insulating sigma bridge. Unfortunately, building this bridge is much more difficult than drawing a theory on paper.

While the donor and acceptor molecules can conduct electricity, there is is presently no way to stop the electrons from suddenly racing across the bridge. And if a successful bridge is built "there is a question if the conduction path will be fast enough and will act as promised—as a very fast, very small and very efficient rectifier," Metzger explained.

"If the organizing of this mono-layer works then we will have a device that could be 500 times smaller than any silicon or germanium-based device," he observed. "And, for micro-miniaturization, that is a fantastic idea."

specific number of machine cycles with the more complex instructions, such as MULTIPLY or DIVIDE, taking more time than a simple instruction, such as ADD.

At the start of a program a special register, called the instruction counter, is set to the address of the first instruction to be executed. The computer now enters what is known as I-time of the instruction cycle. During I-time the following takes place.

1. The op code part of the instruction is brought from memory and placed in the operation code register.
2. The bit structure of the op code is examined by the system in order to determine specific details of the instruction. For example, the op code contains information as to the length of the instruction and its general type, i.e., whether it deals with data in registers, in memory, or in both. Once this is known, the entire instruction may

be brought to the control unit for processing. The control unit then conditions the various circuits that are needed for the specific task.

3. Once the length of an instruction is known, the system can calculate the address of the next instruction to be executed. Branch instructions—those that change the orderly, sequential processing of instructions—pose another problem for the control unit. When instructions of this type are encountered, the system takes the address supplied by the branch instruction itself and uses this as the address of the next instruction to be processed.

The control unit then enters the execution phase (E-time) of the operation, during which the instruction is actually executed. If the instruction requires the use of the arithmetic/logic unit, information may be passed back and forth between this unit and storage areas. At the conclusion of a successful operation the control unit processes the next instruction. During these operations the control unit also checks the validity of the data being processed. If an error is detected and if it can be corrected, processing continues. If not, the system halts and action must be taken by the system operator.

THE ARITHMETIC/ LOGIC UNIT (ALU)

The arithmetic/logic unit contains all the necessary circuitry to perform the various arithmetic operations. In addition to the basic operations of adding, subtracting, multiplying, and dividing, the arithmetic portion also provides for shifting numbers to the left or right, setting the algebraic sign of the result, rounding numbers, and comparing. The primary responsibility of the logic section is to handle the decision-making operations that change the sequence in which instructions are executed. It is this part of the arithmetic/logic unit that tends to capture our imagination and make us believe that the computer has certain "magic" capabilities. The fact is, of course, that no such magic exists.

On the surface, it appears that the arithmetic unit must contain separate circuitry to take care of each arithmetic function, i.e., addition, subtraction, multiplication, and division. Since all arithmetic operations are really forms of addition (multiplication is repeated addition, division is repeated subtraction, and subtraction is reverse or complement addition), the system requires only extensive addition circuits.

ARITHMETIC OPERATIONS

Arithmetic operations inside the computer are generally performed in one of two ways: serially or in parallel. Serial addition is performed in the same way that we do our arithmetic—one pair of digits at a time. Typically, we start with the rightmost pair of digits, do the addition,

	1st Step	2nd Step	3rd Step	4th Step
Addend	1234	1234	1234	1234
Augend	2459	2459	2459	2459
Carry	1	1		
Sum	3	93	693	3693

Serial addition

Numbers being added	00564213
	00000824
Carry	1
Final Result	00565037

Parallel addition

FIGURE 6.2
Arithmetic operations.

hold carries (if there are any) for the next pair of digits to the left, and repeat the process. Accordingly, the time required for serial addition is dependent upon the number of digits involved. The operation is generally slow; but it has the distinct advantage that only one addition circuit is required since each digit is handled separately. Computers that have *character-oriented* memory typically perform their arithmetic serially since each program may have data fields of varying lengths. Most business machines operate in this manner.

Parallel arithmetic operations are common on computers that hold data in the form of storage words (*word-oriented* machines). Each storage word is comprised of a set number of storage positions (even though all storage positions in a word need not be used). Adding-circuitry is established for each digit of the word, and addition is performed on the entire word at one time. All carries are then processed in a separate operation. The two operations are shown in Figure 6.2. (*Note:* Although the numbers are shown in decimal form, all values stored in memory are actually in binary format. For further information on this and other number formats, look in the appendix.)

Arithmetic operations may be categorized in yet another way—in terms of the format of the data. *Fixed-point* arithmetic (binary data format) and decimal arithmetic (packed data format) are performed on data that does not contain a decimal point. Most business data falls into this category even though the information frequently involves dollars and cents, which implies the idea of a decimal point. Actually, the dollars-and-cents data entering memory seldom contains an actual decimal point. Instead, the data is entered as a string of digits and the programmer is required to know the location of the implied decimal point within the string of data. The programmer causes the computer to perform fixed-point arithmetic operations and then *edits* the output to show the proper relationship of dollars and cents. Output editing is the process of putting the output data into more readable form by inserting dollar signs, commas, periods, and by eliminating leading zeros.

For example, in a payroll calculation, the programmer knows that data fields are

Hours Worked
    3 digits with an implied decimal point one place to the left
Rate of Pay
    3 digits with an implied decimal point two places to the left

The actual values entered might be 415 (41½ hours) worked and 675 (6 dollars and 75 cents), but to the computer the data is simply a stream of

FIGURE 6.3
How does a computer work?

digits. After fixed-point multiplication has taken place, the answer is the digit string of 280125. The computer does not "know" that this number represents the gross pay amount. Instead, it is the programmer who knows the size and nature of the data fields. After rounding and editing by the programmer, the output becomes $280.13, which represents the gross pay amount.

Floating-point arithmetic is just the opposite. Here, special arithmetic instructions are available to work on numbers that do contain a decimal point. The term floating-point is literally descriptive since the circuitry is capable of adjusting or floating the decimal point to its correct position within a number at the conclusion of the arithmetic operation. A normal question at this point is: If floating-point operates as outlined here, why have fixed-point? The answer is, though floating-point instructions operate as indicated, they do have at least two major disadvantages for business applications: (1) it is slow compared to fixed-point processing and (2) most output editing is impossible. Since editing is an important part of business data processing, floating-point is seldom used in business (Figure 6.3).

LOGIC OPERATIONS

The decision-making capability of the computer lies in the logic unit and it is this capability that makes the computer an extremely versatile and flexible piece of equipment. It is precisely this capability that leads to pronouncements that the computer is a thinking machine when, in fact, it is not. Computer logic is nothing more than arithmetic testing as ordered by the programmer and carried out by the circuitry.

As indicated earlier, the computer is designed to execute sequentially the instructions stored in memory. In anything other than the simplest problems, however, you do not wish to have the instructions executed sequentially each time you process a unit of data. For example, payroll computations would involve a majority of employees who worked a 40-hour week, but the program would also have to take care of those who worked in excess of 40 hours. The program, therefore, must contain a series of instructions to calculate overtime pay, but only for those who qualify by working more than 40 hours. In the program itself, the programmer sets up a simple arithmetic test (actual hours worked versus 40) and causes the computer to branch or jump to the overtime routine (or set of instructions) if the results of the test indicate that overtime pay is justified.

The computer usually performs its comparisons by simple subtraction and the result of the subtraction triggers, i.e., turns on or off, appropriate internal switches called indicators. For example, the comparison of 43 hours worked versus 40 hours would result in a high or positive condition (the first factor, 43, is higher than the second factor, 40) and the turning on of the positive indicator. The program then branches to one routine or another, depending upon the setting of the high/positive indicator. To illustrate further, a comparison of 40 versus 40 would turn on the equal/zero indicator within the machine and the setting of this switch (indicator) can be tested according to the desires of the programmer. Logical comparisons are entirely reasonable since they are usually based on the *collating sequence* of the characters acceptable to the system. As an example, the number 9 has a higher collating sequence than an 8, which has a higher collating sequence than a 7, etc. For alphabetic characters the normal coding structure is such that the B is greater than A, C is greater than B, etc. Because of this coding structure, alphabetic and even special characters may be compared and manipulated.

EXECUTING A PROGRAM

Keeping in mind how the control unit and the arithmetic/logic unit operate, we can illustrate their interrelationship by a simple problem. The problem is to add together the values found on four data cards and to print the answer. Obviously this is not a very dramatic example, yet it shows the steps that man and machine have to go through in order to arrive at a result. Before starting, we shall make one important and basic assumption. We shall assume that the computer program is written in machine language—the lowest level at which man and machine can interact. Programs can be written in a variety of languages depending upon the type of problem to be solved and the capability of the machine. In this example, however, we are concerned with showing the basic steps in solving a problem, not with a specific model of machine or with the specific language employed. Four data cards are shown as follows:

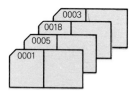

We shall write a program to do the following:

1. Read into memory the value from the first data card.
2. Add the value to a total. (Since we intend to sum the values from four cards, the total area must be set to zero before the first addition is performed.)
3. Read into memory the value from the second data card.
4. Add this second value to the total.
5. Repeat the read–add process for cards three and four.
6. Print the answer, i.e., the total of the numbers from the cards.

Up to now, we have always spoken of entering and temporarily storing data in computer memory but, in reality, memory can hold both data and instructions.

In solving a problem, the programmer specifies a series of instructions that will get the job done and these instructions are stored in the computer along with data. A schematic of the operation is shown in Figure 6.4.

The card reader is the input device in this particular case. Note that it reads in cards containing program instructions *and* cards containing data. Actually, we can break the operation down into a series of steps:

1. The operator initiates the reading of cards by certain console actions—pushing buttons, etc.
2. The instructions are read in and stored in memory. Recognition of instructions (as opposed to data) and storage of the instructions is performed by the control unit. Instructions and data were originally punched into cards with the Hollerith keypunch code. During the read-in process, however, this coding structure is changed or converted to the internal format of the computer being used.
3. Upon recognizing that the last of the instructions has been read in

FIGURE 6.4
Executing a program.

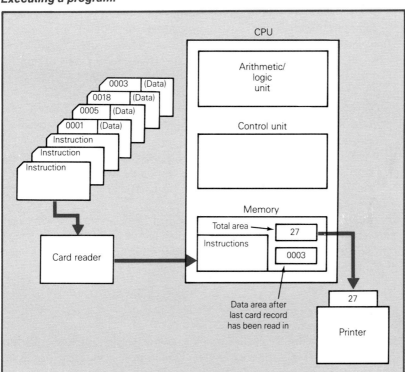

and stored, the control unit causes the stored instructions to be executed.

4. The instructions in the program will then cause the first data card to be read into and stored in memory. The programmer, of course, knows where the data is stored and his/her instructions refer to it accordingly.

5. The next part of the program concerns the manipulation of data. Whenever the control unit encounters an arithmetic operation (such as adding), it makes use of the arithmetic/logic unit. However, the control unit of the central processing unit still directs the overall system operation. You have already noted that the value from the first card is added to a total area which is also in main memory. The logical assumption is that this area should contain 0's prior to the addition operation. Right now we are not concerned with how 0's get into particular locations; but it is important to understand that it is the job of the programmer to see that this area is properly established. In the arithmetic/logic unit the first data field (0001) is added to the 0 value of the total area. When the addition operation is completed, the control unit goes on to the next instruction in the program.

6. The value from the second data card is now read into memory by the execution of the stored instructions. In normal programming, the input data is usually read into the same area in which the first data was stored. *Read-in is destructive;* i.e., it destroys whatever was in that area before. However, this poses no problem for the programmer because the data from the first card has already been added to the total. The reason for programming in this manner is to economize on the amount of computer memory used. Since there is only a limited amount of memory, there is no point in storing data that is no longer needed. The read and add sequence is continued until all the card records have been processed.

7. Eventually, the instruction to cause printout is encountered. The control unit activates the output device (printer) and the answer is printed.

8. If any irregularity occurs during the execution of the program, the control unit stops the action and indicates the difficulty on the operator console and possibly on various machine indicator lights.

As simple as all the previous steps sound, it is imperative that you understand exactly what happens inside the machine. Study each step until you are certain it makes sense. Remember that all machines and all programs generally work the same way.

PARITY CHECKING

Because of the extreme importance of having each bit be in the correct state (on or off) within each byte at all times, computer designers added another switching element to each byte of memory. This extra element, called a *check* bit or *parity* bit, performs automatic checking within the computer. Data is constantly manipulated by the computer system; that is, data is entered into the system and moved, stored, changed, and eventually sent to output or auxiliary storage devices. Data is also created within the machine, as in the case of totals that are derived from a series of additions. With so much data activity going on within the machine, it is imperative that the system have some method for detecting errors in the coding of the individual characters.

During the time a computer is actually being designed, the manufacturer decides whether the system will have odd or even parity. By odd parity, for example, we mean that the machine can only function properly if the total number of "on" bits in a storage location is odd. The EBCDIC coding structure discussed previously actually uses a ninth bit for this purpose. The programmer, however, has no control over or access to this bit.

Whenever data is entered into or created within the machine, the system automatically turns the parity bit on or off in order to generate the proper parity condition. However, whenever data is being referred to *(not entered or created),* the system investigates each piece of coded data to see whether parity is correct. As long as the parity is satisfactory, processing continues.

Bit values sometimes get changed during computer operations. Electrical power surges, excessive heat and/or humidity, malfunctioning parts, or improper operations can cause the loss or gain of bits. Theoretically, it is possible for two bits to be lost from a single storage position: if this were to occur, there is a good chance that the computer would not detect the error. In the vast majority of cases a single bit is lost and a parity error is detected, at which point the system stops, signals an error, and awaits operator intervention (Figure 6.5).

Many of the newer computers have elaborate mathematical methods of checking for parity errors. One of these systems uses not one but five parity bits arranged in such a way that the system can calculate which bit was incorrectly turned on or off *and* correct the error. This system will detect and correct 100% of all single-bit errors and almost 90% of all 2-bit errors. Even if the error is corrected, the system outputs a message to the operator on the system console device. If the error cannot be corrected, the computer halts with a parity error indication.

SUMMARY OF IMPORTANT POINTS

☐ The control unit of the central processing unit has the job of maintaining overall control of the entire computer system. Some of the tasks for which it is responsible are as follows.

Recognize and execute instructions.

Alter or change the sequence of program instructions according to the needs of the program.

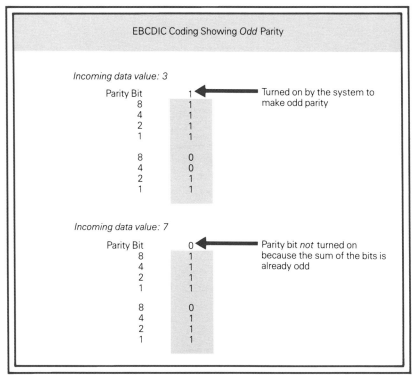

EBCDIC Coding Showing *Odd* Parity

Incoming data value: 3

Parity Bit	1	◄── Turned on by the system to make odd parity
8	1
4	1
2	1
1	1
8	0
4	0
2	1
1	1

Incoming data value: 7

Parity Bit	0	◄── Parity bit *not* turned on because the sum of the bits is already odd
8	1
4	1
2	1
1	1
8	0
4	1
2	1
1	1

FIGURE 6.5
Parity checking.

Provide for temporary storage of answers during processing.
Coordinate input/output operations.
Provide precise electronic timing for all computer operations.

☐ Temporary storage areas called registers are used for many of the operations of the control unit and the arithmetic/logic unit.

☐ Firmware (also called microcode) is special software, often in the form of a removable disk that can be loaded into a computer's control unit to change the basic way in which the machine operates.

☐ Computer instructions generally consist of an operation code (op code) and one or more operands. The op code indicates the exact nature of the instruction (such as add or subtract), while an operand refers to the location of a data field in memory.

☐ The arithmetic/logic unit performs all arithmetic operations by means of addition. Subtraction is done by complement addition, multiplication by repeated addition, and division by repeated subtraction.

☐ Computer logic operations are performed by the arithmetic/logic unit by means of subtraction as ordered by the programmer. Numbers, alphabetic characters, and special characters can be compared logically because each character has a unique place in the character collating sequence.

☐ When a program is executed, the program itself resides in memory, and it is the execution of the program that usually brings in data, manipulates it, and outputs the answers to a printer.

☐ All computers have some form of parity checking, which is the machine's way of checking to see that the contents (bits) of memory are in the proper coded format. All machines use at least one bit for parity purposes for each position of memory. Some machines have more elaborate parity-checking methods that use multiple parity bits for each position of memory.

GLOSSARY OF TERMS

Accumulator—a register used to hold sums during arithmetic operations.

Check bit—see parity bit.

Direct-access device—see random-access device.

Editing—as used by the programmer, editing instructions allow the programmer to place a dollar sign, decimal point, debit and credit symbols, etc., in printed output.

Emulation—the act of executing a program written for one computer on a different computer. Frequently, this is accomplished by read-only circuits.

E-time, or execution time—the time during which the instruction is actually executed by the central processing unit.

Firmware—special software that can be loaded into a computer system in order to emulate a specific task.

Fixed-point arithmetic—operations on numbers without decimal points.

I-time, or instruction time—the time during which the instruction is analyzed by the control unit.

Indicators—internal switches that are turned on or off, depending upon the results of arithmetical or logical comparisons.

Logic elements—various forms of electrical switches within the computer. The term is used interchangeably with switching elements.

Machine cycle—a set period of time in which the computer can perform a specific machine operation.

Microcode—see firmware.

Op code, Operation code—that part of a computer instruction that specifies exactly what operation is to take place, such as ADD or SUBTRACT.

Operand—that part of a computer instruction that refers to data on storage.

Parallel arithmetic operations—a method by which the computer handles entire arithmetic fields at one time. Computers of this type are usually word-type machines.

Parity bit or parity checking—the built-in feature of the machine that allows it to check itself to see whether the bit structure in the storage of data is correct. Odd or even parity refers to whether the system requires an odd or an even number of bits turned on to represent a data character.

Registers—memory elements that function as temporary storage for the computer system.

Semiconductor—memory devices that store information by means of conducting or not conducting electricity.

Serial arithmetic operations—a method by which the computer handles arithmetic fields one digit at a time, usually from right to left.

Software—the general term applied to all programming support applied to a computer system. Specifically, operating system programs supplied by the manufacturer.

THOUGHT QUESTIONS

1. Differentiate between the following terms: software, hardware, firmware.
2. What reasons would a manufacturer have for making extensive use of firmware within a computer?
3. In general, what is the method by which a computer performs "logic" operations? Is this in any way parallel or similar to the way you perform your own logic operation?
4. Exactly what is a computer instruction?

   Make a list of 15 instructions that you would want to have on a computer you would have to program. If possible, put these instructions in order of importance.
5. Why is parity checking so important in computer systems? Explain your answer in detail.
6. Can parity bits fail within the machine? If so, how is this detected?

CHAPTER 7
COMPUTER
INPUT
AND OUTPUT

LEARNING OBJECTIVES

Upon completion of the chapter you should understand the following:

The role of some of the common input and output devices that are used on computer systems.

How card read/punch units operate.

That there are two general classes of printers: impact and nonimpact; That nonimpact devices, such as printer/plotters, have the capability of drawing as well as printing.

The multiple uses of video screen (CRT) units in such diverse applications as data entry, data retrieval, interactive graphics, and computer-assisted instructions (CAI).

The nature and use of magnetic character recording (MICR) in the banking industry.

How voice output capability can be incorporated into computer systems and the application areas that are making use of this technology.

CHAPTER CONTENTS

So far we have identified the major parts of the central processing unit and how it operates under program control. To many, the CPU and its components—memory, the control unit, and the arithmetic unit—are considered to be somewhat "mysterious" devices because they usually are contained within a single boxlike cabinet. Input/output devices, on the other hand, are far more glamorous, or at least more easily photographed and visualized. Let's take a look at some of these devices and where they fit into the makeup of a complete computer system. An astounding number (into the hundreds on some systems) and variety of hardware can be attached to the central processing system. Some, such as card readers, can only be input or reading devices; others, such as printers, are output devices only and still others, such as video screen terminals, can operate as two-way units.

CARD READ/ PUNCH UNITS

As you know from previous chapters, the various input/output devices are activated by specific instructions within the program. If multiple input devices are used, the command of "read a record" is simply too vague for the computer to understand. Instead, the programmer will have to designate which input device he or she wants activated. An instruction to READ given to the card reader causes precisely that—the reading of one card. The instruction causes the information from one card record (80 columns) to be placed into memory in the area designated or named by the programmer. The action of the READ statement is shown in Figure 7.1. Note that our card record is more accurately called a *data record* and the entire stack or deck of data cards will be a *data file.*

The actual reading of a card is done optically. The card passes by a light source that beams the light onto the card as it passes by. Whenever a hole is present, the light falls through and onto a receptor unit. With this method it is possible to read up to 1500 cards per minute. Even at this speed, however, the process is extremely slow in terms of the internal speed of the computer. As you know from Chapter 4, faster and more accurate input methods are available today and card use is becoming rare.

PRINTERS AND PLOTTERS

Although the end result of computations and manipulations performed on data can be output in a variety of ways, most output eventually appears in printed form. Graphical forms of output have

FIGURE 7.1
Schematic: card-read operation.

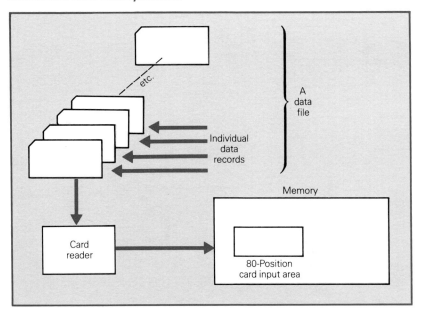

become more popular recently, but it is still the printer on which we turn out invoices, shipping documents, checks, reports, and the like. The output instruction WRITE, when directed to a printer unit, normally causes the printing of *one line* of information. However, before that simple instruction of WRITE can be given, the programmer first has to arrange the characters in memory so that they correspond to the exact format of the output record or line desired. Usually this is done by means of a printer spacing chart on which the programmer figures out the exact layout of each line. This type of work may seem time-consuming, but it really is necessary in order to get the print to appear within specific boxes or areas on preprinted forms (Figure 7.2).

Printers can be classified in several ways, but the broadest designation would be that of impact and nonimpact printers. The term *impact printer* covers any printing device where the printed character is made by a striking or hitting mechanism. The term *nonimpact printer* refers to those devices that form the characters by some method other than striking. The difference in speed, from the slowest printer to the fast-

FIGURE 7.2
Printer spacing chart.

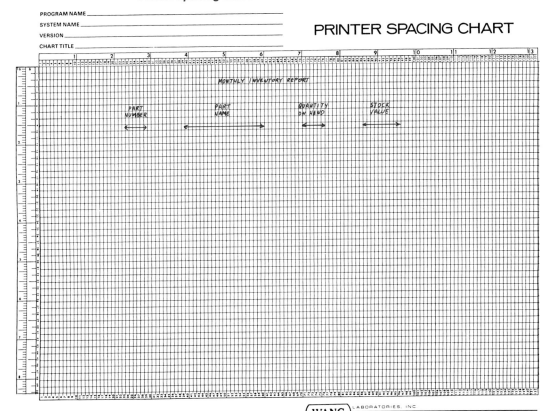

est, is enormous—from 10 characters a second to over 21,000 lines per minute.

IMPACT PRINTERS

The standard high-speed printer attached to a computer system is usually known as a *line printer* because it prints an entire line at a time. The width of the print line will vary depending upon the model of printer used, but lines of 100, 120, 132, or 144 characters are most common. This means that there will be 100, 120, etc., hammers or character-shaping mechanisms across the line, one for each printing position. At least three distinct types of line printers are in use.

Chain printers, or variations thereof, are the backbone of high-speed impact printing because of their speed, the ease of replacing a chain, and the consistency of printing a straight, even line.

As you can see (Figure 7.3), the printer uses a chain arrangement on which the character set is repeated several times. The chain revolves at a constant speed and hammers fire or strike the correct character on the fly, i.e., as it comes around on the type chain. The complicated electronics of the printer unit calculate which characters should be struck in relation to the timing of the moving sets of type. Typical of this kind of printer, the characters are not struck from the front (such as a typewriter); instead, the hammers strike from the rear. Inter-

FIGURE 7.3
Print chain.

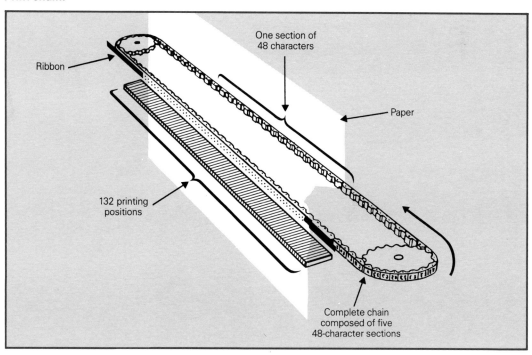

FIGURE 7.4
High-speed impact printer.

changeable type chains with full character sets, numeric sets, or special characters can be used according to the needs of the operation. Printers of this type can achieve a speed of 2000 or more lines per minute (Figure 7.4)

FIGURE 7.5
Pedestal printer.

However, not all printers are large, high-speed devices. Many pedestal type printers operating in the 300 to 1500 lines-per-minute range are entirely adequate for a great many small business applications (Figure 7.5).

In addition to the line-at-a-time devices just described, there are those slower speed devices that print serially, i.e., one character at a time. Typeballs such as those found on IBM Selectric typewriters have been in use for many years, but *daisy wheel* printers are becoming more and more popular. Their particular advantage is that the unit produces "letter-quality" print that cannot be distinguished from output from the best typewriter. Another advantage is that you can change to a different type style simply by changing wheels (Figure 7.6).

Traditionally, daisy wheel and similar devices have been fairly slow, but some of the new serial output devices derive their high output rate because of complex electronics that allow them to print bidirectionally. When the print mechanism gets to the end of the line it does not return to the left margin to begin printing the next line. Instead, printing for every other line is done from right to left (Figure 7.7).

Not all impact printing devices use hammers to strike against solid slugs of type. Many serial printing devices utilize a matrix of grid wires as the impact device. Selected wires are extended from the matrix (5 × 7 or 7 × 9) into the ribbon to form a recognizable pattern of dots. Actually, it is likely that you have seen matrix printing devices for many years but never noticed them. For example, most basketball or football

FIGURE 7.6

Daisy wheel print mechanism.

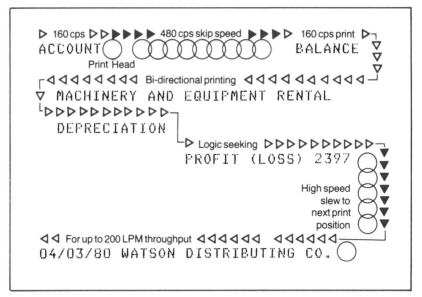

FIGURE 7.7
Bidirectional printing.

scoreboards consist of a matrix of lights that are turned on in appropriate combinations to spell out specific values (Figure 7.8).

Chain printers, and other impact devices, have been limited in their speed because of the necessity of moving all the mechanical parts. For this reason, there have been many attempts to develop nonimpact methods where the major limitation is the speed at which paper can pass through the devices. It is estimated that of today's total high-speed printer market, only 5% of the printers can be classified as nonimpact. However, it is expected that this market segment will grow to 25% by 1985.

NONIMPACT DEVICES (PRINTER/PLOTTERS)

A wide variety of technologies exist for nonimpact printers. Some devices use special paper that reacts thermally, or photographically, while others use plain paper. No matter what technique is used, one major disadvantage, as compared to impact printers, is the limitation of single printer copy.

In electrostatic printing, the characters are sent from memory to the print buffer (which is a small amount of memory retained in the printer) until an entire line has been received. Then, conductive styluses or dot makers, with a density of from 100 to 200 per inch, form the characters from top to bottom as the page moves up. Specially coated paper is charged electrically and passed by rollers that apply a liquid toner or darkening material. The toner sticks to the charged areas to produce printing.

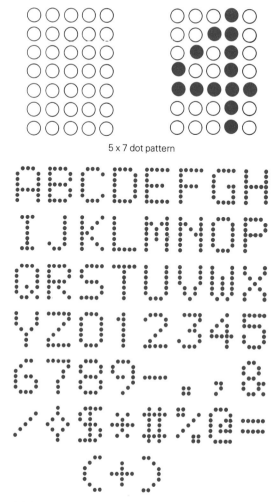

5 x 7 dot pattern

FIGURE 7.8
Matrix dot printing pattern.

Electrostatic devices are often called printer/plotters because the characters are actually drawn on the paper rather than printed. The units are not particularly expensive, but the need for special paper can be bothersome. Speeds range from about 600 to 5000 lines per minute.

One interesting point about this type of device is that we are used to seeing printed English characters wherein we are fortunate to have a very limited character set. In other languages, of course, this is not so, as they may have hundreds or perhaps thousands of characters. By using removable ROMs, or PROM (programmable read-only memory), chips in either the printer or the central processing unit, the printer/plotter can be directed to draw almost any character set imaginable, such as oriental and Arabic characters.

** END OF JOB **
THIS DATA WAS BROUGHT TO YOU IN PART
BY THE FOLLOWING FINE BUSINESS FIRMS

DATA ENTRY SYSTEMS, INC.
ABC PAPER PRODUCTS
NO-SMUDGE PRINTER RIBBONS

FIGURE 7.9
Schematic of IBM electrophotographic printing system.

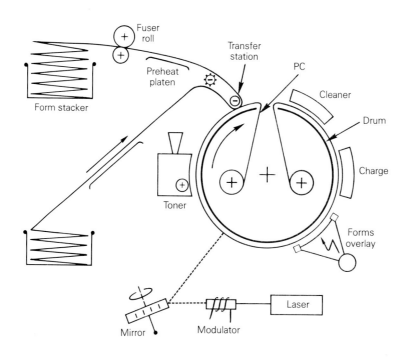

Another variation is known as electrophotographic printing in which a low-power laser forms the character images on light-sensitive material covering a rotating drum (Figure 7.9). As the drum rotates, toner powder sticks to the photoconductor material and is then transferred to the paper. One of the advantages of this printing system is that it can print smaller character sizes if the user desires. This saves on paper costs, although the unit already uses standard, rather than special printer paper.

Another feature of the system is a forms-overlay capability. Complex form designs on film negatives can be projected onto the drum by means of a strobe light. This minimizes the need to keep preprinted forms in stock. The unit prints at 13,360 lines per minute, which makes a second, third, or fourth print run a reasonable and inexpensive way to get duplicate copies. Similar units are available today that print at 21,000 lines per minute (Figure 7.10).

Another device, called an ink jet printer, that has met with reasonable success uses a different form of nonimpact printing. As Figure 7.11 illustrates, drops of ink are sprayed toward the paper. On the way to the page, the ink is electrically deflected into a matrix format for each character and the consistency of the ink is such that it dries almost instantly upon contact with the paper. Its major advantage is that it is virtually silent and therefore usable in applications where noise is a determining factor.

FIGURE 7.10
High-speed laser printer.

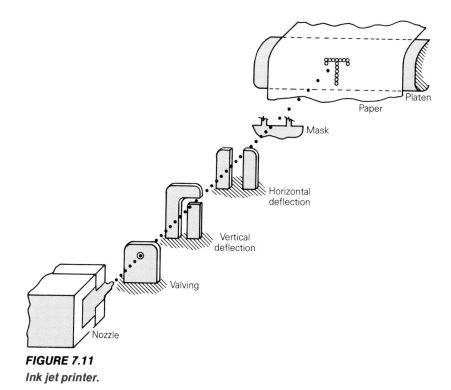

FIGURE 7.11
Ink jet printer.

PLOTTERS

Basically, a plotter is a device for drawing lines on paper. It is particularly useful in situations where pictorial presentations of computer data are more meaningful and/or easier to use than regular printer listings, i.e., sales charts, three-dimensional drawings, etc. (Figure 7.12).

Typically, the ink-on-paper type of plotter produces lines by small movements of the pen relative to the surface of the paper. Figure 7.13 shows a drum plotter and a set of multicolored drawing pens, while Figure 7.14 shows a large flatbed plotter. Input signals coming from the computer are used to produce pen or paper movement or to raise or lower the pen over the recording surface. Alphanumeric characters can be drawn on the plot along with the graphic representation. In addition, plotters can be used both on-line and off-line. For off-line operations the output information is written onto magnetic tape which is later used to drive the plotter.

Figure 7.15 illustrates a special, yet very useful, form of plotter graphics known as digitizing. It consists of a small, movable keyboard, an electronic drafting surface, a free-moving cursor, and a computer-compatible magnetic tape drive. The cursor is positioned, as desired, on the graphic material and the location coordinates are recorded (digitized) automatically into the system. With a minicomputer or microprocessor acting as the graphic processing unit, the system can

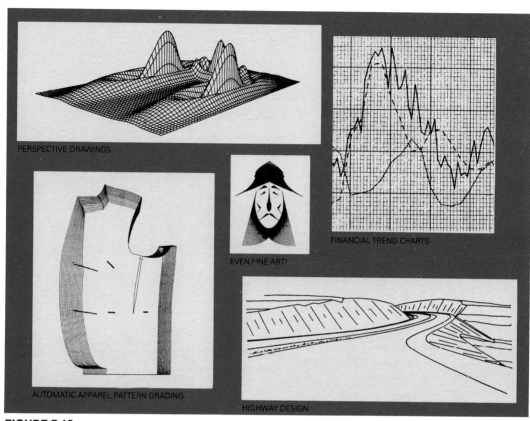

PERSPECTIVE DRAWINGS

FINANCIAL TREND CHARTS

EVEN FINE ART!

AUTOMATIC APPAREL PATTERN GRADING

HIGHWAY DESIGN

FIGURE 7.12
Plotter output.

FIGURE 7.13
Drum plotter.

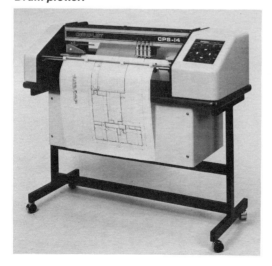

FIGURE 7.14
Large flat-bed plotter.

FIGURE 7.15
Hipad digitizer unit.

KEEPING TRACK OF RUNNERS

This year, the thousands of entrants who ran in the Boston Marathon on April 20th were treated like so many cans of peas. Each runner wore a bar code, very similar to the ones that adorn all the boxes, cans, and magazines at your local supermarket. Upon crossing the finish line, each runner's exact completion time was recorded. Then he turned in his bar-code tag. The tag was read promptly, and before the day was through, all the information the participant would want to know about his performance was already printed on a postcard and on the way to him in the mail.

The bar-code readers were part of a Honeywell Level 6 system that was on loan for the day of the race. It was a Model 47 with 256K words of memory and two 80-megabyte mass-storage units. A 900 lpm printer and five Honeywell VIP7200 terminals, along with the three bar-code readers, were also part of the system.

The information that each runner received included overall rank, finishing time, rank by sex, rank by age group, and average running time for that age group. In previous years, such data were assembled manually. The new method, which was also used in Boston's Bonne Bell National Championship for Women and Tampa's Gasparilla Long Distance Classic, is much faster and eliminates the chances for error.

(Source: *Computer Decisions*, May 1981.)

perform many time-consuming engineering tasks, such as lettering, scaling, cross-hatching, dimensioning, erasing, listing, and calculating. Some systems of this type also permit draftpersons to automatically change scale, make mirror images, rotate images, and repeat commonly used symbols or details by calling them from memory and indicating where they should be placed.

VIDEO SCREEN (CRT) DISPLAYS

Until recently, most computer output has taken the form of characters or lines of characters printed or drawn on paper as described in the previous section. However, Chapter 4 showed that video screen terminals generally operated as both input and output devices. The operator keystroked data (input), which appeared on the screen, and computer responses (output) appeared as the result of system action. Forms overlay and operator prompt messages are typical of this type of output.

Some video screen terminals, however, have graphic display capability. The operator displays the material on the screen and then, if a printed copy is required, a printer/plotter is activated (Figure 7.16).

For a great many years, video output has been in black and white, but there has been a significant trend in recent months to go to color graphics because of a feeling that color allows the user to understand the drawn or plotted output more quickly (Figure 7.17).

In addition to data entry application, another area in which video screen devices are of great importance is interactive graphics. Up to now, CRT's have been shown as more or less static I/O units. By means of a light pen and very complex programming, the video screen can also function as a dynamic I/O device that allows the operator to interact directly with the system. The operator uses keyboard entries to indicate to the system the nature of the task to be performed—drawing, erasing, moving, etc. As interesting and exciting as the CRT light pen seems, you are encouraged to remember that there is no magic involved. The computer has to be elaborately programmed to recognize what is wanted, and to react to specific inputs. The system, by its very nature, is most applicable to scientific uses where programming and development costs can be recovered quickly (Figure 7.18).

One area in which the light pen shows particular promise is that of cartography, i.e., map making. A system developed by IBM's Washington Scientific and Industry Development Center allows direct gra-

FIGURE 7.16
Video screen with hard-copy printout.

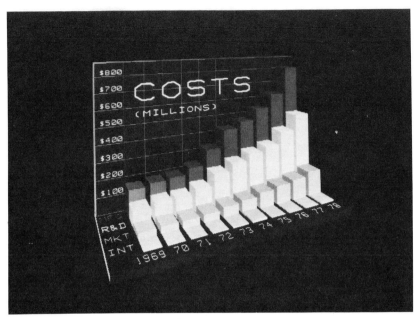

FIGURE 7.17
Three-dimensional video graphics.

FIGURE 7.18
Light pen operation.

phic communication between the cartographer and the computer. The U.S. Coast and Geodetic Survey has the responsibility, among others, of keeping its land and aeronautical charts as current as possible, but a shortage of cartographers, plus slow methods, make the 7- to 28-day schedule of updating charts an impossibility.

Under the old system, a cartographer/draftsperson team worked for several days to redesign a master chart from which prints could be made. Now the cartographer can make changes directly on the CRT screen by means of the light pen. When the satisfactory changes have been made, a button on the console transfers the changes to memory, the updated chart is output on a plotter, and the master copy is sent to the printer for volume production.

Video screen units have been popular in CAI (computer-assisted instruction), where the unit then becomes a sophisticated teaching device that is particularly adaptable to individual or small-group learning. The speed of the unit, plus its lack of print noise, make it an ideal device for school situations. When graphic display capability (with or without the light pen facility) is incorporated in the system, the student is able to communicate directly with the computer on a graphic or visual basis. This is of particular importance to students who have language or cultural barriers that stand in the way of the normal learning process. One of the cardinal principles of education is to indicate immediately that the student has achieved a correct answer or to help him or her find out why the answer is incorrect. With CAI the student not only gets immediate answers but can also cover a wide range of topics that would be beyond the scope of the average teacher. When units of this kind are provided with touch-sensitive screens they can be used in an even wider range of applications (Figure 7.19).

MAGNETIC INK
CHARACTERS (MICR)

During the 1950s the banking institutions in the United States recognized that their current methods of handling checks and other documents would be inadequate in the near future. The very nature of a bank's operation is such that keypunching from source documents is impractical and, since existing input devices and methods were not suited to the banking industry's needs, work was begun with equipment manufacturers to devise a DP method to meet the bank's special requirements. The end result was a set of magnetic ink characters to be used for recording information on a variety of banking documents. The character set, adopted by the American Banking Association, is shown in Figure 7.20.

The MICR-based banking system calls for the preprinting of checks with certain basic information, such as account number and transit

FIGURE 7.19
Touch-sensitive video terminal.

FIGURE 7.20
MICR characters.

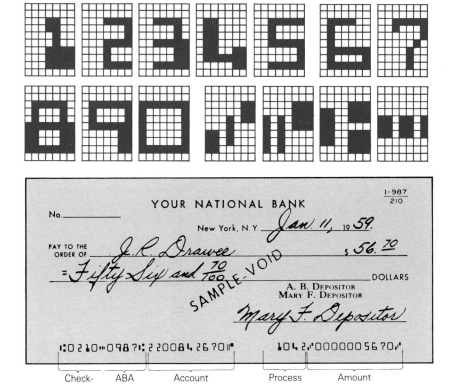

number, but the amount field, of course, cannot be entered until the check is issued, cashed, and deposited in a bank. At the bank the face amount of the check is encoded onto the check using a MICR Encoding Machine (Figure 7.21). Once this is done, the document can be handled by special MICR equipment that reads the data into the computer system for further processing.

VOICE OUTPUT

Perhaps the most spectacular form of output is computerized speech. A very few years ago synthesized speech was the subject of extensive research in artificial intelligence laboratories in university computer centers, where experiments were carried out on large, complex computer systems. The speech that came from these systems was obviously mechanical and often was the subject of ridicule. Today, however, that research has paid off in the form of an ever-increasing array of consumer and industrial products.

Perhaps the most popular of such products are the "Speak and . . ." children's games developed by Texas Instruments. For pre-school-age children, Touch and Tell has a touch-sensitive keyboard and a speech synthesizer that verbally identifies each picture on the board as it is touched. TI's Speak and Read contains over 250 of the most basic English words and is designed to help children recognize words and alphabet letters as they hear the correct pronunciation. In addition, this game can be programmed for three levels of difficulty and can

FIGURE 7.21
MICR proof encoding machine.

even help build vocabulary through the use of syllable sounds and families of words. The unit can be enhanced by a tiny plug-in module called Vowel Power that works on a 140-word list that helps to build pronunciation skills. Speak and Math can present the student with more than 100,000 problems, including word problems that build skills in understanding spoken mathematical concepts such as "greater than" or "less than" (Figure 7.22).

Other consumer applications include talking clocks that announce the time every hour or upon the depression of a key. Many hand-held calculators now include up to 12 preprogrammed melodies that can be played on preset dates (birthdays, anniversaries, etc.). A more complex unit, the Voice Bridge Challenger, announces both the human's and the computer's bids and plays using accepted bridge terminology. Business uses of voice output include special voice warning systems that activate synthesized speech when computer sensing devices recognize dangerous or potentially dangerous situations. Today, air- plane manufacturers are incorporating more and more of these devices to warn of fire, excess heat, low fuel supply, and among other hazards.

How does computerized speech work? Advances in computer technology have made speech synthesis relatively simple. The process starts by having a human record the desired words onto regular audio tape. The audio, or analog signals are then converted to digital form and stored on computer magnetic tape or disk. At this point the speech sounds on the two media are the same. Unfortunately, even a relatively small vocabulary (under 100 words) for an electronic game requires an enormous amount of memory. Even at current memory prices, the product would be priced out of the consumer level.

The solution to the problem is the most complex part of the speech-synthesis process. In the laboratory the number of bits of in- formation required to produce the sound is reduced by a factor of more than 100. This is easy to do, but the secret to the success of the operation lies in retaining enough of the original speech sounds to make the words recognizable to the listener. To do this, each word is analyzed electronically to determine its essential characteristics. Nonessential parts are cut out, the words are reassembled, and, finally, loaded into an integrated circuit chip for assembly into the final product.

BUSINESS APPLICATION: COMPUTER-AIDED DESIGN AND MANUFACTURING (CAD/CAM)

From 1950 to 1965, the average growth in productivity for non-farm business was 2.5%. From 1965 to 1978 the rate dropped to 1.5 percent, a fact that has not been lost on the nations that compete for U.S. busi-

FIGURE 7.22
Electronic learning aids.

ness. One potential solution to this problem is the integration of computers into the production process. CAD/CAM, which is an acronym for computer-aided design/computer-aided manufacturing, can be applied to drafting, design manufacturing, and quality-control tasks over a wide range of industrial activities. For example, CAD/CAM systems are used in computer circuit chip design, mapping, plant layout, piping and wiring diagrams, numerical control of machine tools, tool design, and drafting. The major advantages of CAD/CAM systems are shortened product design times, decreased costs, and increased productivity.

In the early 1970s there were perhaps 200 CAD/CAM workstations in use, primarily by the aerospace and automotive companies, which could afford the expensive hardware and software that were required to drive the system. By the end of the 1970s, the number of workstations had grown to over 12,000. A typical stand-alone system consists of a computer, auxiliary storage, a video screen workstation, a printer/plotter, and a touch-sensitive drawing tablet to accept drawn input.

The process starts when the engineer enters design parameters (starting point on the screen, symbols required, etc.) through the keyboard. In addition to choosing from among a large set of computer-stored drafting and design symbols, the user may also call up previously stored drawings for reference purposes. The heart of the system is the video screen unit where the engineer can enter drafting commands and design changes with a touch of a key or with a single keystroke of the electronic pen. Each entry or change appears on the screen and the operator can manipulate the entire design to produce a three-dimensional drawing, to rotate the parts, produce a mirror image, change the scale, and add text material to the drawing. During the process the system is accumulating data about the location, dimensions, and design descriptions that are necessary to define the part. When the product is finished the design is stored on a magnetic disk or tape. Other output options include plotter drawings and tapes to drive numerically controlled machine tools to produce the part.

Perhaps the most amazing part about CAD/CAM today is that systems of this type are being implemented on small, inexpensive computer systems. Granted, they can't do everything that the large systems can, but they are capable of doing a good job at a relatively low cost. For example, Tri-Digital Systems in Auburn, Washington, markets a hardware/software CAD/CAM package called "Layout" that runs on a Radio Shack microcomputer. "Layout" is an interactive program that helps a machinist calculate complex geometric positions in the design of two-dimensional contours. Figure 7.23 shows examples of plotter output from the "Layout" program.

A further extension of computer-aided manufacturing is shown in Figure 7.24. Here a computer-controlled industrial robot manufactured by General Motors is demonstrating its ability to pick-up and move objects. The unit can not only change tools as required but can be

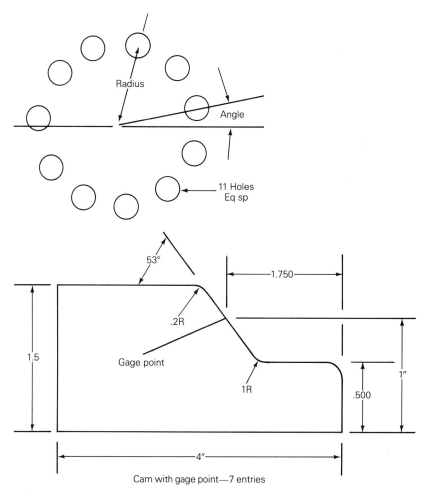

Radius

Angle

11 Holes
Eq sp

53°

1.750

.2R

1.5

Gage point

1R

1"

.500

4"

Cam with gage point—7 entries

FIGURE 7.23
Plotter output—CAD / CAM system.

reprogrammed to perform a wide range of jobs. Today, most industrial robots are engaged in assembly-line activities that are either hazardous or unsuited to humans. The United States currently uses about 3000 industrial robots, but this number is expected to increase at the rate of 35 percent each year.

The two major advantages of industrial robots are that they can increase productivity by working at the same pace all day long and that they are relatively inexpensive ($4.50 per hour) compared to an average labor cost of $18.00 per hour. Figure 7.25 shows a breakdown of costs for various types of industrial robots according to the type of function they perform. Figure 7.26 illustrates the dramatic growth in the robot market that is predicted for the 1980s.

FIGURE 7.24
Computer-controlled industrial robot.

FIGURE 7.25
Typical robot system cost breakdown.

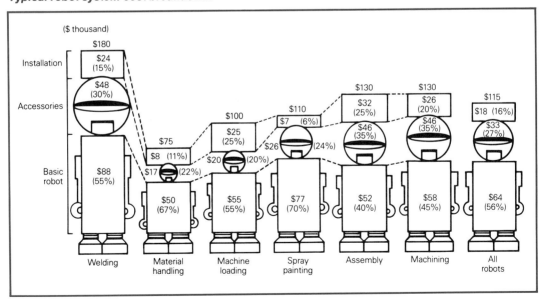

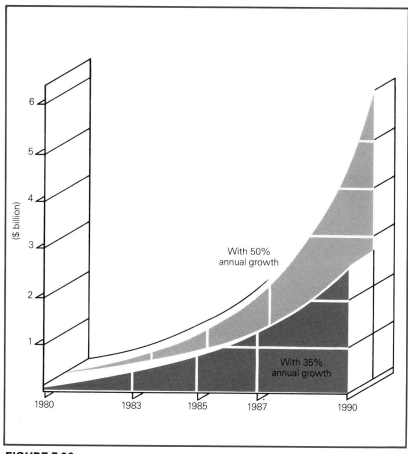

FIGURE 7.26
Growth of robot market in the 1980s.

SUMMARY OF
IMPORTANT POINTS

☐ A standard punched card is a record of data, and the sum total of the records pertaining to an operation is a data file.

☐ The program statement READ causes a record of data to be read into memory from the input device specified.

☐ The program statement WRITE causes the record of data to be written or recorded onto the output device specified.

☐ The standard, high-speed output device used throughout the data processing industry is the line printer, a unit that prints one line at a time.

☐ Serial printers, such as typewriters, print one character at a time.

☐ Impact printers work at speeds up to 3000 lines per minute and can print up to eight copies at one time.

☐ Some printing devices are more accurately called printer/plotters as they are able to print or draw characters and marks by means of matrix print heads as opposed to solid type characters.

☐ Electrophotographic or laser printers can produce output at up to 21,000 lines per minute, which means that it may be faster to run a job four times to get four copies than use an impact printer for one run with four-part paper.

☐ Plotters have been used in scientific and engineering applications to produce detailed drawings, particularly in CAD/CAM (computer-aided design/computer-aided manufacturing). In recent years they have been used with increasing frequency in business applications.

☐ Video screen (CRT) displays offer speed and silent operation as their main advantages. Color units are now becoming more popular because color can show relationships within drawings, charts, etc., more quickly.

☐ Interactive graphics are possible on some video screen systems because the user can enter data directly into the system via a light pen or a touch-sensitive screen.

☐ Magnetic ink characters (MICR) have been used for many years by the banking industry as a way to handle the billions of checks we write each year. The characters and the systems were developed by manufacturers and the banking industry on a cooperative basis.

☐ Voice output has finally come of age due to the changing state of computer technology and the decrease in memory prices. Speech synthesis is being used extensively in electronic games and as an industrial application.

GLOSSARY OF TERMS

CAD/CAM—the acronym for computer-aided design/computer-aided manufacturing, which is the integration of computers into the production process.

Cathode ray tube (CRT)—an output device very similar to television on which the computer system can display numbers, alphabetic characters, and/or lines.

Chain printer—those printers that use a type chain or print chain as their printing mechanism.

Impact printer—any printing mechanism that employs some hitting or striking mechanism, such as hammers.

Interactive graphics—the general term applied to any graphic system where the user and the computer are in active communication.

Light pen—a penlike device used in interactive graphic units to communicate between the computer and the user.

Matrix printer—an output device that prints each character by means of a specially placed series of dots. Usually the dots are made by small wires that press against a ribbon and paper.

Magnetic ink character recording (MICR)—the term applied to the specially devised, magnetically readable characters used in the banking industry.

Plotter—a graphic output device that draws digits, alphabetic characters, symbols, and lines on paper.

Serial printers—devices that print one character at a time (typewriter).

Speech synthesis—a technique in which a human voice is reproduced electronically with enough of the original characteristics to be understood by the listener.

THOUGHT QUESTIONS

1. Explain why CAI (computer-assisted instruction) is viewed by many as an important educational tool. Compare its advantages and disadvantages.
2. Would you use CAI? How do you think you would react to it? Do you think you would get the same benefits from CAI that you do from a regular teacher/student relationship?
3. Other than those examples mentioned in the text, what uses do you see for CAD/CAM systems?
4. The text mentioned a few uses of speech output. You should be able to come up with at least a half a dozen applications other than those mentioned in the text.
5. Which is better, the impact or the nonimpact printer?
6. Do you feel that graphic output would be more meaningful to you than standard printed output?
7. The text did not mention it, but there is at least one drawback to the extensive use of video screen units. What is that?
8. Give some examples of matrix output other than those mentioned in the text.

CHAPTER 8
AUXILIARY
STORAGE
MEDIA

LEARNING OBJECTIVES
Upon completion of this chapter you should understand the following:

How data is recorded on both tape and disk media.

The differences between tape and disk, and the terminology associated with each.

The concept of blocking of data records and why it is done.

The methods that are used to check the validity of data records processed on auxiliary storage media.

How tape and disk files are identified and stored.

The use of microfilm storage in conjunction with computer output.

CHAPTER CONTENTS

Although the point has been made before, it is worth repeating here prior to getting into a discussion of auxiliary storage methods: Data can be manipulated (added, subtracted, etc.) only within the central processing unit. The problem, then, is one of getting the data to the place where processing can take place. Prior to the use of computers, business firms held data in the form of pieces of paper in file folders within filing cabinets. Even the use of punched cards did not change the storage process very much because the data, now in card form, was still held off-line and had to be physically brought to a card reader in order to be used. Tape and disk auxiliary storage, the two major components of this chapter, advance the storage process one step further by having at least some of the stored data on-line or readily accessible to the computer system. Thus, all forms of auxiliary storage are simply areas where data is held until it is needed. Because of the tremendous need for computer-stored information, equipment vendors estimate that user demand for on-line storage is increasing between 45% and 60% annually.

MAGNETIC TAPE

Magnetic tape was the dominant form of auxiliary storage during most of the second generation. In the mid-1960s disk began to come in to the point that today we are likely to see a balance of both types of media on modern computer systems. At one time it was predicted that disk would entirely replace magnetic tape as an auxiliary storage media. However, this has not happened because, among other reasons, tape technology has kept improving with the times. Let's take a look at the makeup of this type of storage medium.

GENERAL CHARACTERISTICS

Magnetic tape can take a variety of forms but the most popular size is half an inch wide, made of acetate or Mylar plastic, and coated with a ferrous oxide or a similar material that is easily magnetized. A full-sized reel holds 2400 feet of tape, although minireels holding about 600 feet are common.

Information is written onto or read from tape by means of a series of magnetic read/write heads. The heads are actually small magnetic coils located very close to the surface. When current is applied a magnetic field is created which, in turn, magnetizes a tiny spot on the tape surface. During reading or writing, tape passes by the recording heads (read/write heads) at a constant speed. Speeds vary from machine to machine, and they can range from a low of about 22 inches per second to approximately 300 inches per second. To prevent the tape from breaking or stretching during reading, backspacing, rewinding, etc., the tape is looped through a transport mechanism that absorbs the shocks of sudden stops and starts (see Figure 8.1).

FIGURE 8.1
Tape transport mechanism.

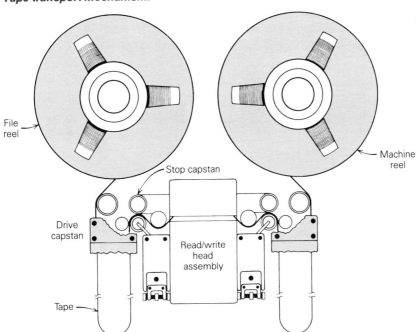

The principles of reading and writing on magnetic tape are the same as they are for home recording tape. Reading is nondestructive, meaning that the data can be read repeatedly. However, writing from memory onto tape is destructive in that it erases or destroys the information that was in that area previously. Generally, data is recorded on tape in bit format in either the 7-bit, second-generation structure or the 9-bit, third-generation pattern (Figure 8.2).

This figure shows several important features of magnetic tape.

1. Data is recorded *vertically* on the tape with the presence of a mark representing a bit turned on and the absence of a mark representing a bit turned off.
2. The bits are not visible on magnetic tape under ordinary circumstances. On rare occasions a systems engineer may have to coat a

FIGURE 8.2

Tape data format.

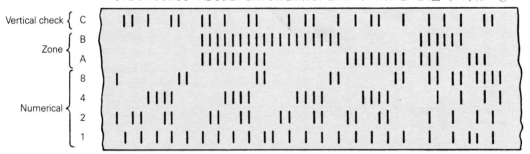

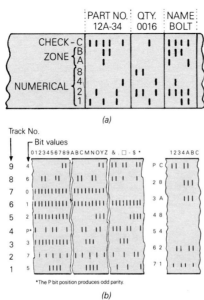

(a)

(b)

*The P bit position produces odd parity.

small area of the tape with an iron solution in order to read the actual bits. If coated, the tape will be as depicted in the illustration.

3. The check bit performs the same function as it does in core memory, except that now we refer to it as a vertical parity or check bit.

4. The rows of bits running lengthwise along the tape are known as *tracks* or *channels* and the illustration shows both 7-channel and 9-channel magnetic tape. Third-generation tape drives usually work with 9-channel tape (8 data bits plus a check bit), although some units have the capability of switching from one coding structure to another.

5. Data is recorded in the form of fields and records just as it is in cards and memory. It is the programmer's responsibility to know the length and order of the data fields.

STORING DATA ON TAPE

Before going any further into magnetic tape operations, you are reminded that a *record* of data is simply a collection of characters or fields that are related in some way. For example, a punched card containing payroll information for a particular employee would be a record. On tape, a record of information can be almost any length depending upon the size of main memory and the capabilities of the tape drive unit—it is not set at 80 characters. (Remember that data has to pass through memory on its way to auxiliary storage.) At the end of each data area on tape the system requires a blank area called an interrecord gap (IRG) or interblock gap (IBG). This gap, which is approximately one-half of an inch, is necessary to allow the drive assembly to come up to the operating speed and to allow it to slow down without breaking the tape. The shock of starting and stopping is absorbed by a vacuum column, or spring mechanism, through which the tape is threaded. A schematic of the record and gap arrangement is shown in Figure 8.3(a).

The illustration shows an example of inefficient tape use. The gaps are almost as long as the records, meaning that only a little more than half of the tape is being used. Figure 8.3(b) shows how tape can be used more efficiently.

In this second example, the data records have been *blocked*, or grouped, to lessen the amount of unused or gap space on the tape. Another important reason for blocking data on tape is to speed up the I/O operation. For example, if the tape records are blocked in groups of 10, all of them can be read into main memory by means of a single input operation. Since the tape unit actually stops and starts every time it encounters a gap, the blocking of data records can save an enormous amount of time on a large job.

Another term used with magnetic tape is that of *recording density*, which refers to the closeness of the vertical rows of bits along the

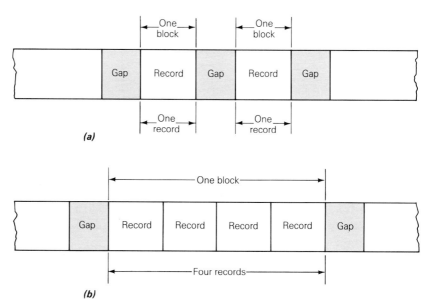

FIGURE 8.3
Tape data format. (a) Unblocked records. (b) Blocked records.

length of the tape. Low-density units record at 800 characters per inch, while high-density units record at 1600, or 6250 characters per inch.

As you can see, the number of characters that can be stored on tape depends upon:

(a)   Recording density
(b)   The blocking of data records.

As a rough rule of thumb, a 2400-foot reel of tape is capable of storing up to 150 million characters. Also, some units are capable of changing recording density by a switch setting and programmed instructions. Figure 8.4 shows how much room a standard 80-column card record would occupy on magnetic tape at a recording density of 800 characters per inch. Think about what it would look like at 6250 characters per inch! One of the major advantages of tape over disk storage medium is that tape reels are relatively inexpensive, about $20 per reel.

Tape *transfer rate* applies to the speed at which a tape unit can move data into main storage. It is usually calculated in characters per second based on the tape speed and recording density. For example, a tape unit that stores 800 characters per inch and which moves tape at 100 inches per second has a transfer rate of 100 × 800 or 80,000 characters per second. Figure 8.5 shows a typical tape unit.

DATA CHECKING AND TAPE PROTECTION

You have already seen one protective device of tape drives, the vertical parity check. In addition, a horizontal or longitudinal parity check is made at the end of each block of data. What actually happens is that

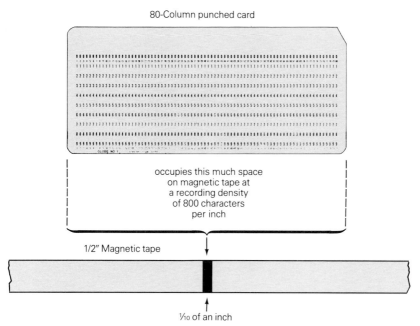

80-Column punched card

occupies this much space
on magnetic tape at
a recording density
of 800 characters
per inch

1/2" Magnetic tape

1/10 of an inch

FIGURE 8.4
Tape recording density.

during a write operation the system keeps track of the number of 1 bits in each channel. After the last column of data is written, the system generates a longitudinal check column on either odd or even parity according to the coding structure used. During a read operation the data is checked both vertically and horizontally, as shown in Figure 8.6.

Some tape drives use dual-gap read/write heads to ensure accuracy. The illustration below shows that the character is written and then read immediately and compared for equality.

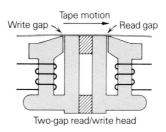

Tape motion
Write gap   Read gap

Two-gap read/write head

Another form of data protection is provided by a file protection ring on the back of a tape reel. When the plastic ring is in, writing can take place. When the ring is removed, the tape can only be read—"no ring, no write." This, of course, helps to prevent valuable data from being destroyed by mistake.

FIGURE 8.5
Magnetic tape drive unit.

Still another protective method is found in error-handling procedures. If a parity error is detected during a read operation, the system usually makes a provision for backspacing and rereading of the block in an attempt to overcome the error. Up to 100 rereads can be attempted before an error condition is signaled to the operator. Proper tape storage and handling procedures are also essential to the elimination of errors. Magnetic tape is particularly susceptible to humidity and dust, and it should be stored under proper atmospheric conditions.

FIGURE 8.6
Tape error checking.

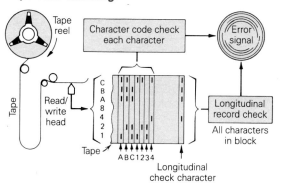

Although tape is not supposed to touch the read/write heads, it does wear a little with each run. Eventually, deposits build up on the surface of the tape and cause read/write errors. When errors begin to occur, the tape may be cleaned, shortened, or destroyed.

TAPE IDENTIFICATION AND HANDLING

In business DP it is not at all uncommon for a large firm to store and use several thousand tape reels. In this situation each tape reel will be numbered or marked for visual identification. Firms making extensive use of tape usually establish tape libraries with full-time personnel (tape librarians) to maintain a record of the use of each tape reel (see Figure 8.7).

Just as camera film requires a certain amount of leader material to allow for threading through the mechanism, so does magnetic tape. The beginning and end of the usable area on tape is indicated by load-point and end-of-reelmarkers. In most cases, these markers are small, aluminized strips glued to the tape and they trigger photoelectric cells, as shown in Figure 8.8. Equally important, however, is the identifying information that is recorded on the tape at the beginning of the data area. Coded in regular bit format, this header label serves to

FIGURE 8.7
Tape library.

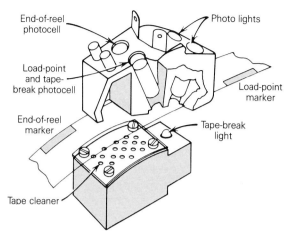

End-of-reel photocell

Photo lights

Load-point and tape-break photocell

Load-point marker

End-of-reel marker

Tape-break light

Tape cleaner

FIGURE 8.8
Tape photoelectric mark reader.

further identify a specific reel of tape. A program that calls for a particular tape reel is then assured of getting the correct spool before any processing takes place. The end of the data area on the tape will also be identified by what is known as a trailer label (Figure 8.8).

Some installations use tape to such a great extent that the sheer amount of time to locate a tape reel, move it to the tape drive, remove the old reel, and mount the new one becomes an important factor in the amount of data that can be processed during a shift. One firm makes an automated tape library that, as the name indicates, takes care of these tasks automatically (Figure 8.9).

MAGNETIC DISK

Magnetic disks resemble phonograph records and can be used singly or in a stacked arrangement in a *disk drive*. Generally, disks are extremely smooth metal platters coated with an easily magnetized substance so that data can be recorded on both the top and bottom sides. Depending upon the number of disks in the unit and the recording density, storage may range from 5 million to over 1 billion bytes on a single disk drive.

Access arms containing read/write heads move in and out to allow reading and/or writing to take place on any part of any surface. As shown in Figure 8.10, the access-arm assembly resembles a comb in that all the read/write heads move in or out at the same time.

Disk storage often is in the form of removable disk *packs* or modules that can be removed and/or inserted in under a minute so that disk storage (like tape storage) is almost unlimited (Figure 8.11).

Access times on disk can vary considerably. On most equipment the

FIGURE 8.9
Automated tape library.

time it takes to read or write on a specific area is determined by: (a) access arm movement delay, and (b) rotational delay (ranging from nearly 20 milliseconds up to 60 milliseconds). In contrast, note that computer memory access time is in terms of 1 microsecond to under 100 nanoseconds.

FIGURE 8.10
Disk schematic.

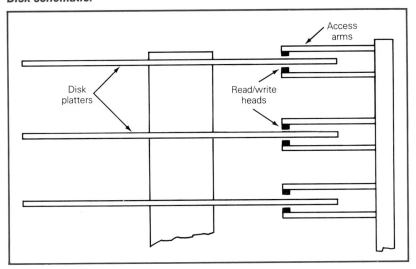

FIGURE 8.11
Disk drives in background with removable disk packs in foreground.

The term *track*, as used with disk, refers to concentric rings or areas on which data can be recorded. Another term, *cylinder*, is commonly used with disk. It refers to the same track on each of the usable disk surfaces. For example, cylinder 45 is composed of track 45 on surface one, surface two, surface three, and so forth. Storage of data is usually done in terms of cylinders rather than tracks. Thus, when writing data records onto disk, the programmer would *not* fill up track 17 on disk surface one and then go to track 18 on the same disk surface, as this would require a considerable amount of time to move the entire set of access arms. Instead, the programmer will fill track 17 on surface one and go to track 17 on surface two and so on until the entire cylinder has been filled. Then, the access arms will be moved to the next cylinder (cylinder 18). Figures 8.12 and 8.13 illustrate the ideas of tracks and cylinders. Depending upon the type of technology used in disk fabrication, storage densities of up to 1000 tracks per inch can be achieved. In general, disk capacities have been doubling every three years while the cost remains the same.

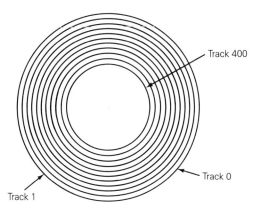

FIGURE 8.12
Disk tracks.

Figure 8.14 shows a different disk arrangement in which the term *sector* is used. Sectors are really conceptual lines that cut across the recording tracks to divide them into smaller chunks, much like pieces of pie. Each sector has an address and can hold a specific amount of information. In either arrangement, when the programmer wishes to

FIGURE 8.13
Disk cylinder concept.

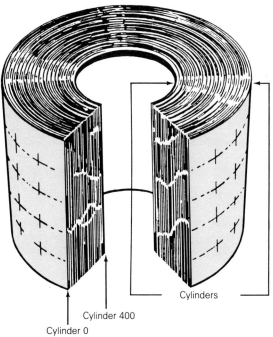

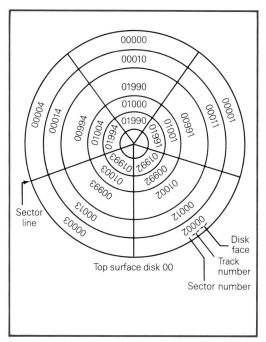

FIGURE 8.14
Schematic of disk showing sectors.

work (read or write) with disk, the computer system locates the track and activates the proper read/write head at the correct moment.

For many years one of the major problems associated with disks has been a "head crash." As the term indicates, the moving heads actually crash into the surface of the disk. Since the disk is rotating at a high speed, the result is loss of the data in the immediate area and possible destruction of the read/write head assembly. In some cases the damage may be so severe that the entire disk is not usable. Although there is no total solution to this problem, it is imperative that operators and computer room personnel be alert to the first sign of disk trouble (often a screaming noise) and shut the disk down immediately. Unfortunately, disk technology is such that the closer the heads are to the surface, the greater the amount of data that can be stored.

In 1973 IBM introduced disks featuring what is now known as Winchester technology. The highly polished disk surfaces are coated with a thin film of material that allows the read/write heads to ride extremely close to the surface—about 20-millionths of an inch! This distance is so small that a particle of dust cannot fit between the disk surface and the read/write head (Figure 8.15). The problem is even further compounded when you realize that, in reference to the head, the disk surface is traveling by at a rate of over 100 miles per hour. To prevent dirt from contaminating the disks, the heads, and access arms

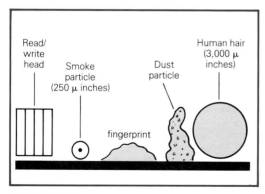

FIGURE 8.15
Disk tolerances. As shown in the figure, the readwrite head is so close to the surface that a particle of smoke cannot fit between the head and the disk surface.

are all contained in a sealed disk pack. When inserted into the disk drive, air is continuously filtered to exclude any dust or dirt particles that are too large. Figure 8.16 shows disk drive units during the manufacturing and fabrication process. Note the "clean room" conditions.

In order to further cut or decrease disk access time, units have been developed that have a read/write head for each disk track. Called "head per track" disks, they permit more rapid access, since the only delay is that caused by the disk rotation. However, these units do not have removable disk packs as do the others discussed so far. A problem then arises when we wish to remove or "save" the data that is stored on nonremovable disk. The solution has been what is known as "streaming" magnetic tape. Figure 8.17 shows a nonremovable, moving-head disk unit that contains its own tape cassette. When a disk

"I discovered why the computers are singing. Read your manual again. It says to insert a disk-pack, not a six-pack..."

(Courtesy Infosystems)

FIGURE 8.16
Disks on production line.

"dump" is needed, the data is "streamed," or written very quickly, to the tape media.

Until recently, hard disk storage has been in the form of 14-inch platters—either single or multiple disks, as shown in the illustrations. However, in a very short space of time the industry has undergone a "revolution." First came the soft or "floppy" disks, which are covered

FIGURE 8.17
"Streaming" tape.

in the next section and which made a deep and lasting impression on the data processing industry. Then the disk manufacturers developed 8-inch Winchester disk drives that have made serious inroads into the traditional 14-inch hard disk market. Just as these devices were about to become a "standard" within the industry, we saw the emergence of 5¼-inch Winchester disks (Figure 8.18). As of this date we are not sure of the outcome, although one prediction indicates that 5¼-inch units will dominate in the mid- to late 1980s.

As far as the future is concerned, one possibility is that of using a laser beam to actually burn holes in the disk surface. The surface is only usable once, but a 14-inch disk could hold as much as 10 billion holes or bits. Optical disk storage, which would not destroy the surface, is still being worked upon and does not appear to be commercially viable at this time.

FIGURE 8.18
5¼ inch Winchester disk drive.

FLOPPY (SOFT) DISK STORAGE

The so-called "floppy" disks or "diskettes," are flexible disks that are made of Mylar plastic and encased in a jacket with openings for the drive spindle and read/write heads. They are used primarily as a cheap storage media for intelligent terminals, data entry systems, office word processing, and small computer systems. (In 1981 a single platter drive cost about $500. Individual diskettes cost about $5 to $10) (Figure 8.19).

As for diskette format, it is like the hard disks described earlier in that the system uses tracks and sectors. Originally, storage capacity was about 250,000 bytes, but some diskettes can now store about 1 million bytes. Sectoring is done by two methods: hard sectoring and soft sectoring. In hard sectoring, tiny holes punched in the disk identify the sectors. In soft sectoring, the sectors are recognized by magnetic codes written onto the disk.

There are, however, two major differences between floppy and regular disks. The original floppies recorded on one side only, but "flippies," that record on both sides, are now available along with increased density of data storage. A second major difference is that the ceramic read/write heads on the floppies actually touch the disk. Consequently, the diskettes do wear out, although most manufacturers guarantee about 2 million passes per track. The read error rate is much higher than hard disk, as a particle of dirt can actually bounce the read mechanism off the surface. Two sizes are now available: the standard 8 inch and the new 5¼-inch minifloppy.

BATTELLE INSTITUTE STUDYING INTELLIGENT CREDIT CARDS

COLUMBUS, Ohio—A six-month research study to examine the future application of wallet-sized plastic cards with built-in microprocessor and computer-type memory is being conducted by the Battelle Memorial Institute under sponsorship from 24 international banking, telephone, oil and high-technology companies.

For $9,000, the institute, a nonprofit research organization headquartered here with facilities in London, Frankfurt, West Germany and Tokyo, will produce a state-of-the-art report on what project manager John Farrell calls "intelligent credit cards."

"I view this as a sort of task force approach where we will have the participants explain their needs and we will see how the cards can be best adapted for their technical, administrative and marketing needs," Farrell said. "What I see happening here is a number of industries being able to use these cards."

The study will forecast near- and long-range uses of the cards by various industries. It will discuss applications that, according to Farrell, could replace traditional payment methods and perform other functions without overburdening large on-line computer networks.

He suggested the cards could be used as convenient substitutes for travelers checks. Instead of carrying bulky notes on long journeys you could purchase a ca'd for a specified amount and use it to buy goods. The card would be inserted into a point-of-sale terminal that would automatically deduct the value of a purchase from the amount programmed into the card.

Though such systems are not in operation anywhere at present, the French government has sponsored a pilot project, to start at the end of the year, where three different intelligent cards, manufactured by European companies, will be tested by banks, shopkeepers and customers.

Farrell said the intelligent cards had security advantages in that built-in self-destruct commands could make duplication almost impossible.

Organizations may still participate in the study. More information is available from Battelle Memorial Institute, 505 King Ave., Columbus, Ohio 43201.

FIGURE 8.19
"Floppy" disk storage.

MICROFILM STORAGE SYSTEMS

Traditionally, microfilm has never been considered to be an auxiliary storage medium. However, increased computer speeds, coupled with relatively static output speeds, have forced manufacturers to search for new output methods that can match the output of the central processing unit. The graphic devices discussed earlier in the text offered much in the way of flexibility and, in some cases, startling savings in time. The vast majority of output operations, however, use the impact printer, which is both slow and costly in terms of paper usage. For some firms, a solution to this perennial problem has appeared in the form of microfilm devices that can be interfaced with computer systems. The term used to describe this alliance is COM (computer output to microfilm).

Generally speaking, a COM device is a piece of hardware that converts computer-generated data into letters, numbers, or symbols on microfilm. On a hardware basis, COMs are of two types: those that work directly with computer output and those that operate off-line with an auxiliary storage media, usually magnetic tape.

As shown in Figure 8.20, magnetic tape data is displayed on a cathode ray tube and photographed by a high-speed microfilm camera. One of the nice features of a COM system is that it can do what is known as "forms overlay." Since business output usually requires special forms, such as those used for billing or shipping, it would be imperative for the COM system to have the ability to overlay the image of the form during the filming process. Microfilm output from the COM system is put into rolls or strips for use with whatever viewing equipment is used by the firm. After processing, a high-speed microfilm duplicator is used to make duplicate copies as required. Figure 8.21 shows a typical computer output microfilmer.

How is COM used? Certainly it is not for everybody, as COM units are fairly expensive. In addition, *micrographics*, which is the general term applied to this technology, opens up a whole new way of handling information and the people involved must be willing to accept graphical methods. Some basic applications include:

1. Business listings that may be referenced frequently but with infrequent changing or updating. Applications of this type include parts catalogs, rate directories, payment records, inventory listings, routing schedules.
2. Engineering drawings of almost every type.
3. Management reports that require charts or drawings, such as sales forecasts, profit ratios, production plans.
4. Special scientific applications that require the creation of film as an intermediate printing step.

FIGURE 8.20
COM operation.

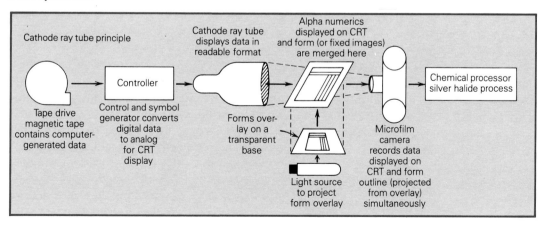

FIGURE 8.21
Computer Output Microfilm (COM) Unit.

Utility companies have been enthusiastic users of COM. Each month they print bills for customers, but at least one copy must be kept in the office in case a complaint or question arises. Records of this type have to be kept for years and sheer size of the storage becomes over-whelming. COM provides the answer by producing a microfilm image of the customer bill. Mounted in rolls or in flat form (called microfiche) the information can be viewed on a screen when needed.

Some of the major advantages of COM systems include a savings of up to 90% in storage space (Figure 8.22), greatly reduced mailing costs,

FIGURE 8.22
Microfilm compared to printed material.

and reduced paper handling costs. Disadvantages include the reorientation of employees to the graphic system and the expense of COM equipment—COM, microfilm viewers, hard-copy printers, etc.

The COM/computer technology has been extended even further in a system installed by the Ohio Bell Telephone Company. The problem was one of trying to answer a directory assistance call by finding the proper telephone number out of a data base of over 1½ million numbers. Obviously, a manual system would not meet the customer's needs within a reasonable length of time. A combination of microfilm and computer technology provided the solution.

8½ by 11-inch pages of telephone numbers were reduced to 1/200 of their original size and stored in groups of 200 on microfilm strips 1.4 by 8 inches. The strips were then stored in cartridges to form the giant data base required by the company. "Lookup" is controlled by a minicomputer that is hooked up to keyboard terminals. The computer stores a reference index that points to any particular strip of microfilm storage. As soon as the caller provides some type of identifier, such as a name or address, the computer searches its index for the location and then starts the microfilm retrieval process. Seconds later the material is displayed on the operator's viewing screen.

SUMMARY OF
IMPORTANT POINTS

☐ Magnetic tape units record in two basic coding structures: 7-channel and 9-channel code.

☐ Recording density refers to the closeness of the vertical columns of bits that are written onto tape. Several different recording densities are available.

☐ Tape data records are usually blocked to save tape space and to permit faster tapehandling.

☐ Tape devices use both vertical and horizontal parity bits to check data blocks that are read or written.

☐ With both disk and tape, the data is recorded as a series of tiny magnetic spots on the surface of the material.

☐ Writing onto tape or disk is destructive in that the data that was already there is written over. Reading of data from tape or disk into memory does not harm the data stored on the auxiliary device.

☐ Disk data is accessed by means of read/write heads located on the end of access arms that can get to any track on any of the disk recording surfaces.

☐ Data is stored on disk in terms of cylinders rather than tracks because this method reduces the amount of time it takes to retrieve data from the file.

☐ Disk technology is changing very rapidly as we go to greater recording densities along with greater system reliability.

☐ Diskettes, or floppy disks, are used extensively on small microcomputer systems because they offer random access storage at a much lower price than hard disk.

☐ Microfilm as a form of auxiliary storage is not a method that is applicable to all business operations. It is appropriate when the firm must retain large numbers of paper documents and make frequent reference to specific items in the file.

☐ COM (computer output to microfilm) occurs when data that would normally be printed is directed toward a microfilm print unit instead. The film may be processed into rolls or flat pieces known as microfiche.

☐ Computer-driven microfilm-retrieval systems can be used to speed the retrieval process.

GLOSSARY OF TERMS

Auxiliary storage—storage devices that can hold much larger amounts of information than memory but with a slower access time.

Blocking—on either disk or tape, it is the act of placing together several data records in order to save storage space and to speed up data transfer.

Channel—Parallel rows of bits running along the length of magnetic tape. Modern computers use 9-channel tape, although earlier computers used 7-channel tape.

COM (computer output to microfilmer)—A device that takes computer output and writes it onto microfilm.

Cylinder—a group of disk tracks that are accessed at one time by a single set of read/write heads. A disk pack having 200 tracks on each disk surface would have 200 cylinders.

Data file—a collection of data records usually organized on a logical basis. For example, all the data records that are created during fall enrollment at a school would comprise the Fall Student Enrollment file.

Data record—a collection of data fields pertaining to a particular subject. A punched card containing payroll information on a particular employee would be a record of data.

Disk storage—a magnetic storage device that very closely resembles a stack of phonograph records.

Diskettes—small, plastic disk platters used as auxiliary storage on many small computer systems.

Floppy disks—see Diskettes.

IRG or IBG (Interrecord Gap or Interblock Gap)—A machine-generated space on magnetic tape or disk that appears after each data record or data block. Generally, the gap is about one-half inch in length.

Magnetic tape—a plastic storage medium that has a thin coating of iron oxide (or a similar material) that is easily magnetized.

Micrographics—the general term applied to the storage of data on microfilm.

Parity check—the general term applied to the act of determining the validity of information stored in a memory device.

Read/write head—a magnetic coil device that is capable of magnetizing or detecting magnetism on a tiny spot on the surface of a magnetic storage device.

Recording Density—the closeness with which data is stored on magnetic tape. The most common densities are 800, 1600, and 6250 characters per inch.

Track—in reference to magnetic disk, the term track refers to the concentric rings on the disk surface on which data is recorded.

Transfer rate—in reference to magnetic tape or disk it indicates how much data can be moved from auxiliary storage to memory per second.

THOUGHT QUESTIONS

1. What are the advantages of floppy disks over hard disks? What are the disadvantages?

2. How would you rate the access times of disk vs tape?

3. In what type of situation would you want your computer system to have the ability to read (or write) 7-channel tape in addition to regular 9-channel format?

4. Discuss the justification of a COM system as opposed to a paper printing system. When would one system be more applicable than the other?

5. Are COM systems likely to involve the retraining of office personnel? If so, how and why?

CHAPTER 9
FILE ACCESS
METHODS

LEARNING OBJECTIVES

*Upon completion of the chapter you should under-
stand the following:*

*The need for sequential access files and the type of
applications that fall into this category.*

*The sequential access process on both tape and
disk files.*

How sequential files are created.

The nature and use of indexed files.

How indexed files are created.

*How random retrieval of data records from an in-
dexed file is accomplished.*

*How disk and tape storage is used in the process of
transferring funds electronically.*

CHAPTER CONTENTS

The previous chapter described the two major types of storage media that are used on computer systems: tape and disk. One of the major tasks of the programmer is that of creating and accessing data files on either medium. The term "accessing," is used here in reference to reading the data records into memory as needed. Therein lies the problem. As you now know, magnetic tape and disk are similar media, but they are accessed in two very radically different ways.

As this chapter shows, magnetic tape is classified as a *sequential* storage device because access to the data is by means of a sequential or serial search through the file until the desired data record is found. Magnetic disk, on the other hand, is classified as *random access* media because the storage media is *addressable*. (The term "addressable" indicates that data can be stored in specific areas on disk that can be referenced or addressed directly.) The difference between the two methods of accessing storage is important because it determines to a great extent how the entire DP operation functions, although most DP systems use a mixture of both types of secondary storage. The fact that magnetic tape is not addressable is not really a disadvantage or limitation as tape files are handled in an entirely different manner than disk. Let's see how a sequential file processing takes place.

SEQUENTIAL FILES: MAGNETIC TAPE

By definition, magnetic tape is a storage medium that does not contain addressable areas. As indicated earlier, this is not a limitation as compared to disk. Beginning students often ask, "Why don't they put addresses on magnetic tape?" and the answer is that, even if the designers could, there is no need to do so. To understand why this is so we start with the simple process of creating a tape file.

CREATING A TAPE FILE

We will start with the storage media with which you are most familiar—punched cards. Suppose we represent ABC Department Store and we have a "Balance Due from Customers" file that consists of many thousands of punched cards. Each card record contains the specific fields of information that would be required in the end-of-the-month accounting process.

Billing number	Customer name	Customer address	Balance due

Getting to a specific card record is fairly difficult with the records in this form. One way of making the records more accessible would be to store them on magnetic tape. The program to do this is extremely simple. It consists of a program loop that is repeated again and again until all the cards have been read and processed.

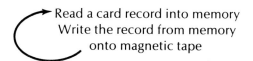

Read a card record into memory
Write the record from memory
onto magnetic tape

The truth of the matter is that you are looking at the "guts" of our "create a tape file" program. Only one other thing needs to be included and that varies from system to system. Somehow, the programmer must tell the computer what name to assign to the tape data file that is being created.

1. The system is informed of the name the programmer wishes to give to the file. The system then writes this and other information into the tape label area at the beginning of the tape.
2. As shown earlier, a card is read into a memory area by the read statement in the program.
3. The write statement causes a copy of the data record in memory to

be written onto magnetic tape. Any data that was in that tape area before is destroyed in the process.

4. The process is repeated until all card records have been written to tape.

5. After the read-write action stops, the system writes an end-of-file (EOF) mark right after the last data record.

As depicted in figure 9.1, the contents of the first card record have been read through the card reader and into memory by the action of the READ statement. (The card then continues in to the stacker.) Next, the WRITE statement actually writes the contents of the 80-byte memory area onto magnetic tape. This process will continue with each card record being written progressively further along tape just as in the recording of songs on a home tape system.

The diagram also illustrates another very important point about tape files. Note that the card records are in ascending order by Billing Identification Number. This is not an accident, as the normal process would be to store the data records in a predetermined order based on a "key" field such as social security number, part number, or customer name. This point is important and comes up repeatedly throughout the remainder of the chapter. Figure 9.2 illustrates the resulting Balance Due file without respect to interrecord gaps or blocking. Note that the tape file is the equivalent to our original deck of data cards but now they are, in effect, laid out end-to-end on magnetic tape.

FIGURE 9.1
Creating a sequential tape file.

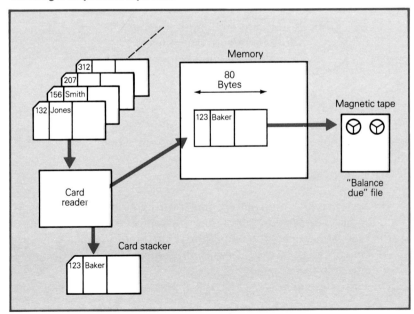

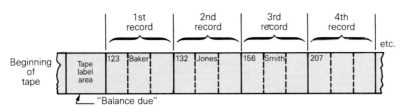

FIGURE 9.2
Tape file format.

USING A TAPE FILE

Magnetic tape has two major uses. First, it is an excellent back-up medium for magnetic disk because it is inexpensive and easily stored. Second, it is used in file processing whenever you need to process *all* the data records on a file. For example, a *monthly* billing operation in which we will send bills to all customers with an outstanding balance is well suited for magnetic tape. Suppose we have the following files (all sorted into ascending order based on the key field Billing Number).

1.   Balance Due—end of previous month.
2.   Monthly Charges by customers.
3.   Monthly Credits and Returns.
4.   Monthly Payment by customers.

As shown in Figure 9.3, the end-of-the-month billing process involves five tape files and a printer. The programmer compares records from the four incoming files until a match is found, calculates the new amount owed by the customer (Old Balance plus Charges minus Credits minus Payments), prints a billing document, and writes the updated record to the new Balance Owed file. The process of matching records from the various files will continue until all data records from the four incoming files have been handled. At this point you may want to think about how all this is done. As you would guess, the matching of records from the different files is a process that requires extensive use of logical testing within the program (i.e., testing to see if a particular record is less than, equal to, or greater than another record based upon a specific field such as customer number or customer name). What makes this possible to do in an efficient manner is that all the files will have been sorted into ascending order prior to the main processing run.

Back-up or security for the new Balance Due file is provided by saving the four tape files from which it was created. The storage period might be a month or perhaps even longer. Then, if the new Balance Due file is destroyed, it can be recreated.

Any file that contains relatively stable or unchanging information is called a "master" file. For example, a payroll file that contains the bulk of the information on employees would be called a Master Payroll File.

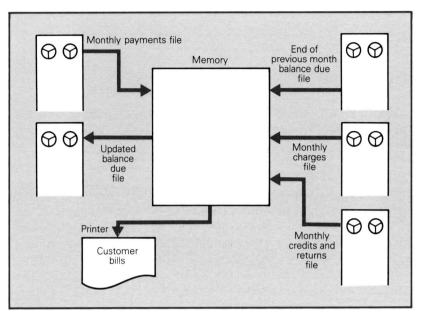

FIGURE 9.3
Sequential file processing.

The weekly file that contains transient information such as hours worked is often called a Detail File or a Transaction File. This terminology applies to both disk and tape and serves to alert programmers and operators as to the nature of the particular file. Destruction of a detail file is awkward because the data in the file probably came from source documents that will have to be rekeyed. Destruction of a master file is one of life's totally unpleasant experiences, particularly if a back-up file is not readily available.

Now that you have seen how a tape file is used, let's use a second application that is totally unsuited to the characteristics of tape storage. Remember, magnetic tape is not addressable; i.e., there is no way that the programmer can go directly to an exact area on tape. Instead, a single record can be located only by means of a sequential search through the file. For example, suppose customer Johnson calls the store and wishes to know the balance owed. To retrieve that information we will have to go through the following steps.

1. Enter the customer name into memory.
2. Execute a program that:
   (a) Reads in a tape record.
   (b) Compares "Johnson" to the name found in the Customer Name field of the first record.
   (c) If the names match, the amount owed is printed.
   (d) If the names do not match, read another tape record.

(e) Repeat the process until a match is found or until the end of the file is reached. If the end of the file is reached before finding the matching record, print a message indicating that no match was found.

3. Rewind the tape to start the process over for the next customer that calls in.

After reading the above, it should be readily apparent that the method shown here is incredibly inefficient. There are several reasons for this, one of which is that the file was created in ascending order based on the Billing Number rather than Customer Name.

The process would have been slightly more efficient if the customers that called had given their billing numbers rather than their names. Then the programmer could have made use of the comparing ability of the computer to allow faster retrieval of records. For example, since the file is in ascending order by Billing Number, we would not have to go to the end of the file each time to see whether a match existed. In addition, a comparing operation would free us from having to rewind the tape every time a new customer request is initiated. We would only have to rewind when the new billing number was less than the last one processed.

Another possibility is that we could batch or hold all customer requests for a few days, and create a second file with the requests sorted into ascending order. Of course, this would not permit quick response to a customer inquiry. However, even if these changes were made, the process would still be inefficient because, in the example we are trying to put tape to a use for which it was not really intended. What you have just seen is an application that is tailor-made for disk because, unlike tape, disk has the capability of being randomly accessed.

RANDOM OR DIRECT ACCESS METHODS

As illustrated in the previous section, some applications are well suited to the sequential access methods offered by magnetic tape. At the same time, this feature of tape can also be a major disadvantage when a random access application arises. Disk storage, however, offers one important feature that tape does not: the ability to go "directly" to a specific area on disk to retrieve a data record.

If the programmer could write a statement that says

Read the data record from disk
area XXXXX into memory

then direct retrieval makes sense. Unfortunately, there is no way that the programmer can know where one particular data record—out of thousands of such records—is stored on a disk. And yet, disk is said to be a direct or random access medium.

How is this accomplished? The answer lies in an *index* that is created as the file itself is being written onto disk.

CREATING AN INDEXED FILE

Indexed files work very much like a textbook: To find a specific topic, you first consult an index that lists the key words or topics and their location in the text. Let's use the same examples that started the chapter. We had a Balance Due file in card form and now we want to create an *indexed* Balance Due file on magnetic disk. The logic of the write-to-disk operation is the same as before.

> Read a card record into memory
> Write the record from memory
> onto magnetic disk

In addition to specifying the file name "BALANCE DUE," we will also tell the system to build an index as the data records are being entered. (Fortunately, the programmer is not bothered with the details of how

FIGURE 9.4
Creating an indexed file.

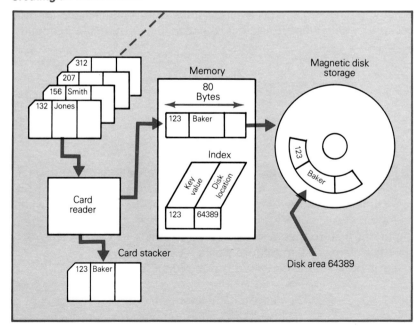

this is done, as a single entry in the program triggers the system action.)

As indicated above, an index is based upon a key field that the programmer identifies. In our case, the programmer would indicate to the system that the index is to be created on the basis of the Billing Number field. The index will contain two columns of entries: the key field value and the disk area on which that record was stored (Figure 9.4).

Several points should be noted in the diagram. First, the system automatically makes an entry to the index everytime a record is read in and then written to the disk file. Second, the index is created within memory and is based upon the key field specified by the programmer. After the disk file has been created, the index will be written onto disk as shown in the following diagram.

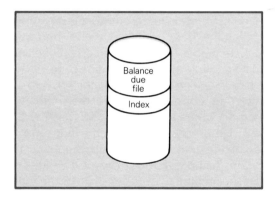

USING AN INDEXED FILE

Those of you who have taken a good look at the last example will have noted that the card records were still in sequential order. Even though we can now access out new file randomly based on the Billing Number, there may be times when it would be convenient to retrieve *all* the records in sequential order. Therein lies one of the major advantages of indexed files. Indexed files, perhaps more accurately called Indexed-Sequential files, allow us the best of both worlds—sequential *and* random retrieval.

Suppose we wanted to run the same end-of-the-month billing application that was illustrated earlier with magnetic tape. Our diagram would be the same as Figure 9.3, except that we would substitute disk symbols for magnetic tape drive symbols. The programmer indicates that he or she wishes to retrieve data records sequentially (rather than randomly) and the system goes through the following steps.

1. The system, upon encountering the file name requested (Balance Due), sees that it is an indexed file and reads a copy of the index from disk into memory.

2. Since the file retrieval method is specified as *sequential,* the system goes to the index *once* to find the disk location of the first record.
3. All future reads from the file are done on a straight sequential basis without further reference to the index.

Since an index was created with the file, random applications can be taken care of with little difficulty. In an earlier example we had customers calling in to ascertain the status of an account. Assuming that a customer provided the Billing Number, we would activate a random retrieval program. Then we would simply enter the number (probably from a video terminal) and await the computer response. What actually takes place within the program is outlined below.

1. The index is read into memory.
2. The Billing Number is entered by the operator.
3. The system compares the Billing Number just entered to the Billing Numbers in the *file index* until a match is found. When a match is found, the system goes to the disk area specified and retrieves the specified data record. At this point, some of you may have thought about the fact that searching a large index to find a specific value may be very time-consuming. When the index itself gets large, another method, called a *binary search,* is used. In a binary search, the system first goes to the middle of the index to see which of the two halves of the index can contain the value for which it is searching. (This technique works only if the index is in sequential order.) Each succeeding test cuts the size of the index in half until the searched-for value is found.
4. The process continues as long as customer requests are entered.

One small problem remains. What if the customer does not know his or her Billing Number? It would be nice to be able to retrieve records based upon more than one key field. That, of course, is exactly what we can do by specifying *alternate* key fields during the file building process. In addition, the presence of an index with a file gives the programmer the ability to add to, to change, and to delete records from the file without having to recreate the entire file every time.

USING DISK AND TAPE: ELECTRONIC FUNDS TRANSFER

The use of MICR encoded documents (discussed in a previous chapter) was the first major assault by bankers on the incredible paper blizzard to which the banking industry was subjected in the 1960s.

Over the years, a few improvements were made on MICR equipment and handling techniques; for example, most MICR sorter/readers can read the MICR characters optically as well as magnetically. However, these minor improvements were small compared to the enormous number of checks being written. In 1980 over 40 billion checks were written, nearly double the number that were written in 1973. Electronic funds transfer (EFT) offers a solution to at least part of the problem.

EFT can be defined as computer systems in which information is sent from one location to another via electrical impulses. The traditional use of checks actually creates two systems: one system for the transfer of payments and another for the clearing of such transactions among the banking institutions involved. This latter task has always been performed by clearing houses, but EFT requires Automated Clearing Houses (ACH) to perform these services.

Conventional clearing houses are organizations through which checks drawn on one bank but cashed at another bank are "cleared," accounted for, and routed back to the original bank. Automated clearing houses are already performing a wide variety of accounting functions, such as automatic deposit of payroll checks and payment of preauthorized fixed monthly bills, such as house or car loans or insurance premiums.

A typical example of EFT for payroll checks operates as follows:

1. The employees of a firm sign authorization cards that authorize the release of paycheck amounts via EFT to specific banks. Obviously, these same banks also must have the capability to handle electronic funds transfers.
2. Assuming that the computer system uses both disk and tape, the output from the payroll program will be in several forms.
    (a) Complete checks for those employees who choose not to go into electronic funds transfer.
    (b) Check stubs for those signed up for EFT as their money has been deposited electronically in their designated bank.
    (c) Information on the whole payroll operation will be written onto disk storage so that it will be immediately available to other programs that are part of the payroll program package. For example, there would be programs to post amounts to various accounts, prepare management reports, etc.
    (d) A magnetic tape will be prepared that shows the net amount to be paid to each employee. The various employees have their accounts with many different banks, but the tape records are not necessarily segregated according to the banks where the deposits are to be made.
3. The tape(s) is sent to the automated clearing house for further processing on the ACH computer system. Here, the deposits for each bank are sorted out and written onto separate tapes for each bank. Tape is ideal for this purpose because a reel of tape is cheap compared to a magnetic disk pack and it can survive the rigors of being mailed or carried from one location to another.
4. Each bank receives its tape and runs the data through its computer system to deposit the funds to customers' accounts. If communication links exist between these various computer systems, the funds can be deposited almost instantly. Otherwise, the tape spools must be physically sent to the next location.

Another EFT activity is essentially the reverse of the system outlined above. Customers can authorize the automatic payment of bills, particularly those that are the same from month to month (garbage bills, for example). The agency electronically sends the bill to the clearing house or bank and the amount is deducted from the customer's account and deposited in the agency account. In most cases, it is not necessary for the agency to send a receipt to the customer, as the customer's bank balance is proof that the payment was made.

An indication of the importance of EFT is that in October 1975, Congress established the National Commission on electronic funds transfer and charged it with the task of drafting a plan "for the orderly

FIGURE 9.5
Cash terminal.

development of electronic banking." From this it can be seen that EFT is here to stay, even though there are many unanswered questions. Both the consumer and DP professionals are extremely concerned over possible fraud, computer errors, how to cope with invasion of privacy, and monopolistic control of the systems. Despite these problems, EFT seems to be the only logical solution to the cumbersome and costly proliferation of paper.

Many of the next steps in electronic funds transfer have already been implemented on a limited scale. Increasingly, computer terminals, such as those described earlier in the text, are being located in supermarkets, retail stores, and post offices to take the place of much of branch banking that has been practiced in the past. This, of course, will give the customer an easier and more convenient way to bank. Electronically encoded credit cards that can provide instant access to cash from special "sidewalk" terminals have been in operation for many years (see Figure 9.5).

Point-of-sale terminals located in retail stores will provide for electronic transfer of funds as well as instant credit authorization. This latter point is of extreme importance to retailers who lose millions of dollars each year because of faulty or tardy credit information. All of these uses of EFT are in operation now and many more will be coming as we eliminate the excessive handling of paper. One of the major benefits to banking institutions from EFT is the chance to reduce "float," or the time lag, between deposit and collection of funds. What is making this all possible is the burgeoning use of intelligent terminals, minicomputers, and communication, networks.

SUMMARY OF IMPORTANT POINTS

☐   Magnetic tape is a sequential storage medium which means that a specific data record can be accessed only by means of a sequential read through all previous records.

☐   Disk is considered to be a random access storage medium because specific areas of a disk are directly addressable.

☐   Disk and tape each have their advantages and disadvantages, and most large computer systems have both types of units.

☐   Normally, files are created on the basis of a key field within the record. This field then serves as the identifying feature or mark of a particular record.

☐   An index is a listing of the data records within a file and the disk locations or areas in which those records are stored.

☐   The index is created in memory but stored on disk for use whenever a user wishes to access the file.

☐   Indexed files have the advantage of being able to be accessed sequentially and/or randomly.

☐   Because of this random access feature, individual records may be accessed and modified or deleted without recreating the whole file.

☐ Electronic funds transfer (EFT) is a processing technique that makes use of tape and disk storage in the electronic transfer of funds from one physical location to another.

☐ All indications point toward increased application of electronic funds transfer in the future.

GLOSSARY OF TERMS

Binary search—a method of searching an index in which the system first goes to the middle of the index to see which half of the index could contain the item wanted. Each succeeding test goes to the midpoint of the remaining part of the index that is being searched. The net effect is that a large index can be searched very quickly.

Detail file (also called a Transaction file)—as opposed to a master file, a detail file contains information that may be used only once. In addition, the detail records are not likely to contain extensive data fields because much of this information is already available in the master file records.

Index—a listing of the data records and the disk areas on which they are stored.

Key—the field or fields on which the indexs is based. Common key fields would be Social Security number, part number, or customer name.

Master file—usually an extensive file that contains relatively unchanging information. For example, a master payroll file would contain many fields that would not be needed in a payroll detail file (date of birth, telephone number, address, etc.).

Random access—a storage retrieval method by which the programmer can, through the use of an index, access separate data records without having to sequentially search through the whole file.

Sequential access—a storage retrieval method that requires a record-by-record reading through the file to find a specific record.

Transaction file—see detail file.

THOUGHT QUESTIONS

1. If disk files can be accessed either sequentially or randomly, why would any computer system use magnetic tape?

2. Describe how you think the computer system would set up an index that was based on two key fields rather than one.

3. If you were retrieving records from an indexed file based upon an alternate or secondary key, what extra statement(s) do you think would be required in the program?

4. Describe electronic funds transfer. What are its dangers to you as a consumer? What are its benefits? Do you use it now? If so, describe the application.

CHAPTER 10 COMPUTER SOFTWARE

LEARNING OBJECTIVES

Upon completion of the chapter you should understand the following:

What software is and how it functions in a modern computer system.

The difference between application and system software.

The general nature and uses of the programming languages listed: FORTRAN, BASIC, PASCAL, COBOL, assembly language, and RPG.

The general makeup of an operating system and the functions of each major category of programs.

Why translator or compiler programs are needed and how the compiling process takes place.

The need for and use of packaged software and the problems of using predesigned programs.

The future potential of application generator programs.

CHAPTER CONTENTS

So far, the term *software* has been used to refer to programs that direct the computer to solve specific, well-designed tasks. A program is a long list of instructions (like the ones you saw in an earlier chapter) that tell the computer, in agonizing detail, precisely what steps to perform and in what order. It is a slow and exacting process that is extremely expensive because it is so "labor-intensive," i.e., dependent upon human effort. For these reasons, computer users are in a constant state of crisis, needing software now but facing long waiting periods before specific programs become available.

THE SOFTWARE CRISIS

Today, well over a million computer systems are being used in the United States, nearly seven times the number that were in use six years ago. For nearly two decades we have witnessed a steady decrease of 20% *per year* in the cost of computing. This declining price has enabled computers to be applied to a torrent of new applications. As rosy as this picture seems, there is a major bottleneck—software. The demands of the new computer users seem to be inexhaustible, as both the users and the manufacturers think up new and more exotic applications every day.

Software costs have not declined over this two-decade period. Instead, they have increased dramatically due to the increase in people-related costs such as salaries and fringe benefits. In 1973 software for a computer system was estimated at twice the cost of the hardware, but in 1985 software is expected to cost ten times as much as the hardware.

According to International Data Corporation, sales of software and other such services by American companies totaled $13.14 billion in 1980 and they expect that figure to grow to nearly 34 billion by 1985. Other data indicates that there are more than 4300 firms in the software or computer services business, with IBM the leader with nearly $600 million worth of sales in 1980.

The current trend toward sophisticated communication-oriented and distributed data processing systems has strained to the breaking point our capacity to produce software. Intel Corporation, one of the leading manufacturers of computer electronics, figures that they have to spend more than $200,000 to develop the software to run a $10 microchip. On the surface the simple solution would seem to be that of hiring more programmers, but the answer to that proposal is equally simple: there are not enough qualified programmers around to satisfy the demand. In 1980 the gap was estimated at 50,000 people and the shortfall would increase to nearly 250,000 by the mid-1980s.

Another way of approaching this software crisis is to increase programmer productivity. But writing software is a highly creative, costly, and time-consuming enterprise that is often thought of as a modern art form. As such it has proved to be highly resistant to assembly-line tactics. The introduction of structure and discipline to programming was tried in the early 1970s and perhaps has helped a little. In general, however, demand has far outstripped any productivity gains that may have been made. According to Werner Frank in a report to *Computerworld* magazine (September 15, 1980):

There are just under 500,000 programmer/analysts in the U.S.

Personnel costs, often equated to software costs, are 40% to 50% of an installation's total DP expenditure.

Software productivity improvement appears to be at a near standstill. Individual programmer differences in (the) rate of program statement generation and in end program efficiency can easily differ by an order of magnitude (that is, by ten to one).

Even the largest corporations are having difficulty developing system software. IBM encountered programming problems or "bugs" in its software for a machine marketed in 1979 and had to delay delivery of the system for well over a year even though the hardware was functioning properly. This is not an unusual case, since virtually every major hardware manufacturer has suffered from software delays. In IBM's case, it was estimated that over 700 software programmers were working on the project and yet the delays still occurred.

System Development Corporation in Santa Monica, California, is a custom software house that is trying to reduce software development costs by using a factory or "assembly-line" approach to the problem. The traditional "division of labor" idea is used to break a job into component parts that can then be attacked by software specialists. One group determines the specifications of the task and a second group converts these functions into specific tasks that are to be automated. A third group translates these functions into design requirements, and group number four programs or codes each of the design modules. Finally, the last group tests the individual modules and sees that the program meets the customer's requirements.

From the above list of tasks we can identify at least four steps through which all software must proceed: analysis, design, coding, and testing. The analysis phase is that of determining exactly what problem the program is supposed to solve. One of the most common difficulties we experience here is that the user, for whom this program is being written, has only a hazy idea of what he or she wants to accomplish. Even when the needs are determined explicitly it may be difficult to convey this information to data processing people, since both groups tend to speak and think in their own particular jargon. Once the exact needs have been ascertained, the next step is to design the solution in terms that are satisfactory to all the parties concerned. Testing involves trying the application first with test data and ultimately with real data. Even the most rigorously planned and detailed programs are likely to contain errors, or "bugs," and this testing process probably involves some degree of "debugging" before the software is released to the user. (The following chapter will go more deeply into the details of these basic steps.)

So far we have grouped together all programming effort under the single term of software. In fact, not all software is the same—some is much more difficult to write and is known as *systems software,* or systems programming, as opposed to *application software.*

APPLICATION SOFTWARE

The term *application software* refers to programs written to perform a specific task (such as payroll or inventory, as previously discussed) for an individual agency or business firm. There are extreme variations in the length and complexity of such programs and their cost is very difficult to estimate. In 1976 it was estimated that a 20,000 statement payroll program cost about $160,000, but today a figure of $300,000 might be more accurate. On the topic of application software, Werner Frank reports (*Computerworld,* September 15, 1980):

The average time to develop a new application is two years.

User's average backlog of number of pending applications awaiting development stands at more than ten.

Only one-sixth of the total effort in developing an application should be devoted to programming; the balance of activity is involved in design and testing.

The application programmer produces 10 to 15 debugged lines of program per day; the system programmer generates about one-third as much. (Note: other sources indicate these estimates are too high.)

Software maintenance occupies 60% of an installation's manpower efforts.

The last of Mr. Frank's observations is well worth noting and falls within the commonly heard estimate of 50%–80% for maintenance work. If we assume this figure to be true, then there is an incredible need to turn out programs that are well planned, well documented and, to a reasonable extent, standardized in their programming structure. Certain computer languages lend themselves to structure, while others do not—a point that has been recognized and that is being dealt with as new languages and improved versions of old languages are developed.

It is doubtful that anyone knows just how many programming languages exist, but by now it is certainly in the thousands, with more appearing each day. To the newcomer this proliferation of languages is confusing and makes little sense. Why not just have one or two or even three languages and end the confusion? The answer is that no one language will satisfy all the applications that arise. Generally speaking, there are three factors that differentiate one language from another.

1. The types of data the language is equipped to deal with. For example, mathematical languages, such as FORTRAN, handle numbers with ease and precision but generally lack the capability to process names and alphabetic characters efficiently or gracefully.
2. The operations that can be performed on the data. As you already know, the computer really is an efficient adding machine which, by program instructions, can be made to subtract, divide, etc. However, some languages are built around powerful *macro* instructions that can save the programmer a great amount of time and trouble. By using macro instructions, the programmer can, with a single instruction, cause the computer to go through a long, complicated series of previously coded steps.
3. The control functions inherent in the language. Programming languages "built" or devised in the 1950s and 1960s had few control functions, which meant that the programmer had to resort to ingenious and often roundabout methods to get a program to execute the statements in the desired order. Most modern languages have a wide range of built-in control functions to ease the burden of the programmer.

In many cases, the so-called new languages are not truly new but are versions of existing languages that have been modified for a special application or industry use. In other cases, a manufacturer or software house feels that the development of a whole new language would be a better approach to customers' needs. Of all the languages that exist, some are older or more popular than others and these tend to form the common base of knowledge of application programmers. Let's take.a quick look at a few of these languages.

FORTRAN (FORmula TRANslation)

FORTRAN was one of the earliest languages of data processing and was developed by a group of people from various organizations headed by John Backus of IBM. The language was based on the laws of algebra plus various syntax rules established by the makeup of the computer. It took about three years and 25,000 lines of coding to develop the language. Since it has been around for such a long time, it has been imitated or modified more often than perhaps any other language. As the name indicates it was designed for mathematical and scientific work—"number crunching"—rather than for sophisticated file manipulation.

In its original version, the language was difficult to read because the names given to fields of data by the programmer were very limited. The more modern version of the language, FORTRAN 77, has corrected this deficiency.

FORTRAN is a high-level, *procedure-oriented* language because it was designed to be machine independent and applicable over a wide range of procedures. Figure 10.1 shows a FORTRAN 77 program that prints an inventory listing from data records contained in a disk file called PARTS. The program reads a record and calculates available stock by subtracting customer orders from inventory on hand. If the remainder is positive, it is multiplied by a part value to give an inventory-value figure. If the result of the subtraction is zero, there are no back orders and no inventory value. If the result of the subtraction is negative, back orders are printed. Totals are accumulated and printed at the end of the report.

BASIC (BEGINNERS ALL-PURPOSE SYMBOLIC INSTRUCTION CODE)

BASIC was developed in the late 1960s by two professors at Dartmouth College for time-sharing applications. Since then BASIC has become an extremely popular language, although some efforts have been made at standardization. Thus, each computer manufacturer or software house promulgates its own version so there is a low portability factor in transporting BASIC programs from one computer to another. It is not surprising that BASIC is very similar to FORTRAN, since the FORTRAN language served as the original model.

```
        PROGRAM FOUR

        INTEGER PARTNBR,ONHAND,CUSTORDERS
        INTEGER AVAILSTOCK,BACKORDERS,STAT
        INTEGER COUNTER,TOTALAVAILSTOCK
        INTEGER TOTALBACKORDERS

        REAL        ITEMVALUE,STOCKVALUE,TOTALVALUE

        CHARACTER PAGE*7

        DATA PAGE/'(' '1' ')'/
        DATA TOTALAVAILSTOCK,TOTALBACKORDERS/2*0/
        DATA TOTALVALUE/0.0/

****                START OF PROGRAM
*****                   OPEN FILES

        OPEN (5,FILE='PARTS')
        OPEN (1,FILE='OUTPUT')

        PRINT PAGE                      /* PRINT TOP OF PAGE */

*****             PRINT HEADINGS

        WRITE (1,200)'PART','AVAILABLE','BACK','INVENTORY'
        WRITE (1,300)'NUMBER','STOCK','ORDERS','VALUE'
        WRITE (1,400)'------','---------','------','---------'

*****              START OF LOOP

    10  CONTINUE

        READ (5,100,IOSTAT=STAT)PARTNBR,ONHAND,CUSTORDERS, ITEMVALUE

        IF (STAT.GE.0) THEN
          COUNTER = COUNTER + 1
          AVAILSTOCK = ONHAND - CUSTORDERS
          BACKORDERS = 0
          IF (AVAILSTOCK.LT.0) THEN
            BACKORDERS = - AVAILSTOCK
            AVAILSTOCK = 0
          ENDIF
          STOCKVALUE = AVAILSTOCK * ITEMVALUE
          WRITE (1,500)PARTNBR,AVAILSTOCK,BACKORDERS, STOCKVALUE
```

FIGURE 10.1
FORTRAN program.   (Continued)

```
        TOTALAVAILSTOCK = TOTALAVAILSTOCK + AVAILSTOCK
        TOTALBACKORDERS = TOTALBACKORDERS + BACKORDERS
        TOTALVALUE = TOTALVALUE + STOCKVALUE
        GO TO 10
    ENDIF

*****               END OF LOOP
    WRITE(1,600)TOTALAVAILSTOCK,TOTALBACKORDERS, TOTALVALUE
    PRINT '(/' 'PROGRAMMED BY WILLIAM HOPP' ')'


100   FORMAT(I4,2(1X,I3),F6.2)
200   FORMAT(1X,A5,12X,A9,9X,A4,12X,A9)
300   FORMAT(1X,A6,13X,A5,10X,A6,13X,A5)
400   FORMAT(1X,A6,11X,A9,8X,A6,11X,A9)
500   FORMAT(1X,I5,15X,I3,12X,I3,12X,F8.2)
600   FORMAT(/1X,'TOTALS',13X,I4,11X,I4,11X,F9.2)


    CLOSE (1)
    CLOSE (5)


    END                        /* END OF PROGRAM */
```

PART NUMBER	AVAILABLE STOCK	BACK ORDERS	INVENTORY VALUE
1111	97	0	1249.36
1355	372	0	7358.16
1883	0	0	0.00
5720	0	419	0.00
6292	366	0	8022.72
1500	0	0	0.00
2463	0	633	0.00
6895	441	0	4828.95
TOTALS	1276	1052	21459.18

PROGRAMMED BY WILLIAM HOPP
**** STOP

FIGURE 10.1 (Continued)

The chief advantage of BASIC is that it is easy to learn so that a beginner can write very powerful and sophisticated programs after learning about a dozen simple statements. It lacks the self-documenting advantages of COBOL and any extensive file-handling capabilities. These two deficiencies are being remedied as new versions of the language appear but, in doing so, the software developers are making a relatively simple language more complex. Traditionally,

BASIC has been the prime language used on minicomputers and home computers, such as those sold by Radio Shack and Apple, Inc. COBOL and PASCAL, however, are rapidly being implemented on these machines as user sophistication and application needs increase. Figure 10.2 shows the same inventory program using the BASIC language.

PASCAL

In the last few years, PASCAL has become one of the more popular programming languages throughout the world. Originally developed by Niklaus Wirth of Switzerland in 1973, its use has spread rapidly to colleges and universities because it allows students to understand computer architecture and structured programming concepts without becoming bogged down in the details of the language. It is not particularly well adapted to business applications, since it lacks the necessary editing and input/output capabilities that business demands. Several versions, including some for microcomputers, exist today, but the most popular form is UCSD PASCAL as modified by the University of California at San Diego. Figure 10.3 illustrates the solution to the inventory program using PASCAL.

COBOL (COMMON BUSINESS-ORIENTED LANGUAGE)

COBOL came into being in 1959 when a group of large systems users formed a committee named CODASYL (COnference on DAta SYstems and Languages) to design a common language. The committee, with representatives from the Department of Defense, IBM, Burroughs, Honeywell, RCA, and Sperry-Rand, devised COBOL to replace the various machine languages then used by each vendor installation. Despite the common design features, the COBOL produced by these vendors contained enough differences to make the transferability of programs from one machine to another quite difficult.

The problems were mostly resolved in 1968 when the American National Standards Institute (ANSI) approved a standard version of the language. Since then COBOL has been significantly modified (in 1974 and 1977) to provide greater standardization to the user. Today, it is the single most popular business language because of several advantages. First, it is relatively easy to learn because it is an English-like language in which statements such as

ADD GROSS-PAY TO TOTAL-GROSS-PAY
or
MOVE INCOMING-NAME TO OUTGOING-NAME
or
PERFORM READ-AND-CALCULATE-ROUTINE
    UNTIL LAST-CARD-INDICATOR = 1

```
100 DEFINE READ FILE #1="PARTS"
110 LET Z,T1,T2,T3 = 0
120 PRINT " ", "ABC PARTS CO"
130 PRINT
140 PRINT
150 PRINT "PART","AVAILABLE","BACK","INVENTORY"
160 PRINT "NUMBER","STOCK","ORDERS","VALUE"
170 PRINT
180 READ #1,P,H,C,D
190 ON END #1 GOTO 340
200 LET A = H−C
210 IF A<0 THEN GOTO 250
220 LET I = A*D
230 LET B = 0
240 GOTO 280
250 LET B = C−H
260 LET A = 0
270 LET I = 0
280 PRINT P,A,B,I
290 LET T1 = T1+A
300 LET T2 = T2+B
310 LET T3 = T3+I
320 LET Z = Z+1
330 GOTO 180
340 PRINT
350 PRINT "TOTALS",T1,T2,T3
360 PRINT "NUMBER OF RECORDS PROCESSED":Z
370 END
```

Output

ABC PARTS CO

PART NUMBER	AVAILABLE STOCK	BACK ORDERS	INVENTORY VALUE
1111	97	0	1249.36
1355	372	0	7358.16
1883	0	0	0
5720	0	419	0
6292	366	0	8022.72
1500	0	0	0
2463	0	633	0
6895	441	0	4828.95
TOTALS	1276	1052	21459.19

NUMBER OF RECORDS PROCESSED 8

FIGURE 10.2
BASIC program.

```
PROGRAM FOUR(PARTS);

CONST SPACE = ' ';

VAR   PARTNBR,ONHAND,CUSTORDERS :    INTEGER;
      AVAILABLESTOCK,BACKORDERS   :   INTEGER;
      COUNTER,TOTALAVAILSTOCK     :   INTEGER;
      TOTALBACKORDERS             :   INTEGER;
      ITEMVALUE, STOCKVALUE,TOTALVALUE        :   REAL;

      DATAIN                      :   TEXT;

BEGIN                             (Start of program)

      TOTALAVAILSTOCK := 0;
      TOTALBACKORDERS:= 0;
      TOTALVALUE := 0;

      PAGE;                       (Gives TOP-OF-PAGE)

                                  (Write headings)

      WRITE('PART':5,SPACE:12,'AVAILABLE',SPACE:9,'BACK');
      WRITELN(SPACE:12,'INVENTORY');
      WRITE('NUMBER',SPACE:13,'STOCK',SPACE:10,'ORDERS');
      WRITELN(SPACE:13.'VALUE');
      WRITE('------',SPACE:11,'---------',SPACE:8,'------');
      WRITELN(SPACE:11,'---------');
                                  (Open file for usage)
      RESET(DATAIN,'PARTS');

                                  (Loop until done)

WHILE NOT EOF(DATAIN) DO
  BEGIN
      READ(DATAIN,PARTNBR,ONHAND,CUSTORDERS);
      READLN(DATAIN,ITEMVALUE);
      COUNTER := COUNTER + 1;
      AVAILABLESTOCK := ONHAND - CUSTORDERS;
      BACKORDERS := 0;
      IF AVAILABLESTOCK < 0 THEN
        BEGIN
          BACKORDERS := -AVAILABLESTOCK;
          AVAILABLESTOCK := 0;
        END;
```

FIGURE 10.3
PASCAL program.   (Continued)

```
    STOCKVALUE := AVAILABLESTOCK * ITEMVALUE;
    WRITE(PARTNBR:5,SPACE:12,AVAILABLESTOCK:6,SPACE:9);
    WRITELN(BACKORDERS:6,SPACE:13,STOCKVALUE:8:2);

    TOTALAVAILSTOCK := TOTALAVAILSTOCK + AVAILABLESTOCK;
    TOTALBACKORDERS := TOTALBACKORDERS + BACKORDERS;
                   TOTALVALUE := TOTALVALUE + STOCKVALUE;

END;                              (End of loop)

WRITELN;
WRITE('TOTALS',SPACE:10,TOTALAVAILSTOCK:7,SPACE:8);
WRITELN(TOTALBACKORDERS:7,SPACE:12,TOTALVALUE:9:2);

WRITELN;WRITELN('PROGRAMMED BY WILLIAM HOPP');

CLOSE (DATAIN);
END.                              (End of program)
```

FIGURE 10.3 (Continued)

are easily read and make obvious sense. Second, because it is readable in English, COBOL is one of the most self-documenting languages available today. This self-documenting characteristic is of special importance when you recall the high percentage of maintenance programming that is common in the industry. Finally, COBOL, a procedure-oriented language, is applicable over a wide range of business functions with relative ease. In most business applications we wish to handle large amounts of data from multiple files, but probably will not get involved in intense mathematical manipulation of the data. This is just the reverse of most scientific/mathematical applications that handle relatively little data but manipulate or process it extensively (Figure 10.4).

OTHER LANGUAGES

Just about every manufacturer has an assembly language for each computer that they produce. There is no standardization in terminology and there is little or no portability of an assembly language from one machine to another. Often this is true even for machines produced by the same manufacturer. Assembly language is so machine-dependent that, for example, a program written for a model X Honeywell machine may not run on a model Y Honeywell machine.

The chief advantage of assembly language is also its main disadvantage. The language is very close to the native language of the machine and is difficult to learn, but allows the programmer to produce programs that are extremely efficient in terms of internal machine operations. Exact comparisons are difficult to make but, for

```
ID DIVISION.
PROGRAM-ID. INVENTORY-REPORT.
AUTHOR. ROBERT-DUGAUE.
DATE-WRITTEN. 05-20-82.
DATE-COMPILED. 05-20-82.
ENVIRONMENT DIVISION.
CONFIGURATION SECTION.
SOURCE-COMPUTER. PRIME-650.
OBJECT-COMPUTER. PRIME-650.
INPUT-OUTPUT SECTION.
FILE-CONTROL.
      SELECT PRINT-FILE ASSIGN TO PFMS.
      SELECT DATAFILE ASSIGN TO PFMS.
DATA DIVISION.
FILE SECTION.
FD   PRINT-FILE
      LABEL RECORD IS STANDARD
      RECORD CONTAINS 80 CHARACTERS
      VALUE OF FILE-ID IS 'REPORT'
      DATA RECORD IS PRINT-LINE.
01   PRINT-LINE                  PIC X(80).
FD   DATAFILE
      LABEL RECORD IS STANDARD
      RECORD CONTAINS 20 CHARACTERS
      VALUE OF FILE-ID IS 'DATA-IN'
      DATA RECORD IS IN-FILE.
O1   IN-FILE.
      03 PART-NUMBER-IN          PIC A(4).
      03 FILLER                  PIC XX.
      03 INVENTORY-ON-HAND       PIC 9(3).
      03 FILLER                  PIC XX.
      03 CUSTOMER-ORDERS         PIC 9(3).
      03 FILLER                  PIC XX.
      03 DOLLAR-VALUE            PIC 99V99.
WORKING-STORAGE SECTION.
01   HEADING-LINE-1.
      03 FILLER                  PIC X(17) VALUE SPACES.
      03 ABC                     PIC X(12) VALUE
                  'ABC PARTS CO'
      03 FILLER                  PIC X(51) VALUE SPACES.
01   HEADING-LINE-2.
      03 FILLER                  PIC X VALUE SPACES.
      03 PART-HEADING            PIC X(4) VALUE 'PART'.
      03 FILLER                  PIC X(6) VALUE SPACES.
      03 AVAIL-HEADING           PIC X(9) VALUE
```

FIGURE 10.4
COBOL program.   (*Continued*)

```
                                    'AVAILABLE'.
           03 FILLER                      PIC X(6) VALUE SPACES.
           03 BACK-HEADING                PIC X(4) VALUE 'BACK'.
           03 FILLER                      PIC X(7) VALUE SPACES.
           03 INVEN-HEADING               PIC X(9) VALUE
                              'INVENTORY'.
           03 FILLER                      PIC X(39) VALUE SPACES.
     01    HEADING-LINE-3.
           03 FILLER                      PIC X(1) VALUE SPACES.
           03 NUMB-HEADING                PIC X(6) VALUE 'NUMBER'.
           03 FILLER                      PIC X(4) VALUE SPACES.
           03 STOCK-HEADING               PIC X(5) VALUE 'STOCK'.
           03 FILLER                      PIC X(10) VALUE SPACES.
           03 ORDER-HEADING               PIC X(6) VALUE 'ORDERS'.
           03 FILLER                      PIC X(5) VALUE SPACES.
           03 VALUE-HEADING               PIC X(5) VALUE 'VALUE'.
           03 FILLER                      PIC X(43) VALUE SPACES.
     01    DETAIL-LINE.
           03 FILLER                      PIC X(1) VALUE SPACES.
           03 PART-NUMBER-OUT             PIC A(6).
           03 FILLER                      PIC X(6) VALUE SPACES.
           03 AVAILABLE-STOCK-OUT         PIC S9999.
           03 FILLER                      PIC X(10) VALUE SPACES.
           03 BACK-ORDERS-OUT             PIC 9999.
           03 FILLER                      PIC X(5) VALUE SPACES.
           03 INVENTORY-VALUE-OUT         PIC $$$,$$9.99.
           03 FILLER                      PIC X(20) VALUE SPACES.
     01    ENDING-LINE-1.
           03 FILLER                      PIC X(1) VALUE SPACES.
           03 RECORDS-LINE                PIC X(28) VALUE
                   'NUMBER OF RECORDS PROCESSED'.
           03 RECORDS-PROCESSED           PIC 999.
           03 FILLER                      PIC X(48) VALUE SPACES.
     01    ENDING-LINE-2.
           03 FILLER                      PIC X(1) VALUE SPACES.
           03 MY-NAME                     PIC X(27) VALUE
                   'PROGRAMMED BY ROBERT DU GAUE'.
           03 FILLER                      PIC X(52) VALUE SPACES.
     01    WORK-AREAS                     USAGE IS COMP-3.
           03 INVENTORY-VALUE-WORK        PIC 9999V99.
           03 TOTAL-STOCK-WORK            PIC 9999 VALUE ZERO.
           03 TOTAL-ORDER-WORK            PIC 9999 VALUE ZERO.
           03 TOTAL-INVENTORY-VALUE       PIC 99999V99 VALUE ZERO.
     01    EOF-INDICATOR                  PIC 9 VALUE ZERO.
           88 END-OF-FILE VALUE IS 1.
     PROCEDURE DIVISION.
```

FIGURE 10.4 (Continued)

```
CONTROL-MODULE.
    PERFORM 010-OPENER.
    PERFORM 020-CALCULATE UNTIL
    END-OF-FILE.
    PERFORM
    030-PRINT-THE-TOTALS.
    PERFORM 040-CLOSER.
    STOP RUN.
010-OPENER.
    OPEN INPUT DATAFILE OUTPUT PRINT-FILE.
    WRITE PRINT-LINE FROM HEADING-LINE-1
        AFTER ADVANCING PAGE.
    WRITE PRINT-LINE FROM HEADING-LINE-2
        AFTER ADVANCING 2 LINES.
    WRITE PRINT-LINE FROM HEADING-LINE-3
        AFTER ADVANCING 1 LINES.
    MOVE SPACES TO PRINT-LINE.
    WRITE PRINT-LINE AFTER ADVANCING 1 LINES.
    PERFORM 015-READ-THE-FILE.
015-READ-THE-FILE.
    READ DATAFILE AT END MOVE 1 TO EOF-INDICATOR.
020-CALCULATE.
    ADD 1 TO RECORDS-PROCESSED.
    COMPUTE AVAILABLE-STOCK OUT = INVENTORY-ON-HAND-CUSTOMER-ORDERS.
    COMPUTE BACK-ORDERS-OUT = 0.
    IF AVAILABLE-STOCK-OUT < 0
        COMPUTE BACK-ORDERS-OUT =
                - AVAILABLE-STOCK-OUT
        COMPUTE AVAILABLE-STOCK-OUT = 0.
    COMPUTE INVENTORY-VALUE-WORK =
        AVAILABLE-STOCK-OUT * DOLLAR-VALUE.
    MOVE PART-NUMBER-IN TO PART-NUMBER-OUT.
    MOVE INVENTORY-VALUE-WORK TO INVENTORY-VALUE-OUT.
    WRITE PRINT-LINE FROM DETAIL-LINE
        AFTER ADVANCING 1 LINES.
    ADD AVAILABLE-STOCK-OUT TO TOTAL-STOCK-WORK.
    ADD BACK-ORDERS-OUT TO TOTAL-ORDER-WORK.
    ADD INVENTORY-VALUE-WORK TO TOTAL-INVENTORY-VALUE.
    PERFORM 015-READ-THE-FILE.
030-PRINT-THE-TOTALS.
    MOVE 'TOTALS' TO PART-NUMBER-OUT.
    MOVE TOTAL-STOCK-WORK TO AVAILABLE-STOCK-OUT.
    MOVE TOTAL-ORDER-WORK TO BACK-ORDERS-OUT.
    MOVE TOTAL-INVENTORY-VALUE TO INVENTORY-VALUE-OUT.
    WRITE PRINT-LINE FROM DETAIL-LINE
        AFTER ADVANCING 2 LINES.
```

FIGURE 10.4 (Continued)

```
WRITE PRINT-LINE FROM ENDING-LINE-1
    AFTER ADVANCING 2 LINES.
WRITE PRINT-LINE FROM ENDING-LINE-2
    AFTER ADVANCING 2 LINES.
040-CLOSER.
    CLOSE DATAFILE PRINT-FILE.
    EXIT PROGRAM.
```

PART NUMBER	AVAILABLE STOCK	BACK ORDERS	INVENTORY VALUE
1111	0097	0000	$1,249.36
1355	0372	0000	$7,358.16
1883	0000	0000	$0.00
5720	0000	0419	$0.00
6292	0366	0000	$8,022.72
1500	0000	0000	$0.00
2463	0000	0633	$0.00
6895	0441	0000	$4,828.95
TOTALS	1276	1052	$21,459.19

NUMBER OF RECORDS PROCESSED 008

PROGRAMMED BY ROBERT DU GAUE

FIGURE 10.4 (Continued)

example, a 600-statement COBOL program might take well over 3000 statements in assembly language (Figure 10.5).

Another language, RPG (Report Program Generator) is, as the name indicates, particularly applicable to the generation and printing of reports and listings. In the past, RPG has often been the major language on small business computers where long or sophisticated programs were infrequent. Lately we have seen the implementation of COBOL on these machines, but RPG is still better suited to the qJ ick generation of reports. It is especially useful for those reports that are produced on a one-time basis, never to be needed again. RPG is considered to be a *problem-oriented* language (rather than procedure-oriented) because it is applicable to specific types of programming applications. The current version, RPG II, is far more versatile than its predecessors and has been implemented on most modern machines.

PL/1 (Programming Language One) was developed by IBM in the mid-1960s as a middle position between the mathematical capabilities

THE ORIGIN OF COBOL: CAPTAIN GRACE M. HOPPER

The origins of COBOL go back to the very earliest days of computing. When the Harvard Mark series of the mid-1940s and the UNIVAC I were, for example, programmed in their own peculiar machine code. At that time, the languages that we now know—FORTRAN, BASIC, COBOL—simply did not exist. Library routines such as those to sort or take square root were also unknown. Instead, programmers had to copy long strings of code from one program to another in order to do these operations.

One of the pioneers in the development of high-level languages was Captain Grace M. Hopper of the U.S. Navy who is still very active in data processing today. She is considered the grand matriarch of computing and was one of the major driving forces behind the creation of user groups that shared their ideas on the solution to these common problems. Captain Hopper presented a paper on compiler construction and since then has contributed over fifty more publications on software and programming languages. Ultimately this led to an appointment on the Defense Department sponsored Committee on Data System Languages (CODASYL) in 1959.

Her work on the committee was instrumental in developing COBOL, a language that, for the first time, was not identified with any specific manufacturer and which could be used on a wide variety of machines. Since that time she has been a leader in language standardization and continues to shepherd COBOL through its many revisions. A holder of a Ph.D. in mathematics, Grace Hopper is today, at age 75 and with 40 years of data processing experience, a highly sought-after lecturer. In her words, "We haven't even begun to exploit its [the computers's] potential." (Source: *Computerworld,* November 16, 1981.)

of FORTRAN and the file handling ease of COBOL. However, it has never caught on with the using public for at least two reasons. First, it is a sophisticated language that has been available only on the large machines. The second reason is that although programs are relatively easy to write in PL/1, they are fairly difficult to correct or debug.

SYSTEMS SOFTWARE

The earliest computer programs were written in a crude system of notation called machine language. Each basic machine operation was

FIGURE 10.5
Assembly language program.

LCC	OBJECT	CODE	ADDR1	ADDR2	STMT	SOURCE	STATEMENT
000C00					1		PRINT NOGEN
000000	0380				2	BEGIN	START 0
000002					3		BALR 11,0
					4		USING *,11
					5		OPEN CARDIN,PRINTER
					14	READLCOP	GET CARDIN
000022	D501	818E	00190	00266	19		CLC DEPT,HOLD
000028	4770	8062		0064	20		GNE NEW
00002C	9240	81DE	001E0		21		MV1 OUTPUT,C' '
000030	D276	81DF	001E1	001E0	22		MVC OUTPUT+1(119), OUTPUT
000036	D202	81F4	001F6	00192	23	INREAD	MVC NEAROUT,NBR
00003C	D213	8201	00203	00195	24		MVC NAMEOUT,NAME
000042	D206	821F	00221	00180	25		MVC SALESOUT,CURSALES
000048	F236	8266	00268	00180	26		PACK CURPACK,CURSALES
00004E	FA33	825C	0025E	00268	27		AP MINORTOT,CURPACK
					28		PUT PRINTER
000060	47F0	8014		0016	33		B READLOOP
000064					34	NEW	EOU *
000064	9101	8256	00258		35		TM SWITCH,X'O1'
					36	* THIS COMMAND	TESTS TO SEE IF THE FIRST BIT IS ON
000068	4780	8096		00098	37		AZ SETSW
					38	* 'ON' PART OF THE LOOP	
00006C	F443	8257	00259	0025E	39		AP FINALTOT,MINCRTOT
000072	F373	826A	0026C	0025E	40		UNPK HEXMINOR,MINOPTOT
000078	96F0	8271	00273		41		DI HEXMINOR+7,X'FO'
00007C	9240	81DE	001E0		42		MVI OUTPUT,C' '
000080	D276	81DF	001E1	001E0	43		MVC OUTPUT+1(119), OUTPUT

LOC						STMT	Name	Op	Operand
000086	D207	821E	826A	00220	0026C	44		MVC	SALESOUT-1(8). HEXMINOR
						45		PUT	PRINTER
000098						50	SETSW	EQU	*
000098	9601	8256		00258		51		OI	SWITCH.X'01'
00009C	9240	81DE		001E0	001E0	52		MVI	OUTPUT.C' '
0000A0	D276	81DF	81DE	001E1	001E0	53		MVC	OUTPUT+1(119). OUTPUT
0000A6	D201	8264	818E	00266	00190	54		MVC	HOLD.DEPT
0000AC	D201	81E8	818E	001EA	00190	55		MVC	DEPTOUT.DEPT
0000B2	D203	825C	8260	0025E	00262	56		MVC	MINORTOT.ZERO
0000B8	47F0	8034			00036	57		B	INREAD
0000BC	FA43	8257	825C	00259	0025E	58	EOJ	AP	FINAL TOT.MINORTOT
0000C2	F373	826A	825C	0026C	0025E	59		UNPK	HEXMINOR.MINORTOT
0000C8	96F0	8271		00273		60		OI	HEXMINOR+7.X'FO'
0000CC	9240	81DE		00180		61		MVI	OUTPUT.C' '
0000D0	D276	81DF	81DE	001E1	001E0	62		MVC	OUTPUT+1(119). OUTPUT
0000D6	D207	821E	826A	00220	9926C	63		MVC	SALESOUT-1(8). HEXMINOR
						64		PUT	PRINTER
0000E8	F394	8272	8257	00274	00259	69		UNPK	HEXFINAL. F(NALTO)
0000EE	96F0	8278		0027D		70		OI	HEXFINAL+9.X'FO'
0000F2	9240	81DE		001E0		71		MVI	OUTPUT.C' '
0000F6	D276	81DF	81DE	001E1	001E0	72		MVC	OUTPUT+1(119). OUTPUT
0000FC	D209	821D	8272	0021F	00274	73		MVC	SALESOUT-2(10). HEXFINAL
						74		PUT	PRINTER
						79		CLOSE	CARDIN.PRINTER

triggered by coded entries comprised of numbers or special characters that were recognized by the electronic circuitry. Memory addresses were handled in this same manner and the solution to even the simplest of tasks required perhaps thousands of such instructions and extreme attention to detail.

Obviously what was needed were programming languages that would be easier for the programmer to use, ones that would be more natural and perhaps even English-like in their structure. Languages of this type, such as those just discussed, were developed, but in return an additional software penalty was imposed. Technically speaking, the only programming language a computer truly "understands" is machine language. The programmer may write a program in one of the many high-level, more natural languages, but the program must be translated into machine language in order for the computer to execute the instructions. This task of translating (more accurately called *compiling*) is performed by higher level programs called *systems software*. It is systems software or systems programs that allow the computer to be used with a reasonable degree of efficiency, as these programs stand between the applications program (such as payroll, accounts receivable, or inventory analysis) and the computer hardware. All this is another way of emphasizing that although both hardware and software are necessary in the makeup of a computer system, it is software that drives the hardware and that it is here, not in hardware, that we are in a state of crisis.

When a computer system is leased or purchased, the manufacturer usually provides the appropriate software to make the system operate to certain specifications. Under one common arrangement, the manufacturer may include a certain minimum amount of software in the hardware price and then charge extra for additional systems programs that are requested. In addition, software may be rented or purchased outright from the equipment vendor or from private software firms. One piece of software is not necessarily as good as another despite the fact that it may have come from one of the larger, well-known DP companies. Any time a weak or inefficient software program is recognized by system users, competitors are quick to bring out better and/or cheaper versions.

OPERATING SYSTEMS

The sum total of all these very sophisticated and expensive systems programs may be called by various names, but the general name applied to it is that of *operating system*. By definition, an operating system is "an organized collection of techniques and procedures for operating a computer." Usually, these programs are delivered to the user in the form of a spool of magnetic tape or a disk pack. No matter what form the software takes, it is stored on disk and known as a disk operating system (DOS). In the case of small business systems the system software may be on a floppy disk that needs only to be inserted in the disk drive in order to initiate system start-up procedures.

One of the major features of an operating system is that the operator can stack the jobs for continuous processing which, of course, greatly reduces the setup time that single jobs would take. The system will then take advantage of all the facilities offered in the software package by calling special programs (such as those that sort or merge data files) as needed. Figure 10.6 illustrates the composition of a typical disk-resident operating system.

The system is comprised of three groups of programs: control programs, system service programs, and processing programs. The first group of programs has the function of initializing or getting the system ready and maintaining the orderly and efficient flow of jobs (programs being executed) through the computer system. For example, let's suppose that the computer has been shut down during the evening hours. In a typical medium-scale data processing operation the morning operator will go through a button-pushing console action that reads a copy of Initial Program Loader that, in turn, reads a copy of Supervisor into memory.

Perhaps the single most important software program of all is Supervisor. Actually, it is not a single program. Supervisor is a group of related programs that normally reside in memory at all times to supervise and control or monitor the action of the system. For example, on a computer system having 64,000 bytes of memory, Supervisor

FIGURE 10.6
Disk operating system (DOS).

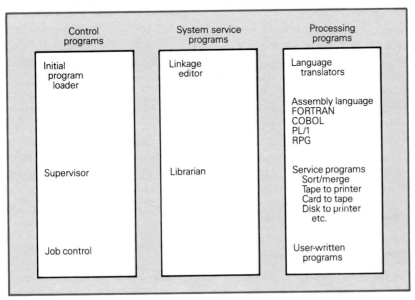

might very well take up 30,000 bytes, which means that programmer-usable memory is about 34,000 bytes. In turn, it is the operator who controls Supervisor via entries made through the system console typewriter.

Jobs or programs may be executed sequentially or, in the case of the more powerful computers, several programs may be executed concurrently. Supervisor and Job Control work together to recognize job priorities and provide the necessary steps to go from one program to the next. As a matter of fact, Job Control itself is so complex that specialists in Job Control Language (JCL) are employed just to work with the Job Control software. Job Control and Supervisor bring in copies of disk programs, clear storage areas, allocate space, etc., as needed.

The second group, system service programs, can perform a variety of tasks. Linkage Editor, for example, takes intermediate output from the language translators and puts it into final machine language form. As you would guess, the Librarian software program has the task of storing programs on disk and maintaining a record of the length and locations of these programs.

The last group, called processing programs, consists of three major parts: language translators, service programs, and user-written programs. The language translators are those software programs that allow the computer to be programmed in specific languages such as FOR-TRAN, COBOL or BASIC. These languages are widely used, and the general rule is that for each language capability you require you will need separate language translator software. The function of a language translator is discussed in detail in the next section of this chapter.

The second group of system software programs are those that often are called *utilities,* as that is exactly their task. There is no point in having each programmer write a different program to duplicate data records from tape to disk, cards to tape, disk to tape, or to sort or to merge records from various files, so most system software includes a set of utility programs. The last part of group three, user-written programs, constitutes what we earlier called "application programs." Frequently used programs would be stored on disk for quick, efficient entry into memory. Figure 10.7 illustrates the relationship of the elements of the operating system. These programs are extremely complex because they act as the go-between or the *interface* between people and machine. The operator calls the parts of the operating system into action by means of job control cards (in a card-based system) or by keyed entries (on terminal-based systems) as shown in Figure 10.8.

COMPILING A PROGRAM

Again, there simply is no way of overemphasizing the importance or the complexity of the system software just described. To get a better understanding of its importance, let's take a brief look at how an

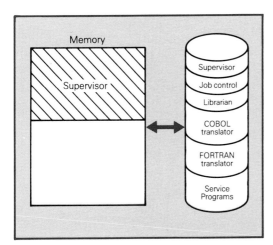

FIGURE 10.7
System software.

operating system works. We will assume that the Supervisor and Job Control software programs are in memory and that the system operator is about to run or execute a program that will perform a typical business operation. To further simplify matters we will assume we will be running an inventory program, written in COBOL, and that the program itself is punched into cards (in the format shown in Figure 10.8). The operator initiates the process by placing the deck in the hopper of the card reader and pressing the start key. Figure 10.9 shows the condition of the system at this point. At this point the COBOL program is known as a *source program.*

It would appear that the COBOL program would be read into memory and executed to produce an inventory report. Unfortunately, the operation is not all that simple. The major problem is that a computer does not truly "understand" COBOL, FORTRAN, or, for that matter, any of the major languages discussed previously. Technically, they are executable only in *machine language,* which is the specific set of instructions applicable to that machine. In the early computers these machine instructions were pure binary—the ones and zeros you encountered earlier in the text. Modern machines have improved a little to the point that we can now use octal, decimal, or hexadecimal symbols for this purpose. Still, programming in machine language is so difficult, so slow, so prone to error, and so expensive that few people will do it.

The solution was to write systems software programs that translate easy-to-write COBOL, FORTRAN, etc., programs into the native language of the machine. Technically, a COBOL program is not executed or run by the machine. Instead, the machine language equivalent of that program is actually executed.

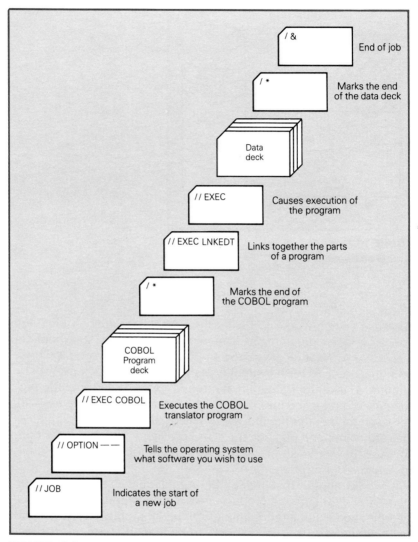

FIGURE 10.8
Job control cards.

The translator programs actually change or translate (compile) statements like

ADD PAY-AMOUNT TO TOTAL-PAY-AMOUNT

into machine language codes for machine execution. The resulting machine language program (derived from the COBOL source program) is known as an *object program*.

Now, let's follow the steps in the compiling process.

1.   Supervisor and Job Control read in the first two cards (//JOB and

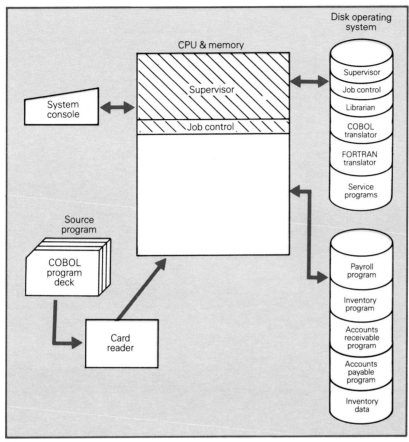

FIGURE 10.9
Relationship of hardware and software.

//OPTION) Which indicates the start of a new task. Supervisor will perform various housekeeping chores in preparation for the new program.

2. Supervisor and Job Control read in the next card, which identifies the program in COBOL (as opposed to a FORTRAN or any other language). Since the services of the COBOL translator software are needed, a copy of the COBOL translator program is read in from disk (Figure 10.10).

By now, some of you have undoubtedly come up with a very valid question. You can see that the COBOL translator is going to read in the Inventory Program and translate it into machine language so that it can be executed. If this is a program that is needed frequently, why must it be translated each time? The answer is that you would be exactly right, a frequently used program would be translated once and then stored on disk in a form such that it can be directly executed. In our example,

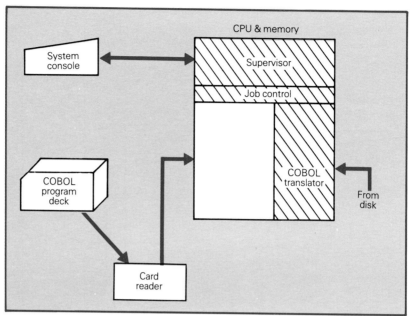

FIGURE 10.10
Translation software in memory.

for the purposes of illustration, we will assume that the Inventory Program is still in COBOL format and must be compiled before it can be run.

3. The translation process is carried out by the COBOL translator to produce an executable, machine-language program (Figure 10.11).
4. After the translation process has been completed, the memory areas occupied by the COBOL Inventory Program and by the COBOL Translator are made available for processing and the machine-language version of the Inventory program is executed. It will read in data records from cards, disk, or tape as specified in the program, manipulate it in memory, and output answers to the printer or onto various auxiliary storage devices. Note that Supervisor and Job Control are still in memory and are under the control of the operator who will initiate another job as soon as this one is finished (Figure 10.12).

SOFTWARE ALTERNATIVES

The solutions to the software problems presented throughout the chapter depend greatly on which side of the problem you face. Today, many, if not most, computer manufacturers are spending one-half of

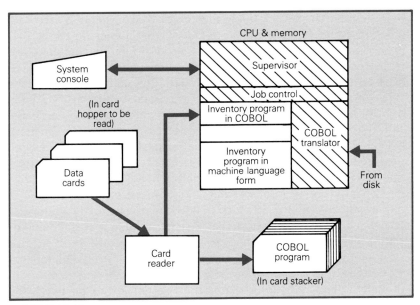

FIGURE 10.11
Translation process.

vice-president of Data General Corporation put it, "We used to write their research and development dollars on software. According to F. G. Rogers, vice-president of marketing at IBM, "Software is the key vehicle to driving the hardware revenues of the future." Or, as a senior

FIGURE 10.12
Executing a machine-language program.

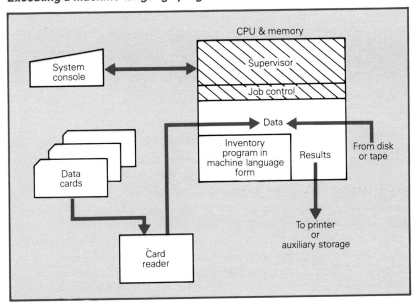

software to sell hardware, but in the long term we will build hardware to sell software." Stephen Gaal of Data General goes on to say that "Today, people evaluate your software—your operating system, your word processing, your networking—then they check your hardware to make sure it's a strong enough machine to drive all that software."

The move to sell software for profit was made by IBM in 1969 when they "unbundled," or separated, their software from the hardware. Until that time the two parts were priced as a whole, which made it difficult to apply a dollar value to either item. Today at Honeywell software represents less than 10% of its total revenues, but that figure is expected to double by 1985. It is estimated that over $1 billion of IBM's gross revenue comes from software and that is sure to increase also.

It is estimated that nearly $200 billion of software exists worldwide today, an amount that is more than twice the value of installed hardware. Much of this software is available for use, free or at a price considerably less than it would cost to produce it yourself. This fact has not been lost on the manufacturers who face staggering increases in software outlays in the immediate future. As you are aware, IBM is the dominant force in the computer industry and spends an enormous amount to produce system software for its computers. Other manufacturers can produce competing hardware but face potential expenditures of hundreds of millions of dollars in order to produce system software that is equivalent to that from IBM. The solution that is being considered by more competitors today is to produce hardware that will run on IBM software and perhaps offer software enhancement programs that promise better, faster, or easier operations. National Cash Register Corporation (NCR) announced this decision in late 1980 after decades of "going it alone" with their own software.

Modifying existing system software is another possibility, but this presents difficulties in the areas of legal ownership, copyright provisions, and is very likely to generate expensive and time-consuming lawsuits within the data processing industry. Those firms that wish to provide some form of security against misuse of their software often will not divulge the actual source code and may implement the software by storing some programs on read-only circuit chips. When this is done, it is usually called firmware to differentiate it from either software or hardware.

Another solution to the software problem presents itself in the form of software packages. For individual firms the question is whether to write the applications program in-house or to license or buy a program from a software vendor. In this discussion we will be talking about application programs, such as inventory or payroll, but many software houses furnish both system and application software. Thus you may decide that manufacturer X's operating system, which was bundled into the computer price, is not particularly efficient and wish to replace it with system software from a private firm. Or, a language compiler may be inadequate and a newer, better version may be available from a software house.

On most of today's microcomputers the application software is relatively simple to go along with simple hardware. As the sophistication of these users increases, however, their demands are forcing the manufacturers to turn to individual software developers and to acquire marketing rights to their packages. *Turnkey* systems—a complete, ready-to-use combination of hardware and software—were necessary to sell these small hardware systems. At first their software was designed to run general accounting functions on single systems, but they soon broadened their efforts to include specialized applications for automobile parts stores, hospitals, pharmaceutical suppliers, real estate offices, dentists, etc., on a variety of computers. It is estimated that over 4000 turnkey vendors have systems available today.

The five leading application areas are (1) accounting, (2) payroll/personnel, (3) manufacturing, (4) banking/finance, and (5) insurance. Despite the apparently large number of packages there are two points to remember. First, software is not available for every application and, second, not every package runs on every piece of hardware. In reference to software packages, a rough rule of thumb says that if a package meets 80% of your prescribed requirements, it is worthy of serious consideration. Let's consider some of the advantages and disadvantages of software packages.

ADVANTAGES

1. Cost. Application packages may cost as little as one-tenth to one-hundredth of what it would cost to develop the same program with in-house personnel.
2. Simplicity. Since the user market consists of many nontechnical, non-DP people, some of the most successful software packages are those that are friendly and forgiving to the user.
3. Continuity. Assuming you have acquired the package from a reputable software house, you have some degree of stability built in. Obviously, jerry-built software produced by itinerant one-person operations is a grave hazard to operational continuity.
4. Documentation. The large, reputable software houses will provide substantial documentation. If the supplier is unwilling to provide such documentation, find another source.

DISADVANTAGES

1. Modification. How easy is it to modify the package when changes are required? Have a professional look it over rather than rely on the word of the salesperson.
2. Functionality. Does the package really do what is promised? Insist on test runs to verify that all promised steps are being performed.
3. Efficiency. Since the package was not written specifically for your firm, you must expect that not all parts of it will be as efficient as if you had written it yourself. However, can you (and your hardware) live with the inefficiency?

Figure 10.13 shows a general list of the types of software packages that are available. This is by no means a complete list since it is estimated that over 5000 different packages are on the market today, of which over 3000 are applications oriented. Over 50% are slanted to micro- and minicomputers, and the percentage is growing to meet the explosive growth in this sector of the data processing economy.

Finally, another possible solution to the software crisis seems to be emerging—application generators. The reasoning is very simple: Why

A consumers' guide to software shopping

Type of software	What it does	Where to buy it	Software price
Data base management system	Organizes data in line with the informational structure of a business. Makes it easier to access and update files	Computer vendors Systems software companies	Starts at $7,000 (for use with a minicomputer) and runs to more than $100,000 (for use with a mainframe computer or for custom programming)
Networking	Enables computers in one building or across the country to communicate	Primarily computer vendors	$5,000 to $75,000 per machine in a minicomputer network and $30,000 to $75,000 for each mainframe computer in a network
Transaction processing	Permits users to carry on a dialogue with the computer —typing information and getting an immediate response. For use with such commercial applications as check processing and order entry	Computer vendors Systems software companies	$15,000 and up
Programming tools	Helps programmers write applications programs by automatically testing software code and identifying errors. Also known as "debuggers"	Computer vendors Systems software companies	$1,000 to $5,000 (for a minicomputer) and $5,000 to $75,000 (for a large mainframe computer)
Queries and report generators	Aids the novice user in extracting information from a computer memory and formating it into a report	Computer vendors Systems software companies	$1,000 to $37,000 for standard software
Applications generators	Generates applications software programs without the need for an experienced programmer	Major computer vendors	$5,000 and up
General financial	Automates the accounting functions of a business, including billing, inventory control, accounts payable, accounts receivable, general ledger, and payroll	Computer vendors Applications software companies	Packages range from $1,000 to $20,000 (for minicomputer systems) and from $20,000 to $70,000 (for large mainframe computers)
Manufacturing resource planning	Helps the user gain better control over the entire manufacturing process from production planning and inventory control to materials monitoring	Large computer vendors Applications software companies	$50,000 and up for standard packages, $100,000 and up for custom software
Financial planning	Simulates profit-and-loss scenarios for a company based on revenues, sales force location, commissions, and other controllable variables	Primarily applications software companies	$5,000 to $45,000 for packages; custom work begins at $250,000
Cash-flow management	Assists financial managers in getting the best use of funds within a business	Primarily applications software companies	$25,000 to $75,000 for packages; custom software begins at $150,000
Management support systems	Combines software packages such as color graphics and business modeling that aid the manager in making decisions	Primarily applications software companies	Depends on the packages selected

Data: International Computer Programs, Inc. BW

FIGURE 10.13
Software packages.

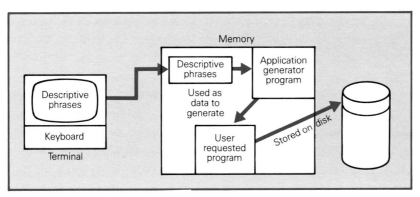

FIGURE 10.14
Application generator.

not write a high-level program that will actually generate a specific application program in response to user requests? A few programs of this type are on the market today and their worth is being evaluated.

In the ideal situation, a person untrained in data processing should be able to enter into the computer the descriptive phrases that would outline a desired program to the application generator software. The phrases then become data to the application generator software in the sense that it uses these entries to generate the program. One such generator, called The Last One, allows the user to input the requests and then asks specific questions in an effort to clarify exactly what is to be done. In addition to generating a BASIC language program, the vendor states that the software can modify an existing program that was created by The Last One.

There are two problems that will have to be overcome with generators if they are to make serious inroads into the backlog of needed application programs. First, the generators will have to be able to be used by those who have no knowledge of data processing terminology and methods. As of now, no generator truly meets that requirement. Second, the generator must be extremely sophisticated in order to handle the bewildering types of requests that will be made of it. Although both these problems seem insurmountable now, a solution may be available in a few years. Figure 10.14 illustrates how an application generator works.

SUMMARY OF IMPORTANT POINTS

☐ We are in a software crisis or, more accurately, a long-term depression that has seen the cost of software for a computer system far exceed the hardware cost.

☐ Hardware costs have decreased because of improved technology and large-scale production. Software production has been resistant to automation because it is dependent upon the skill of the individual programmer.

☐ Application software is written to perform a specific task for an end user—a business firm, a government agency, or the like.

☐ Approximately 50%–80% of all programmer time is spent on program maintenance, that is, changing or modifying existing programs.

☐ FORTRAN (FORmula TRANslation) is a math-oriented language that has been modified extensively as special scientific and mathematical needs have arisen.

☐ BASIC (Beginners All-purpose Symbolic Instruction Code) is similar to FORTRAN, and is the language of time-sharing and is widely used on the small, home computer systems.

☐ PASCAL is an increasingly popular language whose syntax forces or requires structured programming techniques.

☐ COBOL (COmmon Business-Oriented Language) is probably the single most used language in the world, as it is particularly applicable to business needs.

☐ RPG (Report Program Generation) is a problem-oriented language because it is applicable to a specific problem area. COBOL, FORTRAN, and BASIC are procedure-oriented languages because they can be used over a wide range of procedures or applications.

☐ Compiling or translating is one of the major tasks performed by operating systems. The computer truly only "understands" one language—machine language—and language compilers allow application programmers to write programs in specific languages, such as COBOL and FORTRAN.

☐ The term "operating system" is the general name given to the group of system programs or system software that run a computer system. Usually these programs are stored on disk and are known as a disk operating system (DOS).

☐ Supervisor is the single most complex part of the operating system and all or part of it resides in memory to direct the overall operation of the computer system.

☐ Supervisor works closely with another system software program, Job Control, to handle the special requirements of the various types of programs that are run on the system.

☐ One alternative to today's software "crunch" is to make use of either system or application software packages that are available instead of writing your own in-house software.

☐   Software packages offer the advantages of cost, simplicity, continuity, and documentation as weighed against the disadvantages of functionality,—i.e., does it really do the job?—and the necessity of making some modifications to more exactly suit your individual needs.

☐   Application generator programs are offering a hint of the way of the future if actual programs can be generated from user requests.

GLOSSARY OF TERMS

Application generator—a software program that generates an application program in response to user requests.

Application software—programs written to perform particular business functions, such as inventory, payroll, accounts payable, etc., as opposed to system software.

Assembly language—a programming language that is similar to machine language, but at a level high enough to free the programmer from working directly in machine codes.

BASIC (Beginner All-purpose Instruction Code)—a popular language used on time-sharing, microcomputer, and minicomputer systems.

COBOL (COmmon Business Oriented Language)—the most commonly used language in the world today and a language that is particularly applicable to business processing.

Compiler—a software program that translates procedure-oriented or problem-oriented instructions into machine language.

Debugging—the act of removing errors, or "bugs," from a computer program.

Operating system—a collection of programs for operating a computer.

Machine language—the lowest level in a hierarchy of programming languages. At this level, instructions are usually in the form of a string of digits that have particular meaning to the internal circuitry of the computer.

Macro instructions—those instructions that are so complex that a single command generates several machine-language instructions.

Mnemonic—literally, a memory aid. Used in programming in reference to assembly language operation codes.

Native language—see machine language.

Object program—the machine-language program that was derived from the translation of a source program into the native language of the machine.

PASCAL—A modern, structured programming language developed in the mid-1970s by Niklaus Wirth of Switzerland.

Problem-oriented language—a high-level language designed to cover specific programming applications.

Procedure-oriented language—a machine-independent, high-level language designed to cover a wide range of applications.

RPG (Report Program Generator)—a problem-oriented language designed for specific applications in the preparation of business reports.

Source program—the original program submitted to the computer operating system for translation or compiling. Also see Object program.

Systems software—programs that control the internal operations of the computer system. Included would be the language translator programs that translate program statements into a language that the machine can execute.

Translator—see Compiler.

Turnkey system—an entire computer system consisting of both hardware and software and sold to the user as an immediately usable product.

THOUGHT QUESTIONS

1. Briefly describe a problem that would best be solved by a program written in COBOL. Do the same for FORTRAN and assembly language.

2. Describe in your own terms the makeup of an operating system.

3. What features would you look for in a software package? Be specific in your answer.

4. Describe a turnkey system and explain why you would choose it over a non-turnkey system.

5. What personal qualities should an application programmer have?

6. What extra skills would you need as a systems programmer, beyond those required of an application programmer.

CHAPTER 11 PROBLEM SOLVING WITH THE COMPUTER

LEARNING OBJECTIVES

Upon completion of the chapter you should understand the following:

How a program is developed from the time it is first authorized until the finished product is in production on the computer system.

The individual steps in the problem-solving process.

> *Analysis of the problem.*
> *Designing a solution.*
> *Coding the solution.*
> *Testing the solution.*
> *Final documentation.*

The nature of top-down program design and why it is so important in the problem-solving process.

What structured programming is and why programming discipline is necessary.

The use of flowcharting during the design of the program logic.

The importance of good documentation.

The use of structured walk-throughs during the design or coding process to achieve better programs.

CHAPTER CONTENTS

As you know, a computer is really a complex collection of electronic parts that function in accordance with instructions given by the programmer. Each computer has a precise and limited set of instructions that it can obey, and it is from this list that the programmer makes the choices. The sum total of the instructions used constitutes a program that was written to solve a particular problem, such as payroll or inventory adjustment. In fact, a single computer program may not be able to take care of all the details of inventory control or payroll accounting. It may require a series of programs to perform a job of this magnitude.

Although the programmer is the person who actually codes the program for use on the computer, he or she is seldom the one who initiates the action. Instead, there is a sort of chain-of-command procedure that is followed (or should be followed) in the development of a computer program.

PROGRAM DEVELOPMENT

In large business organizations, the initial impetus for computer DP should come from top management. As a matter of fact, the research done by McKinsey and Company, management consultants, indicates that the higher the origin of the action, the greater the chances that the operation will be economically successful. (It should be added that top management must carry through the initial action, not just pay lip service to the plan.)

Once top management has committed itself to a policy of automating inventory operations, customer billing, etc., the firm enters into a chainlike series of events that culminates in the creation of a number of computer programs that will accomplish the specified task. Between this beginning and the conclusion is an almost endless amount of work that can be covered by the terms "systems analysis" and "program development." The newcomer to this part of data processing is often dismayed by the number of meetings, the amount of research, and the length of time that the process takes. Larger complex operations, such as those initiated in computerized airline reservation systems, may take as long as 10 years to reach fulfillment, while small operations may be completed in a few weeks.

Systems development is a kind of filtration process in which the broad ideas of top management pass down through the layers of the organizational structure and are expanded and synthesized into a functional, working system. Eventually, these ideas reach a stage where it is easier to represent them in graphical form than in the traditional written form. These *system flow charts,* as they are called, are drawn by the DP systems analyst. In addition, the systems analyst will break the process down until it is apparent that a certain number of computer programs will have to be written to accomplish the task of customer billing, payroll, and so forth.

During the mental process of recognizing that specific computer programs must be written, the analyst must also realize that each program will be subject to certain limitations. For example, some limitations might include information on the size, type, and general format of the incoming data, the type and format of the output from the program, and the specific limitations of the hardware. Thus, the programmer is never in the dark about what is required. Instead, the design specification, written program requirements, and conversations with the analyst provide all the information needed to get the job done. The how of getting the job done is now up to the programmer and this is what the rest of the chapter is all about.

THE PROBLEM-SOLVING PROCESS

The problem-solving process is not new to you—life actually is a matter of solving everyday problems. As a matter of fact, the steps used to solving your everyday problems are very likely to be the same ones you will use in solving a problem on the computer.

In one way, solving a problem on the computer is much easier than solving many real-world problems. The reason we can say this is that, in programming in a particular language such as BASIC or COBOL, you are limited to a very specific set of instructions or statements that the machine can understand. The BASIC language, for example, offers perhaps a dozen or so commonly used instructions from which you can choose, but in real life there are likely to be a great many more alternatives. This, of course, is what programming is all about. Programmers are paid to find a solution to a problem based upon their knowledge of how a limited number of statements function. In the higher level languages (COBOL, BASIC, FORTRAN) there are relatively few statements to learn and use. Once the nature of these statements is learned, the programmer's job is to determine which statements to use *and in what order to use them* to get the job done.

The problem-solving process involves several distinct steps that you have used all your life, although you may never have thought of them in a formalized fashion. Various texts will describe anywhere from four to six steps, as outlined as follows. Each step will be discussed in detail in this chapter.

1. Analyze the problem.
2. Design a solution.
3. Code the solution into the appropriate language.
4. Test and debug the program.
5. Prepare final documentation.

ANALYZING THE PROBLEM

The art of analyzing the problem will often suggest a solution but, for the purpose of discussion, we will consider the steps separately. The term "analyzing the problem" really means that you have to study the problem to the point that you understand its nature completely. The key word is "completely," because an incomplete understanding of the problem is almost sure to result in failure.

One of the most important things to remember at this point is that the nature of the incoming data is usually known. As a matter of fact, without this knowledge the solution to the problem is not possible. In large DP installations the "filtration" process described earlier in the chapter means that the programmer will be provided with charts, diagrams, memos, etc., that tell, in great detail, just what the input is and what form the output is to take.

One obvious place to start is to see what the input data looks like. For example, if the data were coming in from cards that were prepared in a previous key entry operation, the details would be communicated to the programmer by a specific diagram (Figure 11.1) or on conve-

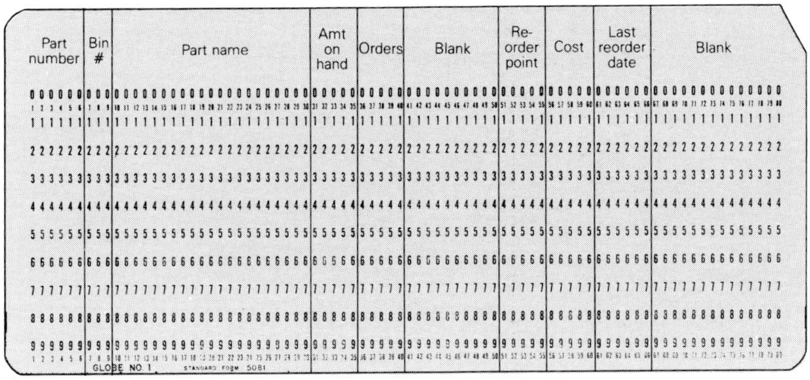

FIGURE 11.1
Data input format.

nient, predrawn charts such as the Multiple-Card Layout Form (Figure 11.2).

Figure 11.1 shows a diagram of the incoming card data record. The diagram is "saying" the following.

1. The first field in the card contains the part number (numeric data) in columns 1 through 6. The programmer now knows that *every* incoming card record will contain this information, with *exactly* this structure.

2. The bin number of the parts is contained in card columns 7 through 9, but the programmer will make particular note that, according to the example and specifications, the "number" is not all numeric. Instead, the field consists of two digits and a letter.

3. The part name or description is contained in the third field, which is in card columns 10 through 30. The format/example shows that the description or name may contain numeric as well as alphabetic characters.

4. Card columns 31 through 35 contain the quantity on hand of that item and is an entirely numeric field.

5. The next field is another 5-digit field containing the amount of customer orders during the past week.

6. Card columns 41 through 50 are blank, probably because of some future need for this area.

7. The reorder point (that is, the quantity below that we would want to reorder from the manufacturer) is punched in card columns 51 through 55.

8. The cost of the part is next. It is punched in card columns 56 through 60 and is a dollars-and-cents figure in the format DDDCC, where D represents dollars and C represents cents. Note that the decimal point is not punched in the card. However, it is the programmer's responsibility to know where the assumed decimal point is during calculations. In addition, the programmer will have to provide for the decimal during output operation.

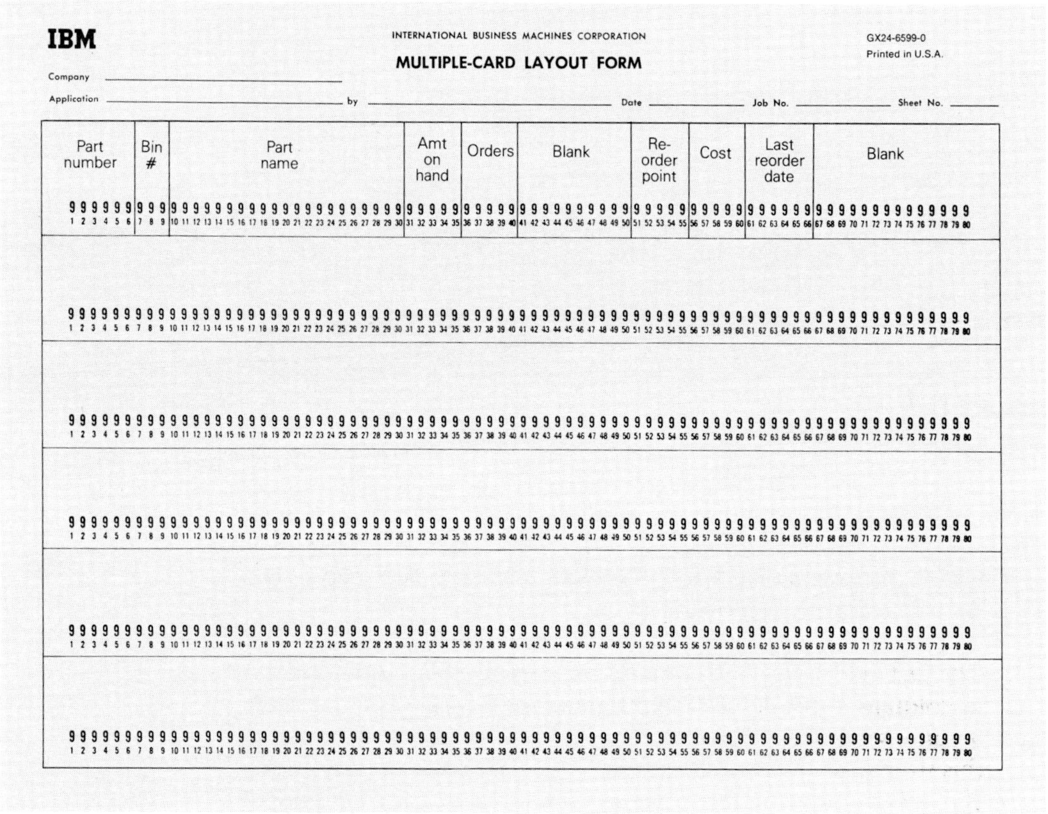

FIGURE 11.2
Multiple-card layout form.

9.   Card columns 61 through 66 contain the date of the last reorder in the form MMDDYY where M indicates the month, D indicates the day, and Y indicates the year.

10.   The remainder of the card is blank.

At this point in our analysis, the programmer understands everything he or she needs to know about the incoming data: the order in which the fields appear in the data records and the nature of each field; that is, whether the data is alphabetic, numeric, special characters, or of combined form. Our example has used cards for data input, but exactly the same process would be used to describe the records in a magnetic tape or disk file.

Now that the programmer understands the makeup of the input data, the next logical step is to look at the output that management requires. In some cases, the output format may be highly structured by the time it reaches this level. This would be particularly true in the case of preprinted forms, such as customer invoices or employee checks.

Here, the output information may be required to fit into exact spaces or areas on the form. In the case of management reports the format may be considerably less formal. The user may simply designate appropriate page and column headings, reasonably spaced material in the body of the report, and normal totals and ending material. Ultimately the programmer will use a printer spacing chart to figure out the exact position of the output material on the line, but for now the point is to simply understand the general format of the output (Figure 11.3).

Along with the description of the input records and general output format, the programmer will get a written description of what is required (Figure 11.4).

Now the programmer is beginning to leave the analysis phase and enter into the design phase. The inputs and outputs are known and the next step is to determine the steps that are necessary to make the input data produce the necessary output.

FIGURE 11.3
Sample output format.

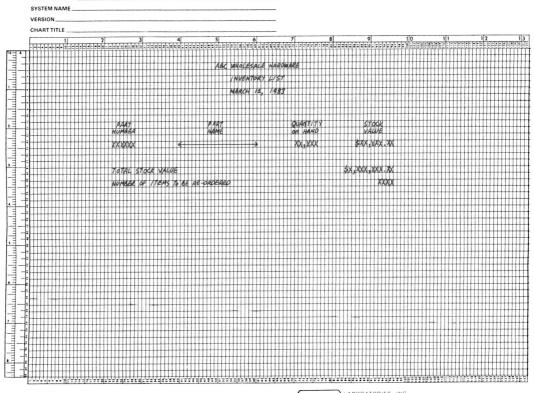

PROBLEM DESCRIPTION: Inventory Report

Using the input card records as described, prepare a listing of inventory items on hand as of the end of the work week.

SPECIFIC INSTRUCTIONS

1. Output will be in the format shown on the attached pages with appropriate heading lines.
2. The quantity on hand and the stock value amounts are to be calculated using the input data described.
3. A total is to be accumulated and printed at the end of the report for·the stock value amount.
4. Those stock items that fall at or below the reorder point are not to be listed in the report.
   (a) A count of the stock items that need to be reordered will be accumulated and printed as shown on the Inventory Report.
   (b) For those stock items that need to be reordered, a record is to be written to magnetic tape. See the programming manager for the format and details of this file.
5. The stock value and total stock value figures are to be edited with a fixed dollar sign and zero suppression as shown.
6. Data records are in part-number order.

FIGURE 11.4
Problem description.

DESIGNING A SOLUTION

As mentioned earlier, quite often the analysis process will itself suggest a possible solution to the problem. Of course, problem solution is nothing new to you, as you do this every day. Usually, your analysis of problems has shown that certain types of problems can be grouped into categories and that a similar approach can be applied to each. Computer-solvable problems almost always involve well-defined, repetitive tasks because this is the type of problem that is specifically suited to the equipment. Humans, on the other hand, are well adapted to solving one-time, poorly structured problems.

Since data records cannot be processed until they have been entered into the computer system and since answers cannot be printed until the processing step has taken place, almost every computer program involves the following three steps in the order given; input, processing, and output. Beyond that, however, outlining the steps may be a bit more complex. To help in the design process, most programmers today use what is known as the top-down approach.

TOP-DOWN DESIGN

In the top-down approach to program design the programmer first considers the functions of tasks that have to be performed rather than

40,000 PROGRAMS FOR COLUMBIA'S TILES

One of the key factors in the success of the U.S. space shuttle program has been the success of the aircraft's heat-resistant ceramic tiles. Lockheed Corporation won the initial contract to produce the tiles that formed the outside skin of the vehicle and they, in turn, subcontracted an initial batch of 200 tiles to a Texas firm, Numerical Control Services (NCS).

NCS originally thought that a single program could be written to drive the numerically controlled (NC) tools that would produce the tiles. However, they soon discovered that this approach would be far too complex so 40,000 separate programs were written to take into account the slight variations in each tile. The programmers/engineers studied the blueprints of tiles and then defined each tile as a set of geometric patterns. Then, a program was written to physically drive or move the numerically controlled shaping tools. Each program required about 300 lines of code or a grand total of nearly 12 million lines for the entire project!

The tiles started as a liquid slurry that was formed into blocks and cooked or cured to required specifications in a microwave oven. Then, the block was mounted in the work bed of the NC device and shaped by the driving action of the program. Following that, the tile was oven cured again and painted with a special heat-resistant silicone coating. The second curing, however, caused the tile to shrink, which meant that the original program had to allow for a specific shrinkage factor for each tile. NCS believes that the expertise it has gained through its computer efforts will allow the firm to be involved in future research and development of tiles used in space projects.

looking at the detailed logic of the program. The nice part of this method is that the programmer attacks the problem in terms of *what* has to be done rather than *how* each task is to be done. This allows the programmer to concentrate on each technique separately. After the individual functions have been isolated and diagrammed, then and only then will they be considered from a logical or *how to* standpoint.

As the name indicates, the programmer will start at the top by identifying the most general function and will get to more specific functions by working downward in a series of layers that break the functions into smaller and smaller tasks. The end result will be a treelike *hierarchy* chart that breaks the total job into a set of related tasks. The chart becomes a visual method of testing the design of the program. Later, the *logical* steps within the individual blocks will be detailed by means of *program flow charts, pseudocode, Warnier/Orr diagrams,* or any of dozens of other program design methods.

Let's apply this technique to the inventory problem that was analyzed earlier. The start of a top-down hierarchy chart usually is a single block that identifies the entire program.

> INVENTORY
>
> LISTING

The next layer will be comprised of blocks that identify the *major* processing tasks that will result in deriving correct output from the specified input. These major processing tasks will be further broken down or refined at successively lower levels until the entire structure of the program has been laid out.

From our analysis of the problem we should be able to identify these major tasks quite easily. We will start with a block labeled "Initialization," which is a general term used to cover all the housekeeping chores that are necessary before any real processing begins. At this point perhaps you cannot think of any such activities that will be necessary but that is of no importance now. All we are doing is recognizing that this is one task that is likely to have to be performed.

The next block is labeled "Inventory Processing," and at this point we are just indicating that the processing of inventory records is a major function of the program design. Obviously, this block will require further breakdown *at a lower level,* but we have not yet finished the level on which we are working. The third box or function identified on this level is the opposite of our first box. It is labeled "Closing Activities" to include any and all program termination tasks. Our top-down design chart is shown in Figure 11.5. Don't be misled by

FIGURE 11.5
Top-down hierarchy chart: first level.

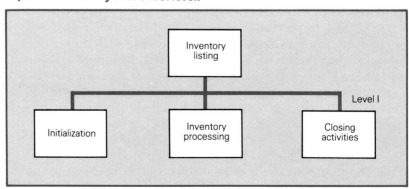

its simplicity—we are just making a start on an extremely valuable design tool.

We can now begin the next layer by expanding each one of the blocks just described. By now you have realized that this method is not applicable to programming alone. It is a general method of breaking large, apparently unmanageable jobs into smaller, more manageable components. The first block, "Initialize," can be divided into three smaller subtasks: "Getting the Files Ready", "Set Up Work Areas", and "Write Report Headings." The problem requires that we work with several data files (card input, printer output, and magnetic tape output), and the task of getting these files ready must be indicated. A second task that comes under the heading of Initialization is that of setting up work areas that may be needed in the program. One obvious need that comes to mind is that work areas must be established for the totals that will be accumulated.

The third function is one that is apparent from the output form sketched in Figure 11.3. The diagram indicated that heading lines were required. Common sense tells us that headings, in the situation we have set up, are not part of main inventory processing but should appear somewhere within the beginning activities. In the same vein, the writing of total lines on our report will be considered to be part of the Closing Activities block.

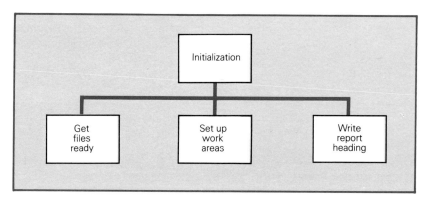

The breakdown of the Inventory Processing block is likely to be the most complex, but we must be careful to identify only the next lower level of functions. Once more, we are only specifying *what* is to be done, *not how* it is to be done. We will list the general processing steps that are invoked or called for by the upper level box. The next block calls for the reading of an inventory card record. As a matter of fact, we are now into the normal processing steps of read-process-print which, in our case, are listed as "Read Inventory Record", "Inventory Calculations", and "Write Inventory Report Line." Note that the Inventory Calculations block does *not* indicate *how* inventory calculation will actually occur in the program, only that they will take place within the Inventory Processing function.

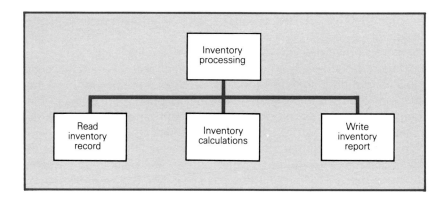

The Closing Activities block can be subdivided into two tasks: writing the totals that are called for at the end of the report and closing the data files that have been used in the program. The top-down design chart for our program is not yet complete, as many of the functions just described need to be broken down further. The chart, as it looks at this point, is shown in Figure 11.6.

A closer look at the second level of blocks in our top-down chart would tell us that all but one of the blocks is functionally complete, that is, needs no further breakdown. The one block that apparently still contains subfunctions that need to be described more fully is Inventory Calculation. At this point we can again go back to our original

FIGURE 11.6

Partial top-down hierarchy chart: inventory problem.

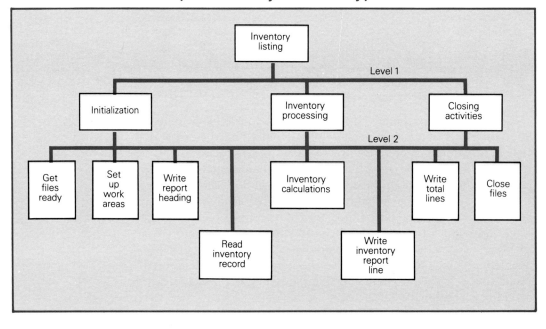

analysis of the program to see what steps will have to be undertaken. Perhaps the most immediate step is that of calculating the current stock-on-hand figure. Next, we would calculate the reorder point, then calculate the value of the stock on hand, and, finally, add to the stock value total that will be printed out at the end of the report. Once more, note that we are not concerned with how these calculations will take place. Instead, we deal with each function at its *own level* and do not worry about the functions of a lower level until we get there.

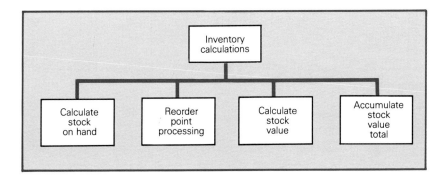

In preparation for the fourth-level activities we again scan the functions just completed. Of the four blocks, only one appears to be complex enough to warrant further breakdown—Reorder Point Processing. The program specification sheet said that if the current stock-on-hand figure was less than or equal to the reorder point, an appropriate record of data was to be written to magnetic tape and one was to be added to a counter or total of reorder items. These two functions are shown below.

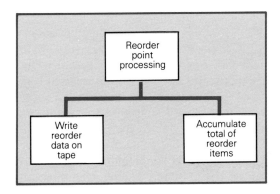

At this point we will end our top-down hierarchy chart because we have succeeded in breaking down each major function into manageable units. All the processing steps have been named and identified and can now be programmed. The complete hierarchy chart is shown in Figure 11.7.

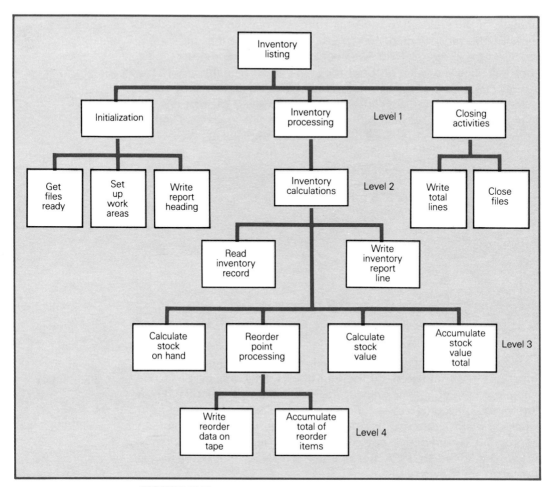

FIGURE 11.7
Completed top-down hierarchy chart.

If you, as the reader, have been thinking that all of this discussion is trivial or hardly worth thinking about, be assured it is an extremely important concept in program design. You have to understand that the sample program was extremely simple and would ultimately involve a few dozen lines of code in one of the high-level languages, such as BASIC or COBOL. In a real-life situation the complexity of the problems encountered will be highly magnified. Consider, for example, the complexity of a top-down hierarchy chart that might involve perhaps 10,000 lines of code, keeping teams of programmers working for a year or two on a single program. In those cases, the value of top-down design is immeasurable because it allows the programmer to verify the program logic as it is being constructed. Program writing proceeds in a top-down fashion, with the higher level modules being written first. Since these modules will be controlling the lower level modules, it is critical that they be correct. Since they are written first and will be used in conjunction with each lower level function, they become the most thoroughly tested parts of the program. As the lower level modules are coded, they are added to the existing code that has been proved to be correct. Thus it is relatively easy to isolate and correct errors in the program. Unstructured programs, by definition, have no structure to them, so code is written in a haphazard manner. This means that program coding has to be complete or nearly complete before any testing can begin. The usual result is that the testing and debugging time may equal or exceed the original coding time. Top-down designed programs are far more likely to run correctly the first time the entire program is tested.

The next step is to find a technique that will allow us to approach the second part of the program design job, that of determining *how* these individual functions are going to be turned into lines of code.

FLOWCHARTING

The top-down hierarchy chart has provided us with *what* it is we want to do in the program and now we want to design the program logic for each of the modules or blocks shown earlier. Many different methods exist, but most of the methods are visually oriented and have the advantage of conveying the relationship between various parts of the program in a quick, easy-to-understand manner.

Before using any of these methods for depicting the program logic you first have to come up with a plan or strategy of how you want to go about solving the problem. This sequence of steps is known as an *algorithm* and must be determined by the programmer *before* writing the program code. Since an algorithm is nothing more than a plan, it is something you have used all your life. You use a variety of algorithms

"DO YOU HAVE ANY 'SORRY YOUR PROGRAM BOMBED' CARDS?

to solve everyday tasks and you certainly realize that, at any one time, there may be several different algorithms or plans that will result in the solution to the problem. The programmer is faced with exactly the same choices except that the choice of algorithms is very likely to be dependent upon the amount of usable memory, machine time available, and other hardware/software limitations. A flow chart is then drawn to reflect the logic or the steps in your plan (algorithm). Most programmers use a flowcharting template (Figure 11.8), but we need not be concerned with the exact meaning of every symbol shown there.

The oval is used to indicate the start or end of a program.

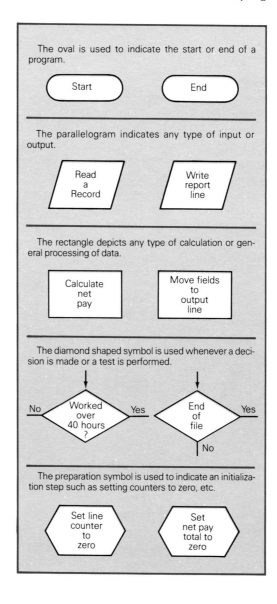

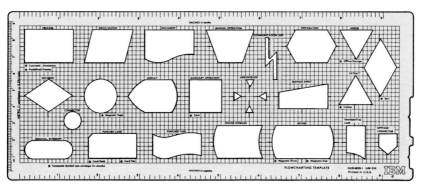

FIGURE 11.8
Flowcharting template.

Usually it is far better to spend the extra time to design a good flow chart than to plunge wildly into writing a series of computer instructions that get you helplessly bogged down. In this sense the flow chart is much like a road map. It is better to look at it before the trip than after getting lost.

By the way, flowcharting is not limited just to use in data processing activities. It is a good technique that can be used anytime you wish to illustrate a process that is likely to be confusing if it were done in narrative form. One example with which many of you may be familiar is that of "exploded view" diagrams that show how parts to various pieces of machinery, games, tools, fit together. Another use that has been around for a long time is that of training aid for new clerical workers. A written job description may be provided, but a diagram that shows the flow of paperwork through the job position is often far more helpful. Figure 11.9 is a flow chart that illustrates the first step in forms processing by an account clerk.

Let's take a look at some of the techniques that aid you in drawing a flow chart:

1. When preparing a flow chart, work with the normal situation first. Follow this mainstream all the way to its conclusion and then go back and pick up the loose ends, one at a time. For example, if you are working on a payroll program, the normal situation concerns those employees working 40 hours per week. After you complete this part of the flow chart, go back and diagram the overtime part of the program for those working in excess of 40 hours.

2. A flow chart should be as machine independent as possible. Theoretically, the logic of the solution should apply on any computer, so try to avoid descriptive terms that apply to a specific computer.

3. A flow chart is *not* supposed to be a detailed description of every program step or command. Each symbol or block should represent a logical step in the program. In addition, each step should be

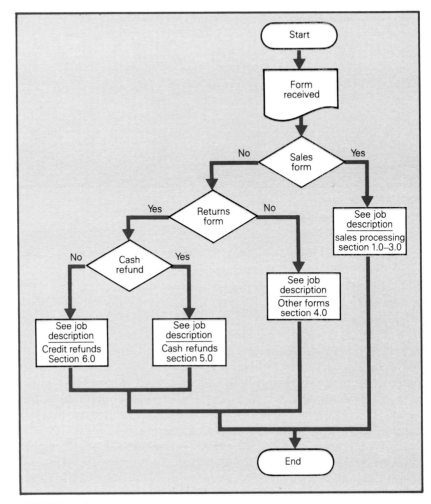

FIGURE 11.9
Job diagram.

broken down to the point that it is meaningful to the reader. For example, suppose that in one part of the program you have to compute the answer to a complicated formula. The flow chart block shown here may be sufficient:

$$\text{Calculate}\quad \frac{-b \pm \sqrt{b^2 - 4ac}}{2a}$$

If this concept is too large in its scope, i.e., that the individual steps in the computation of or solution to the formula are too complex, then break the problem into smaller parts until you are satisfied:

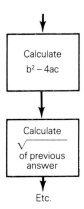

4. Show the lines of logic flow by using arrows on the flow chart. Normally, the flow is from top to bottom and/or from left to right. To illustrate some of these flowcharting techniques, consider the following problem. Suppose that you have a known number of data cards—five, for example—with each card containing the payroll information on a particular person. Data from the first card must be read into memory, processed according to the company payroll formula, and the answer printed. Information from the second card will then go through the same process, followed by the third card, etc.

A top-down design chart of this extremely simple example is shown in Figure 11.10. At least two strategies could be developed for programming the functions of the Payroll Processing block. One plan would be to use the straight linear sequence construct and go through the read-calculate-print operation five times, as shown in Figure 11.11.

FIGURE 11.10
Payroll hierarchy chart.

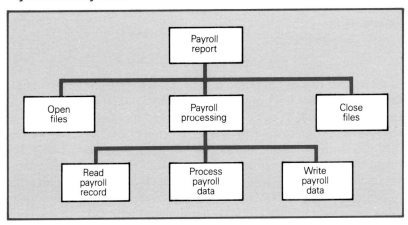

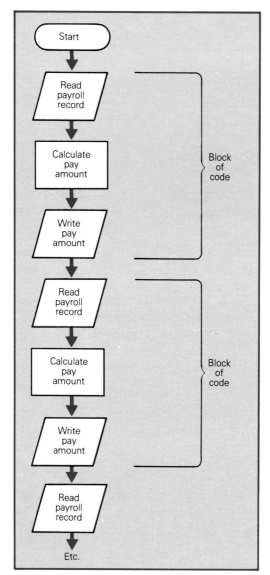

FIGURE 11.11
Repeated blocks of code.

Of course, this first program is so simple that in some cases a single flow-chart symbol does represent one command. This does not contradict the rule stated earlier, because each symbol indicates a program step that must be shown in the overall pattern of logic. A more obvious diffi culty with the flow chart is that the plan is grossly inefficient. It might work for a few data records, but there must be a better strategy for taking care of perhaps thousands of data records. There is no point in writing the READ-COMPUTE-PRINT statements over and over again when an arrangement can be coded that will loop back to a section code over and over again (Figure 11.12). In this particular example, a

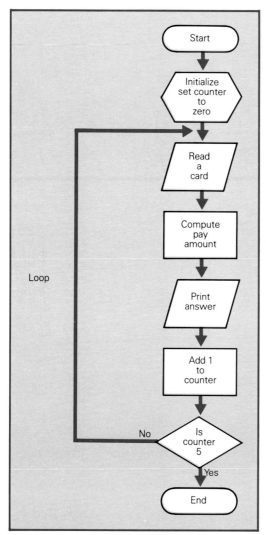

FIGURE 11.12
Program loop: payroll example.

counter is used to keep track of the number of times the block of code has been executed. When the counter indicates that the process has been repeated five times, the program exits from the loop.

STRUCTURED PROGRAMMING CONCEPTS

Historically, top-down or structured design came after considerable effort had been devoted to the concept of structured programming. Programming has been considered something of an art form that

CLASSIC ALGORITHMS
EXPLAINED – $25 ⁰⁰

SANDY

reflects much of the individual style of the programmer. Unfortunately, programs of this type often are "maintenance nightmares" because the design and coding was done in an almost random manner. The object of good programming technique is to produce programs that are easy to read and maintain. As programming costs continued to soar during the late 1960s, it was imperative that a disciplined, structured approach to programming be found.

In 1966 two mathematicians, C. Bohm and G. Jacopini, stated that good programs could be developed using a limited number of logical programming structures, or "constructs"—Linear Sequence, Selection, and Repetition. In addition, certain rules were applied to the use of modules or structures.

1. Each module must have only one entry point and only one exit.
2. A module can never activate another module on its own level.
3. Individual modules should be short, often limited to a single page.

Professor E. W. Dijkstra continued the assault on "art form" programming in a 1966 article to the Association of Computing Machinery titled, "GO TO Statement Considered Harmful." This is perhaps the most often discussed feature of structured programming—that it is "GO TO-less", meaning that the unconditional branch statement GO TO is eliminated.

What is a GO TO statement and why all the concern about restricting its use? Almost every language has a GO TO or unconditional "jump" or "branch" statement that takes the system out of the current set of statements in which it is working and transfers the system to another point in the program. In itself, the GO TO statement is not "bad." The problem is that the GO TO statement was often used as an escape door to get out of a poorly planned section of coding. It is, therefore, the *undisciplined* use of GO TO statements that make the program structure hard to perceive. However, the use or nonuse of GO TO statements is not the real issue. The structure of the program is what counts. Without a proper approach to program design, it is still possible to write poor programs that do not contain any GO TO statements. The questions to be considered are:

> Is the program correct?
> Is it easily understood?
> Is it easy to maintain?

In actual practice, the "structuring" of programmer activity may involve far more than the specific structures just discussed. Other "house" rules may specify such items as the naming of data fields, how they are established, and specific coding rules or conventions.

Dijkstra's ideas were incorporated in the so-called "*New York Times* project" in which an IBM team programmed an on-line retrieval system for the newspaper. Over 80,000 lines of coding were produced in just under two years—productivity that was nearly five times as great as the industry standards. The key point was that the coding was nearly free of errors.

One of the major objectives of structured programming is to get programmers to produce more and better coding that is as error-free as possible. Although it takes traditional programmers about six months or more to adapt to the new discipline, results have generally been good. Exact figures are difficult to ascertain, but unstructured programmer productivity has been in the range of 2000 lines of coding per year (using a high-level language such as COBOL or FORTRAN) with perhaps 1 error per 100 lines of code. Using a disciplined, structured approach, output has gone up to 5000 lines per year with perhaps 1 error in 10,000 lines of coding.

LINEAR SEQUENCE STRUCTURE

The linear sequence structure is nothing more than the sequential execution of one or more program statements, as shown in the flow chart diagrammed below. In flow-chart graphics, the rectangle indicates or stands for any processing function. Note that arrows are used to show the lines of flow of the program action and to connect the processing blocks.

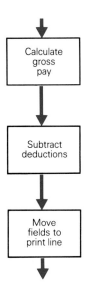

SELECTION STRUCTURE (IFTHENELSE)

Every programming language has some statement that permits the programmer to perform logical (true-false) testing. The statement usually is very simple in its operation and generally is known as an IF statement. The actual statement will be discussed later in the programming chapters, but a typical use of such a statement would be to test whether an employee has worked overtime. If the employee has worked in excess of 40 hours, we would want to follow one set of statements, while a different set of statements would be followed if no overtime was involved.

Although IF statements may be combined in complicated ways, their use in structured programming is severely curtailed. They are to be used in such a manner that there is only one entry point and one exit point from the module, such as shown in the following diagram, which uses the diamond symbol to depict the testing operation.

The following program segment happens to be written in COBOL, but is self-explanatory and follows the Selection Structure format (which is also known as the IFTHENELSE structure). Note that both the true and the false conditions of the IF test end at the same statement (ADD PAY TO TOTAL-PAY) (FIGURE 11.13).

```
IF HOURS-WORKED IS GREATER THAN 40
    COMPUTE PAY = ((HRS—40) *1.5 * RATE) + (RATE * 40)
ELSE
    COMPUTE PAY = RATE * HOURS.
ADD PAY TO TOTAL-PAY.
```

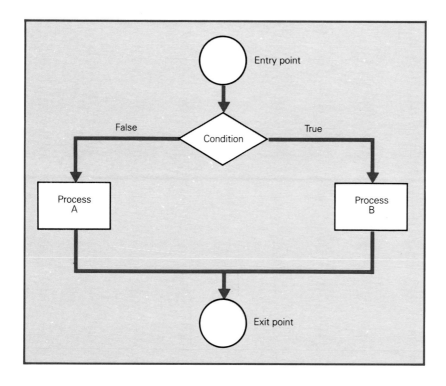

REPETITION STRUCTURE (DOWHILE)

In the repetition, or controlled loop structure (also called the DOWHILE or *iteration* structure), a processing block is combined with a test of some type. The DOWHILE construct says to "Do Process A depending upon the result of a test. When the test condition is satisfied, exit from the loop."

Note that with this structure, it is possible that process A may never be executed at all. In either case, the structure has only one entry and

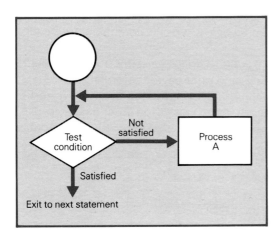

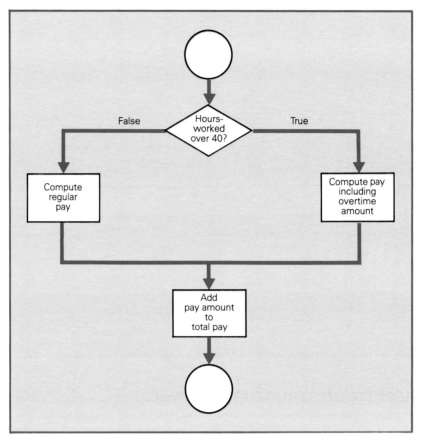

FIGURE 11.13
Selection structure.

one exit point from the module. In COBOL the DOWHILE structure is set up by means of a PERFORM UNTIL statement that says, "PERFORM a certain process UNTIL a specific test is true." Its most common use is in controlling a processing loop until there are no more input records to be processed. In the example below we will assume the following.

1. Process A (PAYROLL-CALCULATION) is a series of COBOL statements that read, calculate, and print payroll information.
2. The END-OF-INPUT-INDICATOR is a field that can be tested to see whether we have reached the end of the input data records.
3. The end-of-data condition will be signaled when the indicator has a value of 1.

  PERFORM PAYROLL-CALCULATION
      UNTIL END-OF-INPUT-INDICATOR
      IS EQUAL TO 1.

        -----Next statement-----

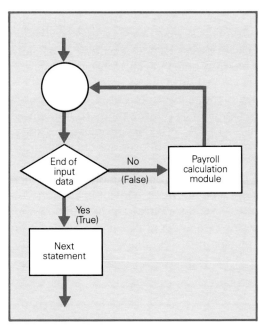

FIGURE 11.14
DOWHILE structure.

Figure 11.14 shows the controlled loop structure (DOWHILE) in a little more detail.

One variation on the DOWHILE format is another controlled loop structure called DOUNTIL.

The DOUNTIL structure says to "Do process A until a particular condition becomes true. Then exit from the loop."

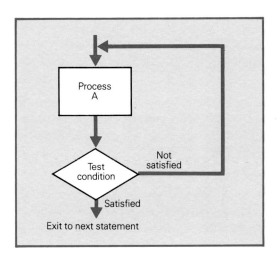

The major difference between the two structures is that with DOWHILE it is possible that Process A may never be executed at all, while with DOUNTIL, Process A is executed at least one time. Note that each of these structures has only one entry and one exit point from the module.

Few programming languages today are truly suited for structured programming. COBOL, for example, has the capability to implement most of the structures but lacks a DOUNTIL. Nevertheless, this situation is changing rapidly as more software houses are creating structured versions of the more popular languages.

Now you know the three basic programming structures with which any problem can be programmed. Before leaving this section you should understand that these three structures can be put together much like building blocks to solve whatever problem you have. It is up to you to use your logical problem-solving ability to decide on the

FIGURE 11.15
Combined structures (1).

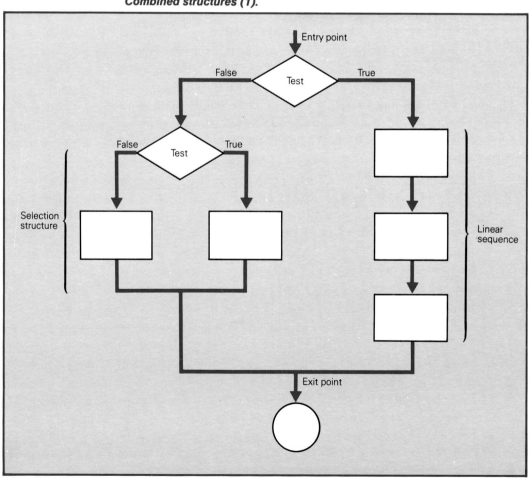

correct structures for your program. Figure 11.15 shows that a linear sequence structure and a selection structure can be combined within a larger selection structure. Figure 11.16 illustrates a repetition structure within a selection structure.

STRUCTURED WALK-THROUGHS

As discussed earlier in this chapter, programming has long been considered to be a solo task. This, of course, has led to individual programming styles that are only now being corrected by the discipline imposed by the top-down approach and through the use of specific programming constructs, such as linear sequence, IFTHENELSE, and DOWHILE. The net effect is that the whole programming process is being structured in an effort to achieve what is often called "egoless" programming.

An extension of this concept is the idea of structured walk-throughs. As you would suspect by the name, a *walk-through* is a

FIGURE 11.16
Combined structures (2).

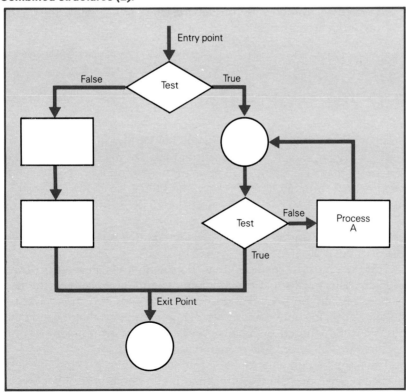

formal review process during which a programmer "walks" or steps through the design and/or coding in front of a group of fellow programmers.

The first walk-through usually takes place before the actual code is entered into the computer, since one of the main objects of the method is to detect design errors before they are coded. Walk-throughs are being used more and more in the larger shops, particularly when teams of programmers are engaged in a group effort. The process follows a fairly standard pattern, as outlined below.

1. The manager informs the programmer that a walk-through will take place at a particular point in the design or coding process.
2. When that point is reached, the manager schedules a meeting of fellow programmers who will act as the review board.
3. Copies of the diagrams, flow charts, coding, etc., are given to the review group well in advance of the meeting so that they have a chance to review the material.
4. At the actual review meeting the programmer explains or, in effect, defends what he or she has done. Questions are asked and notes are taken concerning any flaws that are found in the design or coding.
5. If the changes are relatively minor, they are made and a repeat of the walk-through is not required. If the changes are serious, however, then another walk-through may have to be conducted on the revised material.

CODING, TESTING, AND DOCUMENTING THE PROGRAM

With all the care and patience that has gone into the design of the program, there should be little difficulty in writing the actual lines of code. However, the programmer should keep in mind the oft-quoted statement that 50% to 80% of all programming effort is concerned with *maintenance* programming, that is, modifying or changing existing programs. Therefore, no matter what language is involved, the programmer should be careful to write in such a way that the program is both easily read and understood by someone who is unfamiliar with that particular program.

Test data must be made up that thoroughly tests all aspects of the program. This means that the programmer and/or the supervisor may have to prepare both valid and invalid data. The term "may" is used here because, in some cases, the programmer knows that invalid data has been intercepted by a separate data validation program. If not, invalid data will have to be prepared as well.

The term "documentation" is a frequent battle cry within the field of data processing. The reason is that documentation is of very great importance, and yet there is a great temptation not to take the time to document properly. By the term documentation we generally mean all the paper work, forms, diagrams, approval sheets, flow charts, etc., associated with a computer program. Documentation might not be such a problem within the industry if it were not for the fact that programmers are very mobile, i.e., they tend to move from job to job. It is not at all uncommon to have a 50% turnover or loss of programmers every two or three years, although systems analysts seem to stay put a little longer.

The pressing need for complete documentation is felt when old or existing programs must be modified to meet current needs. The chances are extremely great that the original programmer is no longer available to answer questions so, in these situations, complete documentation is an absolute necessity. Listed here are some items that should be considered minimum requirements for program documentation:

1. A written statement of the problem to be solved and the language required (COBOL, FORTRAN, etc.).
2. Statements or illustrations of what input data is to be used, the reliability of the data, whether or not the data is to be checked before it can be processed, etc. If cards are the input medium, a Multiple Card Layout Form (shown earlier) is an easy way to show the location of card fields.
3. A statement or illustration of the output in the form required by management. For engineering or mathematics problems, it may be necessary to include diagrams of output from various graphic devices such as plotters and video units. Printer spacing charts are usually included in documentation, as a great amount of computer output eventually is printed.
4. A top-down hierarchy chart is a necessity to show the overall design structure. If the design structure is changed by later modifications, the old design, the modifications, and the new design should be shown.
5. Accurate and current flow charts or pseudocode charts showing the logic of the problem. An important point here is that the charts as originally drawn and the program as finally debugged may be two different things. It is the responsibility of the programmer to make sure that the final version of the program is accurately depicted by the logic charts. If a program is revised at a later date, then the appropriate chart pages must be revised also.
6. A final and accurate listing of the program, including computer diagnostic statements (indicating how many memory positions are used, etc.) and linkages (messages telling how various parts of the program are tied together).
7. An illustration of the sample test data for testing the program and a printout of the results. The test data must be such that all logical

and ordinary conditions are tested and the computed results agree with the expected answers.

8. Instructions to the computer operator covering any occurrence out of the ordinary. A list of error messages to the operator and permissible responses should be included so that procedures can be initiated to recover as much of the work as possible in case of program or system failure.

9. A statement to anyone who may have to get into the logic of the program, indicating any unusual programming conventions used. Program decks, tapes, disks, etc., must be marked for identification.

Perhaps the relationship of the preceding topics can be seen in better perspective if we list the sequence of events in the successful preparation of a computer program:

1. The system's flow charts are drawn in sufficient detail to recognize the need for individual programs.

2. The programmer (or perhaps a programmer team) draws the top-down structure chart.

3. The steps of the top-down chart are implemented by means of flow charts, pseudocode, Warnier/Orr diagrams, or other appropriate techniques.

4. The actual program is written on coding sheets and keyed or in some way entered into the computer. Also, it is very likely that test data is generated during this phase.

5. The program is run on the computer until a satisfactory result is obtained. Obtaining a satisfactory result is not always as easy as it sounds, as "bugs" or errors in the program must be noted and corrected (a process that is known as *debugging*).

    What do you do if your program doesn't work? What you do *not* do is make random changes in the program in the hope that one of the changes will make it work. Instead, what you should do is desk-check the program with your mind taking the place of the computer. The partial output or incorrect answers you may have gotten are clues to the location of the error. A thorough analysis of these clues should allow you to concentrate your debugging efforts on a few program modules. Then, corrections are made and the program is rerun.

6. The successful program is documented thoroughly for future reference.

SUMMARY OF IMPORTANT POINTS

☐ Program development is a filtration process in which a program goes through more and more detailed planning as it progresses downward in the organization.

☐ The problem-solving process involves the following:
Analyzing the problem.
Designing the solution.
Coding the solution.
Testing and debugging the program.
Final program documentation.

☐ The data input and output formats are always known to the programmer, and the act of programming is to use the input data to turn out the required output.

☐ In designing the solution to a problem the programmer usually resorts to a number of design tools or methodologies, one of which is top-down design.

☐ In the top-down design process the programmer starts by identifying the highest level of functions or tasks that have to be performed in the program. After that, each successive layer of elemental tasks is developed until all recognizable functions have been identified.

☐ A top-down hierarchy chart is concerned with *what* functions have to be performed, *not how* the function will be coded.

☐ Structured programming techniques were developed to remedy poor, inefficient, and costly programs that were common in the industry.

☐ According to the rules of structured programming, every program can be written in a top-down, modular form using only three basic formats, or "constructs."
Linear sequence.
Selection (IFTHENELSE).
Repetition (DOWHILE and DOUNTIL).

☐ Each one of the constructs has only one entry and one exit point.

☐ Flowcharting was presented as just one of many methods that exist for determining how a particular program module will be processed.

☐ The coding of the program comes after the completion of the design phase and requires the same attention to detail as was necessary in the earlier steps. In theory, if a program has been designed properly, it should work correctly the first time.

☐ Some installations use structured walk-throughs as a method of discovering design or coding errors before they are entered into the computer program.

☐ A program should be tested with data that will cover any and all possibilities that may be encountered when the program is put into production.

☐ Program documentation is the last step in the problem-solving process and is especially important because most programs will be revised at some time in the future. Without thorough and proper documentation, it becomes almost impossible to revise a program.

GLOSSARY OF TERMS

Algorithm—a strategy or plan or series of steps for the solution of a problem.

Counter—a programming device used to control the number of times a program loop is executed.

Debugging—the act of correcting the errors in a computer program.

Documentation—the sum total of the forms, flow charts, program listings, etc., associated with a computer program.

DOUNTIL structure—a form of the repetition or controlled loop structure that permits repetition of a section of code depending upon the result of a test. In the DOUNTIL format the section of code is always executed at least once.

DOWHILE structure—another name for the repetition or controlled loop structure that permits repetition of a section of code depending upon the result of a test. In the DOWHILE format the section of code may not be executed at all.

Flowcharting—a representation of a DP activity by the use of special graphic symbols.

IFTHENELSE structure—another name for the selection or testing structure that uses an IF statement in a simple true-false condition.

Initialize—a programming term that refers to the act of establishing fixed values in certain areas of memory. Generally, the term applies to all the housekeeping that must be completed before the main part of the program can be executed.

Pseudocode—in structured programming it makes reference to English sentence-type descriptions of the processing function to be performed in a logic module.

Program loop—a series of instructions that may be executed repeatedly in accordance with the logic of the program.

Structured programming—a disciplined programming technique that ensures a single entry point and a single exit point from every processing module.

Structured walk-through—a formal review process in which the programmer explains the design and/or logic that he or she used in the preparation of the program.

Top-down design—the term applied to the theory that program design should begin at the top with the largest module and proceed downward to sublevels.

THOUGHT QUESTIONS

1. Why is a top-down hierarchy chart so useful as a program design tool? Explain in detail.
2. Why should a program flow chart be independent of the program language?
3. Take some everyday activity that you are used to doing and describe it by means of a flow chart. If you do a thorough job of it, you may find, to your surprise, that many common tasks are quite complex. Try it on something fairly "simple," such as crossing a street, before tackling a more complex task, such as eating dinner in a restaurant.
4. How would you feel about going through a structured walk-through? Apply this technique to a term project or report that you might have to prepare for another class.

CHAPTER 12
BASIC PROGRAMMING: PART I

LEARNING OBJECTIVES
Upon completion of this chapter you should understand the following:

The general nature of the BASIC programming language, even though it may vary considerably from machine to machine.

How to log on to a timesharing system and how to use its capabilities.

The difference between constants and variables used in your program.

The use of LET to create values and to do arithmetic within the rules of arithmetic operations.

The use of flow charts to diagram the logic of a specific program.

The format and capabilities of the following BASIC statements:

> LET
> PRINT
> END
> REMARK (REM)
> INPUT
> READ and DATA
> GO TO
> IF-THEN

At least three ways of getting data values into a program.

The use of a counter to control a program loop and as an accumulator of values.

CHAPTER CONTENTS

Earlier in the text you saw that perhaps hundreds of programming languages are currently available, but a half dozen or so are in widespread use. Although COBOL (*Common Business-Oriented Language*) is the most widely used language in business, BASIC (*Beginners All-purpose Symbolic Instruction Code*) is perhaps the most popular overall. BASIC was originally designed for use in college and university timesharing systems to service large numbers of mathematics and science students. Here, the computer's great speed could be used to an advantage by devoting a small amount of time to each terminal user on a rotating basis. The language is very similar to FORTRAN (*Formula Translator*) so that a knowledge of one language can be transferred to the other. One major difference exists, however, between BASIC and other languages, such as FORTRAN, COBOL, and RPG. Generally speaking, BASIC is not equipped to handle cards since the principal input-output device is a terminal. This fact has made BASIC the prime language for the ever-growing number of microprocessors—the TRS-80's, Apple's, Commodore's, IBM's, and many others.

A final word of caution regarding BASIC. The language has not yet been standardized, which means that a great many versions are available. This chapter and the following one will illustrate the more common features of the language, but be sure to check your computer for specific details on the format and operation of the various statements.

ACCESSING THE COMPUTER

Gaining access to the computer may be as simple as turning on the system (as in the case of the popular microcomputer systems) or it may involve a series of steps (as in the case of large timesharing systems). There simply is not room here to cover all the logging-in possibilities on the many types of systems that are out there. However, once you are accepted by the system, you have the use of about a dozen *system commands* that allow you to have control over the computer system while accessing BASIC. Some of the more common system commands are discussed below.

1. LOGIN, HELLO (etc.)—used on timesharing systems to gain initial access to the system.
2. LOGOUT, QUIT, BYE, etc.—used in timesharing systems when you are through and wish to leave the terminal. With both microprocessors and timesharing systems, your program that was in memory is no longer available to you.
3. LIST—used on both timesharing and microcomputer systems to print a current listing of your program.
4. COMPILE—used mainly on a few timesharing systems to cause compilation (but *not* execution) of your program.
5. RUN—used on most systems to compile *and* run (or execute).
6. NAME, NEW—assigns a name to a program that you wish to save onto disk.
7. SAVE, FILE (etc.)—stores a program onto disk so that it can be retrieved later.
8. GET, OLD (etc.)—brings into memory a copy of the program that was stored on disk.
9. KILL, PURGE, DELETE (etc.)—deletes a program that had been stored on a disk file.
10. SCRATCH, CLEAR (etc.)—clears memory (not disk) so that you can enter another program.

11.   CAT, CATALOG (etc.)—prints a listing of the programs you have stored on disk.

12.   PASSWORD—used to create a special password so that you can restrict access to your programs.

ENTERING YOUR PROGRAM

BASIC program statements are entered into the computer through the terminal keyboard and will appear on the video screen or on the printer page if a printing terminal is used. At this point we shall assume that you have logged in correctly and are ready to enter your BASIC program, which consists of a series of *statements.*

All statements must begin with a number that is up to four digits in length. (Some systems allow five digits.) These numbers are decided upon by the programmer and they determine the order in which the statements will appear in your program. Generally, statements are numbered by 10's, as shown below.

```
10 _____ CR
20 _____ CR
30 _____ CR
40 _____ CR
```

The CR notation indicates that the carriage-return key (also called ENTER, NEWLINE, among other names) must be struck at the end of each line. This releases the statement to the system for processing. The reason for numbering in this manner is to allow room to insert numbered statements at appropriate places in the program. Thus it is possible to type in the program, decide that you have left out a statement at some point in the program, and still enter it in the correct place without having to retype the whole program.

For example, if you feel that two statements are needed between statements 30 and 40, they can be entered simply by assigning an appropriate number to the statements.

```
10 _____  ⎫
20 _____  ⎪
30 _____  ⎬  Program as originally entered
40 _____  ⎪
50 _____  ⎭
34 _____
38 _____     Statements to be added into the original
                      program
```

How can you verify that these two statements have been placed into your program in the desired position? All you have to do is type in the *system command* LIST and the computer system will print a complete listing of your program statements in ascending numerical order. Note that LIST is *not* numbered. The rule is that *all* program *statements* are numbered; system commands are *never* numbered. Upon typing LIST (note that it is *not* preceded by a line number) this will be the result:

```
LIST
10 _____
20 _____
30 _____
34 _____
38 _____
40 _____
```

To delete a statement from your program, simply type the statement number followed by a carriage return. To delete statement 20, type:

20 (carriage return)

To verify that the statement has been deleted, again use the system command LIST to show the revised contents of your program.

```
20 (carriage return)
LIST
10 _____
30 _____
34 _____
38 _____
40 _____
```

Changing a statement can be done by first deleting it and then entering the new version. However, an easier method is to just enter the new statement. For example, to change statement 10, enter the new version of the statement, which then does both jobs of deleting the old version and inserting the new one.

Most BASIC systems allow the program statements to be written relatively free form, so the programmer may include spaces to improve readability.

For example:

40LETN = H*R-D

is just as valid as

40 LET N = H * R - D

but far less readily understood.

What happens if you make a mistake while keying in a program statement? The process for making corrections varies a little from machine to machine, but just about every system has a key that allows you to backspace to the point of error, make the correction, and continue. If the system detects errors in the syntax or format of a statement, an error message will be forthcoming. On some systems the message appears immediately after the entry of that statement. Other systems wait until all the program statements have been entered. When you enter the system command COMPILE or RUN, the system will then print all the error messages by reference to the statement number.

If, upon typing RUN, the output is not correct, then the program has a logic error(s) that must be modified. If it becomes apparent that the output is incorrect, normally you do not have to wait for the conclusion of the program to correct it. Depressing a special key (check for this on your system) causes an instant stop and you can again make corrections.

Whether you are working at a timesharing video screen terminal or at a microcomputer, you may wish to end the session with a printed copy of the program and its output. On some systems this is accomplished by storing your program on disk, logging off the system and then logging in on a printing terminal, and LISTing and RUNning your program. Other systems permit the use of a special command that causes the program to be listed on the system printing device.

Remember you have the ability to store your program on disk so that it can be retrieved at a later date. Your program does not have to be complete or perfect to be stored. Thus, you can enter part of a program, store it, and return to it later.

ELEMENTS OF THE BASIC LANGUAGE

CHARACTER SET

The character set used with BASIC is essentially the same as the one we use in everyday life, with the addition of a few special characters that are used in mathematical notation. Special symbols include those that have particular meaning in arithmetic operations, those used for punctuation and output, and those used in relational tests:

ARITHMETIC SYMBOLS

    ↑   Exponentiation, or raising to a power
    *   Multiplication
    /   Division
    +   Addition
    –   Subtraction

(*Note:* Some BASIC systems use the double asterisk to represent exponentiation; **)

.   Period (or decimal point)
,   Comma
:   Colon
;   Semicolon
$ Dollar sign
( )   Left and right parentheses
"   Quotation mark (double)
'   Single quotation mark or apostrophe
&   Ampersand
#   Number sign
%   Percent sign
?   Question mark

RELATIONAL SYMBOLS

=	Equal to
< >	
#	Not equal to
> <	
>	Greater than
<	Less than
< =	Less than or equal to
= <	
> =	Greater than or equal to
= >	

(*Note:* Some versions of BASIC allow only one form of the above relations)

NUMERIC CONSTANTS AND VARIABLES

BASIC is capable of handling decimal numbers up to a specific size that is predetermined by the system software. For some systems the maximum is 6 digits, while others go up to 13 or even more. These numbers may or may not be signed and may or may not contain a decimal point.

Examples:

```
7
-12
17.635
-.002
81        (Incorrect: this is a formula to be
           solved, not a number)
64,317    (Incorrect: commas are not permitted)
```

Numbers appearing this way in the program are called *constants,* as their values do not change. Numbers larger than the maximum that can be displayed by the system are represented in another way—by means of what is known as E notation, or Scientific notation. Numbers in this format will be discussed in the next chapter.

Variables are computational elements that change during the execution of a program. In the case of mathematical formulas, the result or answer is unknown to the programmer at the time the program is written. The programmer therefore uses a variable name to represent the unknown answer. In real life we might use the formula

NET PAY = HOURS × RATE – DEDUCTIONS

in which we are using words to represent unknown numerical values. In BASIC the permissible names for variable quantities are a single letter or a single letter and a single digit.

Examples:

X, A, G4, H3

Constants and variables are manipulated by means of the specific arithmetic symbols listed previously. Our same NET PAY formula might look like this in BASIC:

N = H * R – D

Obviously, this is not as easy to read or understand as the previous version, which was more English-like in its makeup. Some of the newer versions of BASIC are correcting this by allowing a greater number of characters for the names of data fields. Since you are the one who knows what these field names represent, it is a good idea to pick names that are as meaningful as possible within the limits of the language.

ARITHMETIC OPERATIONS

Although the arithmetic formula (or "expression") shown earlier is quite correct, the programmer must be careful to specify to the computer the exact order of the operations to be performed. This is necessary because the computer performs arithmetic according to a hierarchy or priority of operations. This means that the system will search through a formula from left to right and do specific operations according to the following set of priorities:

1. Exponentiation (or raising to a power).
2. Multiplication and division.
3. Addition and subtraction.

The programmer may alter this order of operations by using parentheses in the expression. The parentheses have no effect on the formula itself other than to direct the order of operations. The computer will always find the innermost set of parentheses and evaluate the part of the expression it finds there according to the priority of operations. Only after that operation is complete can the result be used in further operations on the expression. In the absense of parentheses, operations on the same level (addition and subtraction, for example) are performed from left to right.

Examples:

$A + B * C \uparrow 2$	Action: C is squared; the result is multiplied by B; A is added to the product
$(A + B) * C \uparrow 2$	Action: A is added to B; C is squared; C^2 is multiplied by the sum of $A + B$.
$(A + B/C * D)$	Action: B is divided by C; the result is multiplied by D; A is added to the product.
$((A + B)/C) \uparrow 3$	Action: A is added to B; C is divided into A + B; the quotient is then cubed.

On this basis, our original formula or expression

$N = H * R - D$

is still correct because the computer will first calculate gross pay (H times R) and then subtract the deductions.

PROGRAM STATEMENTS

So many versions of BASIC are on the market today that it would be impossible to discuss all the various statements that could be used. In 1978 the American National Standard for Minimal BASIC came out with some 26 key words for use in the minimal BASIC. As of this writing, relatively few manufacturers have implemented the standard on their BASIC systems. However, the majority of all problems can be programmed with perhaps a dozen BASIC statements that are relatively standard in format and function. Where considerable differences exist, the most common form will be shown and some other forms noted.

By way of introducing you to these statements and how they function, we will program our payroll problem (NET PAY = HOURS × RATE - DEDUCTIONS) on the computer. The problem to be solved could be worded as follows: "Write a computer program to accept data for employee identification number, hours worked, rate of pay, and deductions. Print the Id Number and the Net Pay amount.

A flow chart of this problem would be:

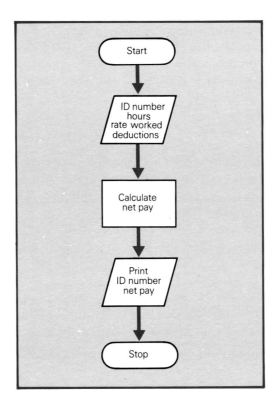

Obviously, you have to read in the data before it can be worked upon and you have to calculate results before they can be printed.

The previous chapter stressed the importance of proper planning before actually coding the solution. It also stressed the idea of a structured approach to programming, and the author believes very strongly in this matter. Unfortunately, the BASIC language has few statements that implement top-down structured programming. Trying to implement some of the structured ideas in BASIC can be done but only by means of awkward or cumbersome coding. Therefore, in these two chapters on BASIC you will see a traditional approach that reflects the unstructured nature of the language. Newer, more powerful versions of BASIC that have statements that permit some structured programming are beginning to appear, but they have not been widely implemented yet.

THE LET STATEMENT

The LET statement is probably the most commonly used statement in BASIC. It is often called the "assignment" statement because it allows us to create a value and assign it to a place in memory. Our sample problem indicated that we needed to enter four data values into the system: Employee Id Number, Hours Worked, Rate of Pay, and Deductions. One method of doing this in BASIC is as follows:

```
10 LET I = 5683
20 LET H = 40
30 LET R = 8.75
40 LET D = 39.57
```

When the program is run, the execution of the LET statements will result in the four values being created and stored in memory as follows:

5683	40	8.75	39.57
I	H	R	D

Perhaps the most important point to note here is that the computer cannot "know" what these values represent. Instead, it is the programmer who knows that a value representing hours worked is stored in memory at a place called H, that the rate of pay is stored in memory at a place called R, and so on. It is the programmer's responsibility to know what values the location of these are and to manipulate them correctly.

A second major use of the LET statement is that of causing the computer to perform an arithmetic calculation.

Earlier you saw an example of arithmetic operation with the formula:

N = H * R - D

In BASIC the actual formula would be written in a LET statement

50 LET N = H * R - D

As a result of this statement, an answer has been created and stored in memory at a place called N. Memory would now look as follows:

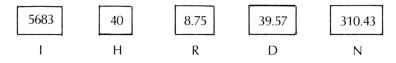

5683	40	8.75	39.57	310.43
I	H	R	D	N

Actually, LET is the only arithmetic statement in BASIC, as there are no specific statements that correspond to add, subtract, etc. Later you will see a variety of ways in which LET may be used. No matter how it is used, it must be formulated as shown. Note that there must be a single variable on the left side of the equal sign, but the formula on the right may be as long and as complicated as the programmer needs. There is no limit to the number of LET statements the programmer can have. Indeed, often it is better to break a complicated formula into a series of LET statements than use one long, complex LET. By doing this it is easier to find errors and make corrections. The program would have been just as correct if you had programmed as follows:

```
50 LET G = H * R    (Gross pay)
55 LET N = G - D    (Less deductions)
```

had you done that, memory would look as follows:

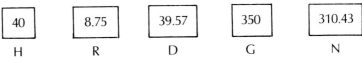

40	8.75	39.57	350	310.43
H	R	D	G	N

Also, it is with the LET statement that the programmer must be particularly aware of the rules of arithmetic and the order of arithmetic operations. Suppose the programmer is to create values for A, B, C, and T and solve the following equation:

$$X = \frac{ABC}{4T}$$

The formula, of course, actually reads as "A times B times C divided by four times T." The correct LET statement is

```
40 LET X = (A*B*C)/(4*T)
```

Note that the formula calls for the quantity above the line to be divided by the quantity below the line. Therefore it is necessary to enclose these parts of the expression within separate sets of parentheses in order to get the system to evaluate them before dividing.

Also, note that it is *not correct* to say

```
40 LET (A*B*C)/(4*T) = X
```

LET can also be used to move values from one place to another. For example, to duplicate and move a value from one place to another you can say

```
LET H = R1
```

which replaces the value that was at H with a duplicate of the value found at R1.

27.5		103.6
H		R1
Value in H before executing the LET statement		Value in R1 before executing the LET statement

103.6		103.6
H		R1
After executing the LET statement		After executing the LET statement

THE PRINT STATEMENT

The PRINT statement is used to output answers and/or to print messages at the discretion of the programmer. At this point we run into a problem that sometimes bothers beginning programmers—the output format. The problem is that BASIC was never designed for "pretty" output. Within certain limits you can get more precise output, but the language is set up in such a way that *reasonable* output can be obtained with little or no effort. Some of the more advanced capabilities of the PRINT statement will be covered later, but for now, the simplest form of the PRINT statement is

    30 PRINT

which causes the system to print a blank line, that is, to advance the carriage down one line. To print the numerical value stored at a particular location we merely have to use the variable name. For example, if we wanted to print the value stored at B, we would say

    50 PRINT B

If we wanted to print the three values stored at A, B, and C, we would use

    50 PRINT A, B, C

By use of the quotation symbol the programmer can cause headings, etc., to be printed with the report:

    15 PRINT "PROBLEM NUMBER ONE"

(*Note:* Some systems require the double quote mark as shown above, other systems use a single quote, and some will accept either as long as they are used in pairs.)

It is also possible to mix messages and numerical data, as the following example shows:

    27 PRINT "THE ANSWER IS", A1

If the current value of the variable A1 is 17, the whole message would be:

    THE ANSWER IS 17

At this time a question normally arises concerning the format of the output items. By means of the comma (,), the colon (:), and the semicolon (;), the programmer can control to a greater degree the format of the output.

On most systems, the output line on the terminal is divided into five print zones, spaced evenly across the page. Output starts at the left-most zone and the comma is a signal to the system to move the next output item to the next output zone. Unless otherwise specified, the end of a PRINT statement causes the terminal to go to the next line. Thus, if we want to print four values A, B, C, and D on the same line, the statement is:

    15 PRINT A, B, C, D

Although another method exists, the simplest way to get the output on four *separate* lines, is by means of four statements.

    10 PRINT A
    20 PRINT B
    30 PRINT C
    40 PRINT D

On many systems the semicolon is used to cause output data to be more tightly packed or spaced across the page. In effect, the semicolon overrides the normal spacing discussed in the preceding paragraph and causes tighter packing of output into a maximum of 12 print zones across the page. The statement

    10 PRINT A; B; C; D; E

would cause packed output of the variables A, B, C, and D.

Unfortunately, not all BASIC systems follow the pattern shown above. For some, the semicolon means that no spaces shall appear between the printed items. To get closer printing on these systems, the *colon* (:) is used to cause *one* space between the output items.

Assuming that we want to print just the identification number and the net pay figure, our PRINT statement would look like:

    60 PRINT I,N

The program at this point is

    10 LET I = 5683
    20 LET H = 40
    30 LET R = 8.75
    40 LET D = 39.57
    50 LET N = H * R - D
    60 PRINT I,N

One more statement is necessary to complete our example—an END statement.

THE END STATEMENT

On some systems the END statement must be the highest numbered statement in the program, as it tells the system when to stop during the execution of the program. Even if END is not required, it is good programming practice to use it anyway. The complete program is shown in Figure 12.1. Note that system command RUN is used right after the program was entered. RUN caused the system to begin execution of the program, beginning with statement 10 and continuing until the END statement was encountered.

THE REMARK STATEMENT

The programmer may insert remarks into a program at any time by use of the REM statement. These remarks will appear only when the program is LISTed; they have no effect on program logic and would not appear on a program flow chart. Note how they can be used in our program to provide documentation for the reader.

```
3 REM SAMPLE BASIC PROGRAM
5 REM USING LET
```

Another important use of the remark statement is to help define the names of the variables used. In long programs, or ones in which you have been interrupted during the programming process, it may be difficult to remember what the names represent.

```
6 REM I IS THE EMPLOYEE ID NUMBER
7 REM H IS THE WEEKLY HOURS WORKED
```

The judicious use of PRINT statements to output headings and other messages will make our program more meaningful and look better. A revised flow chart and program is shown in Figures 12.2 and 12.3.

FIGURE 12.1
Sample BASIC program.

```
10 LET I = 5683
20 LET H = 40
30 LET R = 8.75
40 LET D = 39.57
50 LET N = H*R-D
60 PRINT I,N
70 END

RUN

5683        310.43
```

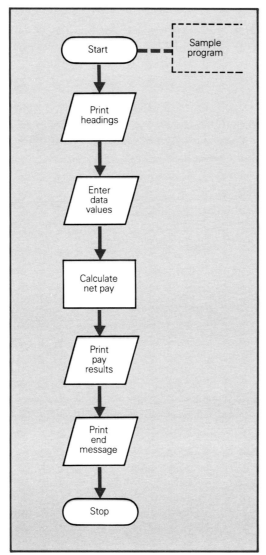

FIGURE 12.2
Flow chart: sample program.

THE INPUT STATEMENT

So far you have seen one way in which data can be entered into a program—by means of the LET statement. A second method is by means of the INPUT statement. It is often called an "interactive" statement because it allows the programmer to enter data values during the actual execution or running of the program. Suppose we change our sample program to enter the data values for the identification number, hours worked, rate of pay, and deductions via INPUT instead of LET statements. We will delete the four LET state-

```
10 REM SAMPLE BASIC PROGRAM
20 REM USING LET
30 PRINT "SAMPLE BASIC PROGRAM"
40 PRINT
50 PRINT "EMP ID","NET PAY"
60 PRINT
70 LET I = 5683
80 LET H = 40
90 LET R = 8.75
100 LET D = 39.57
110 LET N = H*R−D
120 PRINT I,N
130 PRINT
140 PRINT "END OF REPORT"
150 END

RUN

SAMPLE BASIC PROGRAM

EMP ID              NET PAY
5683                310.43

END OF REPORT
```

FIGURE 12.3
Sample program with REMARK.

ments (40, 50, 60, and 70) and insert

```
70 INPUT I,H,R,D
```

Upon reaching the INPUT statement, the terminal will type an exclamation mark (!) (some systems use the question mark (?) and await manual entry of four numbers representing the values of the variables I, H, R, and D. The programmer enters the appropriate values, separated by a comma, and then depresses the return key, which causes the computer to go on to the next statement in sequence. Entry of faulty data or too much data will cause an appropriate error message. Obviously, the INPUT statement is not designed for the easy entry of masses of data. It is particularly useful, however, when the programmer wants to enter data *during program execution* (Figure 12.4). Note that the output is not easily readable since the input values intrude into the middle of the output.

A better plan would be to INPUT the values before printing the headings. To do this, we would move the INPUT statement up between statements 20 and 30.

```
10 REM SAMPLE BASIC PROGRAM
20 REM USING INPUT
30 PRINT "SAMPLE BASIC PROGRAM"
40 PRINT
50 PRINT "EMP ID","NET PAY"
60 PRINT
70 INPUT I,H,R,D
110 LET N=H*R-D
120 PRINT I,N
130 PRINT
140 PRINT "END OF REPORT"
150 END

RUN

SAMPLE BASIC PROGRAM

EMP ID                  NET PAY

!5683,40,8.75,39.57
5683                    310.43

END OF REPORT
```

FIGURE 12.4
Sample program with INPUT

However, there is one more thing we should do. In any situation using INPUT, you would want to PRINT a message just before the INPUT statement in order to let the person at the terminal know what and how many values to enter. Even if you are the only person who will ever run the program, it is easy to forget just what the program needs, particularly if you haven't seen the program in a few days. So, we will revise our program by entering some extra PRINT statements prior to INPUT (Figure 12.5).

THE READ AND DATA STATEMENTS

A third method of entering data into the computer system is by means of a pair of statements: READ and DATA. In the READ statement the programmer assigns names to the incoming values contained in a DATA statement. We can further revise the original sample program that used LET by deleting lines 70 through 110 and inserting the following:

```
70 READ I, H, R, D
80 DATA 5683,40,8.75,39.57
```

```
10 REM SAMPLE BASIC PROGRAM
20 REM USING PRINT AND INPUT
30 PRINT "PLEASE ENTER THE EMPLOYEE ID NUMBER"
40 INPUT I
50 PRINT "ENTER THE NUMBER OF HOURS WORKED"
60 INPUT H
70 PRINT "ENTER THE RATE OF PAY"
80 INPUT R
90 PRINT "ENTER THE DEDUCTION AMOUNT"
100 INPUT D
110 LET N = H*R-D
120 PRINT
130 PRINT
140 PRINT "SAMPLE BASIC PROGRAM"
150 PRINT
160 PRINT "EMP ID", "NET PAY"
170 PRINT
180 PRINT I,N
190 PRINT
200 PRINT "END OF REPORT"
210 END
```

(a)

```
PLEASE ENTER THE EMPLOYEE ID NUMBER
!5683
ENTER THE NUMBER OF HOURS WORKED
!40
ENTER THE RATE OF PAY
!8.75
ENTER THE DEDUCTION AMOUNT
!39.57

SAMPLE BASIC PROGRAM

EMP ID                    NET PAY

5683                      310.43

END OF REPORT
```
(b)

FIGURE 12.5
(a) PRINT with INPUT. (b) Output from program execution.

Just as with the other examples, the value 5683 is stored in memory at a place called I, 40 is stored at H, and so on. Note that the individual data values are separated by commas. Although the example showed

READ and DATA as consecutive statements, it is not necessary to have them together. For example,

    70 READ I, H, R, D
       .
       .
       .
    800 DATA 5683,40,8.73,39.57

is valid and so is the following

    5 DATA 5683
      .
    30 DATA 40
      .
    70 READ I,H
    80 READ R,D
      .
      .
    250 DATA 8.75,39.57

It is important for the programmer to realize the manner in which the READ and DATA statements are handled by the processing system. Before the program is actually executed, the system takes the DATA statements, *in the order in which they appear in the program,* and places them in a special data area. Then, when the READ statement(s) is executed, the data items are pulled from the data area in consecutive order. Observe the following:

    10 READ G, X
      .
      .
    100 READ N1, A, Z3, C
    110 DATA 14, 3, 1.453, 96, 27
    120 DATA 73

Thus, the first READ statement stores the values 14 in G and 3 in X. The second READ statements stores the value 1.453 in N1 and so on through the data list. If the READ statement happens to ask for more data items than are available, the system will detect the lack of data, terminate the program, and print the message "OUT OF DATA IN XX", where XX represents the number of the READ statement.

DATA statements do not have to appear next to READ statements. Most programmers place all the DATA statements at the beginning or end of the program so as not to "cluster" the working or action part of

```
10 REM SAMPLE BASIC PROGRAM
20 REM USING READ AND DATA
30 PRINT "SAMPLE BASIC PROGRAM"
40 PRINT
50 PRINT "EMP ID","NET PAY"
60 PRINT
70 READ I,H,R,D
80 DATA 5683,40,8.75,39.57
110 LET N = H*R-D
120 PRINT I,N
130 PRINT
140 PRINT "END OF REPORT"
150 END

RUN

SAMPLE BASIC PROGRAM

EMP ID                NET PAY
5683                  310.43

END OF REPORT
```

FIGURE 12.6
Sample program with READ and DATA.

the problem. Figure 12.6 shows our same sample program using READ and DATA.

THE GO TO STATEMENT
Several different BASIC statements are available to the programmer to alter or change the straight sequential execution of program statements. By now it should be fairly obvious to you that the same program is hardly worth doing on a computer. Its purpose has been to serve as an example of the format and usage of several common BASIC statements. The real power of the computer comes in doing repetitive tasks. For example, our previous program would be much more useful if we could get it to loop back to the beginning and work with another record of data, and then another, etc. The GO TO statement is one of several that we can use to control the execution of specific blocks of code in the program. The statement shown below is extremely simple—it always causes a branch or jump or transfer of control to statement 60

GO TO 60   (most systems will also accept GOTO 60)

Using GO TO, it is possible to construct an effective but crude looping program. For example, a program to calculate and print the squares of four data values is shown below.

```
10 READ H
20 LET X = H * H
30 PRINT H, "SQUARED IS", X
40 GO TO 10
50 DATA 5,10,15,20
60 END
```

In this case, the loop is uncontrolled because it will never end naturally. Statement 40 always causes the system to go back to READ. Although four correct answers will be printed, the system can never get enough data. The first time the READ statement is executed, it reads the value 5 (the first value in the DATA statement) into memory area H. The answer is calculated and printed and the GO TO forces the system back to statement 10. When READ is executed the second time it takes the second value from the DATA statement, and so on until all the DATA values are used. When the system tries to read a data value the fifth time, the program will stop with a system error message that says "OUT OF DATA IN LINE 10". Note that there is no possible way for the system to reach the END statement (Figure 12.7).

FIGURE 12.7
Uncontrolled looping.

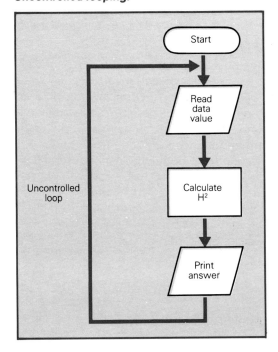

THE IF-THEN STATEMENT

Much more useful and versatile programs can be developed if the programmer can exercise greater control over the decision-making capabilities within the program. GO TO was unconditional, but the IF-THEN statement provides conditional control. The IF-THEN statement is actually a conditional GO TO statement; that is, the branch or transfer of control is executed only if a specific condition is met. The general form is

$$\text{IF} \begin{Bmatrix} \text{formula} \\ \text{constant} \end{Bmatrix} \text{relation} \begin{Bmatrix} \text{formula} \\ \text{constant} \end{Bmatrix} \text{THEN line number}$$

where formula can refer to a single variable or to a complex arithmetic operation, "constant" can be an actual value, and "relation" refers to a test condition. Some systems use the form that requires THEN followed by the word GO TO and the statement number; other systems allow some leeway in the formation of the statement. For example,

10 IF H = 0 THEN 23 15 _____	(If the variable H is equal to zero, the program branches to line 23; otherwise it proceeds to the next statement in sequence.)
20 IF A4 > = Z THEN 140 30 _____	(If the variable A4 is greater than or equal to Z, the program branches to line 140; otherwise it proceeds to the next statement in sequence.)
30 IF ((A/B) ↑ C) > ((C + D) – B) THEN 105 40 _____	(If the formula on the left of the relational symbol is greater than the formula on the right, the program branches to line 105; otherwise it proceeds to the next statement in sequence.)

Note the following example which is *logically incorrect!*

50 IF H = 3 THEN 60 60 _____	(If H is equal to 3, the program branches to statement 60. If H is not equal to 3, the program goes to the next statement in sequence, which happens to be 60.)

How can we use the IF-THEN statement to control the action of a program? Suppose we have the following problem. The manager of a store wishes to have a listing of those employees who worked over 40 hours last week. Those that worked 40 *or fewer* hours are not to be listed. An IF-THEN statement can be used to test for this condition and to bypass a PRINT statement when printing is not required. The flow

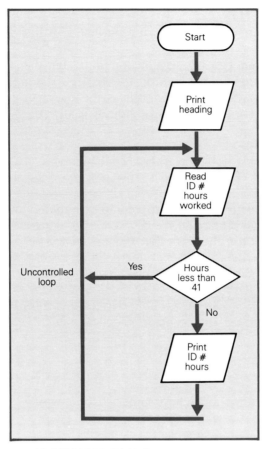

```
10 REM HOURS WORKED PROGRAM
20 REM CONTROLLED LOOP
30 PRINT "ID#","HOURS"
40 PRINT
50 READ I,H
55 IF I = 9999 THEN 140
60 IF H<41 THEN 50
70 PRINT I,H
80 GOTO 50
90 DATA 1234,36
100 DATA 5678,43
110 DATA 6641,40
120 DATA 8905,41
130 DATA 9999,99
140 PRINT "END OF PROGRAM"
150 END

RUN
```

FIGURE 12.8

IF-THEN testing.   (*Continued*)

ID#	HOURS
5678	43
8905	41
END OF PROGRAM	

FIGURE 12.8 (Continued)

chart and program are shown in Figure 12.8. Note that the test condition is shown by the diamond-shaped symbol and that there are always two exits from that block—the True (or Yes) side and the False (or No) side.

The output shows that although we have controlled the execution or nonexecution of the PRINT statement by means of the IF-THEN test, we have not controlled the program looping action.

The difficulty with our Hours Listing program is that we have no way to end the loop properly, since we don't know how many data records there are to be processed. This is not an exceptional case—it is more likely the rule than the exception, since the programmer seldom knows the number of data records that will be read during any particular running of the program. To get around this difficulty a common programming technique is to place a *flag* value or *dummy* value immediately after the last valid data record. This dummy value is usually some easily recognizable number (such as all 9's or all 0's) that *cannot* ever be a valid data item.

Figure 12.9 shows our revised Hours Listing program with the addition of an extra DATA statement and another IF-THEN.

Study the program and flow chart carefully because even though it is simple it contains some very important ideas.

1. An extra DATA statement was added that contained dummy or flag values for *both* fields of the record. If we had not done so, the last time the READ I, H statement was executed it would not have found a data value to satisfy H. At that point we would again have gotten the OUT OF DATA message. Try it on your machine to be certain you understand how it works. Also, if you think about it for a minute, there is another way of getting around the problem, even if you do have only one flag value rather than two.
2. Note that the test for the last item was made at the top of the program, *immediately* after the READ statement. Make sure you understand why it was put there and not down at the bottom of the program.
3. Testing of H for less than 41 was done on the assumption that hours worked would never be a fractional value. If fractional hours had been permitted, the test IF H>40 THEN would have been a better choice.

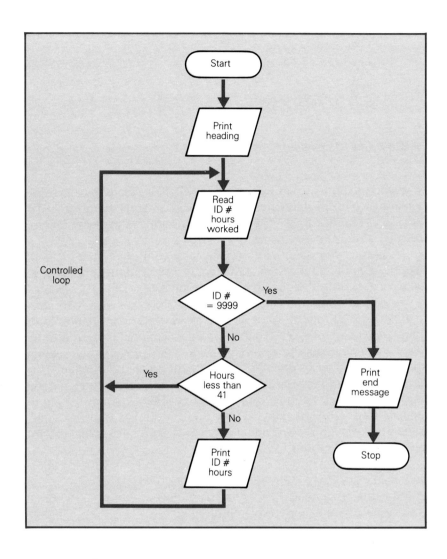

```
10 REM HOURS-WORKED PROGRÄM
20 REM UNCONTROLLED LOOP
30 PRINT "ID#","HOURS"
40 PRINT
50 READ I,H
60 IF H<41 THEN 50
70 PRINT I,H
80 GO TO 50
90 DATA 1234,36
100 DATA 5678,43
110 DATA 6641,40
```

FIGURE 12.9
A controlled loop: last-item testing.   (*Continued*)

```
120 DATA 8905,41
130 END

RUN

ID#                  HOURS

5678                 43
8905                 41

OUT OF DATA IN LINE 50
```

FIGURE 12.9 (Continued)

PROGRAM "BUGS"

Captain Grace Hopper has participated in many notable "firsts" during her long years of work in the data processing industry. Perhaps one of the most interesting of these firsts had to do with the origin of the term "program bug" of "debugging." As she states it, "In 1945, while working in a World War I-vintage non-air-conditioned building on a hot, humid summer day, the computer stopped. We searched for the problem and found a failing relay—one of the big signal relays," she recalled.

"Inside, we found a moth that had been beaten to death. We pulled it out with tweezers and taped it to the log book," Hopper continued. "From then on, when the officer came in to ask if we were accomplishing anything, we told him we were 'debugging' the computer."

(Source: *Computerworld*, November 16, 1981.)

LOOPING AND COUNTERS

As you well know, the power of the computer lies in its ability to loop through or perform a series of instructions over and over again. The programmer must use some technique to control the looping process so that he or she can go through a program loop an exact number of times. The simplest technique is that of a counter, wherein the computer is programmed to add 1 to a counter each time the loop has been completed. Then, when the counter has reached the maximum permitted value, the programmer forces the computer out of the loop into another part of the program. (*Note:* Another term for this repetitive process is *iteration*).

Suppose we wish to read in a numeric value, square the number, take the square root of the number, print the answers, and do this repetitive operation exactly eight times. We will use a counter to count the number of iterations and the IF-THEN statement to test the counter and branch into or out of the loop. Whenever you use a counter, four distinct steps are required.

1. Set up the counter.
2. Increment or modify the counter, usually after one execution of the loop.
3. Test the counter.
4. Take action as a result of the test.

Figure 12.10 and 12.11 show the flow chart and a program that is controlled by a counter.

Note that the counter must be created before entering the program loop. If you were to create it within the loop, the counter would be set back to zero each time. If you have any doubts about how this works, run this program and try moving the LET K = 0 statement to different positions.

In programming it is often necessary to set a number of variables to zero (or any other quantity for that matter), such as shown here.

```
20 LET T1 = 0
30 LET T2 = 0
40 LET R = 0
```

In some systems this can be done with a single LET statement that sets all the variables to the same value.

```
20 LET T1 = T2 = R = 0
```

or

```
20 LET T1,T2,R=0
```

As you already know, in the LET statement the equal sign has a meaning that is different from ordinary arithmetic. Here it means "be made equal to" or "be replaced by." The statement

```
50 LET Q = G * 4 - A
```

is read as "Let Q be made equal to the sum of G multiplied by 4 minus A." With this definition of the equal sign, the LET statement can be used for a variety of purposes. In statement 110 we used it as a counting device to keep track of the number of times an event had taken place. The statement

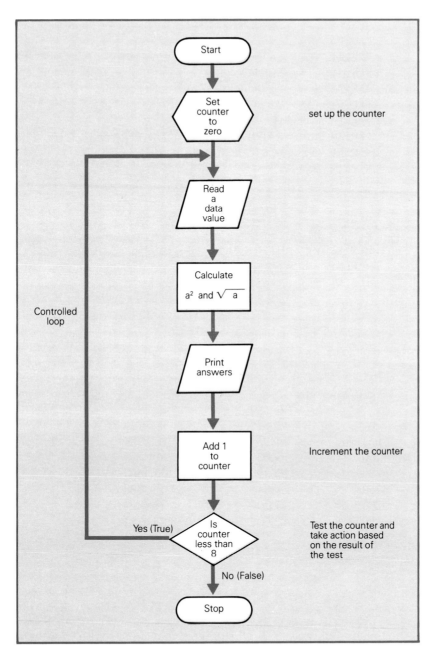

FIGURE 12.10
Using a counter to control a loop.

      LET K = K + 1

says "Let the new value of K be made equal to the old value of K plus
1." The statement, in effect, adds to the counter by ones.

```
10 REM              LOOPING EXAMPLE USING A COUNTER
20 LET K = 0
30 REM              COUNTER K HAS NOW BEEN
40 REM              SET TO ZERO
50 READ A
60 LET B = A↑   2
70 LET C = A↑   .5
80 REM              RAISING TO THE .5 POWER TAKES THE
90 REM              SQUARE ROOT OF A NUMBER
100 PRINT A,B,C
110 LET K = K + 1
120 REM             THIS ADDS ONE TO THE OLD
130 REM             VALUE OF THE COUNTER K
140 IF K<8 THEN 50
150 REM             IF THE COUNTER K IS LESS
160 REM             THAN 8, THE SYSTEM WILL GO
170 REM             TO THE READ STATEMENT
180 REM             OTHERWISE IT WILL GO DOWN
190 REM             TO THE NEXT EXECUTABLE STATEMENT
200 DATA 4,20,67,100,125,152,200,250
210 END

RUN
```

4	16	2.
20	400	4.47214
67	4489	8.18535
100	10000	10.
125	15625	11.1803
152	23104	12.3288
200	40000	14.1421
250	62500	15.8114

FIGURE 12.11
Using a counter.

In the example just shown the programmer chose to use "less than" logic. It is also possible to use "equal" logic with the same program, but testing in this manner requires an extra statement (statement 145). Figure 12.12 shows the revised program.

To emphasize the point that it is the programmer who controls the looping process correctly, consider another possibility. There is no ironclad rule that says that you must test at the bottom of the loop; it is equally correct to test at the top of the loop, as Figures 12.13 and 12.14 indicate.

```
10 REM     LOOPING EXAMPLE USING A COUNTER
20 LET K = 0
30 REM     THE COUNTER K HAS NOW BEEN
40 REM     SET TO ZERO
50 READ A
60 LET B = A↑    2
70 LET C-A↑   .5
80 REM     RAISING TO THE .5 POWER TAKES THE
90 REM     SQUARE ROOT OF A NUMBER
100 PRINT A,B,C
110 LET K = K + 1
120 REM     THIS ADDS ONE TO THE OLD
130 REM     VALUE OF THE COUNTER K
140 IF K = 8 THEN 210
145 GOTO 50
150 REM     IF THE COUNTER K IS EQUAL
160 REM     TO 8, THE SYSTEM WILL GO
170 REM     TO THE END OF THE PROGRAM
180 REM     OTHERWISE THE NEXT STATEMENT
190 REM     WILL SEND IT BACK UP TO "READ"
200 DATA    4,20,67,100,125, 152,200,250
210 END
```

RUN

4	16	2.
20	400	4.47214
67	4489	8.18535
100	10000	10.
125	15625	11.1803
152	23104	12.3288
200	40000.	14.1421
250	62500.	15.8114

DONE

FIGURE 12.12
Looping with "equal" logic.

USING COUNTERS

In previous programs we added 1 to the counter each time through the loop because we wanted a simple count of the number of loop executions or iterations. However, counters may be used for a variety of purposes, limited only by the imagination of the programmer. We do not always have to use the value 1; we can add by any value that is

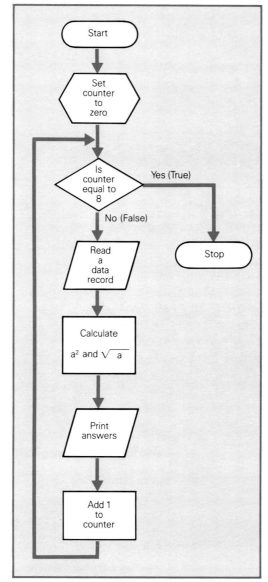

FIGURE 12.13
Test at the top of the loop.

convenient or necessary to the program. The statement

LET K = K + 2

simply adds to the counter by twos. Since the IF statement works this way with actual values (sometimes called "literals"), such as 1 and 2, then it must work the same way to allow us to accumulate a running total of *unknown* values. For example, suppose at the end of the program we wish to print the total of all the values that have been

```
10 REM     LOOPING EXAMPLE USING A COUNTER
20 LET K = 0
30 REM     THE COUNTER K HAS NOW BEEN
40 REM     SET TO ZERO
50 IF K = 8 THEN 210
60 REM     IF THE COUNTER K IS EQUAL
70 REM     TO 8, THE SYSTEM WILL GO
80 REM     TO THE END OF THE PROGRAM
90 REM     OTHERWISE IT WILL GO DOWN TO
100 REM    THE NEXT EXECUTABLE STATEMENT
110 READ A
120 LET B = A ↑ 2
130 LET C = A ↑ .5
140 REM     RAISING TO THE .5 POWER TAKES THE
150 REM     SQUARE ROOT OF A NUMBER
160 PRINT A,B,C
170 LET K = K + 1
180 REM     THIS ADDS ONE TO THE OLD
190 REM     VALUE OF THE COUNTER K
200 GOTO 50
200 DATA 4,20,67,100,125,152,200,250
210 END

RUN
```

4	16	2.
20	400	4.47214
67	4489	8.18535
100	10000	10.
125	15625	11.1803
152	23104	12.3288
250	40000.	14.1421
150	62500.	15.8114

DONE

FIGURE 12.14

Testing at the top of the loop.

stored in R during the looping process. An outline of the process is shown below.

```
  20 LET T = 0            This creates our total area
 100 READ R, X
     IF X = 9999 THEN 500
        .
        .
```

```
          .
190 LET R = _____          Calculates and stores a value in R
250 LET T = T + R                Adds the current value in R to the
          .                      value that is in T
          .
          .
    GO TO 100
500 _____
    _____

540 PRINT "THE TOTAL IS", T
    END
```

Statement 200 says, "let the new value in T be replaced by the old value in T plus the current value in R." If we were to go through the loop three times, a schematic of the operation would look as follows.

	Value in R	Value in T	
Statement 20	—	0	Creates the counter
Statement 190	45		Assume R is 45
Statement 200	45	45	45 is added to the current value in T
Statement 190	110	45	Assume R is 110
Statement 200	110	155	110 is added to the current value in T
Statement 190	50	155	Assume R is 50
Statement 200	50	205	50 is added to the current value in T

Statement 540 prints

THE TOTAL IS 205

We can now use this knowledge of how counters work by setting up the following program. Suppose we have an unknown number of student grade-point averages and we wish to total these and divide by the number of items to get an overall average. We will use the last-value flag of all 9's to get out of the program loop. Two counters will be necessary: one to keep a running total of the grade averages, and one to keep a count of the number of records processed. Then, after exiting from the read-process loop we will divide the total grade-point average by the number of records processed to get the average grade per student (Figures 12.15 and 12.16).

The value of the counter may itself be used in computations within the program. Figure 12.17 illustrates this use of counters, but note that, even though the counters value is *used* within the loop, its value is not changed until the programmer is ready to start the next cycle.

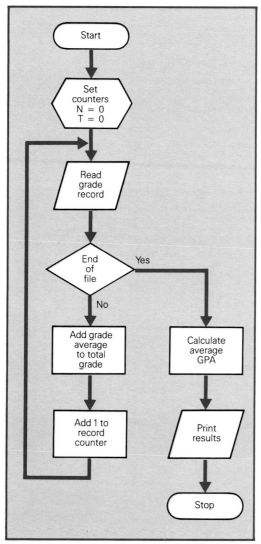

FIGURE 12.15
Using multiple counters.

SUMMARY OF
IMPORTANT POINTS

☐ BASIC was originally developed as a language for use on time-sharing systems, but has become a popular language on microcomputer systems.

☐ The BASIC language is not standardized, which means that a program written on one computer is not likely to run on a different computer without considerable modification.

```
10 REM     PROGRAM TO CALCULATE
20 REM     THE AVERAGE GPA
30 LET N = 0
40 REM     N WILL COUNT THE NUMBER
50 REM     OF RECORDS PROCESSED
60 LET T = 0
70 REM     T  WILL TOTAL THE GRADE
80 REM     POINT AVERAGES
90 READ G
100 IF G = 9.99 THEN 180
110 LET T = T + G
120 REM     STATEMENT 110 AD ¯S TO OUR
130 REM     RUNNING TOTAL OF GRADE AVERAGES
140 LET N = N + 1
150 REM     STATEMENT 140 ADDS TO THE
160 REM     TOTAL OF RECORDS PROCESSED
170 GOTO 90
180 LET A = T/N
190 PRINT "AVG GRADE AVERAGE IS",A
200 PRINT N,"GRADES PROCESSED"
210 DATA 3.56,1.42,4,2.85,9.99
220 END

RUN

AVG GRADE AVERAGE IS          2.9575
4                GRADES PROCESSED

DONE
```

FIGURE 12.16

Using multiple counters.

☐   BASIC is also an unstructured language, although newer versions will have more and more structured formats.

☐   System commands are never numbered; program statements are always numbered.

☐   The LET statement can be used to create values outright or to initiate any and all arithmetic operations.

☐   END normally is the highest numbered statement in a program.

☐   The programmer may use as many of the statements that he or she wishes in a program, with the exception of END.

☐   The INPUT statement is used to enter data values during the execution or running of the program and should be preceded by the PRINT statement.

```
10 REM    USING THE COUNTER VALUE
20 REM    FOR CALCULATIONS
30 PRINT "X","X/10","X/100","X/1000"
40 PRINT
50 LET X = 1
60 IF X = 11 THEN 130
70 LET R = X/10
80 LET Y = X/100
90 LET Z = X/1000
100 PRINT X,R,Y,Z
110 LET X = X + 1
120 GOTO 60
130 PRINT "END OF PROGRAM"
140 END

RUN
```

X	X/10	X/100	X/1000
1	.1	.01	.001
2	.2	.02	.002
3	.3	.03	.003
4	.4	.04	.004
5	.5	.05	.005
6	.6	.06	.006
7	.7	.07	.007
8	.8	.08	.008
9	.9	.09	.009
10	1	.1	.01

END OF PROGRAM

DONE

FIGURE 12.17
Using the counter value in calculations.

☐ READ and DATA are always tied together by the action of the BASIC software.

☐ When the READ statement is executed the system automatically starts to use the values from DATA statements, from top to bottom, in the program in the order in which they are encountered. It is the responsibility of the programmer to make sure the READ variables and the data values match during the data entry process. Arithmetic operations are performed in accordance with an arithmetic hierarchy or order of operations.

☐ The GO TO is an unconditional branch statement.

☐   IF-THEN is a conditional branch statement in which the results of a test are determined to be either true or false.

☐   The real value of a computer program is its ability to perform repetitive tasks and to execute or not execute sections of code, depending upon specific conditions.

☐   A counter was presented as a mechanism to control the number of times a section of code was executed. In using a counter, four steps are always required
(a)   Set up the counter.
(b)   Increment the counter.
(c)   Test the counter.
(d)   Take action as a result of the test.

☐   It was also shown that a counter can be used as an accumulator of values.

GLOSSARY OF TERMS

Branch—the act of causing control to be shifted to another part of the program. The GO TO and IF-THEN statements are branch-type statements.

Constant—a value that does not change during the execution of the program.

Controlled loop—as opposed to an uncontrolled loop, a controlled program loop executes a specific section of code in accordance with programmed instructions.

Iterations—repetitions or repeated execution of blocks of code.

Uncontrolled loop—a program loop that does not reach a logical end.

Variable—as opposed to a constant, a variable is a value that does change during the execution of the program.

THOUGHT QUESTIONS

1.   Explain in detail how the BASIC software links together the DATA values with the variables from the READ statement.
2.   Describe and show an example of the LET statement in the following situations:
     Setting a variable to specific value.
     Setting a variable to an unknown value.
     Moving a value from one place to another.
3.   Explain in detail the action of the BASIC software in the following statement:

     LET Q = $((X+Y)-(N-3.6))/(X-Y)$

4.   Explain why the following statement is syntactically correct yet illogical:

     50 IF L = B THEN GOTO 60
     60 _____

5.   List three occasions or program applications in which the use of the INPUT statement is vital to the operation of the program.

6.   How does a loop iteration counter differ from an accumulator?

BASIC PROBLEMS

1. Using LET, create any five values of your choice, add the values together, and calculate the average. Output is to appear as follows:

> TOTAL IS _____
> THE AVERAGE IS _____
> PROGRAMMED BY _____

2. The formula for the volume of a box is height times width times length. Write a program that READs in three data values (height, width, length), calculates the volume, and prints out the answer. Then your program is to consider three more values and again print out the answer. Output is shown below.

> THE VOLUME OF THE FIRST BOX IS
>
> _____
>
> THE VOLUME OF THE SECOND BOX
> IS _____
>
> (your name and class section)

3. Revise the previous program to use INPUT in place of READ and DATA.

4. The formula to convert temperature expressed in degrees Fahrenheit to degrees Celsius is $°C = 5/9(°F-32)$. Write a program that READs in a value for F, calculates the Celsius value, and prints the answer. Assume you have four DATA values for degrees Fahrenheit: 85, 38, 61, and 99. Use a counter and IF statement to control the program loop. Output format is shown below

FAHRENHEIT	CELSIUS
85	_____
38	_____
61	_____
99	_____

END OF PROGRAM

5. The formula for calculating the length of side C on a right triangle is $C = \sqrt{A^2 + B^2}$.

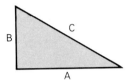

Knowing that you have three records of data, write a program that calculates C for each set of data values. The loop is to be controlled by a counter and an IF statement. Output will be

A	B	C
19	11	_____
25	14	_____
7.3	12.4	_____

END OF CALCULATIONS

6. Management has granted an 8% pay increase to all three of our employees. Write a program that uses a counter and an IF statement to control the loop and that INPUTs the employee identification number and old rate of pay. Data values are: 1234, 7.50, 4567, 6.95, 5678, 10.00. Output for each data record is shown below:

> EMPLOYEE NUMBER _____
> OLD PAY RATE WAS _____
> NEW PAY RATE IS _____

7. Six employees work for our firm and are paid weekly. The data on the employees is given as follows:

Employee Number	Rate of Pay	Hours Worked	Deductions
0503	6.58	40	28.55
0862	5.95	40	32.75
1134	7.00	38	36.27
2068	8.79	41	45.62
4013	7.50	42	41.85
3896	4.90	40	36.22

Write a program that reads a data record and calculates both the gross and net pay amounts. Use a counter and an IF statement to control the loop. Output is shown below

ABC COMPANY

Employee Number	Gross Pay	Deductions Amount	Net Pay
____	____	____	____
____	____	____	____

Etc.

PROGRAMMED BY _____

8. Modify the previous problem by setting up a seventh data record that contains all 9's in each data field. Then, test for all 9's to get out of the read-calculate-print loop.

9. Modify problem 7 to provide for time-and-a-half pay for hours worked in excess of 40. The output format will be the same.

10. Modify problem 9 to print totals of the gross pay, deductions, and net pay amounts at the end of the program.

11. Further modify problem 10 by checking the accuracy of the totals you calculated. If the total deduction and total net pay amounts differ from the total gross pay amount by more than 5 cents, print an appropriate error message. If the answers are within this range, print the message TOTALS ARE OK.

12. Depreciation on capital items, such as machinery, is calculated by the formula

$$\text{Yearly depreciation} = \frac{\text{original cost} - \text{scrap value}}{\text{useful life}}$$

Using the formula, calculate the yearly depreciation for each item and print as shown below.

DEPRECIATION SCHEDULE

ITEM NUMBER	ORIGINAL COST	YEARLY DEPRECIATION
____	____	____
____	____	____
____	____	____

TOTAL COST _____
TOTAL DEPRECIATION _____
DATA 0713,1000,3,200 (Item #, Original Cost, Useful Life, Scrap Value)
DATA 5167,1500,7,400
DATA 6666,975,2,150
DATA 7777,500,4,100

13. Data records concerning the five loans made by our company have the following format.

Loan #	Principal	Int. Rate	Time in days	Class of loan	
567	15000	.085	365	2	Example

Write a program based on the information below:

a. Headings are required, as shown on the output format.
b. Use a counter and an IF statement to control the program loop, knowing that you have five records of data.

c. Interest is calculated by using the formula

$$I = \frac{\text{principal} \times \text{rate} \times \text{time}}{360}$$

d. Keep a running total of the interest and principal amounts, and print them at the end of the program.

e. Your program is to test to see if the time is over 360 days or if the loan is a class-3 loan. If either condition exists, do not add to the totals and do not print anything for that record. In other words, under either of the above conditions, you are to ignore that record and go on to another record of data.

f. Output format is to be as shown below.

LOAN NUMBER	RATE	CLASS	INTEREST
————	————	————	————
————	————	————	————

TOTAL INTEREST _____
TOTAL PRINCIPAL _____

DATA is shown below.

663	35000	.115	90	1
781	10000	.145	180	3
859	5000	.105	30	1
941	7500	.165	500	2
988	9000	.12	30	3

CHAPTER 13
BASIC PROGRAMMING: PART II

LEARNING OBJECTIVES

Upon completion of the chapter you should understand the following:

The handling of program loops by means of FOR-NEXT statements.

The power and flexibility of FOR-NEXT statements, especially when variables are used instead of constant values.

The use of PRINT as a computational statement and how special PRINT functions, such as TAB, permit better looking output.

The capabilities and limitations of string data; how string fields are created, stored, and manipulated.

The nature of data files; how they are accessed and how to exit from a loop using files.

The makeup of tables of data and why tables are necessary in some problems; how data is loaded into tables and how the subscript is manipulated to access table elements.

How and why the STOP and RESTORE statements are used; how the computed GO TO statement can save time and programming steps; how GOSUB and RETURN are used with repeated segments of code.

How PRINT USING can give formatted output.

What E notation, or scientific notation, is and how to convert regular numbers to and from this format.

The need for and use of functions in programming.

The use of special matrix or MAT statements that can perform operations on entire tables with a single instruction.

CHAPTER CONTENTS

The previous chapter covered some of the most commonly used statements in BASIC. Although each statement was simple in its format, they can be strung together in an endless variety of ways to solve some very sophisticated problems. The limiting factor is not the statements themselves. Rather, it is the programmer's inability to see how combinations of statements can be used in individual situations. Once more, you are cautioned to remember that each computer system is different and the exact requirements of the terminal *and* the language must be learned thoroughly.

   The following pages will present a few new statements plus variations on some that you have already learned. Even so, it is not possible to list all the combinations and uses of every statement that is available in BASIC. If you are really serious about learning BASIC programming, plan your programs thoroughly by means of flow charts, pseudocode, or other methods. Test your knowledge by working on the terminal and trying various combinations of statements until you are satisfied as to exactly how each works.

THE FOR-NEXT
STATEMENTS

The FOR-NEXT statements offer the programmer another way to control program looping. In previous examples using IF-THEN and a counter you saw that four distinct steps were required in controlling a program loop.

1. Set up the counter   (LET)
2. Increment the counter   (LET)
3. Test the counter   ⎫
4. Branch as a result of the test ⎭   (IF-THEN)

The FOR-NEXT pair of statements does all these operations by means of two easy statements. Remember the looping program we had earlier? It was controlled by the counter K and an IF statement and looked like this (with the extra statements removed)

```
    10 LET K = 0
┌─► 20 READ A
│   30 LET B = A ↑ 2
│   40 LET C = A ↑ .5
│   50 PRINT A,B,C
│   60 LET K = K + 1
└── 70 IF K < 8 THEN 20
    80 DATA 4,20,67,100,125,152,200,250
    90 END
```

The same program using FOR-NEXT is shown below.

```
    10 FOR K = 1 TO 10
┌─► 20 READ A
│   30 LET B = A ↑ 2
│   40 LET C = A ↑ .5
│   50 PRINT A,B,C
│   60 NEXT K
└── 70 DATA 4,20,67,100,125,152,200,250
    80 END
```

Note the power of this pair of statements. Upon seeing the FOR statement, the system sets the counter K to 1 and then constructs a program loop that extends down to and including the NEXT statement (line 60). When the NEXT statement is reached, K is automatically incremented by 1. As long as the value of K does not exceed 8, the program branches to statement 20. Eventually, K will reach 9 and, instead of branching, the program will go on to the next statement in sequence (END).

Certain logical rules must be followed with FOR-NEXT statements. First, they are always used together—they cannot be used alone. Second, any variable may be used (K was used in the example above), but whatever variable is used with FOR must also be used with NEXT. Also, FOR-NEXT loops cannot be entered from the outside, as this would negate the original purpose of the loop.

```
  ┌─► 80 GO TO 120
  │    90 _____
  │   100 _____
  │   110 FOR Z = 1 TO 20
  └─► 120 LET _____
          _____
          _____
```

Unless specified otherwise, the counter is automatically incremented by 1. On those occasions when the programmer wishes to increment the variable by some value other than 1, the STEP option may be used.

```
15 FOR H = 1 TO 11 STEP 2
   _____
   _____
   _____
   _____
30 NEXT H
```

In this case, the beginning value of H is 1 and, when the program reaches line 30, the NEXT statement will cause the variable H to be increased by 2. Looping will continue to the largest value of H that does not exceed 11. Note the use of the NEXT statement to cause the program to print all odd numbers from 1 to 100:

```
10 FOR X = 1 TO 100 STEP 2
20 PRINT X
30 NEXT X
40 END
```

How do you flowchart a FOR-NEXT loop? Unfortunately, there is no one established way. We could use

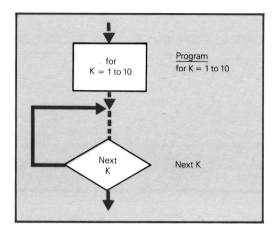

but it has several drawbacks even though it does show correctly that the return is to the statement immediately below FOR. First, it violates the general (although not always followed) rule of flowcharting that the flow chart should not contain actual program statements. In theory, a logic diagram should be independent of the language that is used. A second difficulty with the diagram is that it doesn't show that the counter was incremented, or by what value it was incremented, nor does it show the condition under which the loop was perpetuated. A better approach is shown below using the preparation symbol.

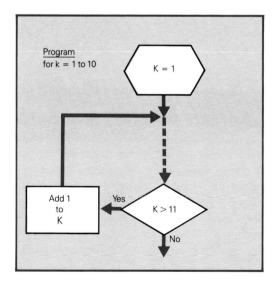

This method not only shows the action of establishing the counter but shows the testing and incrementing steps as well. It also makes it easy to show increments (STEP) other than 1.

All previous looping programs (IF-THEN or FOR-NEXT) that have been shown were based on the premise that we knew exactly how many times the loop was to be executed. Because of this knowledge, we were able to write.

```
LET K = 0                          FOR K = 1 TO 10
     .                                     .
     .                                     .
     .                                     .
LET K = K + 1
IF K < 10 THEN ────               NEXT K
```

What happens, however, when the programmer doesn't know the number of iterations the loop will require until just before the program is to be run? This is a common problem and the way to handle it is to use a variable instead of an actual value to test against. The use of variables becomes an extremely valuable programming tool that adds versatility to programs. As you saw from the previous chapter, the statement that helps us here is INPUT. An INPUT statement placed at the beginning of the program allows us to enter the number of times the loop is to be executed. Note that it works equally well for both IF-THEN and FOR-NEXT loops.

```
INPUT M                            INPUT M
LET K = 0                          FOR K = 1 TO M
     .                                     .
     .                                     .
     .                                     .
LET K = K + 1
IF K < M THEN ────                NEXT K
```

Figure 13.1 illustrates how this works in a program that prints the values from 1 to M.

By now you should be convinced of the simplicity of the FOR-NEXT statements and the ease with which they are used to control program loops. Another possibility in looping is that of having loops within loops or FOR-NEXTs within other FOR-NEXTs. This stacking of FOR-NEXT statements is known as *nesting*.

A common use of this nesting principle is in the printing of mailing labels. Each year department stores normally have several special mailings of advertising material to charge account customers. The appropriate number of mailing labels for these customers can be printed in one run on the computer. The following partial program illustrates the printing of four labels each for 500 customers.

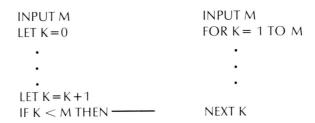

```
180 _____
190 _____
```

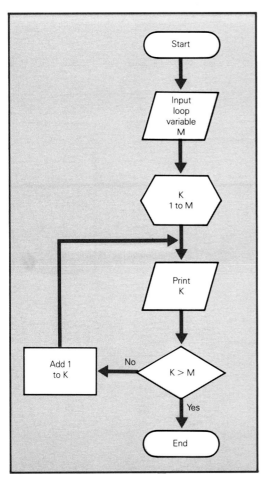

FIGURE 13.1
Executing a loop a variable number of times.

```
200 FOR K = 1 TO 500
210 READ (Customer data)
220 FOR W = 1 TO 4
230 PRINT (mailing label data)
240 NEXT W
250 NEXT K
260 _____
270 _____
```

Several points are worth noting. The outer loop (K = 1 TO 500) gets executed 500 times. The inner loop, however, actually ends up being executed 2000 times (4 times 500). Each time the program progresses down to statement 220 it must go through the inner loop four times before being able to continue.

Certain nesting combinations are illegal, as shown in the following examples.

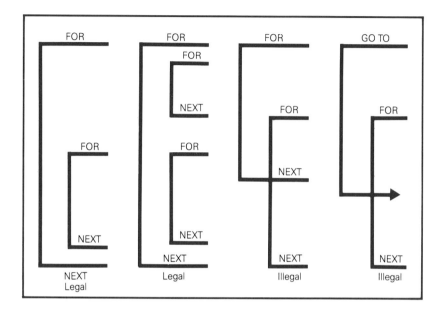

It is permissible to exit from a FOR-NEXT loop and return to it, but it is better to stay within the loop the whole time.

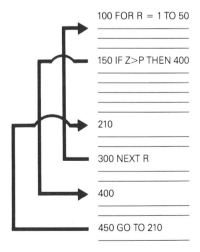

a better arrangement is shown here.

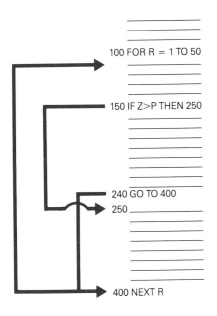

An important consideration is to be sure that the program always returns to the NEXT statement so that the loop is completed correctly.

Figure 13.2 shows an example of nested FOR-NEXT loops to construct a simple multiplication table.

MORE ABOUT PRINT

Earlier you saw a program that illustrated the use of the counter value in a loop. In that case, the counter value was used to do calculations.

```
40 LET X = 1
50 IF X = 11 THEN 120
60 LET R = X/10
70 LET Y = X/100
80 LET Z = X/1000
90 PRINT X, R, Y, Z
100 LET X = X + 1
110 GO TO 50
```

Statements 60, 70, and 80 cause the machine to calculate and store answers at R, Y, and Z. These answers are available for further

```
10 REM USING NESTED LOOPS TO
20 REM CONSTRUCT A MULTIPLICATION TABLE
30 FOR K = 1 TO 3
40 FOR L = 1 TO 5
50 LET X = K*L
60 PRINT K:"TIMES":L:" = ":X
70 NEXT L
80 NEXT K
90 END

RUN

1 TIMES 1 = 1
1 TIMES 2 = 2
1 TIMES 3 = 3
1 TIMES 4 = 4
1 TIMES 5 = 5
2 TIMES 1 = 2
2 TIMES 2 = 4
2 TIMES 3 = 6
2 TIMES 4 = 8
2 TIMES 5 = 10
3 TIMES 1 = 3
3 TIMES 2 = 6
3 TIMES 3 = 9
3 TIMES 4 = 12
3 TIMES 5 = 15

DONE
```

FIGURE 13.2
Nested FOR-NEXT statements.

processing, printing, or whatever the programmer wishes. It is possible, however, to get the PRINT statement to act as a combination of PRINT and LET. The results of statements 60 through 80 can be accomplished in a single statement:

PRINT X, X/10, X/100, X/1000

It is important to realize that, although the printed results are the same, the action of the system is very different. In the latter case, the machine calculates the answers and holds them only long enough to be printed. After that, the results of the calculations are lost and cannot be used in further manipulations. Also, the system is not limited to the simple calculations shown above, as complex calculations of all types can be performed.

PROGRAM LOOPS: LADY LOVELACE

You may remember from Chapter 2 that in the 1830s, Charles Babbage, an English mathematical genius, envisioned a new kind of calculating machine that he called the analytical engine. His machine differed from previous calculators in that it would perform all types of mathematical calculations that could be combined to solve any type of problem. The analytical engine, of course, contained the essential components of the modern computer. Control of the system was to be contained in punched cards that specified the operations to be performed and the address of that instruction. Perhaps most important, his machine was to have the ability to make conditional branches within the program.

Many of his writings were interpreted and expanded by his friend, Lady Ada Augusta Lovelace, daughter of the famous poet, Lord Bryon. A mathematical genius in her own right (in a time when women were not expected to excel in such areas), she mastered his plans to the point of even correcting some errors in his work.

One of her most important ideas was that of recognizing that the same sequence of instructions might have to be repeated many times within the program and that it would be possible to plan for this within the program. Thus, she not only originated the idea of program loops but is considered to have been the world's first programmer.

Her name lives on today in the new Department of Defense sponsored programming language called Ada. (Source: *Computerworld,* July 27, 1981.)

PRINTING FUNCTIONS: TAB, LIN, SPA

The BASIC language supports a wide range of utility and mathematical *functions* that are extremely useful to the programmer. By definition, a function is a prewritten set of statements that perform specific tasks or program operations. Three of these utility functions are available to help the programmer achieve more controlled printed output.

The TAB function tabulates the output device to a specified column before printing the next item.

Example:

    50 PRINT TAB(10);R

Tabulates to the tenth printing position before printing R.

    200 PRINT TAB(5);Z; TAB(50); "END"

Tabulates to the fifth printing position and then to the fiftieth position after printing Z.

The next two PRINT functions, LIN and SPA, are not used as universally as TAB—check your machine to be sure.

The LIN function skips lines down the page before printing the next item.

Example:

        250 PRINT LIN(3)
        260 PRINT B

If the value within parentheses is zero, only a carriage return is generated. If it is less than zero, no carriage return takes place.

LIN can be used with variables in a PRINT statement to simplify the process

        250 PRINT LIN(3); B

The SPA function skips spaces before printing the next item.

Example:

        200 PRINT "THE ANSWER IS"; SPA(10);G

These PRINT functions may be combined to provide more precise output than can be obtained with just the comma and semicolon. However, all print operations are highly dependent upon the particular machine used—check how they work on your system. Another interesting point about the PRINT statement is that you can use it to continue printing on the same line. An extra comma (or semicolon or colon) after the last print variable causes the print mechanism to stay on the same line. Note the difference in output in Figure 13.3a and 13.3b. The only difference is the extra comma in line 30.

STRING DATA

Earlier you saw how the programmer could print messages or headings along with numeric output. Technically, this material is known as string data and must be enclosed within quotation marks. (Maximum string length depends upon the system; some allow up to 255 characters.)

        10 PRINT "THIS IS A STRING"

However, strings may be used in other ways. They may be defined by what is known as a string variable and may be manipulated within

```
10 FOR T = 1 TO 5
20 READ X
30 PRINT X
40 NEXT T
50 DATA 8,13,56,19
60 END

RUN

8
13
56
19
```

(a)

```
10 FOR T = 1 TO 5
20 READ X
30 PRINT X,
40 NEXT T
50 DATA 8,13,56,19

RUN

8            13             56             19
```
(b)

FIGURE 13.3
PRINT options.

certain obvious limitations. Strings may be created by using LET and a *string variable,* which is a single letter or single letter plus a digit followed by a $.

LET G$ = "SPACE TRAVEL"

When the LET statement is executed, the system creates the letters SPACE TRAVEL in a place called G$.

| SPACE TRAVEL |
G$

Note that you do not have to tell the system how many positions of memory to set aside for the string material. The system counts the number of characters between the quotation marks and reserves that much storage. The statement

PRINT G$

will produce the same output as

PRINT "SPACE TRAVEL"

When using string data with READ and DATA, the string data normally is enclosed within quotation marks. (On some systems the quotation marks are not required unless the data contains trailing spaces or commas.) Commas to separate the data items are required.

10 READ A$, X, C$
    .
    .
    .
80 DATA "HAMMER", 57,"JANUARY 12, 1983"

One very important point for you to remember is to make certain that the READ variables and the DATA elements match exactly. If they do not, an error will result.

10 READ N, A$
    .
    .
    .
60 DATA "FRIDAY",19

        Error condition: the data types
          do not match the variables

String and numerical data can be combined in READ, DATA, and PRINT statements to provide nicer looking output.

```
READ N$,H,R,D
LET G = H*R
LET P = G-D
PRINT "FOR";N$
PRINT "NET PAY IS ";P
DATA "JENNY BIRD:,40,9.75,28.50
END
```

Output:

FOR JENNY BIRD
NET PAY IS _____

Duplicating or moving string data is done just as it is with regular variables. In the following example, the string value stored at B$ is moved to X$. On most systems the programmer does not have to worry about the size of the string fields that are used as the system automatically increases or decreases the size of the storage areas needed.

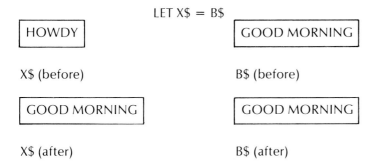

LET X$ = B$

| HOWDY | | GOOD MORNING |

X$ (before)   B$ (before)

| GOOD MORNING | | GOOD MORNING |

X$ (after)   B$ (after)

String data may be compared by means of the IF statement. However, the comparison *has nothing to do with the length of the field.* The comparison is done on the basis of the internal codes of the characters being compared. This coding sequence (called a "collating" sequence) follows the same pattern you already know and follow when sorting values. For example, you know that an 8 is greater than a 6 and that a W is greater than an N. Note the following example.

```
10 LET P$= "ELEPHANTS"
20 LET A$= "XEROX"
30 IF P$>A$ THEN 60
40 PRINT "THE DATA IN A$ IS GREATER"
50 GOTO 70
60 PRINT "THE DATA IN P$ IS GREATER"
70 END
```

Output: THE DATA IN A$ IS GREATER

The ability to test string data is particularly useful in game or CAI (computer-assisted instruction) programs where the user is asked to respond to a question or to provide an answer of some type.

Example:

```
        .
        .
        .
PRINT "DID YOU UNDERSTAND THE LESSON"
PRINT "ABOUT STRING DATA? IF SO,
PRINT "ENTER YES; OTHERWISE ENTER NO"
INPUT A$
```

IF A$ = "YES" THEN ——————

      •
      •
      •

If the answer is YES, then you should branch to a part of the program that either tests the user on the skills learned or goes on to a new lesson. In a CAI situation, if the answer is NO, the program probably would present the material again using a different approach.

Another common string operation is called "concatenation," in which string values can be added together to form new, longer strings.

LET A$ = "PEA"
LET B$ = "NUT"
LET C$ = A$ + B$ (C$ now contains "PEANUT")
PRINT C$ (the system will print PEANUT)

FILES OF DATA

Most versions of BASIC allow the user to write onto and read from data files stored on disk. The immediate advantage of this is that you can now access large amounts of data that would be awkward to do using READ/DATA. Unfortunately, the way BASIC handles files differs greatly from machine to machine, so be sure to consult the manual about the way your system handles them.

A *file* is defined as an area of storage external to the program where data in the form of numbers and strings is stored. In a sense, you have already used what amounts to "internal files" when you used READ and DATA. For example, you have seen a sample program that read in a payroll *record* from a DATA statement. You were told that each record consisted of four fields: Identification Number, Hours Worked, Rate of Pay, and Deductions Amount. Knowing that, the programmer would read in a record

    READ I,H,R,D

and process it accordingly. In this type of program, the DATA values were the file—an internal file rather than an external one.

If this same file were stored on disk, it would appear as follows

In the previous example the system really never had to "look" very far for the data values; they were always within the program in DATA statements. The problem is that this approach of "just" READing won't work for external files since a great many files can be stored on disk (we are making the assumption here that the data file you want has been created and stored on a disk). Before you can read, you must let the system know the name of the data file or files you want.

This is done by means of a statement that differs radically from system to system. Some systems use the following:

    10 FILES OWED, CHARGES

or

        50 DEFINE READ FILE #1 = "OWED"
        60 DEFINE READ FILE #2 = "CHARGES"

The exact format of the statement is not important in our discussion; you can find the format for your machine. What is important is that you are saying that you wish to access or READ from those files. Furthermore, you will, from this point on, *not* refer to either of the files by their name (OWED, CHARGES) but by number. In the FILES statement, OWED will be file #1 because it was mentioned first and CHARGES will be #2. Other than that, the action of the program is essentially the same as before. Let's assume our payroll data is in a file called PAYROL. To read in a record we will program as follows:

        10 DEFINE READ FILE #1="PAYROLL" (or whatever
             •   format your
             •   machine requires)
             •
        50 READ #1,I,H,R,D

Note that the only change to the READ statement is that we used the pound sign (#) followed by the file number. If we were reading from a second file (DEFINE READ FILE #2="CREDITS"), we would use the following:

        READ #2, ————————

Undoubtedly, we will want to use the traditional looping process to keep accessing record after record. The problem now is how do we get out of the loop? BASIC has a statement designed just for this event and generally follows the same format on most machines.

        ON END #1file number GOTO statement number
with this knowledge, we can now complete the looping process

        10 DEFINE READ FILE #1="PAYROL"
             •
             •
             •
        50 READ #1, I,H,R,D
        60 ON END GOTO 210
             •
             •
             •
        200 GOTO 50
        210 ————————

How does the system know when it has reached the end of the file? When the file is created, the system writes a special configuration of bits (End of File—EOF) immediately after the last data record. Then, every time you READ a record, the system *automatically* checks to see whether it has encountered this combination. If so, the ON END statement is executed. If not, the system drops down to normal processing.

When working with a sequential file, it is sometimes necessary to go back to the beginning of the file. This is accomplished by a statement that—you guessed it—varies from machine to machine. However, it is easy to use and looks something like this.

REWIND #1

HANDLING DATA IN TABLES

So far in the text we have always dealt with one data element at a time. Typically, the program reads in the data pertaining to a single transaction, manipulates it arithmetically, outputs an answer, and branches back to the beginning of the loop to do the same process all over again. Not all problems can be handled this way, however. In statistical work, for example, it is often necessary to work with various data items over and over again. When the programmer encounters this type of problem he or she generally stores the data in table form to facilitate the task of repetitive handling.

A table is nothing more than the storage of a series of values in consecutive areas of memory. For example, the storage of six test scores in the table called R would look as follows:

| 78.5 |
| 90.1 |
| 75.3 |
| 90.0 |
| 85.4 |
| 84.7 |

When working with tables, the first thing you must do is let the system know the size of the memory area to be set aside. This is done by the DIM statement.

10 DIM R(6)

On most machines the system automatically reserves some memory areas for the tables. However, you can't always count on this, so you should always DIMension your tables. Note that the DIM statement does not necessarily put any values into your table—you have to do that. The difficulty is that if you ask the system to work with R, it doesn't know what you are talking about since there is not *one* place called R. Instead, there are six places called R. In order to get to a specific element within the table, you must use a subscript.

Table elements are known as *subscripted* variables because the only way they can be accessed is by means of the subscript.

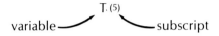

$$T.\,(5)$$

variable⟋   ⟍subscript

For example, the variable G(3) refers to the third element or data item in the table called G, while B7(16) refers to the sixteenth element or data item in the table called B7.

Table called R

78.5	R(1)
90.1	R(2)
75.3	R(3)
90.0	R(4)
85.4	R(5)
84.7	R(6)

An example of the type of data that would be stored in a single-dimension table would be the maximum temperature for every day of the year. Assuming the data is already in a table called T, we could print the data for the 260th day by saying;

    80 PRINT T(260)

How are data values entered into a table? Several methods are possible. You could use the INPUT statement (or READ and DATA) and enter the values directly from the terminal (Figure 13.4). A quick look at this method should tell you that it is inefficient, since the only thing that changes in each of the INPUT statements is the subscript. (Imagine loading a 500-element table this way!) A better method is shown in Figure 13.5.

In this second example, note that we used a variable to do the work for us. Each time you INPUT a value, it is entered into the Kth element of the table called R. The first time through the loop K is 1 and data goes into the first position of the table R; the second time K is 2 and data goes into the second position, etc. Once the data is in the table

```
10 REM      LOADING A TABLE USING INPUT
20 DIM R(6)
30 INPUT R(1)
40 INPUT R(2)
50 INPUT R(3)
60 INPUT R(4)
70 INPUT R(5)
80 INPUT R(6)
90 REM      THE TABLE HAS NOW BEEN LOADED
100 REM
110 REM      THE NEXT STATEMENT PRINTS THE
120 REM      VALUE STORED IN R(5)
130 PRINT R(5)
140 END
```

FIGURE 13.4
Loading a table with INPUT (the hard way!).

there is no reason to "Read" it again as it is now ready to be manipulated by the normal BASIC statement.

How do you use data in tables? You use it the same way you have always used data. The only difference is that whenever you make reference to a table item, you *must* use a subscript. Note the following examples.

PRINT T(65)   Prints the value in the sixty-fifth "slot" or element of the table

LET R(5) = 99.6   99.6 is moved into the fifth element of the table called R

IF Q(3)<(H*M) THEN 500

The value in the third element of the table called Q is compared with the sum of H times M

FIGURE 13.5
Loading a table with INPUT (the easy way).

```
10 REM      LOADING A TABLE USING INPUT
20 REM      (THE EASY WAY!)
30 DIM R(6)
40 FOR K = 1 TO 6
50 INPUT R(K)
60 NEXT K
70 REM      THE NEXT STATEMENT PRINTS THE
80 REM      VALUE STORED IN R(5)
90 PRINT R(5)
100 END
```

LET B3(N) = 0   Zero is moved into the Nth position of the table called B3

Certain "horse-sense" rules must be followed when using tables. The most important of these is that the subscript value must be within the range of the table. For example, it is considered bad form to try to access the seventy-fifth element of a 60-element table. Loading a table with data from an external file follows the same pattern we used before. In the next example (Figure 13.6), we will assume that the file contains exactly 365 temperature values.

The BASIC language also permits the use of two-dimensional tables that not only go down but across as well. We might use a table of this type to store monthly sales data from five branch stores. Schematically, this two-dimensional table would consist of 5 rows down and 12 columns across.

	Col. 1	Col. 2	Col. 3		Col. 12
Row 1	Store 1 Jan.	Store 1 Feb.	Store 1 Mar.		Store 1 Dec.
Row 2	Store 2 Jan.	Store 2 Feb.			Store 2 Dec.
Row 3					
Row 4					
Row 5	Store 5 Jan.				Store 5 Dec.

To set up the table we would use a DIM statement as before.

DIM S(5,12)

Reading data into a two-dimensional table is accomplished by using two FOR-NEXT statements. One FOR-NEXT is used to change the row variable and another to change the column variable. The following example illustrates how data would be read into a 3-by-4 table (3 elements down and 4 elements across) using READ and DATA.

	Col. 1	Col. 2	Col. 3	Col. 4
Row 1	1	2	3	4
Row 2	5	6	7	8
Row 3	9	10	11	12

Just as with a single-dimension table, data may be manipulated as before, except that a position in the table is referenced by the table

```
10 REM        LOADING A TABLE FROM AN
20 REM        EXTERNAL FILE
30 DIM T(365)
40 DEFINE READ FILE #1 = "TEMP"
50 FOR M = 1 TO 365
60 READ #1, T(M)
70 NEXT M
80 PRINT "TABLE LOADING IS COMPLETE"
90 END
```

FIGURE 13.6
Loading a table from an external file.

name followed by a *double subscript* that corresponds to the row and column location (Figure 13.7).

Some BASIC systems allow the programmer to create string tables. They follow the same rules as numerical tables; just remember to use a dollar sign ($) when creating and referencing the string table:

DIM A$(5)

Figure 13.8 illustrates the use of string data in a table.

FIGURE 13.7
A two-dimensional table.

```
5 REM A 2-DIMENSIONAL TABLE
10 DIM A(3,4)
20 FOR R = 1 TO 3
30 FOR C = 1 TO 4
40 READ A(R,C)
50 NEXT C
60 NEXT R
70 PRINT A(2,3)
80 PRINT A(1,4)
90 PRINT A(3,1)
100 DATA 1,2,3,4,5,6,7,8,9,10,11,12
110 END

RUN

7
4
9
```

```
10 REM A ONE-DIMENSION STRING TABLE
20 REM FILLED BY READ AND DATA
30 DIM A$(5)
40 FOR K = 1 TO 5
50 READ A$(K)
60 NEXT K
70 PRINT A$(3)
80 PRINT A$(1)
90 DATA "CINDY","JAMES","REGINALD","SUSAN","RALPH"
100 END

RUN

REGINALD
CINDY
```

FIGURE 13.8
String data in a table.

MISCELLANEOUS STATEMENTS

THE STOP STATEMENT

You already know that on many systems, END must be the highest numbered statement in your program. It stops program execution and is physically located at the end of the program. The STOP statement is used to provide *logical* (rather than a physical) stopping places in your program. For example, it may be that you want to end your program at one of several places, depending upon some condition. Rather than having IFs to test and branch, you may simply use STOP. Execution of the STOP statement causes, in effect, a branch to END and terminates the program.

In the following example, if X is greater than zero, the program branches to the statement 180 for further processing. If X is not greater than zero, the program is ended (stopped).

```
150 IF X>0 THEN 180
160 PRINT "ERROR - EXECUTION TERMINATED"
170 STOP
180 ————————
190 ————————
```

.
.
.
300 END

THE RESTORE STATEMENT

You will recall from Chapter 11 that READ and DATA are related statements. DATA is a "nonexecutable" statement in that it exists to provide data values to READ. Its placement is important in the program only in that data is read in sequence from first to last DATA statements and from left to right within the statement.

When the RUN command is executed, the system automatically sets a *pointer* to the first data item. As the items are read, the pointer moves through the data to point out the next data item that can be read in. The RESTORE statement is used to reset the pointer back to the first item so that the data can be read in again. This sample program shows how RESTORE can be used (Figure 13.9). Two variations on the RESTORE permit restoring numerical values only or string values only:

RESTORE #   restores numerical values only
RESTORE $ restores string items only

```
10 FOR K=1 TO 5
20 READ N
30 PRINT N,"CUBED IS",N↑3
40 NEXT K
50 RESTORE
60 FOR I=1 TO 5
70 READ P
80 PRINT "THE SQR RT OF",P,"IS",SQR(P)
90 NEXT I
100 DATA 1,4,9,16,25
110 END
```

1	CUBED IS	1		
4	CUBED IS	64		
9	CUBED IS	729		
16	CUBED IS	4096		
25	CUBED IS	15625		
THE SQR RT OF	1	IS	1	
THE SQR RT OF	4	IS	2	
THE SQR RT OF	9	IS	3	
THE SQR RT OF	16	IS	4	
THE SQR RT OF	25	IS	5	

DONE

FIGURE 13.9
The RESTORE statement.

THE COMPUTED GO TO STATEMENT

The simple GO TO statement you have used so far is common to every
version of BASIC. Most versions, however, have a second version that
goes by a lot of different names and formats. It is called the "ON GO
TO" or "GO TO depending" or "computed GO TO" because the place
to which the program branches depends upon the value of a variable.
Consider the following situation. Employees work one of three
different shifts: day shift—code 1; swing shift—code 2; or a graveyard
shift—code 3. We want to read in an employee record and branch to
one of three diffierent places in the program, depending upon the
value of the code field K.

```
100 READ A$,I,K
110 IF K = 1 THEN 300
120 IF K = 2 THEN 500
130 IF K = 3 THEN 700
140 (error routine)
```

The same steps can be accomplished by a single computed GO TO
statement that is, in effect, a combination of IF-THEN and GO TO, by
saying:

```
100 READ A$,I,K
110 ON K GO TO 300,500,700
120 (error routine)
```

GOSUB AND RETURN

GOSUB and RETURN are paired statements that allow a program to be
written in a modular form. The statements are used extensively with
large programs or in programs requiring many repetitions of similar
blocks of code. The similar blocks of code are called subroutines and
the following schematic illustrates the straight-line approach to using
a subroutine. For example, suppose we had a situation in which the
programmer had to sort data values into ascending order many times in
the program. Each time the sort routine (or block of code) is needed, it
is inserted into the mainstream of code.

sort routine

sort routine

At some point it becomes more efficient to handle the sort routine statements as a subroutine by using the GOSUB and RETURN statements. GOSUB transfers control to the specified block of code (subroutine) and RETURN brings the computer back to the next statement *below* the *sending* GOSUB.

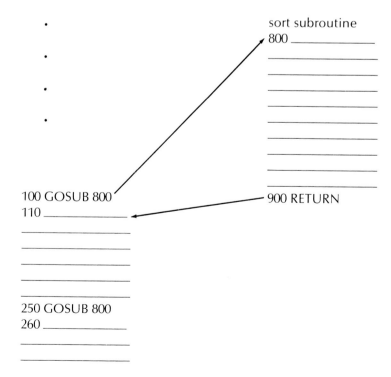

420 GOSUB 800
430 _____

_____
_____

When the program is executed, statement 100 GOSUB 800 sends the program out to the sort subroutine and at the conclusion of sort subroutine, the RETURN statement (900) sends control back to statement 110. Statements 250 and 420 follow the same pattern. Note that the RETURN statement always sends the system back to the statement immediately below the GOSUB that did the sending.

Using this method it is possible to set up highly modularized programs in which each major task is performed in a subroutine. These smaller programs can be written and checked independently of the main program, which could consist of almost all GOSUB statements (Figure 13.10).

PRINT USING

By now you must have noticed one of the major drawbacks of output from a BASIC program: numerical data is *not* aligned on the decimal point. Instead, it is left aligned or left justified.

Most versions of BASIC have some way of providing for finer control of output characters than discussed earlier. The additional formatting capabilities are generally called PRINT USING because the system makes reference to a field of special characters that precisely define the format. Depending upon the machine involved, PRINT USING takes one of two general forms. In one form, the characters that indicate the format of the output are contained within the statement itself. In the second form, the PRINT statement always makes reference to another statement that specifies the format. (Sometimes the term "image" is used because symbols are used to specify an image of how the output should look.)

Since this feature varies widely from machine to machine, we will just take a quick look at how it works. From there you should be able to figure out how it operates on your system. Figure 13.11 shows a program that lists the employee identification numbers and gross pay. Note that the gross pay amount is aligned to the left.

Obviously, the gross pay amounts would look better if they were aligned on the decimal point. On most systems the main formatting character is the pound sign (#). If we wanted to print *just* the employee identification number with PRINT USING we would code as follows for statement 50.

50 PRINT USING "# # # #",I

```
10 REM USING GOSUB AND RETURN
20 REM MAIN CONTROL MODULE
30 REM
40 GOSUB 220
50 GOSUB 430
60 GOSUB 630
70 STOP
200 REM *****************************************
210 REM SETTING UP TOTAL AREAS
220 LET G1 = 0
230 LET D1 = 0
240 LET N1 = 0
250 REM
260 REM PRINTING HEADINGS
270 REM
280 PRINT "PAYROLL DATA"
290 PRINT
300 PRINT "ID","GROSS","DED","NET"
310 PRINT
320 RETURN
330 REM END OF PRINT MODULE
400 REM *****************************************
410 REM MAIN PROCESSING MODULE
420 REM
430 FOR K = 1 TO 5
440 READ I,H,R,D
450 LET G = H*R
460 LET N = G-D
470 LET G1 = G1 + G
480 LET D1 = D1 + D
490 LET N1 = N1 + N
500 PRINT I,G,D,N
510 NEXT K
511 DATA 1234,40,4.57,23.45
512 DATA 2222,41,5.75,19.72
513 DATA 3765,39,6.95,41.35
514 DATA 4893,42,5.75,56.14
515 DATA 7568,40,6.55,35.19
520 RETURN
530 REM
540 REM END OF READ-PROCESS-PRINT
550 REM              MODULE
560 REM ***********************************
600 REM ***********************************
```

FIGURE 13.10
GOSUB and RETURN. *(Continued)*

```
610 REM PRINT TOTALS MODULE
620 REM
630 PRINT
640 PRINT "TOTAL GROSS",G1
650 PRINT "TOTAL DEDUCTIONS",D1
660 PRINT "TOTAL NET PAY"," "," ",N1
670 PRINT
680 PRINT "END OF REPORT"
690 RETURN
700 REM
710 REM END OF PRINT TOTALS MODULE
720 REM
730 REM *************************************
900 END

RUN

PAYROLL DATA
```

ID	GROSS	DED	NET
1234	182.8	23.45	159.35
2222	235.75	19.72	216.03
3765	271.05	41.35	229.7
4893	241.5	56.14	185.36
7568	262	35.19	226.81

```
TOTAL GROSS      1193.1
TOTAL DEDUCTIONS            175.85
TOTAL NET PAY                          1017.25
END OF REPORT

DONE
```

FIGURE 13.10 (Continued)

The statement says "PRINT the value stored in I USING the format within the quotation marks." The four pound signs specify four positions in the print line and are filled with the four digits from the ID field. Of course, we really haven't gained anything by doing this since normal BASIC output would do this anyway.

If we wanted to print *just* the gross pay amount and align the values on the decimal point, our statement would look as follows:

PRINT USING "# # # #.# #",G

```
10 PRINT "ID NUMBER", "GROSS PAY"
20 PRINT
30 FOR K = 1 TO 4
40 READ I,G
50 PRINT I,G
60 NEXT K
70 DATA 1001,97.36
80 DATA 1234,142.91
90 DATA 2569,8.75
100 DATA 3425,1031.82
110 END
```

ID NUMBER	GROSS PAY
1001	97.36
1234	142.91
2569	8.75
3425	1031.82

FIGURE 13.11
Regular BASIC output.

Output:

```
     97.36
    142.91
      8.75
   1031.82
```

If we wanted even prettier output, we could include a dollar sign and a comma in addition to the decimal point:

```
PRINT USING "$#,###.##",G
```

Output:

```
$    97.36
$   142.91
$     8.75
$1,031.82
```

Note that in both examples we were careful to account for the maximum number of digits that the Gross Pay field could contain. To get *both* fields (I and G) printed under the column headings, we will have to set up a format for the whole line.

```
40 PRINT USING "####          $#,###.##",I,G
```

The system will put the value from I into the first set of pound signs and the value from G into the second set of pound signs. The number of spaces between the sets of pound signs determines the distance between the printed output. Figure 13.12 shows the complete program.

An even easier way for the programmer to use PRINT USING is to set up the formatting information as a string item. For example, in the previous example we used the following.

> 50 PRINT USING "# # # # $#,# # #.# #",I,G

Instead, we could have programmed as follows

> LET X$ = "# # # # $#,# # #.# #"
> PRINT USING X$,I,G

and the system will take the formatting information from the X$ string field.

String output can also be handled by PRINT USING. Suppose a total area called T1 contains the value 248. The statement to print the word TOTAL and the value in T1 is shown below.

> PRINT "# # # # #   # # #","TOTAL",T1

Output:

TOTAL   248

FIGURE 13.12
PRINT USING with multiple fields.

```
10 PRINT "ID NUMBER", "GROSS PAY"
20 PRINT
30 FOR K = 1 TO 4
40 READ I,G
50 PRINT USING "# # # #          $#,# # #.# #",I,G
60 NEXT K
70 DATA 1001,97.36
80 DATA 1234,142.91
90 DATA 2569,8.75
100 DATA 3425,1031.82
110 END
```

ID NUMBER	GROSS PAY
1001	$ 97.36
1234	$ 142.91
2569	$ 8.95
3425	$1,031.82

MORE ABOUT
ARITHMETIC VALUES

Chapter 12 showed that BASIC handles numerical values up to a system-specified size with no difficulty, but eventually the number will be loo long to be handled in regular format. At that point the format of the number will be changed into exponential or scientific notation.

E NOTATION (SCIENTIFIC NOTATION)

In E or exponential notation, large numbers are expressed as a decimal value times a power of 10. The examples shown on the next few pages assume that our system can handle numbers up to six digits in length. Suppose that the result of a series of arithmetic calculations was the value 12345678 and we wished to print this. Since the value is larger than six digits, the answer will be printed in E notation. The system will do the following:

1. Convert the number to a one-digit whole number plus a decimal fraction. The resulting number is known as the mantissa.

> 12345678. becomes 1.$\underbrace{2345678}$
>
> mantissa

Note that the decimal point was shifted left seven places.

> 12345678.   1.$\underset{\smile}{2345678}$
>
> original decimal point   decimal point is moved to the left
>   7 places

Unfortunately, since the system can only handle six digits, the last two digits are dropped off and our mantissa now looks like this:

> 1.23456

Obviously, a six-digit size limitation can become an important factor if you wish a reasonable degree of accuracy in arithmetic computations. This one feature may determine which BASIC software to purchase for a particular application.

2. Each place that the decimal was moved to the left is equivalent to multiplying by 10. For example:

> 978 is the same as 97.8×10^1

or

> 978. is the same as 9.78×100 (or 10^2)

3. The system shows this movement of the decimal by the letter E
    (which stands for exponent), a plus sign (to indicate that the
    original number was greater than 1.0), and the number of places
    the decimal was moved to get the number into E notation form.
    Thus,

$$12345678 \text{ becomes } \underbrace{1.23456}_{\text{mantissa}}\underbrace{E+07}_{\text{exponent}}$$

which is read as "one point two three four five six times 10 to the
seventh power."

Very small numbers (less than 1.0) are represented in the same
manner but, since the decimal shift is to the right, the sign of the
exponent is negative:

$$.0913546 \text{ becomes } \underbrace{9.13546}_{\text{mantissa}}\underbrace{E-02}_{\text{exponent}}$$

In the above case, the E–02 tells us that the decimal was moved
two places to the right.

$$.3187649 \text{ becomes } 3.18764E-01$$

One of the disadvantages of E notation is that, since digits after the
sixth place are dropped, there is a loss in accuracy. If this point
were to cause difficulties in your business, you would either go to a
different language or find a version of BASIC that offers greater
precision. Negative values are represented by a negative mantissa,
as shown below:

$$-14863921786 \text{ becomes } -1.48639E+10$$

To find out how your system handles E notation, try a simple
program similar to the one shown in Figure 13.13. Make the
numbers larger and larger until they are changed into scientific
notation.

MATHEMATICAL FUNCTIONS

Some of the many mathematical functions available are shown below.

SQR(X) finds the square root of a positively valued expression. For
example, the square root of $37 + B^3$ can be found by the statement LET
A = SQR(37+B↑3)

The square root of an expression can also be found by raising to the
.5 power

LET A = (37+B↑3)↑.5

```
10 REM EXAMPLES OF E NOTATION OUTPUT
20 PRINT "LARGE POSITIVE NUMBER", 11223344
30 PRINT
40 PRINT "LARGE NEGATIVE NUMBER", -12345678
50 PRINT
60 PRINT "SMALL POSITIVE NUMBER", .000593641
70 PRINT
80 PRINT "SMALL NEGATIVE NUMBER", -.003459876

RUN

LARGE POSITIVE NUMBER      1.12233E+07
LARGE NEGATIVE NUMBER   -1.23457E+07
SMALL POSITIVE NUMBER      5.93641E-04
SMALL NEGATIVE NUMBER   -3.45988E-03

DONE
```

FIGURE 13.13
Scientific notation.

A program to print the first 100 integers along with the square root of each is

```
10 FOR X = 1 TO 100
20 PRINT X, SQR(X)
30 NEXT X
40 END
```

INT(X) finds the largest integer *not larger* than X. For example;

```
50 A7 = INT(2.32)        A7 is equal to 2.
90 L = INT(-2.32)        L is equal to -3
30 G4 = INT(7.96)        G4 is equal to 7.
```

and

```
LET A = INT((G*H↑2)↑3)      is also valid.
```

(*Note:* The INT function is useful in rounding numbers to the next higher digit.) Example: LET B = INT(X + .5). Thus, if X were 2.9, INT(X + .5) would be 3.

In statistical programs it is often necessary to generate random numbers to represent chance occurrences. The flipping of a coin or the dealing of a card is perhaps an even more common example of random number generation. The statement

```
50 LET X = RND(0)
```

generates a random number between 0 and 1, that is, it will be in the form .385612.

To get a whole integer random number it is necessary to multiply the random number by 10 and use the integer function (INT) to produce the integer value.

```
LET X = INT(10 * RND(0))
IF X = 0 THEN _____
```

An almost endless series of variations can be obtained in this manner. For example,

```
LET X = INT(2 * RND(0))
```

will produce zeros and ones (to represent the flipping of a coin). Zero is produced if the answer is less than .5 and 1 if it is over .5. A more efficient program is produced by combining the LET and IF into a single statement.

```
IF RND(0) < .5 THEN _____
```

The RND function actually generates a series of pseudorandom numbers such that the same values will be generated each time the program is run. A more random set of values can be achieved by using the RANDOMIZE statement in addition to the RND function

```
50 LET X = RND(0)
60 RANDOMIZE
```

Assuming that these two lines are part of a program loop, the system will generate different random values each time through the loop.

Other BASIC function are listed as follows:

LOG(X)	Finds the natural logarithm of X.
ABS(X)	Finds the absolute value of X.
EXP(X)	Finds the exponential function (e) by raising e(2.718218) to the power of the expression.
SGN(X)	Finds the sign of X: plus if X is greater than zero; minus if X is less than zero; zero if X is zero. For example, IF SGN(X) = 0 THEN 500.

MATRIX OPERATIONS

The term *matrix* is often used in mathematics to refer to a table or an array of data. Most BASIC compilers have a set of special MAT statements that deal with an entire table of matrix with a single statement that follows the rules of matrix algebra. The system automatically takes care of setting up the subscripted variable(s) and providing loop control. Although most business operations are not likely to use MAT operations, the more common ones are included here for your interest. Let's take a look at some of these operations.

The MAT READ statement is used to read data into a matrix. Suppose we have a 3 × 4 matrix (3 rows down, 4 columns across) and wish to store 12 values. Note the difference between doing this operation with regular BASIC statements versus a MAT READ (Figure 13.14). Note

FIGURE 13.14
Using MAT READ.

```
5 REM           A 2-DIMENSIONAL TABLE
10 DIM A(3,4)
20 FOR R = 1 TO 3
30 FOR C = 1 TO 4
40 READ A(R,C)
50 NEXT C
60 NEXT R
70 PRINT A(2,3)
80 PRINT A(1,4)
90 PRINT A(3,1)
100 DATA 1,2,3,4,5,6,7,8,9,10,11,12
110 END

RUN

    7
    4
    9

DONE
```

(a)

```
5 REM           A 2-DIMENSIONAL TABLE
7 REM           USING MAT STATEMENTS
10 DIM A(3,4)
20 MAT READ A
70 PRINT A(2,3)
80 PRINT A(1,4)
90 PRINT A(3,1)
100 DATA 1,2,3,4,5,6,7,8,9,10,11,12
110 END

RUN

    7
    4
    9

DONE
```

(b)

that the MAT READ statement places the data values into the matrix positions in the order in which they were read in.

The MAT PRINT statement prints out the entire contents of the matrix *in the form in which it was dimensioned.* Different systems follow different rules, but the general rule is that the matrix must be dimensioned as large or larger than the number of data items entered. The next program shows the same data entered into a 4 × 3 matrix and the resulting output (Figure 13.15).

FIGURE 13.15
Matrices with different dimensions.

```
5 REM           A 2-DIMENSIONAL TABLE
7 REM           USING MAT STATEMENTS
10 DIM A(3,4)
20 MAT READ A
70 MAT PRINT A
100 DATA 1,2,3,4,5,6,7,8,9,10,11,12
110 END

RUN
```

1	2	3	4
5	6	7	8
9	10	11	12

```
DONE
```

(a)

```
5 REM           A 2-DIMENSIONAL TABLE
7 REM           USING MAT STATEMENTS
10 DIM A(4,3)
20 MAT READ A
70 MAT PRINT A
100 DATA 1,2,3,4,5,6,7,8,9,10,11,12
110 END

RUN
```

1	2	3
4	5	6
7	8	9
10	11	12

```
DONE
```

(b)

```
5 REM            A 2-DIMENSIONAL TABLE
7 REM            USING MAT STATEMENTS
10 DIM A(4,3)
20 MAT INPUT A
70 MAT PRINT A
110 END


RUN


?1,2,3,4,5,6,7,8,9,10,11,12
   1              2              3
   4              5              6
   7              8              9
   10             11             12


DONE
```

FIGURE 13.16
MAT INPUT.

The MAT INPUT follows the same format as the MAT READ statement (Figure 13.16).

Matrix addition and subtraction can be performed with two matrices that have the same dimensions, as shown in Figure 13.17.

FIGURE 13.17
Matrix subtraction.

```
5 REM              MATRIX ADDITION AND SUBTRACTION
10 DIM A(2,3),B(2,3),C(2,3)
20 MAT READ A
30 DATA 1,2,3,4,5,6
40 MAT READ B
50 DATA 10,20,30,40,50,60
60 PRINT "MATRIX A"
70 PRINT
80 MAT PRINT A
90 PRINT
100 PRINT "MATRIX B"
110 PRINT
120 MAT PRINT B
130 PRINT
140 PRINT "MATRIX C"
150 PRINT
160 MAT C = B-A
170 MAT PRINT C
180 END
```

(Continued)

RUN

MATRIX A

1	2	3
4	5	6

MATRIX B

10	20	30
40	50	60

MATRIX C

9	18	27
36	45	54

DONE

FIGURE 13.17 (Continued)

SUMMARY OF IMPORTANT POINTS

☐ FOR-NEXT was discussed as a pair of statements that permitted the programmer to control the actions of a program loop more easily than by using a counter and an IF-THEN statement.

☐ The FOR-NEXT statement is not only easy to use but particularly adaptable to use with variables that give greater flexibility in programming.

☐ The PRINT statement could act as a combined LET-PRINT to perform complex arithmetic operations in certain circumstances.

☐ Another form of PRINT, PRINT USING, can be used to provide decimal alignment and other editing activities on numeric data.

☐ String data requires that a dollar sign ($) be used in the variable name. Other than that, it can be created, read, written, moved, and even tested, but it cannot be worked on arithmetically.

☐ Files are an easy way for the programmer to handle masses of data. Unfortunately, each BASIC system is likely to have its own special file-handling statements. Generally, all systems require that the file to be accessed be named or defined in the program. From that time on the file is referenced by number, not by name.

☐ For some types of problems it is simply not feasible to program with the regular read-calculate-print progression. Instead, some problems require that the data be accessed repeatedly in order to derive the answers. Tables take care of this problem by providing an area in memory for the temporary storage of data. Once the data is in tables, individual elements can be accessed over and over very quickly by means of subscripts.

☐ The GOSUB and RETURN statements allow the programmer to work with blocks of code or routines that are "sub" to the main program. These two statements are particularly adaptable to structured programming because programs can be written in modular form.

☐ BASIC systems can handle numbers up to a preset maximum. When numbers in excess of the maximum are encountered, the system converts them to E notation (or scientific notation).

☐ Various mathematical functions, such as SQR (square root), are prebuilt into the language and are available for use by the programmer.

☐ Almost all BASIC systems have a series of MAT or matrix statements that work on entire matrices with a single instruction. The use of these statements is usually reserved for applications that are highly mathematical.

GLOSSARY OF TERMS

E notation—also known as scientific notation. E notation is a format for the representation of numbers that are larger than a maximum preset in the system. The notation consists of two parts: a mantissa and an exponent.

Exponent—the rightmost part of a number that has been converted into E notation. This position shows the power of 10 to which the original number had to be raised in order to generate a correct mantissa.

Function—in programming, a function is a prebuilt series of instructions that can be used or called by means of a single word or term. Typical functions are SQR—to do square root and INT—to find the integer value of a variable.

Iteration—the act of repeating a section of code. In this chapter the term has been used in reference to a program counter that keeps track of the number of times a section of code has been processed.

Mantissa—the leftmost part of a number that has been put into E notation. In the mantissa portion, all numbers are reduced to single-digit whole number plus a decimal fraction.

Scientific notation—see E notation.

Subroutine—a block of code that may have to be executed repeatedly by the main program or routine.

THOUGHT QUESTIONS

1. In theory, the GO TO statement should be used sparingly. First, why is this true, and second, what other BASIC statements or constructions can be used in its place?

2. In narrative style, write down exactly what takes place in the following FOR-NEXT loop.
    50 FOR K = 1 TO 10 STEP 3

.
.
.

100 NEXT K

3. Why is it generally incorrect to branch into a FOR-NEXT loop? Under what conditions would it be permitted?

4. What would be the general rule or circum-stances under which you would use tables as opposed to not using tables? It might be useful to set up a problem to illustrate the conditions that would affect your choice.

5. Why is a subscript necessary with tables?

6. Illustrate the difference between a MAT READ statement and a FOR-NEXT loop to accomplish the same data input task.

BASIC PROBLEMS

1. The Galactic Sales Corporation wishes to pay end-of-the-year bonuses to its sale-speople. Data records on the company's five employees have the following format:

ID Number	Code Number	Sales Amount
1306	1	140350
4219	1	35000
5667	2	180800
6402	1	50000
8345	2	28500

You are to write a program to print a list of the employees and their bonus amounts based on the following rules.

a. Senior salespeople (code value of 1) will get a bonus of 4% of their sales that *exceed* $50000 *plus* a flat bonus amount of $6000. If their sales do not exceed $50000, they are to get only a bonus of $3000.

b. Junior salespeople (code value 2) will get a bonus of 3% of their sales that *exceed* $65000 *plus* a flat bonus amount of $4000. If their sales do not exceed $65000, they are to get only a bonus of $2000.

c. Use a FOR-NEXT to control the looping action of the program. Output is to be as follows:

GALACTIC SALES CORP

Number	Sales	Code	Bonus Amount
1306	_____	1	_____
4219	_____	1	_____
etc.			

TOTAL BONUS AMOUNTS _____

2. Inventory Report
Inventory data for the ABC Parts Company has the following format

Part Nbr	Inv. on Hand	Cust. Orders	Dollar Value

Write a program according to the following instructions.

a. Print the main and columnar headings as shown on the diagram below.

b. The Available Stock figure is calculated by subtracting Customer Orders from In-ventory on Hand. If the answer is negative, a zero is to be printed in that area.

c. Back Orders originate when there are more orders than Inventory on Hand. If the company is able to satisfy the order, there will be no Back Orders and a zero is to be printed in that area.

d. Inventory Value is calculated by multi-plying Dollar Value times the Available Stock figure. Obviously, if there is no

Available Stock, a zero will go into the Inventory Value output area.

e. Be sure your logic considers all possible conditions of Available Stock, i.e., positive, zero, or negative.

f. Total the Available Stock, Unfilled Orders, and the Inventory Value columns and print the amounts under the appropriate column after the last data record has been processed.

g. Since there are an unknown number of data records, the end-of-the-file condition will be detected by testing for all zeros in the part number field.

ABC PARTS CO

Part Number	Available Stock	Back Orders	Inventory Value
1111	97	0	1249.36
1355	___	___	___
etc.	___	___	___
Totals	___	___	___

Data

Part Nbr	On Hand	Orders	$Value
1111	873	776	12.88
1355	509	137	19.78
1883	314	314	45.31
5720	430	849	24.63
6292	565	199	21.92
1500	713	713	21.85
2463	264	897	13.21
6895	785	344	10.95
0000	000	000	00.00

3. Property taxes are usually paid on the basis of assessed value. The method of calculating the property tax is to apply a percentage assessment rate to the cash value of the property, which then gives the assessed valuation. Next, the property is taxed at a fixed rate per $100 of assessed valuation. Thus, if a piece of property has an actual cash value of $50,000, is assessed at 25% rate, and has a tax rate of $11 per each $100 of assessed value, the property tax is calculated as follows:

(Cash Value) $50,000 times .25 (assessment rate) = $12,500 (assessed value)

12,500 ÷ 100 = Amount To Which The Rate Is Applied

125 times $11.00 (tax rate) = $1375 property tax

Write a program to calculate the property tax as shown above. Data are given below.

DATA 107, 40,000, 11.91 (Parcel #, Cash Value, Tax Rate)
DATA 108, 58,500, 12.50
DATA 109, 95,000, 10.48

Note: In all cases, assume that the assessment rate is .25. Output is as follows.

PROPERTY TAX CALCULATIONS

Parcel	Value	Tax Rate	Tax Amt
107	___	___	___
108	___	___	___
109	___	___	___

TOTAL TAX ___

4. One common measure of a firm's financial stability is what is known as the *current ratio*. This figure, which is a relationship between what the firm has (assets) by current liabilities. Write a program to find the current ratio for the Gismo Manufacturing Company, using the following data.

Year	Current Assets	Current Liabilities
1980	$550,000	$420,000
1981	697,000	590,000
1982	487,000	545,000

GISMO MGF CO

Year	Current Ratio
1980	___
1981	___
1982	___

DIFFERENCE IN RATIO 1980–1981 IS ___

5. Twenty values, representing test scores, are to be read in one at a time and tested to determine the largest. Use a counter and an IF-THEN statement to control the loop. Output is shown below.

   LARGEST OF 20 SCORES IS _____.

6. Revise the preceding problem to print out the first 10 scores on one line, the next 10 on the next line, and then the largest as shown above.

7. Input four values, a, b, c, and d. Find the largest of the four and print it.

8. Revise problem 10 from the previous chapter by replacing the employee number field with an employee name.

9. The following values are to be read into a table so that they can be manipulated arithmetically.

   1, 19, 17, 23, 46, 18.5, –3, 42, –17.3, 0, 56, 97

   Write a program to

   a. Sum all the values from the even-numbered positions or "slots" in the table.

   b. Sum all the values from the odd-numbered positions.

   c. Sum all the positive values in the table. Output is to be as follows:

   ODD TOTAL _____
   EVEN TOTAL _____
   POSITIVE TOTAL _____
   PROGRAMMED BY _____

10. Create a 10-element table that contains the following test scores:

    78, 96, 88, 80, 72, 70, 81, 97, 62, 74

    Write a program that prints out:

    a. The average test score.

    b. The highest score.

    c. The lowest score.

    d. The difference between the highest score and the average and the lowest score and the average.

11. Modify the previous problem to print a listing of the test scores in ascending order (i.e., from highest to lowest).

12. In statistical work it is often necessary to find the largest and smallest numbers in a set of numbers. In this problem you will be working with two sets of *twelve* numbers. The 24 data values are stored in a *file* called

*MANIP. Write a program to do the following.

a. Read the first 12 data values into a one-dimensional, 12-position table.

b. Search the table to find the largest and smallest number.

c. Calculate the range of the data (i.e., the difference between the largest and smallest numbers).

d. Output your answers and perform the same operations on the second data set. output will be as follows:

Smallest	Largest	Range
_____	_____	_____
_____	_____	_____

PROGRAMMED BY _____

13. Here you will need a two-dimensional table that contains temperature information for 10 cities. Specifically, we have two items of temperature data for each city: lowest temperature and highest temperature. Read the data into a 10-by-3 table and then perform the following data manipulations:

    a. For each of the cities, calculate the range of temperatures (highest minus the lowest) and store these values in a 10-position, single-dimensional table called A.

    b. Print a listing of all cities whose average temperature (highest + lowest ÷ 2) is below 70°, using the format shown.

    c. Assume the data is in a table called TEMP and has the following format:

City Number	Lowest Temp	Highest Temp

Or if your instructor wants you to use READ and DATA, here are the data values:

DATA 1,41,91
DATA 2,15,87
DATA 3,23,96
DATA 4,0,80
DATA 5,–5,61
DATA 6,45,103
DATA 7,–12,106
DATA 8,51,107
DATA 9,60,112
DATA 10,19,88

d. Output format is

City	Average Temperature	Range
_____	_____	_____
_____	_____	_____

14. A file called *GRPS contains customer billing information and each record has the following format:

Account Number	Amount of Purchase
56832	126.19 Ex:

The data records are grouped on the file according to customer number and each customer may have more than one record of data (reflecting the fact that they may have made more than one purchase during the last billing period). Between each set of customer records will be a dummy record consisting of all 9's in the data field. Your program logic will test for all 9's in the account number field to determine the end of a particular group. When the end of a group is detected, you are to print out a total of the purchase amounts and then go on to the next group. When the end of the file is detected, you are to print a grand total of all the purchase amounts. Output will appear as follows:

BILLING DATA

ACCT NBR	AMT OF PURCHASE
56832	126.19
56832	54.03
56832	97.86
	TOTAL 278.08
66289	_____
66289	_____
	TOTAL _____

etc.

GRAND TOTAL _____

(*Note:*) If your instructor wants you to use READ and DATA, use the following values.)

ACCOUNT	AMT OF PURCHASE
56832	126.16
56832	54.03
56832	97.86
99999	999.99
66289	100.55
66289	29.48
66289	59.88
66289	14.05
99999	999.99
77423	561.25
99999	999.99
78431	98.99
78431	258.22
99999	999.99

15. A file called SCHOOL contains an unknown number of records with the following format:

STUDENT NAME	GRADE POINT AVERAGE	SEMESTER IN SCHOOL

You are to write a program that reads in a record and prints a letter grade according to the following rules:

A GPA of .00 to .99 is an F, 1.00 to 1.99 is a D, 2.00 to 2.99 is a C, 3.00 to 3.50 is a B, and 3.51 to 4.00 is an A. Any value outside of the range of 0.00 to 4.00 is to generate an error message.

Output

STUDENT NAME	LETTER GRADE
_____	_____

(*Note:* If your instructor prefers to use READ and DATA, use the following data values.) Note that you will exit from the loop when the program encounters a name of all As.

DATA

"SMITH", 3.52,7
"JONES", 1.86,1
"GREEN", 2.75,3
"ADAMS", 3.05,6
"JOHNSON", –2.89,3

"LEE", 1.01,2
"JOHNSON", 4.02,5
"BAKER", 6.42,4
"BIRCH", 3.92,3
"AAAAA", 0,0

16. Modify the previous problem as follows:
a. Your program is to INPUT a student name and then read through the file to see if a match exists. If it does, print the letter grade. If not, print an error message.
b. Output is to be as follows:

NAME   GPA   COMMENT (if required)
____   ____   ____
____   ____   ____

c. Note that for each succeeding name that you enter, the file will have to be restarted and read through again. This is not an efficient way to do things but illustrates how a sequential file operates.
d. Use the following names for input:

SMITH, GREEN, BAKER, LEE, JONES, AAAAA

17. Modify Problem 16 to use the following student names:

JONES, BIRCH, NAGLE, JOHNSON, LEE, AAAAA

If the end of the file is reached before a match is detected, print the message

NO MATCH FOR STUDENT _____

and continue the processing of INPUT records.

18. A file called RATE contains billing data for the Watt Now Electric Company. Each record has the following format:

Acct Nbr	Type of Acct	Old Meter Reading	New Reading
1026	3	738642	740262

Write a program to calculate monthly electric bills based on the following information:
a. Basic charge for every customer is $7.50, even if no electricity is used.
b. The charge for electricity usage is:

(a) First 100 KWH   9.1 cents per KWH
(b) Next   200 KWH   9.5 cents per KWH
(c) Next   700 KWH   10.3 cents per KWH
(d) Next 2000 KWH   12.7 cents per KWH
(e) Next 3000 KWH   13.1 cents per KWH

c. Maintain a running total of the KWH used and charges and print these totals at the end of the program.

WATT NOW ELECTRIC CO

ACCT   KWH USED   CHARGES
1026   ____   ____
____   ____   ____

TOTAL KWH USED _____
TOTAL CHARGES _____

d. If your instructor prefers to use READ and DATA, use the following values. Use an account number of all zeros to get out of the program loop.

ACCT. #	OLD METER READING	NEW METER READING (KWH)
1026	738642	740262
1247	444328	444328
1569	543211	553211
1743	994321	994385
1896	334455	334705
1943	564321	664321
0000	000000	000000

19. Fibonacci Series
The series of numbers that starts 1, 1, 2, 3, 5, 8, 13, and so on, is known as the *Fibonacci series*. It is calculated by summing the two previous numbers. Write a program that prints the first 30 Fibonacci numbers.

20. Factorials
A special numerical quantity known as a *factorial* is written N!. The factorial of any given number, 5 for example, is found by multiplying 5 times 4 times 3 times 2 times 1. Write a program to calculate the factorials of the numbers shown below. Your program is to stop whenever a factorial of over 9 is detected. That factorial is not to be calculated and the program is to stop.

DATA 7,5,8,9,12

Output:

THE FACTORIAL OF _____ IS _____

21. The calculation of automobile mileage is a simple matter—miles driven divided by the number of gallons used. However, some variations on this basic formula can provide useful information.

    A retired couple living on a fixed income have been keeping very careful records of their gasoline expenses. Last year they spent $650 on gasoline (average price $1.30 per gallon), driving a car that averaged 30 miles per gallon. Today they are increasingly concerned about the rising cost of gasoline. Prepare a report for them that calculates the number of miles that they can drive (obviously a decreasing amount) with the same car and the same total gasoline expense. Do so in 5-cent increments, starting at $1.30 and going to $1.80 per gallon. Output is to take the following format:

    GASOLINE/MILEAGE REPORT

MPG = 30	TOTAL GASOLINE EXPENSE $650
PRICE	MILES
1.30	15000
____	____

22. The report that you prepared in Problem 3 was so useful to the people concerned that they want you to do the same for six of their friends. Do the same for these other people, based on the following DATA statements that show miles per gallon and dollar amount to be spent. Assume that the average price per gallon of gasoline is $1.30.

    DATA 16.7,500
    DATA 21.4,400
    DATA 30.1,350
    DATA 18.5,650
    DATA 24.3,425
    DATA 19.3,550

23. Write a program that INPUTs the following string values: COW, ZEBRA, and HORSES. Find which string is higher in the collating sequence and print the answer.

24. Use the random number generator to simulate the flipping of a coin—heads or tails—25 times. Keep track of the number of heads or tails and print this amount at the end of your program.

25. Use the ramdom number generator to simulate the tossing of dice. (Obviously, only values 1 through 6 will be valid, and there are several ways you can generate such answers.) Print 10 answers in the following form:

TOSS	DIE 1	DIE 2	TOTAL
1	3	4	7
2	____	____	____

26. In business situations, it is often necessary to know how much money must be invested now in order to return a certain number of dollars at a future date. The formula is

    $$P = F \frac{i}{(1+i)^n - 1}$$

    where P = present amount to be invested
    F = the amount that you wish to accumulate in the future
    i = the interest rate
    n = the number of years

    For example, if you wished to accumulate $5000 ($F$) at the end of 20 years (n) at 8% interest (i), the computer would solve the equation

    $$P = 5000 \frac{.08}{(1+.08)^{20} - 1}$$

    Write a program to enter values F, i, and n through the INPUT statement. Use GOSUB and RETURN to branch to a calculation subroutine. Use another GOSUB and RETURN to branch to a print subroutine. Your program is to continue accepting data as long as the player responds with YES when asked if he or she wants to enter data. Run through your program several times to be sure that the answers are reasonable. Finally, when the player enters NO, the program is to terminate and print out your name. Output format is shown below.

    ____ DOLLARS INVESTED FOR ____ YEARS
    AT ____ PERCENT WILL GIVE ____ DOLLARS

27. Write a program to compute depreciation using the sum-of-the-years-digits method. Total depreciation of an item is found by subtracting scrap value from the original cost. The amount of *yearly* depreciation is calculated by means of the sum-of-the-years-digits method. For example, for an item with a usable life of 5 years, the sum of the digits 5-4-3-2-1 is 15. The first year's depreciation is found by taking 5/15 of the total depreciation: the next year is 4/15, then 3/15, 2/15, and so on. Note the following formulas, where

N = usable life in years
T = total depreciation (Cost−Scrap)
Y = sum of the years is found by the formula

$$N \times \frac{N+1}{2}$$

For example, if in the preceding case, N is 5

$$Y = 5 \times \left(\frac{5+1}{2} \right) = 15$$

first year depreciation $D = \left(\dfrac{N-2}{Y} \right) * T$

second year depreciation $= \left(\dfrac{N-1}{Y} \right) * T$

third year depreciation $= \left(\dfrac{N-2}{Y} \right) * T$

Output is to include the item name, cost, scrap value, usable life, and depreciation for each year.

DATA

ITEM	COST	SCRAP VALUE	USABLE LIFE
Drill Press	$15,000	2,000	8 years
Truck	4,500	200	4 years
Furniture	700	50	12 years
Building	50,000	10,000	15 years

or same data stored on a file.

28. A file called RATE contains the following data.

EMPLOYEE NAME	ID #	RATE OF PAY
JONES, EDNA	1234	4.75
BLACK, ED	1896	8.55
JOHNSON, PAUL	1999	4.50
ALBERT, TONY	2314	4.75
FONG, ROBERT	2891	5.90
CUMMINGS, RON	3002	4.85
LLOYD, LLOYD	3533	5.15
MERIDITH, FRANK	4111	6.25
PORTER, CHARLES	4681	7.50
SASANO, MARY	4879	6.75

Write a program to read the data and to store the ID # in a table called I and the rate in a table called R. After you have read all the data into the tables, search through the tables to find and print the ID numbers of all employees whose rate of pay is either below $5 per hour or over $7 per hour. Also, keep track of the number of employees who fall into this category and print out this figure at the end of the program. Output is shown below:

ID NUMBER	RATE
————	————
————	————
————	————

TOTAL   ABOVE   OR   BELOW   LIMITS
————

29. Two 15-record files called FILE1 and FILE2 have the following format.

PART NAME	PART NO
WIDGIT	1234

Ex: FILE1

COST PRICE	RETAIL PRICE
8.75	16.95

Ex: FILE2
File data is as follows

FILE1

PART NAME	PART NUMBER
Widgit	1234
Fender	8163
Bolt	4987
Frame	1000
Crank	7563
Starter	4876
Bumper	5555
Distributor	2468
Spark plug	4646
Cable	7322
Headlight	1857
Windshield	3924
Tail light	8598
Smog unit	9857
Gas cap	2591

FILE2

COST PRICE	RETAIL PRICE
$ 2.00	$ 4.00
85.00	160.00
.25	.75
500.00	750.00
45.00	75.00
18.30	29.75
65.00	110.00
15.00	30.00
.47	1.00
3.20	4.80
3.90	5.60
73.40	155.00
4.00	8.70
49.00	75.00
1.25	‾.50

Write a program to do the following steps.

a. Read FILE1 and store the Part Numbers in the odd-numbered slots of a 30-slot table called Z.

b. Read FILE2 and store the Cost Price in the even-numbered slots of the same table.

c. In a separate loop, search through the table to find those Part Numbers whose Cost Price exceeds $5. When you find this condition, print out the Part Number and the corresponding Cost Price.

PART NUMBER	COST PRICE
_____	_____
_____	_____
_____	_____

CHAPTER 14
SMALL COMPUTER SYSTEMS

LEARNING OBJECTIVES

Upon completion of the chapter you should understand the following:

The origins of the microprocessor and the terminology associated with it.

The difference between a microprocessor and a microcomputer.

The applications of microprocessors and microcomputers in today's world.

Be familiar with the term minicomputer and recognize that the definition of these terms is at best "hazy."

Know the makeup of the hardware and the software for small computer systems; recognize the extent of and use of small desktop or personal computer systems in a wide range of applications.

CHAPTER CONTENTS

Several of the earlier chapters discussed how the computer functioned: the structure of memory; the relationship of the various types of input and output devices; and how programs are handled by the hardware. The key point is that all these previous ideas related to how the system functions, but had nothing to do with the size of the components. As the size of the semiconductor components decreased, they became faster, required less power, and needed less packaging which, in turn, made the components less expensive. Prices dropped dramatically and end-users began to see more applications for these tiny chips. As demand soared, the price was again pushed down and new, better production technologies emerged to satisfy much of the demand. Today we are still in this situation, which is giving us a continually cheaper, better, and faster product. According to Jim Edlin, director of Micro-Marketing Consultants, "The microcomputer is a watershed technology—like the electric light, the automobile, and the telephone, it stands to change our everyday lives more than we can know."

MICROPROCESSORS

Originally, semiconductor logic circuits were designed to perform exact functions and the central processing units of third-generation computers were made up of hundreds and even thousands of these chips. These "hardwired" logic chips were then soldered onto printed circuit boards and plugged into the system.

FIGURE 14.1
Microprocessor chip and holder.

Intel Corporation had been one of the founders in the development of semiconductor memory chips for use on the large, third-generation computers. In 1970 one of their engineers decided that he could condense basic computer functions down to three silicon chips. The CPU itself was placed on a single chip and was called a "microprocessor" (Figure 14.1). Texas Instruments produced a fully operational chip in mid-1971 and by 1976, engineers could demonstrate that a single silicon chip had computing power equivalent to that of ENIAC produced 30 years earlier. The power of IBM's first commercially built computer, the IBM 701, today can be duplicated in a single chip costing $19 each. This point is particularly interesting when you consider that the original IBM 701 computer system cost about $1 million in the 1950s.

For logic and systems designers, the invention of the microprocessor amounted to a revolution. First, they began to replace the inflexible hardwired circuits in hand-held calculators with microprocessor chips. The most dramatic change came when the manufacturers developed *microprogrammable* microprocessors. A microprogrammable microprocessor is one in which the instruction set is not rigidly fixed in the hardware chip. Instead, the instruction set is defined in memory, the contents of which are activated when an instruction is decoded and executed. Since the interpretation of the instruction resides in memory, its meaning can be changed if this special area of memory can be changed. Application of the ultraviolet light causes the electric charges stored in the PROM (programmable read-only memory) portion to leak away prior to reprogramming.

In essence, manufacturers were now able to mass-produce logic chips that, with little effort, could be used for thousands of different applications. Microchips are now small enough and cheap enough that they can be incorporated into almost any device, machine, instrument, or appliance that can make use of the ability to store data and instructions and/or to perform calculations. For example, more and more of these chips are being incorporated into the fabrication of the 1982 automobile models to provide the driver with better information about the condition of the car's vital functions. Delco Electronics, a division of General Motors, turns out 20,000 microprocessors per day and on this basis, claims to be the world's largest computer manufacturer. One of the major characteristics of the microelectronics industry is the rapid and continuing decline in the cost of components. In 1960 approximately 500 million transistors were manufactured. By 1977, annual usage had increased 2000 times. This mass production has led to amazing cost reductions. For the reader, the most obvious example is the hand-held calculator, which has declined in price by a factor of 100 over the last decade.

Microprocessors vary in their architecture depending upon a variety of factors, but mainly upon the length of storage or data "word" that the user wishes to process. This, of course, depends upon the specific task the user has for the microprocessor. Generally, 4-bit microprocessors are used to control electronic games, appliances, and items such as cash registers. Eight-bit (byte) microprocessors are better suited to more complex tasks in automotive, educational, and "smart" instrumentation applications. Sixteen-bit processors are often used in sophisticated applications, such as data acquisition or in the upper range of desktop computer systems.

MICROCOMPUTERS

Intel then went one step further on their microprocessor idea by including additional chips to take care of the other basic functions of a computer and was able to incorporate all the necessary chips on a single board. This single-board *microcomputer* was crude when compared to full-scale computers, but the individual chips had a price between $5 and $30, and could be mass-produced. A microcomputer consists of the microprocessor chip combined with memory and input/output circuits so that it can perform some useful function (Figure 14.2).

As the prices of components decreased, a new market emerged for the home hobbyist who wanted to build a single-board computer from kit components (Figure 14.3). The mail order computer store led to retail computer stores that at first catered to the hobbyist trade. In 1978 there were about 750 such stores with 2000 or more predicted for 1983. However, the market changed rapidly as buyers became more sophisticated and less willing to play at the "nuts and bolts" level. Today the strength of the market lies in small business applications.

Large, single-board microcomputers were a notable achievement, but they were soon doomed to obsolescence by the incredible onslaught of computer technology, particularly LSI (large scale integration) and now by VLSI (very large scale integration). Current manufacturing techniques can now integrate the equivalent of several hundred thousand transistors on a single chip. This is far more than the

FIGURE 14.2
Microcomputer on a single board.

number of elements required by the microprocessor alone. With VLSI technology, memory, input/output, and other functions can reside on the same chip with the microprocessor. This means that the *entire* microcomputer can be placed on a *single chip* rather than a single board (Figure 14.4). The chip shown in the illustration was developed by Bell Labs and is used in a variety of telecommunications applications.

Despite its small size, the microprocessor shown in Figure 14.4 contains all the components of a full size central processing unit. Some

FIGURE 14.3
Microcomputer in kit form.

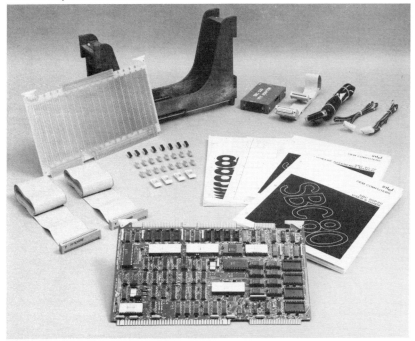

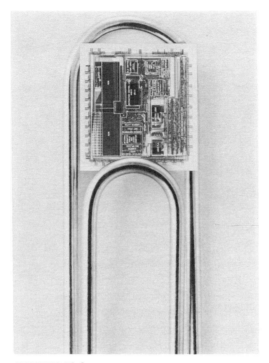

FIGURE 14.4
Microcomputer on a chip.

FIGURE 14.5
Microcomputer components.

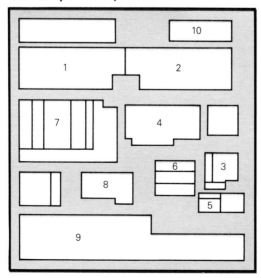

of the components are diagrammed in a schematic of that same chip (Figure 14.5).

1. Random access memory (RAM) for the manipulation of data.
2. Read-only memory (ROM), which contains the instruction set.
3. Arithmetic logic unit.
4. Instruction control logic array.
5. Instruction register decoder.
6. Program control register, which records the instruction being executed.
7. Internal register array and event counter.
8. Data control logic array.

Both microprocessors and microcomputers are generally incorporated into other devices. Indeed, a majority of the micros produced go to OEM's (original equipment manufacturers) for just that purpose. The chips and boards are used in a staggering number of products that are visibly changing the way we live.

Some of the uses of these microchips include cameras with built-in light meters; sewing machines that embroider complex designs at the touch of a button; home record players that allow the user to choose which songs to play from a record; video games on TV; chips that determine the proper detergent level and water temperature for washing machines; programmable chips that turn electrical devices on and off; talking clocks; and so forth (Figure 14.6). The possibilities in the automotive industry alone are endless. Engineers in Japan have been experimenting with microunits to activate and control lights, direction indicators, windshield washers, heating, ventilation, and other functions, all in response to orders from the vehicle's microcomputer. According to reports, by using micros the Japanese are able to save over 300 meters of wiring and to cut 113 electrical connections down to 37. Here in the United States we are already using microcircuitry to control ignition and carburetion functions on some cars. With computer performance increasing at the rate of approximately 30% per year it is possible for the manufacturer to tailor the terminals to the amount of "intelligence" required by the user. Intelligence is rapidly becoming part of every item we use and make.

A *microcomputer system* consists of the microcomputer, I/O interfaces, power supply, cabinetry, input/output devices, auxiliary storage units, programs, etc., and has general computing capability. Thus, microcomputers are essentially a smaller version of the so-called minicomputer (discussed in the next section). Their cost is about one-half to one-third that of a mini, and they use only a fraction of the power of a mini. Normally, they are slower than minis, with typical instruction execution time of 1 to 4 microseconds. At one time the distinction between a mini and a micro was determined by their price, language capability, processing power, internal bit size, and ability to

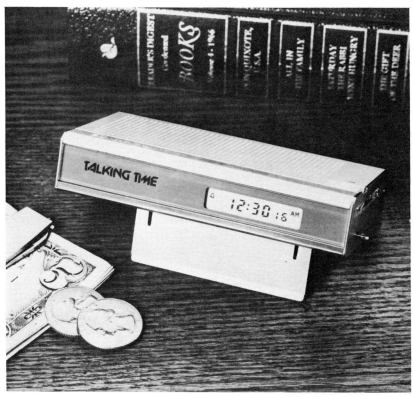

FIGURE 14.6
Talking clock.

attach peripheral equipment. These distinctions have fallen away one by one, until now several microcomputer systems currently on the market (such as the Radio Shack Model 16) operate in the area once thought to belong to the mini.

This early model of Bell Labs' 32-bit digital micro-processor contains 100,000 transistors, and is intended for use in telecommunications products. A Bell Lab spokesperson says that a smaller chip available later this year will have three-quarters the processing power of current medium-sized computers.

(Courtesy Infosystems)

"That's a great innovation ... microprocessors so small they're invisible ... unless, of course, you're putting me on."

MINICOMPUTERS

The minicomputer evolved in the 1960s because of a need for an inexpensive computer to perform specific processing tasks. The large computers of that era were quite efficient at "number crunching" in mathematical and scientific applications, but their costs could not be justified for most small business and industry uses. At that time a "mini" was defined as costing under $20,000 with a word length between 8 and 32 bits and with a memory range of 4000 to 56,000 bytes. Today, the term "mini" is an anachronism, as it has lost its original meaning, but the problem is that we really don't have a valid, current definition.

The name, however, had nothing to do with performance; only with size. As we became able to cram more and more circuitry into a smaller and smaller area, the power and capability of the mini increased while its size remained the same. The first minis were used to control or monitor sophisticated test and production machinery, but they quickly outgrew those uses.

The mini makers expanded their line of computers both upward and downward until the top-of-the-line systems became competitive on a hardware basis with such powerful machines of the 1970s as the IBM 370/158. The reason that these top-line minis did not totally compete with the "maxi" machines is that most mini manufacturers did not provide full system support, particularly in the software area. That changed rapidly, however, as the mini manufacturers gained experience in broad application areas. As the minis became more powerful, they migrated upward, while microcomputers took their place at the low end of the spectrum. Figure 14.7 shows a low-cost Hewlett-Pack-

FIGURE 14.7
Hewlett-Packard 1000 minicomputer with optional peripherals.

ard mini with a wide range of peripheral equipment that can be attached to the system.

One of the more important design aspects of the minicomputer has been its modularity, which permits expansion and flexibility of the system. While most microprocessors and microcomputers are sold to other manufacturers, minicomputer systems are normally sold on a "turnkey basis." Under a turnkey arrangement, a user acquires a computer system complete with auxiliary storage, input/output units, software, and communications capability for a specific application.

The advantage of a turnkey system is that a user who wants to acquire computer power and capability can do so without deep computer commitment. The vendor provides the hardware, software, training, and general "handholding" that is necessary in such an application. In actual fact, it is not always the manufacturer who sells turnkey systems. Often, the hardware is purchased by software houses that add the software solution to the hardware as a turnkey package.

As an example, consider the minicomputer system installed in the public library system in Boise, Idaho. The turnkey system was marketed by CL Systems, Inc., a firm whose only product is library systems. The system was designed to handle circulation transactions, reserves and overdue-book processing, inquiry into book status, and high-volume check-in and check-out. Special bar-encoded labels (much like those used in supermarkets) were placed on each book and read by means of a light pen reader.

The most important aspect of the system was that it required a minimum of computer expertise on the part of the librarians and clerks to operate it. Minimum training was provided by the vendor for the few people who had to have some knowledge of the system operation. Service is always a problem on any computer system, but CL Systems has an interesting solution. They maintain a telephone "trouble desk" to answer maintenance and operational questions. Generally, they are able to diagnose the problem by having library personnel display register contents by means of color-coded sense switches. The problem is then recreated at the vendor's site and a solution found.

The success of minicomputers and the turnkey approach was particularly evident when the industry leader IBM brought out several computers in this area. One of these was designed around what IBM called an "Industry Application Package." Each package was designed for a particular industry or application: Distributors, Food Industry, Billing, Inventory Control, Accounts Receivable and Sales Analysis, Financial Applications, etc.

In its simplest form, a small business computer consists of a central processing unit, a video screen and keyboard, disk storage, and a printer. Memory size can range from a low of about 4000 bytes to over a half a million storage characters. The low-end-of-the-line systems use floppy disks in multiple drive configurations, which store perhaps a million or more characters. The top-of-the-line systems use hard disk and store over a hundred million characters.

In terms of applications, small business computers generally fall into at least three broad categories: accounting machines, batch systems, and transaction-oriented systems. Historically, small accounting machines were the first devices to make inroads into small business. Earlier systems used magnetic-strip ledger cards, but newer units can process a variety of media.

Small, dedicated, batch processing systems featured expanded capability using magnetic disk and better, faster printers. Transaction-oriented systems are generally able to handle both data entry and processing concurrently. Single-user entry systems are not particularly complex, but multiuser systems require more sophisticated software and hardware. Still, these applications are well within the range of mini capabilities (Figure 14.8).

FIGURE 14.8
Minicomputer business system.

DESKTOP/
PERSONAL COMPUTERS

Today the term minicomputer tends to be used in reference to fairly sophisticated business and industrial applications. Even a quick look at any of the data processing magazines will show that the distinction between microcomputers and many of the minicomputer systems has been lost, particularly as microcomputers get more and more powerful and versatile. In place of these two terms we are hearing the terms "desktop computers" and "personal computers," which describe quite accurately how they are used. The consumer is looking for a microcomputer package that may be used for any one of several purposes.

1. Personal enjoyment through games such as Space Invaders.
2. Learning via special-skill games or CAI (computer assisted instruction) drill and practice session.
3. Personal management of records, checks, and general cataloging of information.

" WE'RE INTERESTED IN A MINICOMPUTER.
DO YOU HAVE ANYTHING IN
EARLY AMERICAN? "

4. Controlling other devices, such as security devices, lights, appliances, etc.
5. Word processing activities, encompassing letter and report writing, mailing lists, and the like.

The size of the personal/home computer market is staggering. The importance of this market is illustrated by the fact that in 1978 in its first year of personal computer sales, Tandy Corporation (Radio Shack) sold between 150,000 and 200,000 of its TRS-80 personal computers. In one year it became only the third company to ever sell that many computers, and it sold more than all the other microcomputer manufacturers combined (Figure 14.9). By 1980, micros accounted for one-third of the number of computers sold and according to *Popular Computing,* in 1981 nearly 800,000 units were delivered. (*Note:* Other sources put the number of deliveries at 1.2 million.)

Apparently, the only thing holding back a virtual flood of sales is the price. As one observer put it, "You don't spend $3000 to balance your checkbook." Prices, however, are dropping rapidly. Knowledgeable industry people predict that a home computer selling for $1500 in 1982 will be $700 in 1987. In the same time frame, small business computers will drop from $4500 to $2500.

The micro manufacturers face a problem in that they are having a hard time defining exactly what is "the market." Of the 800,000 machines delivered by 1982, only 25% were purchased for home applica-

FIGURE 14.9
Radio Shack personal computer.

tions. The rest went to widely varied business applications. To reach this market the Hewlett-Packard HP-85 is advertised as a "personal computer for professionals" (Figure 14.10).

The HP-85 is designed for personal use in business and industry by professionals such as engineers, scientists, accountants, and investment analysts. Because of its price, ease of use, and compactness, it also can be used in the home by serious hobbyists and as an instructional computer in secondary schools, colleges, and universities. This new computer is aimed at users who need computing power in dedicated applications at a reasonable price.

The biggest news in the personal computer market occurred in mid-1981 when IBM brought out its long-awaited entry, the IBM Personal Computer. For years IBM had ignored this market, but the success of Apple, Radio Shack, and Commodore showed that the market demand was not just a passing fad. Perhaps most important, IBM's entry has lent legitimacy to the personal computer market. The importance of the move is further underscored by the fact that it is being sold through special IBM Product Centers, Sears, Roebuck Business Centers, and the Computerland chain of retail stores. This represents a major departure from the traditional IBM approach to selling its products. In an even

FIGURE 14.10
Hewlett-Packard HP-85 personal computer.

more radical move, IBM's Personal Computer relied heavily on both hardware and software produced by others. They not only openly invited independent software applications but made their technical specifications known so that private hardware houses could devise and manufacture system enhancements. The advantage to this approach is that the Personal Computer has access to a great amount of existing software. All estimates place IBM in the top three in the microcomputer world, along with Tandy/Radio Shack and Apple. Most industry observers feel that IBM will be number one very shortly, if, indeed, it has not already reached that position (Figure 14.11).

But IBM was not the only manufacturer to decide that the micro market would be a large source of potential revenue. In mid-1982, Digital Equipment Corporation (DEC), acknowledged as number two in the DP industry, announced its entry into the micro market with three machines ranging from $3500 to $5000. At the same time, Burroughs and Victor Business Products made similar decisions. These new entries, however, differ from the earlier microcomputers in that they are based on a 16-bit microprocessor. The 16-bit machines have so much processing power that they are taking the place of the traditional minicomputer. Not everyone will need this extra capability but, as one manufacturer says, "Whatever you give people, they need twice as much."(Figure 14.12.)

FIGURE 14.11
IBM personal computer.

FIGURE 14.12
DEC personal computer.

"TO PLAY OR NOT TO PLAY"

A sign of modern times is the increasing concern of today's adults over the younger generation's interest in computer games, particularly the arcade games. To many adults, this interest is seen as an unhealthy, all-consuming preoccupation that transcends any rational explanation. But, like it or not, the fact of the matter is that computer video games have infiltrated their way into almost every nook and cranny of America. Jorge Schement, writing for the *Los Angeles Times,* has done an excellent job of placing all this into perspective in an article titled "Arcade Critics May Miss Crucial Issues." In the article he points out that video games are the leading edge of our move to a technological information society. His feeling is that this move is so swift that our educational system has not been able to adapt fast enough and that, in effect, video games are filling this void that has been created. As he puts it,

Students who have no formal instruction in computers or programming will find a video game is the first computer they can learn to control. In fact, the video games' teaching potential has already been tapped by the military and used effectively in numerous organizational settings for computer-use training.

His point is well taken. Many writers have pointed to the fact that these so called games are much more complex than they may seem. They require a high degree of mental concentration, strategy formulation, manual dexterity, and quick thinking. Jorge compares video games to what the automobile did for earlier generations. Just as the automobile prepared Americans for an industrial society, video games may be preparing today's youth for the information society.

His biggest complaint is that most adults have persisted "in seeing video games as simple substitutes for pinball machines or, worse, as passive replacements for social and intellectual activities." Part of his solution is that they are an excellent teaching device and that "we ought to demand more of the computer games our children play."

Micro users cover a wide range of uses. At one end you have the sophisticated uses made by investors who use the machines to access financial data bases (discussed in a later chapter), to plot market trends, rates of returns on complex investments, tax effects of long- and short-term holdings, and the construction of "What-if?" investment strategies. At the other end of the spectrum are the microcomputer products aimed at the youth market. Schools have become the most direct way to reach today's students who, in a few years, will become micro purchasers. The micro manufacturers aren't the only ones in the game. The toy manufacturers, led by Mattel, are deeply committed to producing micro products that have educational value. The secret, of course, is to develop a product that convinces the user, and the parent or the school, that the product is fun but worthwhile. Mattel's Discovery System is advertised as "computerized-learning fun" and features plug-in learning modules on mathematics, word games, logic, geography, science, economics, and social science. Children, however, are sophisticated users and want products that match their sophistication as they become more and more computer literate (Figure 14.13).

The versatility of the personal computers on the market today is astounding. Apple computers (see Figure 14.14), one of the "big three," has perhaps more software available for their system than any other manufacturer. Some of the applications include:

Small business	payroll
	accounts receivable
	general ledger
Financial planning	forecasting
	budgeting
Engineering/science	Modeling of physical processes
	data analysis
Education	to develop courseware
	teach computer science
Home	managing the household budget
	helping with school homework

FIGURE 14.13
ATARI® 800® home computer with Caverns of Mars® game.

FIGURE 14.14
Apple computer.

The key to the popularity of the personal desktop computers is the wide range of software that is available. Just one of these programs, Visicalc, has been credited with selling more Apples and Radio Shack machines than any other factor. Visicalc is a program that provides the user with an electronic ledger sheet for words, numbers, and formulas. It allows executives to plan budgets, compare actual expenditures with forecasts, and answer "What if?" questions based on changing values within a complex mix. The key, of course, is not that Visicalc does this: The success of this software, and others like it, is that it is easy to use and "friendly" to the operator.

A second major piece of software that contributed greatly to the popularity of microcomputer systems was an operating system called CP/M (Control Program/Microcomputer) developed by Digital Research, Inc. When microcomputers first entered the scene, each had its own software operating system. Thus, programs written for an Apple computer could not run on a Radio Shack machine, and so forth. For some software, such as Visicalc and others like it, the demand was so great that it was worth the time and effort to rewrite the program so that it could be run on perhaps a second or third brand of microcomputer.

Digital Research provided the solution by writing an operating system (CP/M) in the mid-1970s that was designed to run on most 8-bit microprocessors. The product was so good that by 1981 it had become the de facto industry standard microcomputer operating system. Now, software houses could write a program to work on CP/M rather than on a specific brand of microprocessor. With the coming of 16-bit machines, CP/M has been modified and is known as CP/M-86. The impact of CP/M is seen when you realize that it has been adopted by several hundred domestic and foreign microcomputer manufacturers.

Tandy/Radio Shack, a leader in the personal/desktop market has a wide range of systems to offer the prospective buyer. The low-end-of-the-line appeals to the home-hobbyist, but the top-of-the-line is a full-fledged business system that can handle sophisticated word processing tasks as well. Word processing will be covered in detail in a later chapter, but increased public demand for the ability to process words easily has forced the makers of small systems to offer this capability. One reason for the great success of the Radio Shack TRS-80 line of computers is that they offer extensive upward expansion of the system in addition to an incredible array of software, some of which can be applied to the full range of hardware. Some of the more popular software packages are listed below.

Real Estate	Mortgage and Cash Flow Analysis. Appreciation and Depreciation. Income and Expense.
Statistics	Multiple Linear Regression Analysis. Time Series Analysis. Chi Square Analysis.
Mailing List	Sorts up to 990 names in any logical sequence.
Payroll	Prints checks, Payroll Register. W-2 Forms.
General Ledger	Up to 600 accounts with three levels of summary and 50 entries per document.
Inventory Control	Up to 15,000 items and 200 vendors.
Accounts Receivable	Tracks up to 800 customers and 100 general ledger accounts.
Accounts Payable	Tracks up to 150 transactions per vendor.
Computerized File System Languages	BASIC; COBOL; FORTRAN; PASCAL

Schools are making extensive use of Radio Shack and Apple computers because they can be used as dumb terminals connected to minicomputer systems or they can function as stand-alone desktop microcomputer systems. As a matter of fact, in some school applications it may be cheaper to provide students with individual desktop computers than to set up an extensive terminal-oriented system using a large computer.

But perhaps the most surprising use of these personal microcomputers is coming from industry itself. More and more managers are becoming aware of the need for computers in the managing process. They are finally realizing that information is a resource to be managed and that the computer is the precise tool for that purpose. This realization plus the widespread development of "friendly" computer systems has broken through the traditional fear of computers held by many. These managers have then approached the data processing department with requests for programs that will provide information that will help them to manage better. Unfortunately, most corporate data processing centers have a tremendous backlog of program

FIGURE 14.15
Xerox 820 desktop computer.

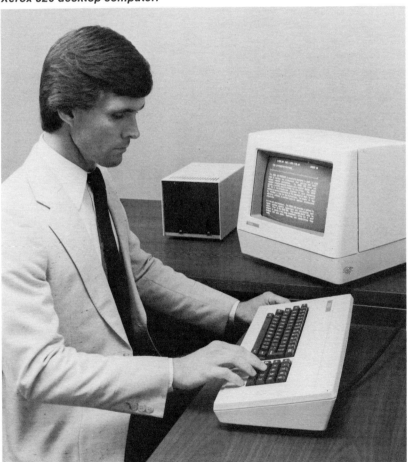

requests—up to two years in many cases. In desperation, these executives have been turning to Radio Shack, Apple, and similar computers to serve their immediate needs. Currently we are seeing such a steady stream of reports that managers are asking their corporations to provide them with a personal computer. In cases where their request,is denied, they often buy the computer with their own money and take it to the office. These users have come to realize a point that was developed in the first chapter of the book, that the computer is a tool for accessing and manipulating perhaps the most valuable of all assets—information.

Professional data processing workers are concerned that they will have to spend significant amounts of time in "bailing out" the beginner who gets in over his or her head. However, the benefits may well outweigh the disadvantages. One immediate gain is that these users became computer "literate" and will understand far better than before exactly what the computer can and can't do. In turn, this should lead to better communication between data processing and the rest of the company.

FIGURE 14.16
Pocket computer.

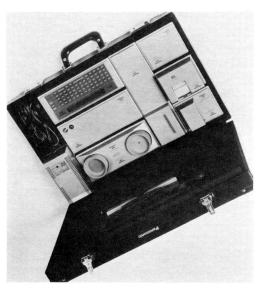

FIGURE 14.17
Pocket computer with accessories.

POCKET COMPUTERS

As of the time that this section was written, at least three firms are marketing what they call "pocket computers." These hand-held devices are not play things, but are designed to fit a need. They differ from traditional calculators in that they are programmable (in BASIC) and can operate alone or with adapters for a printer and a cassette recorder (Figure 14.14). The Panasonic version (called The Link) starts at 16K of memory but can be upgraded to 48K, depending upon the needs of the user. More important, it is part of a modular system that includes a printer, a TV adapter for video output, and communications capability (Figure 14.15).

BUSINESS APPLICATIONS

In contrast to the turnkey library application described earlier, real estate sales people in New York are using a minicomputer in an interesting way. The system, located at Multiple Listing Service (MLS) of Long Island, is making the job of finding the right house for the right client more efficient. MLS is a group of over 600 participating real estate offices in the area that store real estate data on a minicomputer. Agents in the field, equipped with portable terminals, are able to access the machine to take advantage of a number of supportive services.

One service that seems to greatly aid sales is the residential sales analysis. The prospect provides the amount of his current monthly rent and an estimate of annual income. Once the data is entered, a mini-system program prints out the price the client can afford without spending more than the amount currently being spent. The program also prints a listing of the tax benefits that will accrue and the amount of equity over a long-range period.

Perhaps the key application on the system, however, is the listing update. As each new listing is entered into the system, it immediately becomes available to all salespeople. The agent can also enter the prospect's requirements as to number of rooms, location, etc. Other agents can then search through these coded entries to see if they have a matching parcel for sale. The system also lists what similar houses sell for when the client puts a house up for sale.

A second example illustrates one of the most common uses of a minicomputer system: inventory control. Kent Beverages of Grand Rapids, Michigan, is a beer and wine wholesaler that, like all liquor dealers, must abide by a huge number of federal and state liquor laws. All sales and inventory data, for example, must be kept for seven years.

The wine inventory list is preset in that buyers choose from an existing list. When wine is ordered, inventory is altered and a customer picklist is generated for warehouse personnel.

Beer, however, is sold on an entirely different basis, and a different set of programs had to be written to take care of this type of transaction.

Actually, a complete turnkey package was not available for beer/wine wholesalers, so Kent Beverage wrote most of the programs with their own personnel who had no previous experience in data processing. Initial cost of the system (CPU, slow printer, one CRT terminal, and one floppy disk) was $17,000, low by almost any pricing standards, yet enough computer power to do the job.

A third application illustrates the fact that even though you have a fairly large minicomputer system, you may still have use for desktop computers. Lee Pharmaceuticals in southern California has 50 Radio Shack computers in addition to a Basic Four minicomputer system. Lee is a specialized manufacturer of dental and orthodontic materials and biomedic adhesives and has a staff of 40 engineers. However, the engineers are not the only ones who use the desktop computers. The owner, Dr. Henry Lee, has two, the heads of data processing and public relations each have two, most of the scientists have them, the sales-people have them, and a good many of the secretaries have them.

Knippers Rental Center in Santa Ana, California, spent $15,000 for a Durango F-85 desktop system that has enabled them to escape from under an ever-increasing mound of paperwork. In addition to doing traditional accounting work, such as accounts receivable, accounts payable, and general ledger, the system has special software tailored to the equipment-rental business. This software provides them with re-turn-on-investment reports, utilization of equipment records, and notification when a piece of equipment is not being fully utilized.

SUMMARY OF IMPORTANT POINTS

☐ To a very great extent the computer revolution has taken place at the microchip level, where technology has enabled us to etch thousands of circuits on tiny chips.

☐ This technology led to the birth of the microprocessor, a functioning central processing unit on a single silicon chip. The immediate outgrowth of this was that a small computer, a microcomputer, could be placed on a single board.

☐ Advances in chip technology then led to the placement of a complete microcomputer on a single chip.

☐ Most microprocessors or microcomputers are integrated into a bewildering array of devices to give them varying degrees of "intelligence." The most frequent buyers of these devices are OEMs (original equipment manufacturers), who incorporate them into their products.

☐ The so-called minicomputers of a few years past are now very difficult to distinguish from high-powered microcomputers. Together they have revolutionized the data processing industry.

☐ The original demand for small, personal computer systems led to the eventual development of retail computer stores, which at first served the home-hobbyist market. In recent years this market has been overtaken by the personal computer users, who want a fully functioning system.

☐ Turnkey, or fully functional systems consisting of the proper hardware and software are extremely popular today and account for a great portion of the sales to small business operations.

GLOSSARY OF TERMS

Microprocessor—a complete, functioning CPU on a single integrated circuit chip.

Microcomputer—a functional computer, usually on a single board or on a single chip.

Minicomputer—no standard definition exists today because of the rapid change of the industry. Generally, however, the term "minicomputer" refers to a physically small computer that is relatively inexpensive ($20,000 to $100,000).

OEM (original equipment manufacturer)—a manufacturer who buys microprocessors or microcomputers in large quantities for incorporation into the items they market.

Turnkey system—an operational computer system that comes complete with both the hardware and software for a particular application. The user only has to "turn the key" to make the system work.

THOUGHT QUESTIONS

1. What uses do you think you personally would have for a microprocessor? Try to list at least a half a dozen uses that you can envision.

2. Assuming that you have a full- or part-time job, what uses do you see there for a microprocessor?

3. Have you had any experience using small computers either directly or indirectly?

4. What do you think microprocessors and microcomputers can be used for in the future.

5. Other than cost, why would a small business wish to use a microcomputer rather than a larger system?

CHAPTER 15
DATA
COMMUNICA-
TIONS

LEARNING OBJECTIVES

Upon completion of the chapter you should under-stand the following:

The need for data communications.

The nature of four basic transmission facilities:
 Telephone lines.
 Coaxial cables.
 Microwave.
 Satellites.

About the basic problem that exists in sending digi-tal information over facilities designed for the trans-mission of the human voice.

The use of modulators/demodulators to change the format of digital data to analog form.

The three general modes under which data can be transmitted: simplex, half-duplex, and full duplex.

The use of and the need for multiplexors in a data communications system, and the differences be-tween synchronous and asynchronous transmission.

That we are experiencing a staggering growth in the need to communicate data and that more and more complex networks are being created to serve this need.

That local networks using private branch exchanges are springing up as business firms in localized areas make use of computer facilities.

A combination of hardware and software proce-dures or protocols are used to interface the com-ponents of the networks.

The nature of two communication methods: real-time systems and timesharing.

CHAPTER CONTENTS
DATA TRANSMISSION

TRANSMISSION FACILITIES
TELEPHONE LINES
COAXIAL CABLES
MICROWAVE SYSTEMS
COMMUNICATION SATELLITES

COMMUNICATION SERVICES
MULTIPLEXING
ERROR CHECKING

NETWORKS
COMMUNICATIONS-ORIENTED SYSTEMS
REAL-TIME SYSTEMS
TIMESHARING

BUSINESS APPLICATIONS
 FUTURISTIC HOME USES APPLES

SUMMARY OF IMPORTANT POINTS

GLOSSARY OF TERMS

THOUGHT QUESTIONS

People have always had a need to communicate and, to a great extent, the history of our society has been a history of communications. For a great many years our needs were relatively modest and even the first mechanical device, the telegraph, was a simple form of communication. That form of communication dominated the industry for a period of nearly 40 years until the invention of the telephone in 1876.

As time passed, however, our communication needs became more complex. First the train, and then the automobile and then the airplane fostered the development of a mobile population that became increasingly anxious to communicate rapidly over long distances. In the 1940s and 1950s business firms followed this trend by decentralizing their operations to outlying division and branch offices. The need for large, complex communication systems during World War II added to the already increasing demand for communications capability, but now a new element was added—the computer. The need to communicate to and from the computer has dominated the second half of this century and this need has forever changed the nature of our society.

Our problem then becomes one of getting the information to the place or places where it can best be used. In this chapter, therefore, the emphasis will be on how data communication takes place and on the makeup and use of communications facilities. According to Edgar C. Gentle, *Data Communications in Business,* the term data communications is "The movement of encoded information by means of electrical transmission systems."

Unfortunately, communications technology and hardware often are alien topics to even the most experienced data processing professional. Perhaps even more unfortunate is the fact that, because the technology is complex and uses its own jargon, the subject tends to be omitted from the training of data processing students. But the fact of the matter is that the two technologies are coming closer together and, in the near future, it will be difficult to say where one ends and the other begins. The following pages will acquaint you with the basics of data communications.

DATA TRANSMISSION

At this point you may be tempted to say that data transmission is not really anything for you to be concerned about. However, you may get more deeply involved in this than you suspect. Chapter 1 mentioned the possibility of working at home on a remote terminal that is connected to the corporate computer system. The term "electronic cottage" was coined by noted futurist and author Alvin Toffler, who envisions the potential for a dynamic change in our society arising from the marriage of computer and communication technology.

More and more companies can be described . . . as people huddled around a computer. Put the computer into people's homes, and they no longer need to huddle . . . It is worth recognizing that if as few as 10 to 20 percent of the workforce . . . were to make this historic transfer over the next 20 to 30 years, our entire economy, our cities, our ecology, our family structure, our values, and even our politics would be altered almost beyond recognition. It is a possibility—a plausibility, perhaps—to be pondered.[1]

TRANSMISSION FACILITIES

Earlier in the text you studied the steps of the data processing cycle and you may recall that data had to be collected before being processed, and then it had to be distributed to those who could make use of the information. As long as these two steps can be performed in close proximity to the computer system, there is relatively little difficulty. The word "close" is a bit ambiguous but most terminals, for example, can be attached to a computer at distances up to about one-quarter mile with simple cable connections. When done in this manner, the terminals are said to be *hardwired,* since each unit will have an actual wire connecting it to the host processor. Systems of this type are common in schools, manufacturing, and business operations involving centralized office facilities. Beyond the quarter-mile distance, however, we encounter problems because simple wire connections cannot carry the messages accurately.

It appears that the obvious solution to the problem is to use the telephone system to transport information to and from remote terminals. The traditional telephone system, however, is only one of several transmission facilities that can be used. Let's take a quick look at some of the options that are available.

TELEPHONE LINES

Telephone is the oldest transmission medium and consists of a pair of wires (often called a "twisted pair") strung on poles. We all recognize that telephone systems are generally reliable and can be used for the transmission of data, but therein lies the problem: Telephones were designed to handle the transmission of information in voice or *analog* form rather than data in digital form. Before computer data can be sent to a remote terminal device it must be changed into analog form in order to go over the telephone lines.

Electronic devices called "data sets" perform the task that is technically known as "modulation" and "demodulation" (changing from digital to analog and back to digital form). In abbreviated terminology they are usually called *modems* and simply look like an electronic "black box" (Figure 15.1). Several modulation methods are used, but Figure 15.2 shows the general method by which a modem converts the digital data into analog form.

Terminals come in a bewildering assortment of types and capabilities. Most of the terminals are of the stand-alone variety with varying characteristics, but with speeds in the range of 30 to 100 characters per second. However, not all terminals are of the stand-alone type. Both regular terminals and portable terminals, of the attache-case size, can be connected into telephone lines by means of *acoustic couplers.* An acoustic coupler is nothing more than a specialized modem whose connection with the telephone system is made by means of a microphone.

Portable terminals with acoustic couplers (Figure 15.3) are extremely useful in situations where the salesperson does not get back to the main office for days or even weeks. With a portable terminal, the salesperson can make calls on several customers and then call the orders in to the main computer through the regular telephone system.

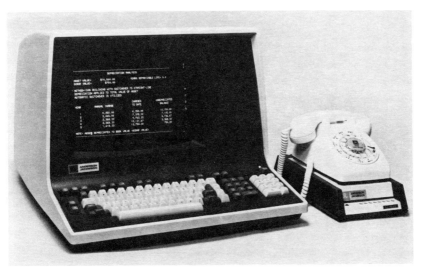

FIGURE 15.1
Terminal with telephone and modem.

Since sales may take place in different time zones, the main computer may be run on a 24-hour basis. In addition to just placing the orders, the portable terminal may be used to verify that a specific quantity is on hand or that special credit terms are authorized. However, units of this type do have at least one major disadvantage. The most important limitation on the performance of these units is the quality of the telephone itself. Unfortunately, there is a wide range in telephone characteristics that cannot be compensated for in the acoustic coupler. Figure 15.4 shows a typical computer system using all the facilities discussed so far.

By now you are probably aware that transmission facilities are enormously varied. However, there are three basic modes in which data can be transmitted over standard two-wire circuits: simplex, half-duplex and full-duplex.

FIGURE 15.2
Converting digital data to analog form.

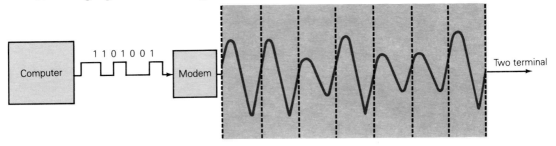

FIGURE 15.3
Portable terminal with acoustic coupler.

A simplex channel can carry information in one direction only. The most common use of this type of channel is in situations involving receive-only terminals located at branch offices or warehouses.

A half-duplex circuit or channel can carry information in either direction, but in only one direction at a time. A circuit of this type is used in inquiry-oriented systems where the computer sends information back to a terminal user in response to a request. Banks, investment firms, law enforcement agencies all typically use two-way inquiry/response systems. After a message is sent to the receiving device, the line is reversed or turned around so that the receiving device can acknowledge that the message was received. The time delay is appreciable (in the neighborhood of 150 milliseconds), but acceptable for most terminal-oriented systems.

Full-duplex channels normally use four-wire telephone circuits to carry information in both directions at the same time, and normally are used in extensive, high-speed communications networks (Figures 15.5 and 15.6).

COAXIAL CABLES

Twisted pairs of wires work well up to a point but, as the communication needs of the company expand, the wires will no longer be able to handle data at the higher and higher speeds that are necessary. A

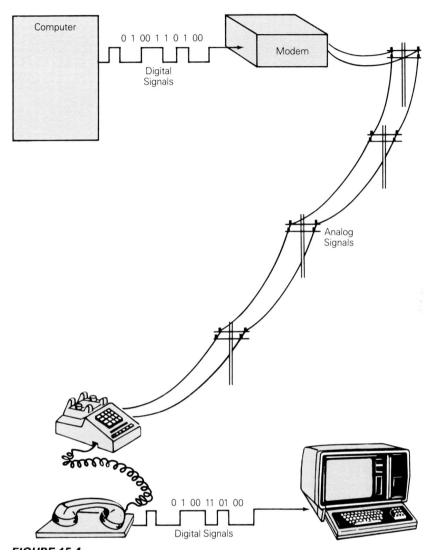

FIGURE 15.4
Data communications using telephone lines.

coaxial cable consists of a central cylinder surrounded by a series of wires that can carry data at a much higher rate than twisted pairs. Typically, they are used in large data processing centers and run under the floor or overhead in false ceilings. It has even been laid on the ocean floor to provide data transmission facilities between continents. In some cases, coaxial cables are being replaced with cables that are made up of thin glass fibers that can carry enormous amounts of data at high speeds. For the most part, these fiber-optic cables are being used experimentally in some of the major "hub" cities to evaluate the feasibility of the method. Their future, however, looks extremely promising at this point.

FIGURE 15.5
Transmission modes.

MICROWAVE SYSTEMS

Frequently, coaxial cables are tied into microwave relay systems that transmit high-frequency radio waves above ground. Undoubtedly you have seen the familiar dish-type antennas typical of these microwave systems located on the roofs of tall buildings and on remote hilltop locations. This method of transmission is expensive because, even

FIGURE 15.6
Communications modem.

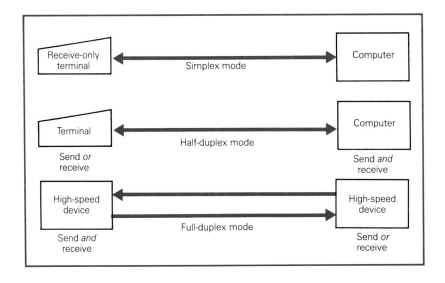

though it transmits much faster than coaxial cable, the repeater antennas must be located in straight-line sight of each other. Since microwaves travel in a straight line, the transmission facility is made up of a series of towers spaced 25 to 30 miles apart. One of the largest single users is, as you would suspect, the federal government, but many states, particularly those that cover a wide geographical area, have extensive microwave systems.

COMMUNICATIONS SATELLITES

Far less visible to us are the communication satellites that have been blasted into space and placed into stationary orbit above the earth. Earth stations beam precisely aligned microwave transmissions to the satellites, which relay them on to another earth station, as shown in Figure 15.7.

Satellites have been used since 1963 when the U.S. Communications Satellite Act established Comsat Corporation, which was the United States' part of an international network of communication satellites (Intelsat). Today, the Intelsat system encompasses 260 earth

FIGURE 15.7
Satellite system.

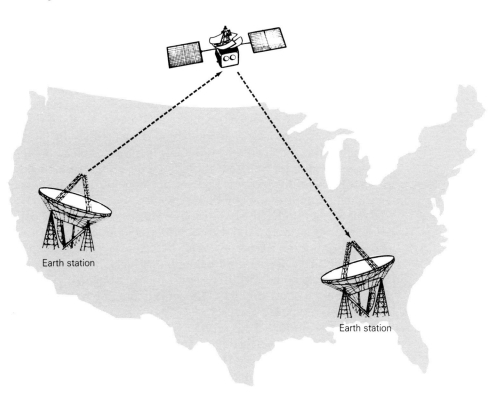

Earth station

Earth station

stations in 130 countries and can carry 12,000 simultaneous telephone conversations and two television channels. The satellites orbit the earth at a distance of about 22,000 miles, which means that an earth-to-satellite-to-earth transmission must travel at least 44,000 miles.

By early 1982 there were 12 satellites in orbit with 17 (7 as replacements) scheduled for launch within the next 4 years. In addition to the telephone companies, at least eight firms are involved in the domestic satellite business, and four actually have devices in orbit. Satellite communication, however, does have its problems, among which is that it must compete with excellent terrestrial communication facilities.

COMMUNICATION SERVICES

Data transmission services are available from *common carriers,* such as the Bell Telephone Company, or from various private carriers. In past years private carriers have offered specialized communication services that were not in direct competition with the major telephone companies. Recently, however, some of the larger computer companies have come out with services rivaling those of the telephone systems.

Most of the communication channels discussed earlier belong to the Bell Telephone system and are of the twisted-pair, dial-up variety. However, some large business firms have extensive communication needs that cannot be adequately served by dial-up lines. They then use special *dedicated* lines (also called *leased lines*) for this purpose. These lines are generally of higher quality than dial-up lines since they do not go through the normal switching process with which we are familiar. Modems are still required, but dialing is not necessary since the line serves only one customer. For low-volume traffic, dial-up lines are usually appropriate and cost considerably less than dedicated lines. A point to remember here is that the telephone system was never designed to handle digital data, and yet our demands for this type of traffic are increasing at the rate of 35% per year.

Earlier we mentioned the basic problem of converting digital data to analog form in order to send it through the telephone lines. This has been a major bottleneck because the characteristics of the telephone line are such that data cannot be handled at high speed, as the wave form tends to become distorted as it proceeds down the wire. For voice communication this has little effect, but for transmission of digital information it is critical.

Recently, a solution to this problem of distortion has been found in the construction of special facilities just for the transmission of digital data. Called DATAPHONE Digital Service (DDS), it offers higher reliability and greater accuracy to the user. In DDS there is no need for data conversion equipment because the signal is carried in binary form. The system uses regenerative repeaters or boosters placed at intervals in the communication links to reshape the signal to the proper form.

Voice-grade communication channels have long been used for thr transmission of pictures, drawings, and handwritten material. Strictly speaking, this is not necessarily part of a computer system, but it does illustrate the range of communications capabilities, particularly when combined with computers. Called *facsimile transmission* (FAX), it has typically taken from three to six minutes to send a copy of a business document from one location to another. The 3M Corporation has a new facsimile transmission unit that can transmit a 300-word business letter in 20 seconds. The chief element in this system is a microcomputer that compresses or condenses graphic data into digital form. After being compressed, the data is converted to analog and sent over voice-grade channels to a FAX unit at the receiving end.

MULTIPLEXING

So far we have described a data communications system as consisting of three major parts.

1. Terminals and a central processing unit.
2. Modems to convert signals from one format to another.
3. A communications channel for the transmission of information.

Using this information, we set up a relatively simple data communications system in Figure 15.4. If we had three terminals and, assuming that we are communicating beyond the local area, we would need the terminals, six modems (one for each end of the transmission line), three channels or telephone lines, and the central processing unit, as shown in Figure 15.8.

The data communication system shown in Figure 15.8 probably is cost-effective because we have only three terminals using three, relatively low-cost communications channels. However, if we were to expand the system to 30, 40, or more terminals, the cost of all the low-speed lines could become prohibitive. At this point it may be more efficient to use *multiplexors* in the system in conjunction with a single, high-speed transmission line.

A multiplexor is an electronic device that takes the data coming from or going to each terminal and combines it into a single stream for transmission over the channel. The messages do not get mixed because of separator codes inserted into the data stream by the multiplexor. Figure 15.9 shows the use of multiplexors in a communications system.

ERROR CHECKING

So far we have disregarded the problem of how a data communications system handles errors. Errors are a big problem because communication facilities seldom are as accurate as the movement of data

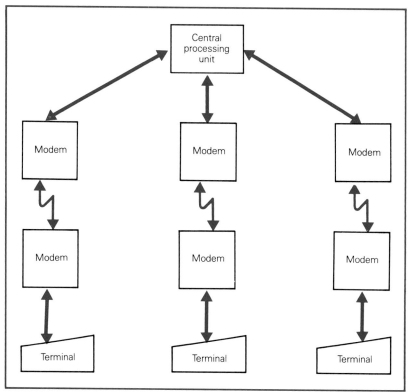

FIGURE 15.8
Data communication system with multiple terminals.

within the computer itself. A great many terminal-oriented systems send data *asynchronously,* that is, without any synchronization between the characters being sent. For example, the user of an inquiry system may be entering a customer name by striking one or two keys quickly and then, after a pause, three or four more. This type of transmission is often called *start-stop* because each character is headed by a start bit and trailed by one or more stop bits. Error detection is accomplished by having the receiving device "echo back" the character just sent.

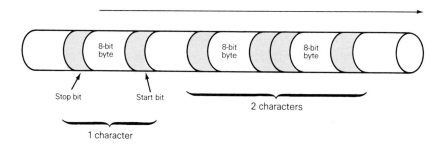

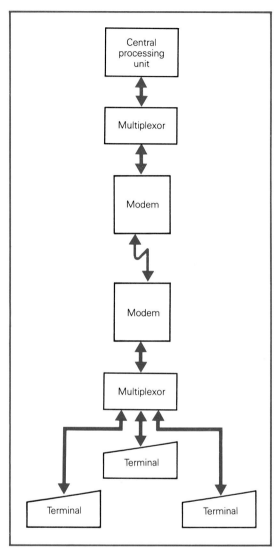

FIGURE 15.9
Multiplexor in a data communications system.

Synchronous transmission usually involves communication between high-speed devices such as tape and disk drives and the central processing unit. With this method, blocks of characters are sent at regular timed intervals. The modems are kept synchronized by the periodic transmission of a sync bit from the host computer and its communication components. Errors are detected through the block header and trailer and parity bits. If an error is detected, the block is sent again. After a specified number of tries, transmission is halted and the system alerts the operator.

"Henderson here has some terrific ideas on controlling our communications costs."

The task of putting together a data communications system is not easy, as the various components—terminals, modems, and the central processing unit—may each have come from a different manufacturer. Originally, each manufacturer has its own internal standard for interconnection of parts, but today most companies adhere to a standard interface for the connection of terminals. As defined by the Electronics Industries Association (EIA), it is the EIA RS-232 "Interface Between Data Processing Terminal Equipment and Data Communications Equipment."

NETWORKS

With a few major exceptions, the era of the centralized, stand-alone, large-scale computer system has been replaced by an era of data communications using a wide variety of methods and media. All signs point to the fact that it will be increasingly hard to differentiate between data processing and data communications, since they have merged in all but name. As a matter of fact, several new terms, including "telematics," have been coined to more clearly represent this relationship.

The systems described so far cannot really be called networks. Although several definitions are used, a network today is considered to

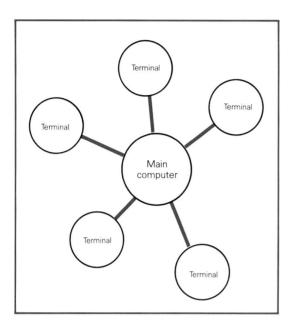

be a system of linked terminals that can operate independently and yet share data and other resources, such as printers and peripheral storage. The earliest networks consisted of terminals (known as "nodes") in the network connected to a main computer in a starlike arrangement.

More recent network variations use a "ring" or "bus" arrangement that eliminates the need for a main central processing unit. The powerful new microprocessors described in an earlier chapter perform a dual function as both terminals and central processing units.

In a bus arrangement (Figure 15.10), all the units are connected to a single cable or bus that does not originate from a central point. Each unit in the network has as much local hardware (diskettes and printers) as it needs, but all the users can share data from the hard disk. The big problem with this type of network is that the network hardware/software must be able to resolve conflicts when two users try to send messages at the same time.

A local network is a data communications system that interconnects terminals and computers within a single building or within a local area. As with regular long-distance networks, they make possible the sharing of computer power and data files by users at remote locations. Most networks of this type are implemented by using Private Branch Exchange (PBX) or Centrex telephone systems. In this situation, a microcomputer terminal is substituted for the telephone switchboard and a regular voice-grade channel is used to carry the information.

The federal government has created incredibly large and complex communication networks in its SAGE system (Semi-Automatic Ground Environment), which watches over the air space of North America. The

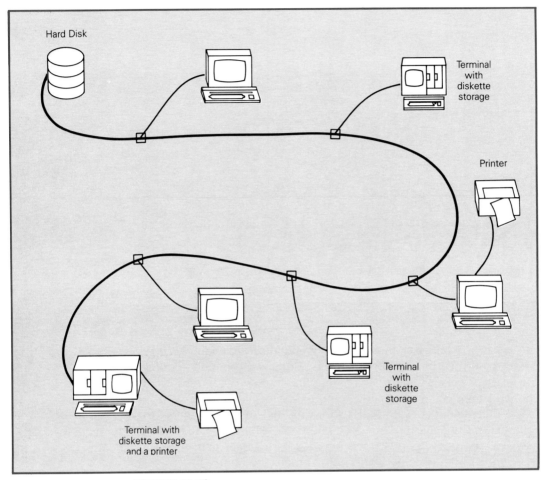

FIGURE 15.10
Bus network.

Ballistic Missile Early Warning System (BMEWS) and the system main-tained by our Strategic Air Command (SAC) are further examples of integrated communications systems. Since the advent of television coverage of our manned space flight series, it is almost impossible for anyone to be unaware of the extent and importance of a system of global communications.

In a business setting, Westinghouse Corporation has long been a leader in large automated networks. They have actually set up a Tele-Computer Center to provide communications with and control of their chain of warehouses and sales offices throughout the United States. In the transportation industry, railroads have had all the facilities for establishing complete communications networks but, generally speaking, they have only recently started to automate their systems. The airlines, particularly American Airlines with its complex flight re-

THE ARPAnet SYSTEM

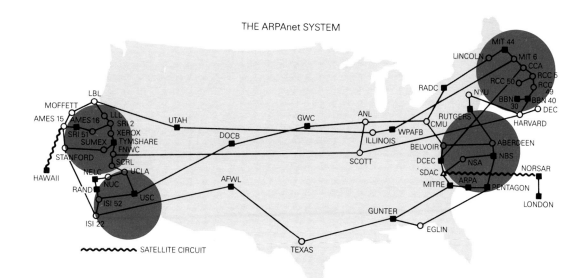

FIGURE 15.11
ARPA communications network.

servation system, are in a continual state of modification, expansion, and improvement of their systems.

A variety of hardware and software methods are used to interface the computer and its equipment with that of the communication channel. These interface control procedures are called *protocols* (or "hand-shaking") and are essential to the construction of a computerized network. Most mainframe computers are not designed to handle data communications activities, so special communication processors are used just for this purpose. Called *front-end processors,* these specialized minicomputers relieve the host computer of many if not all of the tasks associated with data communications.

One of the earliest networks was one called ARPANET, which was designed for the Department of Defense in the 1950s. As shown in Figure 15.11, it transmitted data between military installations scattered throughout the United States.

Unfortunately, networks of communicating machines—central processing units, terminals, multiplexors, facsimile devices, modems, front end processors, etc.—have evolved in a totally disorganized way. In 1974 IBM introduced its System Network Architecture (SNA) in an attempt to bring some sense of order to its own communications offerings. At that time it had over 35 different network access methods and standards for establishing physical and electronic connections. IBM is not alone, however, in devising networks. General Electric, Motorola, Digital Equipment Corporation, Xerox, General Telephone and Electronics, International Telephone and Telegraph, and others are already into or plan to get into the network business.

"YOU HAVE REACHED AN EARTH STATION LINKED TO A SATELLITE IN THE 6GHz BAND. PLEASE HANG UP AND DIAL AGAIN."

COMMUNICATIONS-ORIENTED SYSTEMS

Data processing systems that involve communications activities are, for the most part direct-access systems because of the need for a quick response. Two distinct types of communications-oriented systems will be covered here: real-time systems and timesharing. A third candidate, distributed data processing will be covered in the next chapter.

REAL-TIME SYSTEMS

The term "real-time" means many things to many people, so we must be careful in its use. The traditional definition of a real-time system is one in which a response to an on-going activity is generated in time for the user to take appropriate action. Most business operations do not require a quick response in terms of time, but there are a few to which real-time is important. In some cases, both the time element and the certainty of getting a response at all is so important that a backup computer is employed to take over in case the "first string" computer malfunctions. Typical of this application are airline reservation systems.

All passenger airlines faced a critical situation in the early 1960s. As a regulated industry, they began to come under more and more criticism over their methods of handling flight reservations, and at the same time they had expended huge amounts of money for jet aircraft that they were having difficulty filling. Today, some 20 years later, the problem is still the same, only caused by high fuel costs, intense industry competition, and a change in economic conditions. At that earlier time, part of the answer lay in the installation of a real-time reservation-response system. With a break-even factor of about 55% (i.e., 55% of the seats on a flight had to be filled in order not to lose money), it was imperative that a method be found to solve the problem. American Airlines, with its SABRE system, was one of the pioneers in this area, but all the major airlines now have similar systems.

The key point in airline reservations is that the customer wants reasonably quick response to questions concerning seat availability and connecting flight information. The system not only gives these answers, but it can provide many more services to the customer, including reservations for particular seats on a flight, airport car rental reservation, and special service provisions during flights. The process starts when the reservation agent keys in the request for information on a terminal that is part of the network system. Within a few seconds the response is available at the unit so that the agent can complete the reservation process. For the airline, the payoff comes when seats become available because of late cancellations. What it means, of course, is that seat availability is known right up to the moment that the aircraft takes off. Figure 15.12 illustrates an on-line airline reservation system that shows the real-time aspect of the operation: two central processing units are available, but the second, or standby computer is not idle. Among other things, it performs various types of batch processing jobs that can be delayed or postponed in the event this computer has to take over the primary on-line, real-time operations.

TIMESHARING

Another processing method is known as timesharing, and the terminology is exactly descriptive, since it refers to the idea of many users sharing access to a computer. During the early years of computer development it was obvious that computers were getting larger and faster, but that the I/O devices could not match the increased speed and power of the central processing unit. Although many people were involved along the way, Christopher Strachey is generally given credit for proposing (in 1959) the idea of sharing time on a computer. He suggested that the computer, because of its fantastic speed, could be used more efficiently by giving its attention to many users on a timesharing basis.

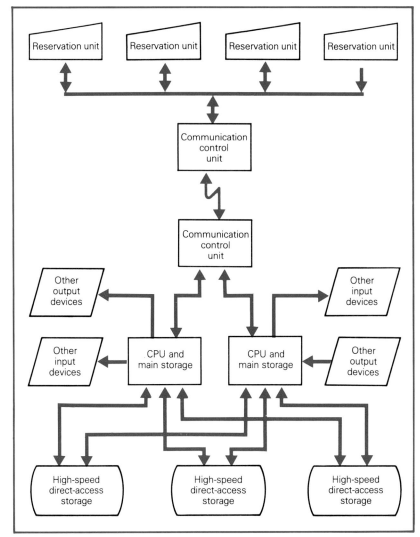

FIGURE 15.12
Real-time airline reservation system.

With the aid of federal money, the first true timesharing system was initiated at the Massachusetts Institute of Technology in 1961, where the CTSS (Compatible Timesharing System) serviced eight users through an IBM 7090 computer. At that time, computer memory was partitioned into eight segments, one for each user. A software "clock" allocated, in turn, a brief portion of time to each of the eight terminals. On today's computers, the time allocated to each terminal may be as little as 1/100 of a second or as much as 1/10 of a second, which is very little by our standards, but which is an extraordinary length of time in relation to the speed of the CPU.

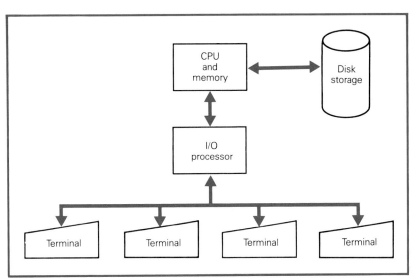

FIGURE 15.13
Timesharing system.

Two general methods of timesharing are in use today. In one method, each terminal user gets full use of memory during his or her slice of time that has allocated. A separate CPU (called an input/output) processor takes care of the job of determining which user shall have access to the main computer. During this time, the system completes as much of the program as it can, stores the program and any results that have been generated, and then goes on to the next user in sequence. This process is repeated for each active terminal until the system returns to the original user. The first user's program is then read in from disk and processing continues until the time has expired and, once more, the program is stored on disk. This process continues with the new users coming onto the system when others have finished and left their terminals (Figure 15.13).

A second method of timesharing uses a large amount of memory that has been partitioned into segments for each one of the user terminals. In this case, the users' programs remain in memory but are serviced on the same rotating basis.

BUSINESS APPLICATIONS

The scope or sheer physical size of a communications network often is difficult to see. This is particularly true in the case of the Missouri Pacific Railroad (Mo-Pac), which has a communications complex that

FUTURISTIC HOME USES APPLES

A home near Greenwich, CT has been built with a microcomputer system that controls everything from the home's solar heating to evening entertainment. It can even help the kids with homework.

The Sun/Tronic House, the creation of Copper Development Association, Inc. (New York), uses an Apple II to continuously monitor the energy performance of all solar components. All mechanical systems in the house, including lighting systems, emergency lighting systems, alarm systems, and motorized window shades, are controlled and monitored on the system, which is located in the library. All such information can be called up onto the G. E. 13-inch color TV, which is used as a display terminal.

A second personal computer is located in the family room, and it is dedicated to fun and learning. It is connected to a 45-inch TV set, also from G.E., which provides computerized games, plus information children may need for help with their homework.

Remote terminals are located in the kitchen and the master bedroom. Information such as menus, recipes, or the wine cellar's inventory can be stored on the computer.

Sun/Tronic's Apple II system cost $7,200, and this price includes the software operating system. All other software for the house was custom-designed by W. W. Gaertner Research, Inc. of Stamford, CT. W. W. Gaertner, company president, plans to make the software available for close to $15,000, plus needed interfacing hardware.

In addition to the latest energy and computer technologies, the home also features the most up-to-date architecture and interior design. (Source: *Computer Decisions,* March 1981.)

is larger and more complex than that used by the largest airlines or by the government in the Apollo space program. Mo-Pac uses several different types of communications networks to keep track of 1100 locomotives and 96,000 freight cars in 12 states being loaded or unloaded at 100,000 customer sidings. Each day the system handles 135,000 incoming and 160,000 outgoing messages.

Mo-Pac uses a variety of point-to-point and star networks in its communications system. Its needs are so large and so varied that it not only uses the facilities of the telephone system and Western Union, but it also has its own microwave system.

Called the Transportation Control System (TCS), the system uses over 400 on-line terminals in the network. The headquarters office alone has 91 CRT terminals for use by the executives that manage the railroad. The CPU, utilizing continuous reporting of railroad transactions, keeps track of every car and every train on the railroad. In addition, inventory information on various train yards and industrial areas (shops) is maintained on the system.

One of the more impressive subsystems is that of central car control. Through the network system the operators are able to match empty car supply with demand. This up-to-the-minute inventory of supply and demand makes it possible for the operations personnel to communicate distribution decisions quickly and directly to the yard offices.

In addition to maintaining a record of Mo-Pac's cars, the system also tracks "foreign cars," i.e., cars of competing railroads. The object is to move these cars back to the owner as fast as possible because Mo-Pac is charged a daily rental fee on each car kept in the system. So far, network operation has led to a 10–20% time reduction of rental fees. Along with that, another major benefit is an increase in cash flow because the system provides for easier and faster production of shipping and billing documents.

A second example of an outstanding communications network is that used by the State of Ohio in its Law Enforcement Automated Data System. Like the previous example, it is also a large system. Nearly 800 terminals at remote sites throughout Ohio are linked to a multiprocessor computer system in Columbus. The Ohio State Highway Patrol is responsible for 400 of the terminals, while the Bureau of Motor Vehicles uses the remaining I/O units. Specifically, some 60 terminals are installed at Highway Patrol stations, while nearly 300 units of various types are installed at police and sheriffs' headquarters.

With a system of this size, and due to the nature of data messages processed, it is imperative that the system keep running at all times. Two CPUs are used but one can take over the critical task should the other fail. Two separate communications controllers are used to handle the bulk of the message load from the network terminals. The system supports a vast collection of communication lines. High-speed lines go to other CPU's in Ohio's major cities, while medium-speed lines are used to link small CPUs that, in turn, support the terminals. Low-speed lines are generally used to connect local police departments with Teletype or similar terminals. In addition, special circuits connect the system with the FBI's National Crime Information Center (NCIC) and the National Law Enforcement Teletype System (NLETS).

On stolen cars alone, the highway patrol averages 200,000 inquiries a month, with an average response time of 3 to 5 seconds. In total, the system handles nearly 175,000 transactions daily. Typical of these transactions is the real-time check with the computer to ascertain that the person applying for a driver's license is eligible and not under suspension. The 3- to 5-second response time is quite an improvement over the old 30- to 60-day wait.

SUMMARY OF IMPORTANT POINTS

☐ The need to communicate has always been present but never to the degree that we are now experiencing. Much of this is due to the changing nature of our society, which has become communications oriented.

☐ Computers and terminals can be hard-wired or physically connected by cables up to a distance of about one-quarter mile. Beyond that a specific type of communications channel is needed to handle the data transmission.

☐ The four major data transmission facilities are telephone lines, coaxial cables, microwave, and satellites.

☐ The main barrier to the transmission of data over telephone networks has been the fact that these networks were designed to transmit analog signals (voice) rather than computer signals (digital).

☐ Special digital transmission systems are now being built specifically to handle the overload that has been placed on the older, traditional communication system.

☐ There are three different modes of transmission: simplex, which transmits one way only; half-duplex, which transmits in both directions, but only one way at a time; and full-duplex, which transmits both ways at the same time.

☐ Multiplexing is a process in which streams of data from many slow-speed devices are combined into a single stream for more efficient transmission.

☐ Transmission may be synchronous—that is, at set intervals—or asynchronous—in a random time pattern. Most high-speed transmission is synchronous, while most slow-speed transmission is asynchronous.

☐ Historically, communications networks have been established to handle transmission over long distances. In recent years we have seen the emergence of local networks to take care of communication needs in large buildings, downtown office operations, and the like.

☐ Interface control in communications networks are handled by specifically defined hardware and software procedures called protocols.

☐ As networks grew more complex, the burdens placed on the main processor began to degrade its performance. The use of special communications processors, called front-end processors, has relieved the host computer of this burden.

☐ The two main communications-oriented systems are real-time systems, which require a quick response, and timesharing systems, which allow many users to share the computer facility on a rotating basis.

GLOSSARY OF TERMS

Acoustic coupler—a special form of modulator that connects terminals (usually portable) with regular telephone equipment.

Analog signal—the signal is proportional to the electrical equivalent of the original communication.

Asynchronous transmission—as opposed to synchronous transmission, individual characters, or messages are sent at random intervals.

Coaxial cable—a special type of communications cable that permits the transmission of data at high speed.

Common carrier—a company that offers data and/or voice communication facilities for public use.

Communications channels—paths over which data is moved. These paths or links are usually described in terms of their speed and capacity to carry information.

Data set—a device that performs modulation/demodulation and control functions to provide compatibility between business machines and communications lines.

Dedicated lines—telephone-grade lines that are used by a single firm on a leased basis.

Digital signal—a binary process restricted to either the presence of absence of a signal.

Duplex channel—a communications path that can carry messages in both directions at the same time.

Facsimile transmission (FAX)—a system of telecommunication for the transmission of images for reproduction on a permanent form.

Half-duplex—a communications path that can carry a message in either direction, but only one way at a time.

Hardwired—the physical connection of two pieces of electronic equipment by means of a cable. Usually the maximum distance for hardwiring is about one quarter of a mile.

Interface—a connecting point between two systems.

Leased lines—see "dedicated lines."

Modems—see modulators/demodulators.

Modulators/demodulators—communications terminal equipment that changes signals from one form to another because of the incompatibility of computer and communications signals.

Multiplexor—an electronic device that takes data streams from many slow-speed devices and combines them into a single, high-speed output stream.

Node—a terminal or connection point in a network.

Protocols—interface control procedures for data transmission.

Real-time processing—the term used to describe a computer system in which there is very rapid response to a question, communication, or situation. The term quick-response system is sometimes substituted for real-time.

Simplex channel—a communications channel that can carry messages in only one direction at a time.

Synchronous transmission—a transmission arrangement in which data is sent through the channel at regular intervals.

Timesharing—a computer system in which a great many users have access to the central processing unit on a timed, rotating basis.

Voice-grade channels—telephone-grade communications channels that provide for medium-speed transmission of data.

THOUGHT QUESTIONS

1. How do you feel about the idea of an "electronic cottage" industry, as described by Alvin Toffler? Do you think you could work this way?

2. Why would a business firm want to establish a computer network? What are the advantages and disadvantages?

3. What are some of the dangers inherent in communications networks? How can these dangers be at least partially overcome?

4. Why are line protocols necessary? Why are there so many different protocols and who establishes them?

5. To many people, real-time and timesharing systems appear to be the same. Indicate how they differ and how they are alike.

6. What use would you make of a facsimile (FAX) system?

CHAPTER 16
DATA BASE
SYSTEMS

LEARNING OBJECTIVES

Upon completion of the chapter you should understand the following:

The importance of information as a corporate resource.

That management operates at three levels: at the lowest, or tactical level, the computer is of great help to management; at the strategic, or middle level, the computer is of some help, but is of limited value in areas involving qualitative data; at the top, or personal level, it is of little or no help.

Management Information Systems (MIS) are computer-driven systems designed to aid management in the process of running the company. Results to date have been mixed, partially due to management reluctance to use the system and partially due to the inadequacies of the system itself.

Data base systems are software/hardware systems designed to provide users with rapid access to the available data of the corporation.

Data base systems rely on a software program called DBMS (Data Base Management System) to provide user access to the data.

The success of a data base system is dependent upon the accessing method employed by the DBMS and the way in which data is stored.

The main goals of a data base system are data independence, data reduction, data security, and data integrity.

CHAPTER CONTENTS

The previous chapters pointed up the fact that, although we have been processing data in a variety of ways for centuries, we now have computer systems that can be used in an almost infinite number of combinations on an equally infinite number of applications. And therein lies the problem. Since computer equipment exists that allows us to automate almost any facet of business operation, the number of choices facing management is enormous. The payoff, however, comes not as a result of system capability but because management has learned to make efficient use of the information obtained.

Industry leader John Diebold, president of the prestigious Diebold Group, made the point quite clear when he stated that companies must recognize information is as much "a corporate resource as its workforce, its capital or its plant and equipment." He went on to say that "the way a company manages and regards its information is a relatively new concept called *information resource management.*"[1] Further, since information flows cut across all the business functions, such as marketing, finance, and production, there is considerable thought that data processing people should not automatically be the practitioners of information resource management (IRM). Instead, a professional IRM manager, one who understands the goals and directions of the corporation within the business environment, may be better situated to promote and maintain a viable management information system.

MANAGING WITH THE COMPUTER

With the coming of the computer age, management has had a fantastic decision-making tool at its disposal. This point was recognized in the early 1960s when the computer's success in routine clerical operations became established. The practitioners of data processing became eager to apply the computer to almost every task, including that of managing. Thus, the tasks that were generally considered to be qualitative in nature were being attacked in quantitative terms by a new discipline—management science.

We now recognize that many of these attempts were too bold or ill-planned, and the abundant enthusiasm of the 1960s gave way to a more logical and rational approach. Experience has taught us that not all management problems can be solved by quantitative methods. Arjay Miller, former president of Ford Motor Company and Dean of Stanford University's Graduate School of Business, outlined an approach based on various levels of management:

1. *Tactical level.* This is the lowest level of management where decisions are made about production and distribution problems. Management at this level is very likely to be replaced by computer management techniques. A classic example is the area of inventory control. By job definition, inventory managers are responsible for determining how many products should be ordered and when. In some businesses this requires an inituitive "feel" for the product and the market. But in a great many business applications, perhaps 90% of inventory ordering follows set patterns that are easily programmed into a computer. Today, the more sophisticated programs take into account quantity discounts, delivery costs, lag time before delivery, costs from alternative suppliers, insurance charges, and seasonal demand variations.

2. *Strategic level.* Middle-level management is involved in areas such as marketing and long-range financial planning. Some of these decisions involve quantifiable information and, as such, are prime candidates for computer solution. Here we can use the computer to prepare forecasting information, particularly information that involves many variables. Of course, the accuracy of the forecast is dependent both upon the accuracy of the input data and the relationships among the variables.

   Other decision areas, such as advertising, marketing, or public relations, involve decisions based on guesses, experience, feelings, and qualitative data that is beyond the scope of computers.

3. *Personal level.* At the very top levels of management the computer is of little or no help, as decisions are based almost totally on qualitative data. Thus, the corporate president can get little help, if

any, from the computer system when he or she tries to lead, to motivate people, or to make personnel choices.

MANAGEMENT INFORMATION SYSTEMS (MIS)

The term management information system (MIS) has been used for a long time in data processing, yet we lack a definition that would be acceptable to the majority of MIS practitioners. Rather than try to define it, we can list or discuss what management should be able to do if a computerized system of this type were available.

1. First, and perhaps most important, is that the MIS computer system would store all the data that management might need to perform its task effectively. The term *data base,* a topic that will be covered in detail a little further along in this chapter, is used to describe a collection of data that is shared by multiple users.
2. The data base would contain detailed information about the company, its structure, the environment in which it operates, and the competition. This data would be organized in a formal, logical way so that the data base could be expanded and modified as the need arises.
3. The data base would be dynamic—that is constantly updated so that all data would reflect the most current current condition.
4. Management would have rapid on-line access to the data base and be able to receive special, one-of-a-kind reports upon request.
5. The system would not only provide management with normal periodic reports but automatically with *exception* reports when situations reach certain predetermined limits.
6. Management would have the ability to communicate the data and reports to specific users and/or functional areas in the company organization.
7. Data security would be built into the system to prevent access to or manipulation of specific data items by unauthorized personnel.

The problems in setting up a system with these characteristics are enormous and today no one company has a complete or total management information system. This is entirely reasonable because, as author Ben-Ami Lipetz puts it: "In other words, the system is created in anticipation of needs that are not fully known. Yet the measure of the adequacy of a system is its ability to satisfy its users' needs as they arise."

The function of MIS is similar to that of other corporate staff functions—to aid in the day-to-day line operations of the corporation to achieve a specific goal (Figure 16.1).

FIGURE 16.1
Management information displayed on terminal.

MIS is far more than just a matter of collecting assorted pieces of hardware; it is a DP system idea that encompasses many parts of the company operation. In terms of hardware, such a system is likely to include keyboard and CRT terminal devices, and have a communications capability to allow managers to interrogate the computer system for answers to specific questions concerning inventories, budget status, sales, and the like. Most early management information systems were developed for a specific purpose within a single specific business. Today, the term MIS refers to a far more extensive computer software system that results in better and more timely information for management.

Robert G. Brown, IBM consultant in advanced management systems, lists some key questions in designing management information systems:

1. What kinds of information are needed? What facts should be reported routinely or occasionally? Computers are very effective in storing and retrieving great masses of routine information, but people are best at obtaining odd, disassociated facts on demand. Within the set the computer can best furnish, what types of data are clearly vital and which are only relatively important?
2. Should the information be in absolute terms, such as quantity sold or price paid? Would it be more meaningful if it related to some standard of comparison? These standards may be past trends, year-to-year accumulation or budgets.
3. How often would new information be needed? A sales report by the minute is meaningless, but a report once a year allows too much scope. How current should the data be?
4. How accurate should the data be? Many business decisions must be based on information that is late, incomplete, and inaccurate. If these defects are too great the decisions may be wrong. It is possible, however, to make good decisions based on information somewhat less than perfect. Accuracy itself may not be expensive. But when it is combined with rigid time constraints, the cost can rise.[2]
5. What sorts of decisions will be based on the information?

Once these questions are answered, a viable management information system can be built. Even then, the system is subject to several hazards:

1. Management is not always sure exactly what information it needs in order to practice the art of management.
2. Will the system be used? Too often we have seen elaborately structured systems fail because managers don't really want to manage with the aid of the computer. Part of the reason for this reluctance can be laid to fear of a new technology that is infringing upon their area of expertise. In effect, they feel that they may be replaced by a machine. In the case of some low and middle management positions, this fear is well-grounded because the computer can be programmed to perform many of the *routine* management functions. For example, inventory reorder point decisions are routinely done by computers now, as are mathematical simulations that are used to model complex management problems.
3. The management information system must remain flexible if it is to survive. Remember that the system was devised for the current group of managers for the current situation based on the current state of the system art. There is no guarantee that future managers will operate in the same manner.

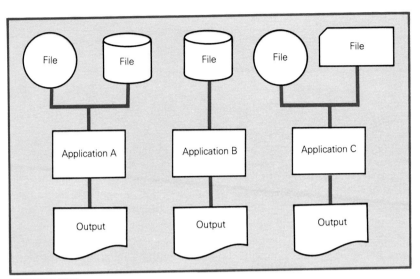

FIGURE 16.2
Conventional file system.

DATA BASE SYSTEMS

In order to understand data base systems you must first understand the difficulty in setting up the data in a usable form. Historically, DP systems have been built around *files* of *data* that are organized to meet a specific application (Figure 16.2). By definition, a data file is a group of related data records. Each record within the file is made up of a series of data fields that are of an exact length and type (alphabetic, numeric, or alphanumeric) and order. Using a simplified example, a payroll file would contain payroll records made up of fields containing the employee name, address, social security number, salary amount, and deductions (Figure 16.3).

FIGURE 16.3
Fields within a record.

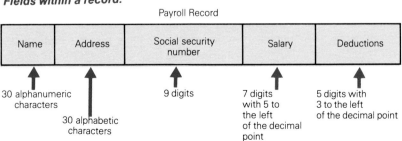

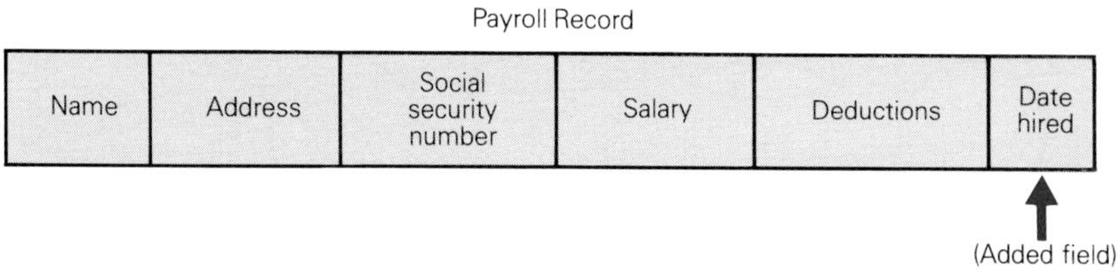

Payroll Record

Name	Address	Social security number	Salary	Deductions	Date hired

(Added field)

FIGURE 16.4
Changed data record.

As depicted in Figure 16.3, each field within the record must be described in terms of its length, the type of data it contains (alphabetic or numeric), and the location of a decimal point (if any). The key point is that this description appears within the program itself. Unless the fields are described *outside* of the program, managers and other non-programming people would have a difficult time understanding the layout of the data fields. However, as long as each file was accessed by only one program, such as shown in Figure 16.2, the problems were minimized. In real life the problem is that a particular data file seldom is used by just one program. Multiple programs are likely to access the data and any change in the structure of the record means that *every* program using that file will have to be modified. For example, suppose that we add a six-digit field that reflects the date on which the employee was hired. As shown in Figure 16.4, many application programs may have to be changed to account for the added field, *even* if these programs do not use that data field. This is one of the major reasons why a lot of business firms fought the move for a nine-digit postal ZIP code.

The reluctance to add or change fields in a record is not always due to just the cost of reprogramming. For example, suppose we maintain sales records with the following field format.

Salesperson's Name
Social Security Number
Customer Account Number
Date of Sale
Product Description
Product Number
Sales Dollar Amount
Sales Commission Rate

The accounting department then decides to automate its inventory accounting procedures. They learn of the sales file and realize that most of the data they want is already on the record. All that is needed are fields for

Cost Price of the Item Sold
Retail Price of the Item Sold
Delivery Date

A request made to add these fields to the record may be turned down for two reasons: (1) the cost of reprogramming and (2) that the data concerning the Commission Rate is sensitive and should not be available to those who handle inventory records.

The end result is that data records are duplicated because the accounting department will now set up its own file to be processed by a separate application program (Figure 16.5).

In addition to duplicate or redundant data, multiple files pose yet another problem—data integrity. The term data integrity refers to whether the individual data fields contain valid information. For example, customer addresses may be contained in several files: accounts receivable, advertising, sales, shipping, etc. If the customer moves or changes the work location, the update or change should be made in every file that contains that field of data. With multiple files there is a good chance that one of the duplicate fields may not get updated.

In the 1960s these problems were recognized and partially handled by special software developed to provide data analysis, interrogation, file management, and reporting. These systems, as depicted in Figure 16.6, attempted to develop a corporate control system by relating the output from a number of separate applications.

These integrated management imformation systems did provide management with better access to data, but at the cost of large, cumbersome data files that involved much sorting, moving, and manipulation.

James Martin, perhap /the most widely followed industry leader in the area of communications and data base, explained the problem in these terms:

The computer has been hailed as one of the most versatile and flexible machines ever built, but in many corporations, because of the difficulty and cost of changing programs and data bases, it becomes a straitjacket that precludes change and even constrains corporate

FIGURE 16.5
Redundant data fields.

SALES DATA	INVENTORY – DATA
Salesperson's Name	
Social Security Number	
Customer Account Number	
Date of Sale ———————————	Date of Sale
Product Description ———————————	Product Description
Product Number ———————————	Product Number
Sales $ Amount	
Commission Rate	
	Cost Price
	Retail Price
	Delivery Date

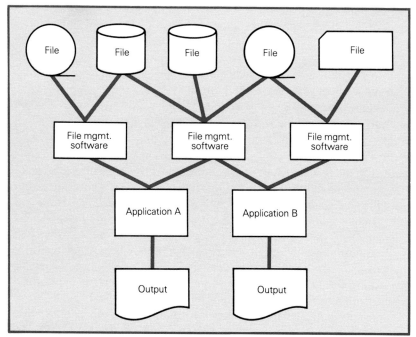

FIGURE 16.6
Early integrated management information system.

policy. The comment is often heard, 'We cannot do that because change is too difficult with our computer system.' [3]

The next change came with the idea of a data base and data base management systems (DBMS).

DATA BASE MANAGEMENT SYSTEMS (DBMS)

A *data base* is defined as an integrated source of data that is accessed by many users and that is controlled by a data base management system. In turn, the data base management system is a package of software programs designed to operate interactively with a collection of computer-stored files or data base. The DBMS has the function of locating those data base records that have in common whatever characteristics are specified by the user and to retrieve them for further processing.

The basic parts of a data base are listed below:

1. *Schema.* The schema is high-level computer language that the data base administrator uses to define the exact structure of the data base. This language enables the administrator to establish the location, contents, relationships, and security level of the data.
2. *Data manipulation routines.* These routines are software programs that are callable or used from the more common programming

languages such as COBOL or FORTRAN. Because of these routines, regular application programs are able to link into the data base management systems whenever necessary. In essence, it extends the normal capability of COBOL, FORTRAN, etc.

3. *Utility programs.* These programs are used to actually create the data base within the framework set up in the schema. They provide for data storage, movement, and extraction.

4. *Query language.* Some data base systems employ a special English-like language that provides for easy use of the data base system.

The key, innovative point for DBMS is that the definition and control of the data base is independent of the applications. The data items or data files are *logically* rather than physically connected, which means that the data is accessible to all application programs that have proper security clearance. The advantage of this approach is that it reduces the time and cost of writing programs to store and retrieve data. This point is particularly true when you consider that, in data management, a great many of the tasks are repetitive, time-consuming, and error-prone.

As of the end of 1981 it was estimated that there were more than 600 data base systems on line and the industry was expected to achieve a compound annual growth rate of 38%. Figure 16.7 shows a schematic of a data base system.

FIGURE 16.7

Data base management system.

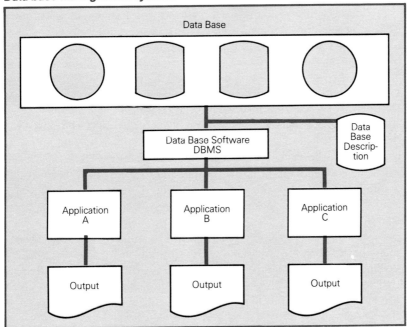

One of the items in the diagram needs further explanation. The data base description software system serves DBMS as a dictionary and as a directory. As a *dictionary,* it does the following:

1. Provides a data item and data record description that indicates the characteristics of each unit of data.
2. Identifies redundant items, that is, items that occur more than once.
3. Defines the relationships of the contents of data items to data records and records to other records.
4. Provides a cross-reference relating uses and/or applications to various data items.

As a *directory,* it has the job of doing the following:

1. Records the physical location of data.
2. Provides an interface with the data base management system software. The directory software takes the data definitions assigned to it and builds and maintains internal tables and indexes for the total system.

A quick look at the actual makeup of the data base should give you a good idea of the system. The smallest accessible data element is a *data item,* which would roughly correspond to a field of data. Each data item has a data name, as defined in the schema.

A *data entry* is an ordered collection of related data items as defined by a listing in the schema. These data items would roughly correspond to data records and would be stored on direct-access storage devices.

A *data set* is a collection of data entries that share a common definition as defined in the schema. A data set name references all of the entries in a data set and corresponds roughly to a data file. A data base is a named collection of related data sets. In some data base systems, the sets are further designated as master sets or detail sets. One of the important aspects of a master set is that it serves as an index to the location and relationship of detail data sets.

The point of the above description is to show that each item, entry, or set is carefully integrated into the system in such a way that it points to other related data items in a chainlike fashion. Data base interrogation software permits an inquiry made by a user to be traced through the system to retrieve the required data. Thus, a manager can ask for one-of-a-kind, nonrecurring reports rather than resorting to the traditional request for a special program to be written.

A data base management system tends to solve or to at least by-pass many of the problems involved with information storage and retrieval. Because of its structure, it allows the file to be manipulated in ways that were not anticipated at the time the data was created. Obviously, the key to this solution lies in the organization of the data base from the beginning.

Data base systems avoid the problems associated with traditional data files because of the way the data is handled by the software.

1. *Data independence.* Data independence is achieved because users see the data in terms of English descriptions or key words. Internally the description of the data may change, but the programs accessing the data do not. If a new field is added, a specific program must be changed only if it needs to access the new field. Each user has a different perception of the data base. To any one user, the data base system consists of one data file that contains exactly the fields that are needed. In other terms, the data base is shared by multiple users, each of whom has a different perception of its contents.

2. *Data reduction.* Data reduction is accomplished because the data base software recognizes and eliminates duplicate fields.

3. *Data security.* The data base system provides for security of individual data items by means of software protection. For example, gaining access to a data file does not necessarily mean that the user can automatically access each field. Further, protection is provided by separating the read and write operations. Permission to read a field does not automatically give permission to transfer or write it to another location.

4. *Data integrity.* Integrity of the data within the system is preserved because each item appears only once.

5. *Provision for change.* Perhaps the most important characteristic of a data base is the provision for constant change. In a true data base system, the data base is dynamic, i.e., constantly changing.

Note that the data base approach provides each user with a consistent view of the data and that the DBMS software does not itself contain any application programs. For the programmer, access to the data base is through special data base programming languages mentioned earlier.

The individual who has the job of overall control of the data is the *data base administrator,* often abbreviated as DBA. In a large corporation the task of coordinating or managing the activity of the data base may require a group of people specially trained in data base methods. Some of the jobs performed by the data base administrator are listed below.

1. Develop the structure of the data base itself by consultation with present and potential users.
2. Provide extensive documentation of all aspects of data base use.
3. Manage the activity of the data base and resolve conflicts among user requests.
4. Upgrade the schema, data manipulation routine, and utility programs as required.
5. Provide for data base interaction with new languages.

6. Maintain liaison with the suppliers of the data base software.
7. Maintain security over the data base so that certain data elements cannot be accessed by unauthorized users.

ACCESSING THE DATA

Since a data base consists of a number of segments of data stored on a fast access device, such as disk, the key to the success of a data base system is how the data segments are organized for retrieval. Prior to the use of data base systems most retrieval involved either sequential or direct access methods. Sequential access, typical of all magnetic tape and of some disk operations, requires a sequential reading of the data segments until the proper one is found. Direct access, on the other hand, involves some way of going directly to a specific data segment, that is, the fiftieth item in the file or the seventy-first item, etc.

Second-generation systems relied on ISAM (indexed sequential access method) to locate specific data elements. The ISAM method is shown in Figure 16.8. Note that the key fields are arranged alphabetically in the index and the disk location tells where the record containing that key is located on disk. The figure also illustrates the point that the index could have been set up on the basis of the "Purchased From" field. It is also possible to set up multiple indexes based on different key fields to access the data (Figure 16.9).

Random access methods often involve the use of a mathematical "hashing," or randomization routine, to both store and locate data. When the data is being stored, the key value is given to the software, which uses a hashing technique to convert the key into a disk record location. Retrieval is accomplished the same way; providing the system with a key will initiate the hashing routine that results in a retrieval location on disk.

Most data base access methods use a form if ISAM plus chaining or linked lists to retrieve the necessary data. Chaining or linking is accomplished by providing each record with a data field that points to the next occurrence of the key. For example, suppose a customer placed an order (#6835) for several different products and that the data has been entered into storage. Now we wish to have access to all the items that were on that order. Reference to the ISAM index tells us where the first item is stored. That record will then chain or point us to the other items. The last item may then refer or point back to the zeroth item, which indicates to the software that data retrieval is complete (Figure 16.10).

As indicated previously, one method of data accessing is by means

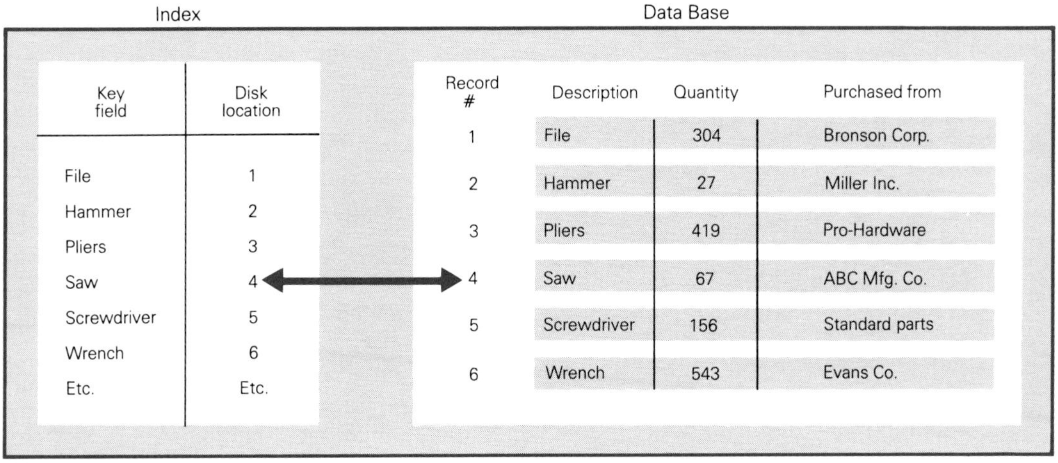

FIGURE 16.8
Indexed sequential data retrieval.

of application programs such as those written in COBOL or other business languages. Typically, these standardized languages do not have the capability of accessing the data base directly because each brand of data base software may use its own peculiar statements. The gap is bridged by a vendor-supplied precompiler that "intercepts" the nonstandardized instructions before they get to the language translator. The precompiler then inserts the proper instructions into the programmer's code *before* the program gets to the regular compiler.

A second method of accessing some data bases is by means of a *query* language, which provides for access by nonprogrammers. Instead of learning an actual programming language, the user only needs

FIGURE 16.9
ISAM method: different key.

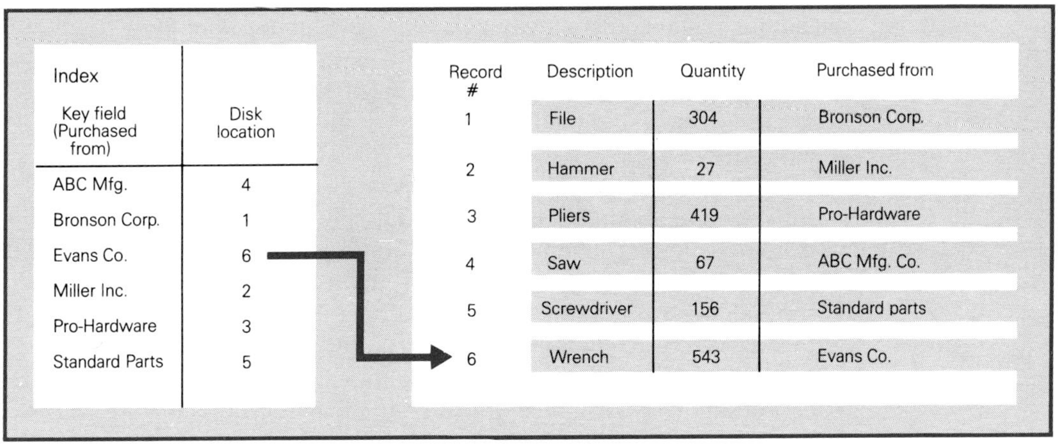

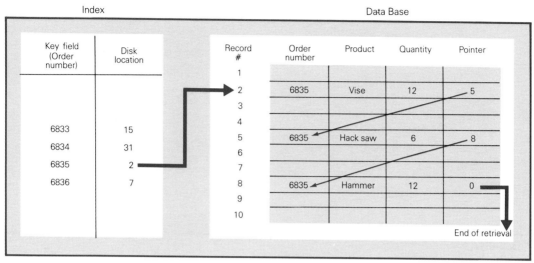

FIGURE 16.10
Chaining, or pointing, access method.

to learn a few simple commands that can be entered at a local input/output terminal. Thus, a manager can enter requests in a simplified form, as shown in Figure 16.11.

DATA BASE SYSTEMS: PROS AND CONS

The ideals of a perfect data base system have not yet been realized. Although there are many data base products on the market, few, if any, of these offer true ease of retrieval. Vendors of the so-called relational data base systems that are now beginning to appear on the market state that they have overcome the access problems of the past. The ideal data base would be set up and accessed in a way that the programmer could concentrate on the logic of the application program rather than on the manner in which the data is represented.

This same idea would have to apply to a user of a query language; that he or she could specify *what* is wanted rather than *how* to get it. To do this, however, means that the DBMS would have to be sophisticated enough to access collections of data records rather than a single record, a feat that is difficult to do on much of the existing data base software. Since data base systems are a combination of data files and linking structures that permit access to data elements, the software is extremely complex. Today, no single data base software system is perfect in its operation. Some are efficient in retrieval of certain types of data structures, but inefficient in others. In addition, some data base systems are more hardware oriented than others, and this is evidenced by the use of "back end processors" or specialized computers that take over the data base processing from the main computer. As shown in Figure 16.12, the back-end processor is a combination hardware/software device that does the actual search

RUN, QUERY	(initiates execution of the inquiry language processor)
•———	
NEXT?	(inquiry processor prompt)
DATA-BASE = MANPOWER	(defines data base to inquiry)
•—————————————	
SECURITY CODE = 7 × P309	(user defined password)
•———	
NEXT?	
FIND SEX IS "F" AND STATUS	(actual inquiry request)
*IS "HEAD OF HOUSEHOLD"	
AND DEPENDENTS IS "2" END;	
1 ENTRY QUALIFIED	(only one entry in the data base satisfies the inquiry conditions)
REPORT ALL	(user requests a report of the one entry that satisfied the inquiry conditions)
•———	

NAME: Dale Fischer
SEX: F
STATUS: Head of Household
DEPENDENTS: 2
ADDRESS: Poplar St., Denver, Colorado
TELE. NO.: 303-963-1986

NEXT?	(additional inquiries could be made at this point)

*Underlining indicates dialogue entered by the user

FIGURE 16.11
Inquiry mode of a data base system.

through the data base—in effect, the task has been off-loaded from the host computer.

At this point the question becomes, "Is a data base system worthwhile?" The answer is clear, as more and more firms are responding with a yes answer to that question. Theoretically, these firms know the trade-offs that are involved and feel that the disadvantages of a data base system are more than offset by the advantages. Let's take a look at both sides of data base systems.

ADVANTAGES

1. Eliminates redundant data.
2. Programs are independent from the data.
3. File access follows a set, predetermined pattern.
4. A central agency provides security for and control over the files.

5. Users have greater access to the data.

DISADVANTAGES

1. Data base systems are expensive in terms of software, additional hardware that is required, and for the programmer and administrators to run the system.
2. Learning to use a data base system efficiently requires the training of both users and programmer.
3. Creating the data base is a time-consuming and expensive process.
4. Although a data base system eliminates redundant data from storage, it is likely to require more storage than was eliminated because of the overhead generated by the data base system itself.
5. Extensive security measures may have to be set up to protect against unauthorized use of certain data and to guard against malfunctioning of the data base itself.

Who are the vendors of data base systems? In 1979 six suppliers accounted for 80% of the market and that trend is continuing today. In terms of dollar sales, IBM's two entries, IMS and DL/1, put it in the number one position followed by TOTAL (from Cincom); IDMS (from Software AG) and Inquire (from Infodata). Every indication is that the market for data base systems will expand dramatically during the 1980s.

FIGURE 16.12
Back-end processor.

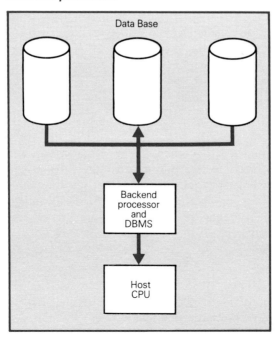

"THE DATABANK WOULD BE GLAD TO GIVE YOU INFORMATION ABOUT YOURSELF, BUT, UNFORTUNATELY, THE DATABANK IS NOT CONVINCED THAT YOU ARE REALLY YOU."

DISTRIBUTED
DATA BASE SYSTEMS

One of the most important data processing ideas to come out of the late 1970s was that of distributed processing. The term itself has many definitions, but it is a variation on the old rule that the processing power should be placed where at least 80% of the work is being done. The term should not be used to describe a simple mixture of minicomputers and network terminals. Instead, DDP means placing a substantial portion of the processing work load and data access at the places where the data originates and is needed.

This approach is now economically possible because of the increased processing power of minicomputers coupled with cheap, larger, and faster memories and auxiliary storage devices. By using various network forms and communications facilities described in the previous chapter, distributed data processing is a popular solution to many of our information needs.

By using sophisticated yet inexpensive minicomputers at each node or terminal point in the network, the local manager has the ability to process a local data base independently of the main computer site. The advantages of this method of operation are a faster response than going to the main data base, which is likely to be loaded down with similar requests, and the ability to store information that is peculiar to customers in the local area. The main computer would still contain the corporatewide data base for access by the local minicomputers.

In some distributed systems there may not be a central, main computer. One of the local minicomputers then acts as the network controller. The distribution of the data base then follows one of three patterns. Each mini may have its own exclusive data base, one mini may maintain the data base for the network, or the data base may be segmented with each mini controlling a part and all mini's having access to it.

Two of the leading practitioners of the distributed approach are New York's Citibank and the Bank of America. Citibank, for example, once had one huge data center filled with some very large maxicomputers. They now have 6 centers and about 100 minicomputers. Reportedly they have cut the EDP force by 20% and lowered DP costs by $1 million per year. Despite Citibank's example, there is some feeling that no true, distributed data base system exists today. In a true distributed data base system the DBMS should perform in such a way that the user can access data without knowing where it is located. In addition, the DBMS must maintain data integrity and security in all the data base locations.

The difficulty comes in deciding how to implement distributed data bases. Should each local office have its own data base system that operates independently of the headquarters system? Should local offices have access to the main data base? Should the main data base be duplicated at each local node? Should a proliferation of DBMS methods and hardware be permitted? Who is responsible for the security and integrity of the data? How much data redundancy should be permitted? All these questions need to be answered in designing and implementing a true, distributed data base system.

BUSINESS APPLICATIONS

The Bell Telephone system maintains extremely sophisticated computer data base systems that deal with data bases of a billion or more segments. One of their systems—Trunks Integrated Records Keeping System (TIRKS)—keeps track of special services circuits, message trunks, and carrier systems. It helps the Bell operating companies in forecasting circuit requirements, tracking circuit orders from customers, assigning circuit components, and distributing work orders. The work load is enormous when you consider that TIRKS contains more than 100 on-line data bases, representing more than 25 billion pieces of data. Not only does the system work but it is constantly being fine-tuned to answer more than 100,000 inquiries per day.

The *New York Times* Information service and the *Boston Globe* newspaper have just introduced an on-line data base system that provides users with quick access to summarized news and editorial items from the *Boston Globe*. The data base, called "Globedata," abstracts virtually every article printed in the *Globe* except certain syndicated question and answer columns and sports statistics. Users are charged an hourly connect rate, which works out to be about $1.50 per minute of computer time.

Searching the data base is done by means of a 900-word vocabulary or by using key words that might appear in the body of the abstract. When the particular abstract is found, the computer prints bibliographic data that indicates the date and page of the publication. Then, if the user decides that reading the whole article is worthwhile, the actual article must be retrieved separately through a different system.

COSTS VERSUS BENEFITS

A final point needs to be made here concerning the use of computers, particularly large MIS-oriented, data base systems. The mere fact that a corporation has a computer system is no guarantee that the investment was or is profitable. As a matter of fact, it is extremely difficult in some cases to ascertain whether a computer system pays its way when compared to other business expenses.

When the computer is used for a direct reduction of clerical costs, that is, when a manual operation is automated, the application is usually economically justified. Typical applications would include billing, receivables, payroll, inventory, budget control, and financial statements.

The next level of computer cost justification normally involves the performance of tasks that would have required the hiring of additional clerical workers at some later date. Thus, we have a built-in capability for future expansion, but how much is that worth and how much does it cost now?

Perhaps the most difficult area in which to ascertain the cost of the computer *vs* its benefits has to do with the performance of tasks that would not have been possible without the computer. This is one of the most important areas of computer usage and yet the most difficult to document. If the process of management decision-making is not aided directly or indirectly, then the computer system is of dubious value.

Studies made in the 1960s concerning profitability of computer usage were not flattering toward management. At that time only one-third of the largest and most sophisticated corporate computer users were able to justify their expenditures on a cost/benefit basis. The key to the profitable use of large computer systems lay in management involvement. Generally, when top management was involved they took the time and effort to learn and understand the potential of computer DP. They did not view it as just a faster piece of mechanical equipment. Instead, they realized that parts of the business might have to be reorganized to take advantage of the computer's capability. They realized that here they had a tool that could be of significant value to the whole company, not just the accounting section. Naturally, once this concept was understood by the senior managers, they had the power and willingness to change company operations. While the less successful companies were shuffling accounts receivable, accounts payable, and payroll accounting faster than ever before, the successful users were going into the area of inventory control with automatic reordering of low-stock items, sales forecasting, engineering analysis, production control and scheduling, simulation, product-mix analysis, etc.

As improbable as it sounds, many managers do not really have a clear grasp of how their own company operates. Companies that prospered in the long period of good times had never really taken a close look at their operations. According to a McKinsey and Company study ("Unlocking the Computer's Profit Potential"), in order to get maximum results from the computer effort, the top executive must:

1. Approve objectives, criteria, and priorities for the computer effort, with special attention to the development program.
2. Decide on the organizational arrangements to carry out these policies and achieve these objectives.
3. Assign responsibility for results to the line and functional executives . . . and to see to it that they exercise this responsibility.
4. Insist that detailed and thorough computer system plans are made an integral part of operating plans and budget.
5. Follow through to see that planned results are achieved.[4]

Perhaps the most important point to be gained from the last few paragraphs is that these ideas are probably even more true today than they were 15 or 20 years ago. The increasing use of mini- and microcomputers without any management direction is possibly worse than no solution at all. In this case, the computer would only add to the company's problems rather than detracting from them.

SUMMARY OF IMPORTANT POINTS

☐ More and more, business firms are beginning to recognize that information may be their most important asset and that information resource management is the way of the future.

☐ As a tool of management, the computer is not equally usable at all levels of management.

☐ At the lowest, or tactical level of management, the computer is a necessary tool because most of the decisions are based on quantifiable elements.

☐ At the middle, or strategic level, the computer is of less help because some of the decisions will be based on qualitative issues rather than quantitative items.

☐ At the top, or personal level, the computer is of little help because most of the judgments will be based on personal or qualitative points.

☐ Management information systems (MIS) use a wide base of computer-stored data about the company operations and the environment in which it operates. Management has access to the system through on-line terminals and can get answers to almost any question.

☐ The system should be dynamic, that is, it should be changed to meet current conditions. Its value is in the ability to meet user's needs as they arise.

☐ Traditionally, data storage systems have been built around the idea of files and records of data. Each file contains a collection of related data records and may be accessed by one or more programs.

☐ The difficulty with regular files is that even a small change in the data structure means that all programs accessing that file will have to be changed.

☐ Programming problems and difficulty in maintaining the security of data led to data redundancy, that is, multiple files containing many duplicate fields.

☐ Data base systems avoid most of the problems encountered with traditional files by incorporating the data into one integrated data source, which is accessed through a data base management system.

☐ A data base management system is a collection of programs that operates interactively on the computer-stored data. It stands between the data base and the programmer and relieves the programmer of most of the chores of data manipulation.

☐ Users interact with the data base by means of a query language that allows quick, on-line access to the data.

☐ Data base systems offer the user the advantages of
Relative ease of data retrieval.
Data independence.
Data reduction.
Data security.
Data integrity.
Provision for change.

☐ Disadvantages of data base systems include
Increased hardware expense.
Increased software expense.
Additional work load placed upon the central processing unit.
Additional costs of setting up the data base and in maintaining
staff to support the system.

☐   Access to the data is dependent upon how the data base is organized. Most data base systems use a combination of an indexed method plus a pointer that chains the user to the next appropriate record.

☐   A data base administrator (DBA) is a person or staff group that has the task of maintaining control of the data base system.

☐   With the increased use of minicomputers in communications networks and the decentralization of data processing, there is added need for a similar distribution of the data base. Thus, we are seeing the emergence of distributed data base systems.

☐   The computer is a tool of business and, like any other tool, should be evaluated in terms of its costs vs its benefits. Unfortunately, the benefits are often intangible and difficult to measure.

GLOSSARY OF TERMS

Backend processor—a specialized computer that takes over, or off-loads, the data base processing from the main computer.

Data base—an integrated source of data that is accessed by many users, and that is controlled by a data base management system.

Data base administrator (DBA)—the person or group responsible for control of the data base system.

Data base management system (DBMS)—a package of programs designed to operate interactively with a collection of computer-stored files.

Data entry—an ordered collection of related data items (similar to a record) as defined by a listing in the schema.

Data file—a group of related data records.

Data item—the smallest accessible element in a data base. It corresponds roughly to a data field in traditional data files.

Data set (in a data base)—a collection of data entries that share a common definition as defined in the schema.

Exception reports—reports to management that are generated automatically when a certain condition has been reached.

Hashing routine—a mathematical formula that is applied to a key field to determine where the record is stored.

Indexed sequential access method (ISAM)—a file access system that employs a key field and an index to provide access to the data record in auxiliary storage.

Information resource management (IRM)—the way in which a company manages and handles its information. Today, more and more firms are thinking of their data as a corporate asset and are managing it accordingly.

Key—a particular field such as customer name or social security number that is used to identify a unique record of data.

Management information systems (MIS)—an information storage and retrieval system that provides management with the information it requires in the performance of its function.

Pointer—a data value that points to the next record of data that contains the same key field.

Relational data base—a data base system that operates with a high-level language that allows the user to access data without knowledge of how the data items are stored.

Schema—a high-level computer language used by the data base administrator to define the structure of the data base.

THOUGHT QUESTIONS

1. The chapter included a statement that information is a corporate resource just like plants and machinery. Exactly what is the term "information" referring to? Give some specific examples of what this information is.
2. In reference to the previous question, how would you place a value on such information? What measuring would you use to determine value?
3. Why is it so difficult to set up management information systems?
4. Assume that you are the sales manager of a firm that sells goods nationally. Make a list of some of the kinds of information that you would have to have in order to manage effectively.
5. List the major elements or characteristics of a traditional filing cabinet file system, a traditional computer disk file system, and a computer data base system.

CHAPTER 17
OFFICE AUTOMATION

LEARNING OBJECTIVES

Upon completion of the chapter you should understand the following:

Why there is such a pressing need for office automation today.

That people costs are rising at an extraordinary rate while the cost of electronic components is steadily decreasing.

That in a society whose rate of change is speeding up, there is a corresponding need for faster and more efficient communication in the office.

Historically, the points at which word and data processing have come together is in the use of the typewriter and in the storage of data on magnetic media.

The word processing (WP) cycle involves the four steps of origination (input), production (output), reproduction (copy processing or reprographics), and distribution (storage).

Although machine dictation is a less expensive and more efficient form of creating documents, most executives today still write their letters or dictate to a secretary.

Optical characters recognition (OCR) is another form of input that requires the use of typewriters equipped with OCR readable type.

WP systems are primarily text editors, which means that they allow the operator to add, delete, move, and modify text that has been entered into the system.

The major advantage to word processing is that typed material need only be entered into or stored on the system once. After that, it can be manipulated at computer speed.

Complex office automation systems offer WP and DP capability, extensive document printing options, and electronic mail service.

CHAPTER CONTENTS

In the past we have always spoken of data processing with obvious reference to those machines and systems that process numerical data used in accounting, inventory, statistical, and similar activities. The reporting medium has long ignored the other side of the house—the office—where a comparable "revolution" was also taking place but which, until recently, has gone relatively unnoticed.

New terms are being used to describe this phenomenon—"Office of the Future," "Paperless Society," "Dataword Processing," "Office Automation"—in an effort to better describe what is actually happening. Fundamental economics have been the driving force behind this change. As people costs have exploded upward, computer hardware costs have plummeted. This combination of events triggered the shift from an age of data processing to an age in which words and numbers have equal status.

INTRODUCTION

Previously we have focused on the computer as an information processing tool of incredible value if used wisely. Indeed, a presidential commission reported in 1977 that from one-third to one-half of our gross national product (GNP) is derived in some form from the production of information and knowledge. And yet, in this "Information Age" we have done little to speed up the process by which managers disseminate decisions that are based upon computer-processed information.

Various studies have shown that managers spend up to 80% of their time in some form of communication. Of that 80%, approximately one-half of that time is spent in communicating with people in another physical location. In the average business firm, internally generated correspondence accounts for 90% of the paper that crosses an employee's desk.

Approximately 25% of the U. S. work force is tied up in paper processing, and this group is expected to grow to 40% by 1990. During that time, however, the U. S. work force will decline and there will be a 10% shortage of white collar workers unless office automation takes hold. Unfortunately, spending by businesses to modernize this area has been extremely low. The average U.S. factory worker is supported by $25,000 worth of laborsaving devices, such as computerized assembly lines. Each farmer is backed by $52,000 of laborsaving machinery, but the average office worker is backed by only $2000 in equipment.

In addition to purely economic factors, other forces are driving the larger corporations and government agencies to install more and more complex office information systems. For example, the scope of management is broadening while business organizations get increasingly complex. Consequently, there is greater need for more rapid and accurate communication of ideas. A marriage of the techniques of the office and of the computer seems to be the solution.

HISTORICAL PERSPECTIVE

The history of office automation is inextricably entwined with that of data processing because both systems use the same processes to produce the final product. The original patent for a typewriter was issued to Henry Mill of England in 1714, but the first working model was developed by Christopher Sholes, a Milwaukee newspaper editor and printer, in 1868. A few years later, in 1874, E. Remington and sons produced the first commercially successful typewriter.

Thomas Edison worked on an electric version of the typewriter in 1872, but his version was too expensive to manufacture. However, his original work on methods of reproducing sound led to another device that has become a mainstay of office automation—the dictating machine. In 1888 Alexander Graham Bell, Chichester Bell, and Charles Tainter combined their talents to produce a commercially usable dictating machine. As crude as these devices were by any modern standards, they were successful and by 1906 the Dictaphone Corporation had a considerable lead over its competitors (Figure 17.1).

In the 1920s, at the same time that punched-card data processing was dominant, the first automated typewriter was brought onto the market. The Hooven Company combined the typewriter with dictating machine technology to produce a typewriter that could make repetitive copies. The words were typed and simultaneously stored on an embossed cylinder that permitted automatic playback of as many copies as needed. Later, paper rolls, much like those seen on old player pianos, were used, but neither system permitted the typist to make changes to the original typed material.

Until 1933 four companies shared approximately 90% of the U.S. typewriter market—Remington, Royal, Underwood, and Smith-Corona. Then IBM entered the typewriter marketplace by acquiring the rights to manufacture the electromatic typewriter from Northwestern Manufacturing Company. IBM was able to get an edge on the electric typewriter market when they became the only typewriter manufacturer allowed by the government to continue production of its electric

FIGURE 17.1
Early dictaphone with waxed cylinder.

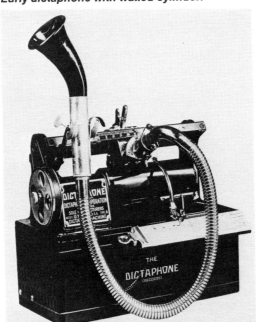

typewriters during World War II. By 1976, IBM held an estimated 65% of the $600 million office electric typewriter market.

IBM continued to play a key role in the development of dataword processing equipment. The company was the first to use input/output typewriter terminals for their computer systems and, in 1961, introduced the Selectric typewriter. The Selectric used a movable typeball, or element, that contained all the letters and symbols found on the traditional movable typebars. The invention of this element allowed the printing of 15 characters per second without the possibility of jamming the keys (Figure 17.2).

In 1964, IBM introduced another first, the Magnetic Tape Selectric Typewriter (MT/ST). As the keys of the typewriter were depressed, the words were not only printed on paper but were also recorded in electronic code on magnetic tape. If an error was made, the typist backspaced and retyped the word correctly, erasing the incorrect material on the tape by recording over it. When the typing was completed, the tape was rewound by using the controls on the console. It then became possible for the console to read the codes on the tape and to send electronic signals to the typewriter, allowing the document to be printed at the rate of 150 words per minute (Figure 17.3).

PREPARING FOR THE AUTOMATED OFFICE

As indicated in the previous section, almost unreasonable demands for increased productivity are being placed upon today's office. The technological changes of the past decade offer a way of solving this problem, but it is meeting with resistance by the very people who ultimately stand to benefit the most. Unfortunately, some of the early

FIGURE 17.2
Selectric typeball elements.

FIGURE 17.3
IBM magnetic tape selectric typewriter (MT/ST).

attempts to set up word processing centers were not successful and "horror" stories of such attempts continue to survive. Most of these failures were due to poor management planning and/or poor choice of vendor equipment. Yet the potential for savings is enormous. Studies have shown that an average of 15% of a manager's time can be saved through office automation—a saving that amounts to $125 billion per year. In addition, survey respondents identified what they considered to be "wasteful activities" that consume 15% to 40% of their time.

Why the reluctance to move into office automation? One reason that immediately comes to mind is that the formation of a typing or WP work center is seen as a loss of status by the executive who must give up a private secretary. Office automation is not a narrow approach to the problem. Instead, it is likely to encompass the installation of a wide range of word processing equipment, as well as significant changes to the office environment and in the office organization. In many cases these changes will actually replace the traditional way in which offices have been conducting their work.

Perhaps the single most important part of the change involves people rather than equipment. There simply is no way of overemphasizing the point that the office people must be prepared for change and be deeply involved in the planning and implementation of office automation.

Employee attitudes ultimately will be crucial to the success or failure of the office automation system. For example, it should come as no surprise that not all office employees care whether or not productivity is increased. Others will be prepared to fight the process, some will be involved only under duress, and others will welcome the change. A preliminary study will go a long way toward determining the needs of the company and the feelings of the employees.

The study will define the work applications that are actually being used in the office. Generally, office documents fall into one of five categories.

1. *Original documents.* Letters, memorandums, or any form of written communication that contains the originator's ideas.
2. *Repetitive documents.* This category would include original documents that are sent to different people, that is, form letters.
3. *Revised documents.* Original documents that have been changed fall into this group.
4. *"Boiler plate" documents.* Documents that are made up of prerecorded paragraphs that are selected from a group of such paragraphs and used to create a "new" document.
5. *Lengthy documents.* Generally this category includes documents longer than a certain preset amount, such as 5 or 10 pages. Manuscripts, company reports, legal briefs, etc., would fall into this category.

Implementation of the new system can be a trying time, but the critical point is that people will have to make the system work. If employees see the equipment as an ally that will help them perform their jobs better and faster, if they see their improved performance in the light of promotional opportunities, if they see both the opportunity for growth and the sense of security, then, and only then will the equipment of the automated office be accepted and put to work. The ultimate goal is to have people using procedures and equipment in a cost-effective way to create, produce, reproduce, and distribute documents. Or, another way of looking at it is that productivity means operating the office such that costs are minimized, customers are satisfied, and employees are happy.

THE WORD PROCESSING CYCLE

In the 1940s, letters were written by hand or personally dictated to a secretary who transcribed them from shorthand. A draft copy was typed, revised, and retyped. Eventually, dictation equipment was introduced into the office scene but, even today, the majority of letters, reports, memos, etc., are still drafted by hand. Thus, we are still using old-fashioned techniques for the processing of data in word form. The cost of processing words keeps mounting every year, with over $50 billion spent annually on typing. There are over 8 million electric typewriters in the United States but the bottleneck lies in the 50–60-word-per-minute typing speed and the editing, proofreading, and re-typing cycle with which we are familiar.

In the 1960s, however, IBM created a new term, "word processing," and new techniques to apply to this area. Word processing techniques and equipment are designed to take advantage of computer tech-nology to permit input, storage, editing, and output of typewritten material using computer components. Word processing is *not* simply a machine that types the same letter over and over again, nor is it just an automatic typewriter. Instead, it is an entire system composed of people, procedures, and automated, electronic equipment to more effectively produce written communication.

Unfortunately, this view is not shared by all businesses. A survey conducted in 1980 of 400 middle managers of Fortune 500 companies revealed that 63% defined word processing as "memory or auto typ-ing." Only 41% understood the use of word processing in its larger role of text correction and manipulation.

The word processing cycle consists of four distinct stages, some of which directly correspond to similar stages in the data processing cycle discussed much earlier in the text.

1. *Origination or input.* Origination covers the creation of ideas and putting those ideas into a usable form. So far we have discussed only the written form, but a vocal or dictated form is equally usable.
2. *Production or output.* In this stage the information is formatted into a form that is acceptable for output, usually on the printer.
3. *Reproduction.* This phase involves making multiple copies and is known as copy processing or reprographics. The most comparable counterpart in data processing would be printers that can make multiple copies or COM—computer-output microfilm—which produces output in a film form.
4. *Distribution or storage.* Distribution involves the filing, mailing, and distribution of office automation output.

WORK FLOW

The actual flow of the work in a word processing operation is vis-ualized in Figure 17.4.

1. The author puts his or her ideas into a form that the word processing operator can understand. Some of the forms would include written letters, dictated material, or copies of previously used letters with additions and deletions.

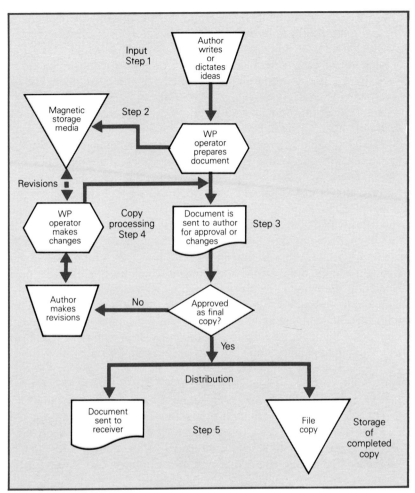

FIGURE 17.4
Work flow cycle.

2. The WP operator prepares or types the idea in a traditional, readable form. This step also shows that the document is both typed *and* stored on magnetic or electronic media.
3. The author reviews the typed copy and makes any needed corrections. If no corrections are required, the document is distributed. If corrections are required, the document is returned to the word processing operator for further work.
4. The word processing operator makes additions, corrections, and/or deletions using the copy stored on the electronic media. The corrected document is then returned to the author for approval. These steps are repeated until the document is approved and distributed.
5. The file copy of the approved document may be in paper form or stored on magnetic media for future use.

Input into the system can take several forms, the most prevalent of which are handwriting or dictation to a secretary. In 1979 it cost $5.59 to produce a letter that was dictated to a secretary, while a machine dictated letter cost only $4.19. Machine dictation is about six times faster than writing longhand and about two to three times faster than dictating to a secretary.

Dictation equipment is one of the least appreciated office tools available today. One reason for this has already been given—the loss of a secretary and corresponding loss of status. Another reason for this resentment is that early dictation equipment was awkward and difficult to use, which resulted in a "bad name" in office automation. A third reason for its lack of use is the uncomfortableness that many feel when using machines.

A third way of entering material into the WP system is by means of optical character recognition (OCR). The topic of OCR was discussed in an earlier chapter, and you may recall that this method had been used for years in specialized applications involving the entry of massive amounts of data from credit card slips, insurance premium notices, etc. In an office situation, the originator writes or dictates a letter that is typed on an electric typewriter using a typeball with an OCR type font. The author may approve the copy or may make corrections by writing in special symbols such as pound sign (#) or slash symbols (/) to indicate appropriate changes.

The edited copy is then run through the OCR device, which reads the characters and the correction symbols. The output from the OCR device is transmitted to the text editor that prepares the final form of the material. Video screen terminals attached to the WP equipment allow the operator to verify that the output corresponds to the originator's requests. If it does not, the operator can enter further changes right then.

The major point to understand in this discussion is that we can increase overall productivity significantly by cutting down on the amount of original typing that is required. It takes 12 to 15 *uninterrupted* minutes to type in a 3-page document at 60 words per minute. However, original typing can be done at "rough-draft" speed as opposed to "final copy" speed, which is used if each typing is expected to be the final copy. Furthermore, if each tiny revision requires that the document has to be entirely rekeyed, the amount of wasted time is extraordinary. WP systems avoid this problem by capturing the keystrokes in storage and, under computer control, allowing the operator to make corrections without rekeying the whole document (Figure 17.5).

WHAT CAN WP DO?

The capabilities of word processing equipment are truly astounding. The general term *text editing,* already used in this chapter, itself covers a wide range of activities. Three basic steps are involved.

1. Rough draft material is typed as input to the system and stored magnetically.

FIGURE 17.5
Word processing system.

2. Corrections, additions, and deletions are entered via typewriter or video units. CRT devices have the advantage of allowing the user to see the whole page at a glance and to enter corrections at selected points by positioning a pointer or cursor.
3. Output is printed at high speed on quality printers, some of which permit the use of special forms and multiple copies.

Sales material produced in this manner has the look of hand-typed letters at a greatly reduced cost. In addition, the more sophisticated word processing systems permit the user to "personalize" letters by picking appropriate sentences or paragraphs from hundreds stored on the system.

However, within the term of text editing we can include such features as the following.

Insertion, addition, and deletion of words, phrases, sentences, paragraphs, and pages.
Automatic paragraph indention; automatic carriage return; automatic page numbering.

CARTER TACKLES NEW CAMPAIGN BY WRITING MEMOIRS ON-LINE
By Bill Laberis, CW Staff

PLAINS, Ga.—There was a time not long ago when the nation's chief executive, upon completing his tenure at the White House, would retire to the tranquility of the family compound and begin banging out his memoirs on an old manual Remington.

By the harsh glow of an old brass lamp, he would dredge up the glorious images of days past, interrupted at times by the clickity-clack of typewriter keys as he put it all down in black and white.

So much for the past. Today the glow on former President Jimmy Carter's face as he sets down his memoirs is a dull, luminescent green. And the only sounds floating out the windows of his study here are the barely audible "tic-tics" from his all-plastic keyboard.

The Carters, both Jimmy and Rosalynn, are composing, editing and rewriting the sagas of their public lives on two leased word processors.

King said the former president was a particularly eager student, picking up the intricacies of the system in half the time it takes most of her students, while dazzling her with a typing speed she estimated at about 50 words per minute.

"I guess I never thought a president of these United States could type at all," she remarked. "I don't imagine he got much practice at the White House." (Source: *Computerworld*, May 4, 1981.)

Automatic centering.

Ability to transfer part or all of one document into another document.

Column printing; column deletion—automatic reformatting of pages to change the width of the copy or to modify vertical spacing.

Automatic underline.

Printing of bold characters.

Change in type size (pitch) from 10 to 12.

Right and left justification of margins.

Global search to pick out each occurrence of a particular word or phrase. This feature is very useful when a term that was used repeatedly in a long document needs to be changed.

IBM's Displaywriter (Figure 17.6) features an electronic dictionary that checks the spelling on 50,000 commonly used words. In addition, the user has the option of adding another 500 words that are used in specific applications, such as law and medicine. When a request for a

FIGURE 17.6
IBM displaywriter WP system.

spelling check is initiated, misspelled words are checked at up to 1000 words per minute and highlighted on the screen. No, there is not yet a machine that can automatically make the appropriate corrections. The operator must go back to the highlighted words and make the appropriate corrections (Figure 17.7).

Some systems even have mathematical capabilities that the WP operator can use. Figure 17.8 shows how this feature can help. The operator has entered a column of figures and wants to be certain that

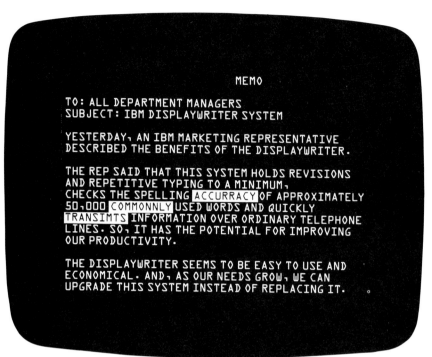

```
                          MEMO

TO: ALL DEPARTMENT MANAGERS
SUBJECT: IBM DISPLAYWRITER SYSTEM

YESTERDAY, AN IBM MARKETING REPRESENTATIVE
DESCRIBED THE BENEFITS OF THE DISPLAYWRITER.

THE REP SAID THAT THIS SYSTEM HOLDS REVISIONS
AND REPETITIVE TYPING TO A MINIMUM,
CHECKS THE SPELLING ACCURRACY OF APPROXIMATELY
50,000 COMMONNLY USED WORDS AND QUICKLY
TRANSIMTS INFORMATION OVER ORDINARY TELEPHONE
LINES. SO, IT HAS THE POTENTIAL FOR IMPROVING
OUR PRODUCTIVITY.

THE DISPLAYWRITER SEEMS TO BE EASY TO USE AND
ECONOMICAL. AND, AS OUR NEEDS GROW, WE CAN
UPGRADE THIS SYSTEM INSTEAD OF REPLACING IT.
```

FIGURE 17.7
Spelling verification.

the total is correct before entering it. In this example on the IBM Displaywriter the operator has invoked the addition function and the system shows the total of the high-lighted numbers. If this figure matches the one the author indicated, then the entry will be made.

The features described so far are common to almost all the major WP systems on the market today. Of far greater importance are the selection and report-generating capabilities of some of the more sophisticated systems. For example, some systems allow the operator to sort a file, such as a mailing list, into a particular order. This means that with the touch of a few keys he or she get an alphabetical list, a list based on postal ZIP code, or city, or state, etc. Files can be sorted on the basis of balance owed, bin number, part number and, most important, data records can be extracted based on tests like "if last charge amount was over fifty dollars."

The significance of these capabilities is enormous because in the past these capabilities have been available only through full-scale computer programs. It means that we are seeing the first true overlapping of DP and WP activities. For the executive, it opens up a whole new world because word processing machines are now becoming true "information processing" devices. Traditionally WP systems have had the mailing list capability, but it now means that the executive can get certain types of management reports without having to go to the DP department with the request.

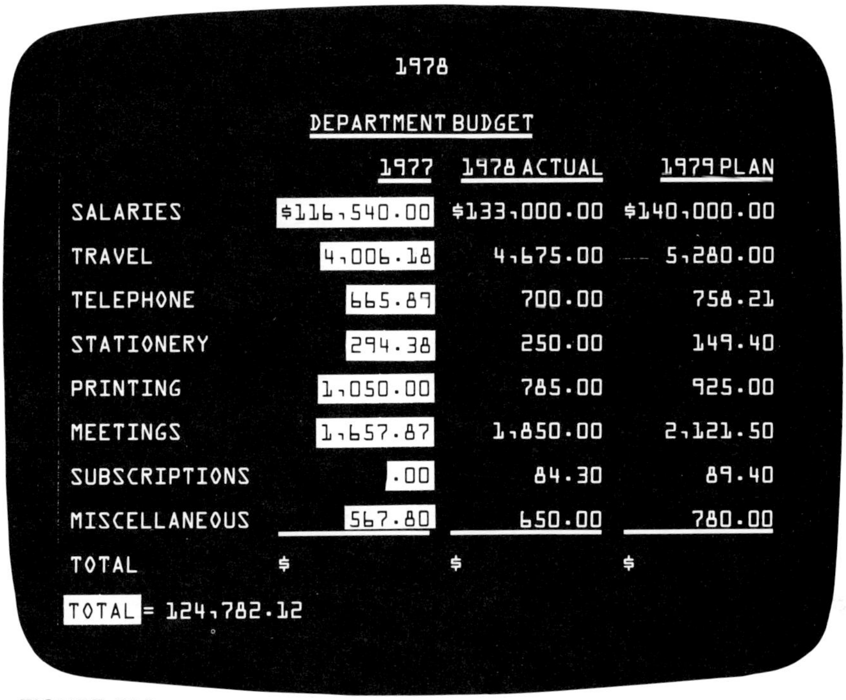

```
                         1978

                  DEPARTMENT BUDGET
                      1977    1978 ACTUAL    1979 PLAN

  SALARIES     $116,540.00   $133,000.00   $140,000.00

  TRAVEL         4,006.18       4,675.00      5,280.00

  TELEPHONE        665.89         700.00        758.21

  STATIONERY       294.38         250.00        149.40

  PRINTING       1,050.00         785.00        925.00

  MEETINGS       1,657.87       1,850.00      2,121.50

  SUBSCRIPTIONS      .00           84.30         89.40

  MISCELLANEOUS    567.80         650.00        780.00

  TOTAL        $              $             $

  TOTAL = 124,782.12
```

FIGURE 17.8
Arithmetic capability.

WORD PROCESSING SOFTWARE

How does the operator use the capabilities just described? Actually it is not all that difficult when you realize that the operator does not program the system. Instead, the operator is merely a user who interacts with the word processing software. As a matter of fact, most small WP systems do not have any capability for modifying or changing the software—they are turnkey systems in the true sense.

Since word processing systems are often devoted to just one task, their software is likely to be smaller and more simple. For example, the act of turning on the system and/or striking a single key may be enough to bring the WP software into memory from auxiliary disk storage. Another possibility is that the main WP software programs may be small enough that they can be kept in memory or on preprogrammed ROM chips. Additional software routines would be stored on disk and brought into memory when needed. Figure 17.9a illustrates how this would look.

When the system is activated, the main WP software displays a "menu" of operator options on the video screen (Figure 17.9b). The highlighted first letter (shown within box) indicates the key that the operator is to strike in order to enter that mode of operation. If Editing were desired, the E key would be struck and the page or screen of information last worked upon would be sent to the printing device. After printing was complete, the menu page would again appear as the system awaits further instructions.

As WP systems get more complex, a hierarchy of menus is used to allow the operator greater control over system actions. In this case, pressing the E key may bring in a complete edit routine from disk that displays its own submenu, which offers choices of adding or deleting a word, moving, replacing, etc. (Figure 17.9c). When the operator is finished, control is returned to the main WP software that again presents the original menu to the operator.

WORD PROCESSING SYSTEMS

Word processing systems fall into four broad categories.

1. *Stand-alone hardcopy devices.* Here we have the relatively simple devices that were typical of the 1960s. This would include IBM's famous Magnetic Tape Selectric Typewriter (MT/ST), which came out in 1964. These are mechanical systems with no video or CRT capability. Typically, these systems are used to eliminate much of the retyping that occurs during the drafting, correction, and retyping process. The data (letter) is stored on magnetic media (tape, card, cassette, or diskette) and can be recalled for future use. The more sophisticated systems can switch between media stations,

FIGURE 17.9A
WP SOFTWARE EXAMPLES.

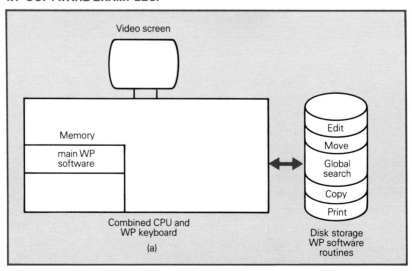

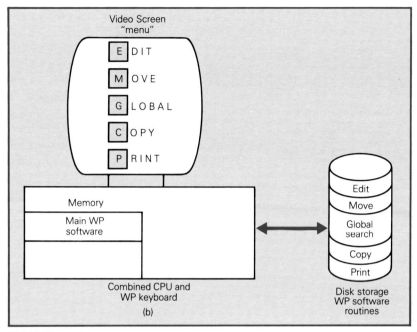

FIGURE 17.9B

FIGURE 17.9C

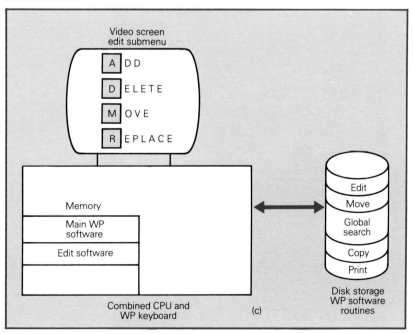

select fields from a data base, etc. Long, frequently revised documents require special repagination software routines as well as search, merge, and sort capability. A later IBM entry, the memory typewriter (Figure 17.10), had electronic storage for one full page plus magnetic tape storage of nearly 50 pages. The dial on the right allows the operator to play back specific pages at 150 words per minute.

2. *Stand-alone word processing equipment.* At this level, the word processing systems usually include full-page CRT display, magnetic storage media, such as cassette or floppy disk, and a fast, letter-quality printer. These systems are really microcomputer-based units with PROM or ROM chips for special functions. Actually, many of these stand-alone display word processors started out as small business computers but were adapted into the word processing area. The Wang Office Information System (Figure 17.11) not only functions as a stand-alone system but has the additional capability of being programmed in BASIC. Thus it can

FIGURE 17.10
IBM memory typewriter.

FIGURE 17.11
Wang office automation system.

be used as a small business computer as well as for word processing.

Word processing, however, is not limited to the larger machines, as many of the microcomputer systems described in Chapter 14 are excellent word processing devices. Much of the software available today for these machines (such as SCRIPSIT, WORDSTAR, ELECTRIC PENCIL, etc.) has gone through several revisions to improve its reliability. Even spelling checkers, originally designed for the larger WP systems, are now available for the micros. A stand-alone system from any of the microcomputer companies costs about $5000, including a letter-quality printer. Even at the personal rather than office level, the time and effort that can be saved by one of these systems is truly amazing. For example, the manuscript for this book was prepared on a Radio Shack TRS-80 microcomputer using SCRIPSIT (Figure 17.12). Here are the steps that are involved in producing a final copy of the manuscript.

FIGURE 17.12
Word processing on a microcomputer.

a.   The original material is written or dictated on a chapter-by-chapter basis. Included in this are special notes to the operator, indicating special spacing, indenting, room to be left for drawings, figure numbers, etc.

b.   The operator prepares a rough draft of the material and stores the chapter on diskette. A copy is printed on inexpensive, fan-fold paper and given to the writer.

c.   The writer indicates words, sentences, paragraphs to be added, moved, or deleted. In addition, figure numbering may have to be changed throughout the whole chapter because of the addition or deletion of an illustration. The changes are made by bringing to the screen a copy of the page that is to be revised. Revisions are made on the screen and to the diskette-stored pages. Then, a copy is printed on bond paper. For safety's sake, the operator "backs up," or duplicates the original disk material to a second disk in case the original gets destroyed.

d.   This process is repeated, chapter by chapter, until the manuscript is complete. At this point, the author may send the printed copy to the publisher but that would leave him or her without a hard copy of the manuscript. Since the author probably wants a visible reference on hand, a second copy can be made by photocopying, but it is usually cheaper to print another copy on your system.

e.   The publisher photocopies the manuscript and sends it to several reviewers who write back with suggestions and comments. The reviews are sent to the author, who then repeats Steps 3 and 4 to produce a revised version of the manuscript. The review-rewrite steps are repeated until the publisher feels that the manuscript is in a publishable form.

Note that these are the classic steps in any text-editing process and would apply to term papers as well as business reports. As more and more writers and publishers get experience with WP equipment and, as the equipment becomes more compatible, authors will be able to send manuscripts in diskette form rather than printed form. The next step after that is to send the material electronically from the writer's computer to the publisher's computer.

3. *Shared logic word processing.* The term "shared logic" means that a number of simple, hardcopy or display terminals share the storage and capabilities of a central processing unit. The main advantage of such a system is the overall dollar savings by spreading the system cost over many stations or terminals. Systems of this type are usually configured in a clustered arrangement so that several units can share a common printer (Figure 17.13). One feature that is shared by all types of word processing systems is a printer that produces letter-quality output either by means of a golf-ball unit or a daisy-wheel mechanism.

FIGURE 17.13
Clustered workstation arrangement.

4. *Communicating office automation systems.* Some of the new so-phisticated WP systems, such as that offered by A. M. Jacquard, have incorporated multiple functions into one system that offers text editing, OCR capability, phototypesetting, diskette and magnetic card input, plus telecommunications capability.

IBM's 6670 Information Distributor is another example of the versatility and flexibility of these systems. The unit links word and data processing functions into a single system. As shown in Figures 17.14 and 17.15, it is a printer/copier unit that gives exceptional flexibility to the distribution function. Its laser printer can change typestyles in the middle of a page, condense oversize output, customize output formats, print on both sides of a page, collate documents, and communicate to and from a variety of devices. With systems of this type it would be possible to merge information from data base storage (names, addresses, etc.) with text material stored on diskettes for applications such as mass mailings.

FIGURE 17.14
Automated office system.

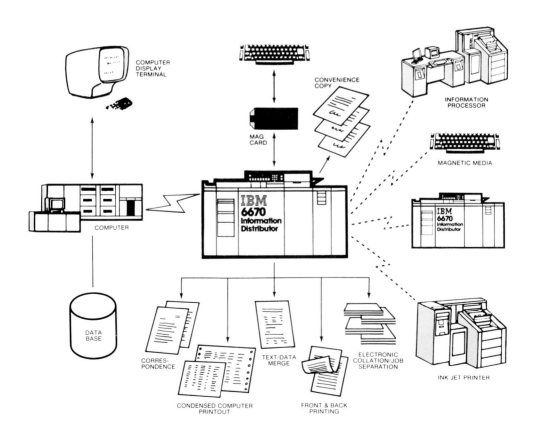

FIGURE 17.15
IBM information distributor.

In effect, one of the most obvious tasks of the computer is that of functioning as a limitless, high-speed address book.

One of the most innovative systems to appear is the Xerox Star Information System. As shown in the Figure 17.16, the system is unique because it allows a user to pick the functions desired by referencing a series of symbols or visual displays on the right of the screen. The system permits not only the normal word processing functions but also the capability of electronic mail, graphics, filing, and communications through the Xerox Ethernet communication network (Figure 17.17).

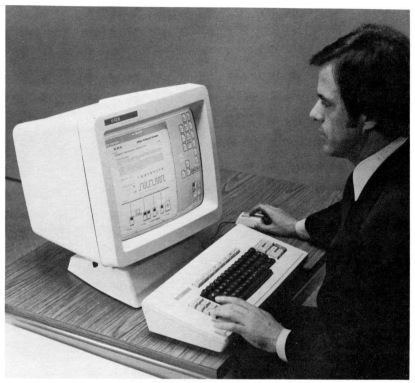

FIGURE 17.16
Xerox star information system.

ELECTRONIC MAIL/MESSAGE SYSTEMS

Although word processing is at the heart of the automated office, the equipment can be used for other purposes as well. Electronic mail systems (EMS) are already a reality in many large corporations. Generally, EMS is used in computer networks or within a large office complex. The purpose of the system is to speed the dissemination of information from one point to another within the corporate structure.

In its simplest form, messages, documents, drawings, etc., are sent from one location to another via facsimile transmission devices that operate over conventional communication networks. With facsimile transmission the document is inserted into a device that reads the dark areas on a document, digitizes the data, and transmits it to another facsimile unit at the opposite end. Here, the dark areas are reproduced onto paper and the message is then distributed to the proper person in the organization.

Electronic mail, however, goes beyond just facsimile transmission. It

FIGURE 17.17
Xerox Ethernet communication network.

can operate from one office to another office, but it is more likely to operate on a person-to-person basis. Under this arrangement each person has an electronic "mailbox" in the message system. A message is sent from Ms. Jones to Mr. Smith and deposited electronically in Smith's computer-based mailbox. One nice feature of the system is that it is not necessary for Smith to be there to receive the message. When Smith arrives at his desk, he activates the terminal and requests that his messages be displayed either in the order in which they were received or according to an urgency code placed on it by the sender (Figure 17.18).

Some messages may be for information only and some may require that an answer be returned to the sending party. Other messages may require the calling up of information from the corporate data base before the answer can be formulated.

A further extension of electronic message systems is electronic

FIGURE 17.18
Video terminal showing electronic mail message.

"conferencing." Participants at remote locations may enter and store their comments, responses to questions, etc., for use at a later date. One nice feature of this method is that the "attendees" can input their messages and read the notes and comments of other attendees at convenient times rather than at a specific time of the day.

A question that should be asked here is "Why is it taking so long to combine the word processing and data processing functions?" As with many questions in the processing world, the answer is not simple. Part of the answer has to do with tradition—the processing of numbers by a highly trained, isolated group of practitioners who "look down," so to speak, on office data processing. A second part of the answer has to do with the unfamiliarity of each group with the activities of the other. As

Willoughby Walsche, executive editor of *Word Processing Systems* magazine says, DP and WP people "live in two different worlds. One doesn't talk to the other and when they do, it is in different languages." Finally, it also has to do with economics. Manufacturers have been reluctant to "jump in feet first" for fear of making a massive and costly mistake. Instead, the entry has been slow and cautious. Amy Wohl, executive editor of the office systems group at Datapro Research Corporation said in mid-1979 that "the integration of word processing components and other information processing equipment into a smoothly functioning single system is perhaps one of the thorniest problems today."

BUSINESS APPLICATIONS

Word processing has made a drastic change in the way things are done at Public Service Electric and Gas Company of New Jersey. Office work of all types is being produced faster, more accurately, with fewer typists, and less overtime. In addition, some jobs that were handled before only with considerable difficulty are now being done in a routine fashion.

Their Wordstream III minicomputer system operates on a time-shared basis to a network of 12 terminals and 3 printers. Both system software and data (letters, reports, etc.) are stored on floppy diskettes. Data from a diskette in one terminal may be transferred to the diskette at another terminal, a feature that permits two or more operators to work on the same project at the same time.

The system, upon simple, straightforward commands from the operator, can edit text in almost any conceivable way. Some of these commands cause the adding and deleting of characters, lines, paragraphs, or columns, moving lines or columns in all four directions, duplicating text from one location to another, deleting text from the CRT display without destroying the file data, merging text, changing margin setting, and printing hard-to-spell technical words.

The word processing system was originally installed in the personnel department, but its success there has led to the introduction of similar but different systems in the financial and statistical department and the engineering and construction department. Productivity in the personnel department has increased by 56% since the installation of the system. Output volume is large when you consider that the department produced 1.3 million lines of typing in 1976.

The most elaborate WP center is in the engineering and construction department. Originally the department employed 76 secretaries and typists to handle a work load of letters, internal correspondence, bid letters (of up to 150 pages each, with specifications), engineering reports, manuals, etc. Today, the job is being done by eight WP specialists. For this department alone, annual savings of over a half a million dollars are predicted.

The key to the success of the new WP system was training and planning. Particularly, managers had to be trained to use dictation cassettes. Standard form letters were designed and stored in the computer. The writer of the letter now calls for it by number and adds the new fill-in data (name, address, etc.) as required. Currently, operators are averaging 1200 lines of typing per day, compared with 400 lines under the old system. In addition, the company has two terminals hooked up to a New York City timeshared word processing service.

SUMMARY OF IMPORTANT POINTS

☐ Information processing is rapidly becoming the major business of the United States, yet comparatively little money is spent on the office worker.

☐ Competition is placing increased pressure on business people to communicate rapidly and accurately, and office automation is a method that is ideally suited to the task.

☐ Historically, the typewriter and dictation equipment evolved at approximately the same time as punched-card processing. The path of the two technologies merged with the use of magnetic media for the storage of typed data in 1964.

☐ IBM typewriters have long been used as computer console devices, and the Selectric model became the unofficial standard for office use in the early 1960s.

☐ Word processing involves far more than just the introduction of automated devices into an office situation. If anything, office automation—word processing—is more concerned with the people who have to make the system operate. Both managers and workers may feel threatened by office automation and their entry into this world should be planned very carefully.

☐ The word processing cycle involves four distinct steps: origination or input; production or output; reproduction of documents; distribution or storage.

☐ Input into the work flow process may be in the form of written documents, personally dictated material, or machine dictated letters. Word processing printed output usually is of higher quality (letter-quality) than DP output because the document is going outside the firm.

☐ "Text editing" is the general term applied to word processing activities. Text editing includes the ability to insert, delete, move, and change words, phrases, sentences, paragraphs, and pages within a document.

☐ A "cursor" or pointer on the video screen is used by the operator to position the system for the activity desired.

☐ Word processing systems generally are not capable of being programmed by the user. Instead, they are turnkey systems that are "menu" driven.

☐ The WP operator interacts with the system software by making choices from a series of menus or possible actions that are presented on the video screen. These choices might include the pressing of a key to indicate deletion of a character or the movement of a block of text from one place to another.

☐ Some WP systems can perform arithmetic manipulations while operating in a word processing mode. Other systems have an extensive electronic vocabulary that allows them to check the spelling of a great many commonly used words.

☐ Word processing systems fall into four general classifications:
Stand-alone, hardcopy devices, such as the IBM MT/ST typewriter and the IBM memory typewriter.
Stand-alone systems with full video display and printing capability.
Shared logic systems that can support multiple terminals.
Communicating office automation systems that combine WP and DP into a single integrated system with a telecommunications capability.

☐ Electronic mail/message systems are rapidly becoming part of office automation. Facsimile transmission was the forerunner of today's systems that allow electronic messages to be sent to individual computer "mailboxes."

GLOSSARY OF TERMS

Electronic message/mail service (EMS)—a means of transmission in which data is sent and deposited in electronic mailboxes assigned to specific parties.

Menu—in word processing applications, it is a list of alternative actions that the system can take, depending upon the choice of the operator.

Text editing—the general term that covers any additions, changes, or deletions made to elec-

tronically stored material.

Typeball—a typewriter striking element that is formed like a golf ball. It contains all the usable characters and cannot possibly jam "keys," since only one character at a time can be printed.

Word processing (WP)—is a system comprised of people, procedures, and automated electronic equipment to more effectively produce written communication.

THOUGHT QUESTIONS

1. Currently there is considerable difficulty in actually merging the two areas of word and data processing. Assuming that you believe this statement, why is it so?

2. Why does the chapter keep stressing the importance of people rather than machines in office automation?

3. Do you think electronic mail could work on a larger scale than that described in the text?

4. In term papers or reports you have had to prepare for various classes, what text-editing features would you like to see on a word processing system? Be specific when compiling your list.

CHAPTER 18 SYSTEMS CONSIDERA- TIONS

LEARNING OBJECTIVES

Upon completion of this chapter you should under-stand the following:

That a business firm is very similar to a computer in that it has its own form of inputs, internal processing, and outputs.

That a business consists of a series of nine subsystems that are highly interrelated.

The four basic steps in systems analysis and design.

How the existing system is studied in order to de-termine its strengths and weaknesses.

How systems flowcharting is used as a study tool to graphically represent the way in which the business operates.

How the study team analyzes the data and presents alternative choices of action to management.

How the systems design phase proceeds through hardware selection.

The need for follow-up after a system has been installed.

CHAPTER CONTENTS

At this point you should be fairly familiar with both the hardware and software components of a computer system. In addition, the last few chapters should have made you aware that data files can be set up and processed in many different ways, particularly with the new data base capabilities that are extending down to smaller and smaller machines. To make things even more complex, you have just seen how tele-communications can extend the power of the computer by permitting relatively inexpensive remote access capability. The next step is to put all these elements together into a data processing system that is effective for a particular firm or application. Before getting to the system analysis and design phase, we need to take a quick look at the overall structure of a business.

THE STRUCTURE OF BUSINESS

In order to understand how the computer is used in processing business data, we need to get a clearer picture of the makeup of a corporation. In a way, the corporation is much like the typical computer system described earlier in the text. Professor L. N. Killough states that the corporation is a data processing system in itself and diagrams the structure as shown in Figure 18.1[1]

Note the similarities between this and a computer system. Input is in the form of resources that are subject to specific operating conditions and operating methods. Typically, the economic resources of money, material, and labor are limited by certain operating conditions

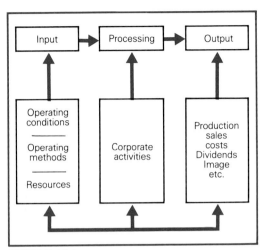

FIGURE 18.1
The corporate system.

imposed by the environments that surround the corporate structure. The existing resources and operating conditions are further constrained by the operating methods imposed by the management, which may be likened to an internal corporate pacemaker.

These inputs are then filtered through the various layers of corporate activity. Processing takes place at every level and probably involves far more manual processing than automatic handling. The computer is simply a machine technique that is part of what is known as "corporate activities."

However, the concept of corporate activities is much too broad to be handled effectively either by computer or manual methods. Several large corporations have tried to use a single computer system to service the entire company operation. Almost all attempts have failed and costs have run into millions of dollars, but business has learned a valuable lesson from these failures: no one computer system can satisfy all users.

BUSINESS SUBSYSTEMS

Perhaps a better way to look at the overall corporate structure is to view it as a series of smaller subsystems that, in total, comprise the business organization. Some of the identifiable subsystems are as follows.

1. Manufacturing systems.
   a. Buying.

  b. Receiving.
  c. Stockkeeping.
  d. Production.
2. Marketing systems.
  a. Selling.
  b. Delivery.
3. Accounting systems.
  a. Billing.
  b. Collecting.
  c. Disbursing funds.

Schematically, the relationship of these business subsystems is shown in Figure 18.2. As simple as this breakdown seems, it should be obvious

FIGURE 18.2

Nine key operations of business.

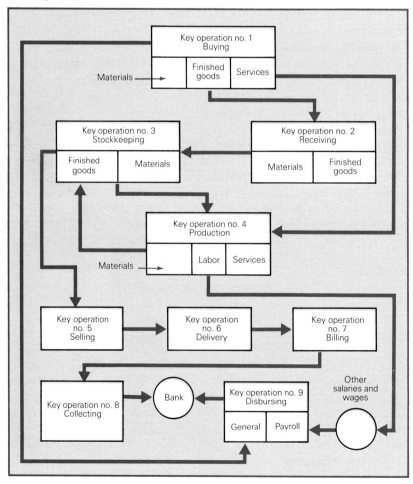

that most of the subsystems are closely interrelated with the other systems. Each needs the other to function adequately. Buying involves receiving and disbursement of funds, and it provides the raw materials for production. In turn, production is as much dependent upon sales as sales is upon delivery and billing. The accounting functions tend to stand alone, and it is in this area that business has traditionally focused its DP effort. Stockkeeping (inventory control) is usually the next area to be automated, while some of the marketing functions, which are highly personal in nature, are often neglected.

Armed with this knowledge of the corporate structure, business managers generally do not try to automate all aspects of the corporate operation. Instead, they concentrate their efforts on the area(s) that is either the easiest to implement (to gain experience) or that will give the greatest return for the effort expended.

One of the first areas that is likely to be automated are those operations that directly involve the income or outflow of cash. Thus, Billing (key operation #7), Collecting (key operation #8), and Disbursing (key operation #9) are the most likely candidates. After that we will probably automate the Stockkeeping (key operation #3), because it is a relatively easy task that can result in sizable savings.

SYSTEMS ANALYSIS AND DESIGN

By definition, a *system* is an orderly arrangement of parts into a whole based upon some rational principle. In data processing terms a computer system is made up of all the hardware and software components discussed so far plus, and perhaps at least equally important, a mixture of people, techniques, and procedures that act as a sort of "lubricant" to make these parts function effectively.

At this point we will assume that our firm does not use computers and that we are now ready to consider implementing a DP system. How do you choose one system over another? Which system is better? Should we have centralized or decentralized data processing? Will communications be involved? Which area or areas of corporate activity should be automated first? Where do we start?

The answers to these questions are at the heart of what is known as systems analysis and design. The subject area of systems analysis and design is very difficult to pinpoint because there are few established rules of the game. However, there are some overall ideas that occur in almost every analysis and/or design of a new DP system. Usually, four basic parts of the process can be identified:

1. Studying the existing system.
2. Considering alternatives.

3. System design and development.
4. Implementation and follow-up.

STUDYING THE EXISTING SYSTEM

The request for a systems study may arise for a variety of reasons, two of which might be that the company's profits are not what they should be, or that operating efficiencies are becoming more difficult to attain. Reasons that are this broad in scope necessitate a very broad corporate systems study. On the other hand, pressures outside of or external to the corporate structure may force an evaluation of specific subsystems, such as production or marketing. Then, too, management may feel that data processing is needed to meet expanding work loads, etc.

The list can be expanded, but the basic point is that the systems study is a review process that attempts to isolate the corporate problem areas and to make suggestions for their solution. Since a full-scale study is a very expensive and time-consuming process (perhaps taking a year or more), a fairly common practice is to initiate a *feasibility* study. This is a limited systems study that is done to narrow the scope of the full systems study so that time, energy, and money are not wasted. It is during this process that management has the chance to think more thoroughly about short-term goals and long-range objectives.

The process may stop at this point if the feasibility study indicates that a further study is not warranted or if such a study is too expensive. The most likely occurrence, however, is that the results will serve as a guide to a full systems study. In looking for a solution to the problem we must be sure that the study considers all feasible methods. Obviously, this includes methods that may be unpopular and out of the ordinary. The end result of the systems study is a set of proposals or alternative solutions presented to management. It is possible that a valid solution may be to restructure one of several operating departments or to shift personnel or corporate responsibilities.

Joseph Orlicky, in his book *The Successful Computer System*, feels that the systems study should be concerned with three basic questions:

1. The technical questions as to whether the problem can be solved with existing computer technology. With the rapid changes in the whole field of data processing, that which was impractical yesterday may be standard practice tomorrow.
2. The economic questions of whether the job should be done by data processing. This point is often overlooked on the assumption that because a job can be done by data processing, it should be done by data processing. Often, the economic expenditure is not worth the result.
3. The operational question as to whether the system, as proposed, will actually work. This point may seem ridiculous on the surface,

but a proposed system is not always a working system. A system that works for one company may not work for another company that appears to be in exactly the same situation. The difficulty is one of manpower, morale, and management.

Conduct of the Study. The systems study may be conducted in a variety of ways depending upon the problem at hand. An in-house study group has the advantage of being familiar with the company structure, its products, and/or services and problems; however, it tends to be stable, biased and, to a certain extent, influenced by corporate politics. An outside study group does not have these disadvantages, but it probably will take longer to get to the core of the problem because of this group's unfamiliarity with the situation. By the way, this latter disadvantage may be lessened by dealing with an outside consulting firm that specializes in the same area of operation.

The scope of the study has already been defined by the feasibility study conducted earlier. Because of that, the study probably will be restructured to specific areas rather than trying to encompass all company operations. The depth of the study will, to a great extent, dictate the methods used. In turn, the depth of the study is really determined by the type or quantity of information required. How is a study conducted? Some of the techniques are listed below.

1. *Interview.* For example, it may be that the information requirements can be satisfied by interviewing company executives who operate at the decision management level. Interview techniques work well at this level and on down through operating management (department managers and supervisors).
2. *Questionnaires.* At lower levels within the company structure, interviewing is likely to be too expensive in terms of both time and money. Carefully constructed questionnaires are often used at this level.
3. *Analysis of corporate records, reports, etc.* The purpose of this approach is to provide historical data to see what has been done in the past. Actually, data of this type serves a second purpose, as it will be used as comparison data in the event a new system is actually implemented.
4. *Forms and records survey.* This part of a systems study tends to be dull, but is an important part of the process. By gathering samples of various records and documents used within the company, the systems study people can perform an analysis of how the work flows through the corporate structure.

The systems study is a well-planned operation designed to gather raw data on the business firm, much as a doctor gathers data on a patient during the examination. Just as the patient should be made aware of the nature of the examination, so should the company employees be informed of the purpose of the systems study. This point is particularly important if data processing is being considered, as employees are understandably apprehensive of "being replaced by a machine." Early in the study, management should make every effort to gain employee cooperation rather than breed hostility by being secretive.

To what kinds of questions will the study team be seeking answers? A broad list is outlined below:

1. What are the present objectives of the particular department or section?
2. Are these objectives being met by present methods?
3. What is the cost of the present method?
4. Is the data that is currently being collected accurate enough to do the job?
5. How is the data collected?
6. Who does the collecting?
7. Is mechanical equipment used now?
8. What forms are generated?
9. Who processes the data?
10. Who uses the data?
11. Is data generated more than once?
12. What controls are maintained over the data and its processing?
13. Who has access to the data?
14. What are the work loads during peak periods? During slack and average periods?
15. How much work is duplicated at each phase of the operation?
16. What are feelings of management toward the workers?
17. How do the workers feel about management?

It is apparent that during the study itself a great amount of data will be amassed by the study team. If the data is assembled in the traditional narrative form, it may be difficult to grasp the relationships of the various subsystems to the system as a whole. It is, then, at this point that another technique, systems flowcharting, is used.

Systems Flowcharting. *Flowcharting* is defined as the graphic representation of a solution to the problem at hand by means of symbols. Many different terms are still being used (block diagram, flow diagram, process flow chart, run diagrams), but two basic types of flowcharting can be identified: systems flowcharting and program flowcharting. *Systems flowcharting* is concerned with diagramming or showing graphically the flow of information in a business system or business organization. A *program flow chart,* on the other hand, is a graphic representation of how a programmer intends to solve a particular problem on the computer. The systems flow chart, therefore, is much broader in its scope and does not get down to the detail that is a necessary part of a program flow chart.

Flowcharting has become a kind of universal language of data processing for a number of reasons. First, it is a great time-saver in that one can describe a system graphically in a very few symbols, while a written description of the same system would be both expensive to create and time-consuming to read. A second advantage of flowcharting is that the symbols usually represent particular kinds of equipment or specific functions that are rather well defined. Once these symbols and functions are understood, even a difference in language is no barrier to communication. At one time there was little or no standardization of flowcharting symbols. Now the symbols have become fairly well standardized through the efforts of the International Organization for Standardization (IOS) and the American National Standards Institute (ANSI). Their symbols plus one or two extra ones used by IBM are shown in Figures 18.3 and 18.4.

The next illustration, Figure 18.5, shows a very simple form of a system flow chart depicting the handling of incoming company mail from customers. Remittances are credited to the customer's account and then go through further processing in the treasury section. Both operations are shown enclosed in dark lines to indicate that they are handled by data processing rather than by manual methods. The same is true for customer billing; and it is even possible that the credit checking operation can be done this way, too. Each one of the blocks in the flow chart, in turn, may be flowcharted further until the operation gets down to a desired level of detail. Ultimately, the automation of customer billing may involve the writing of several computer programs. The advantage of flowcharting is that it allows us to grasp quickly the relationships between the divisions and departments of the company, to see how the individual jobs are interrelated, to understand how documents and reports flow through the life stream of the company, and to see how the business firm is actually managed and operated.

CONSIDERING ALTERNATIVES

After the facts have been gathered, the systems team must analyze them. The first step is to take the raw data that has been amassed and to synthesize it to the point that it depicts a true picture of the area being studied. From these facts the team should be able to spot both the strengths and weaknesses of the present system.

The next step is to draw up a set of alternative solutions for management consideration. Note that several solutions to a problem should be offered. The proposal to management should include:

1. A restatement of the objective of the study.
2. A brief summary of the study methods used.
3. Conclusions drawn from the facts as gathered by the study.
4. Proposed solutions that detail the benefits to the company versus costs to be incurred. These costs, by the way, should be broken

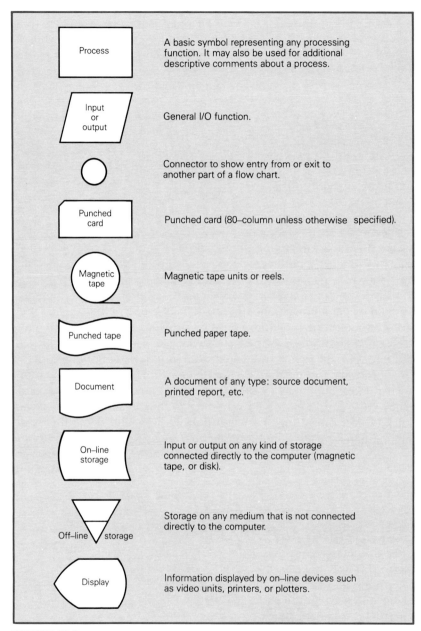

FIGURE 18.3
Flowcharting symbols (USASI).

into immediate and/or one-time costs as opposed to long-term, continuing obligations. The term costs covers a variety of items, such as equipment expenditures, plan facilities, and people costs (training, relocation, etc.).

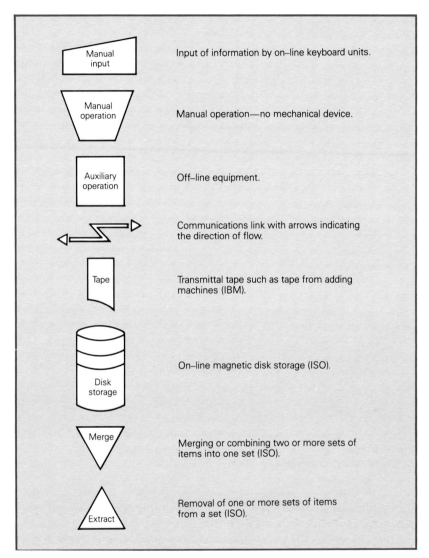

FIGURE 18.4
Additional flowcharting symbols.

5. A listing of the advantages and disadvantages of the proposed solutions (on the assumption that every proposal does have some disadvantages).
6. A realistic time schedule for the fulfillment of each solution.

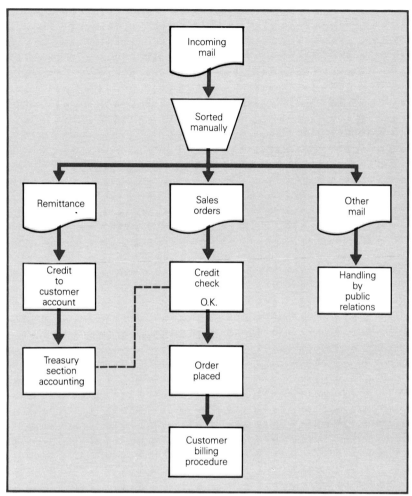

FIGURE 18.5
Systems flow chart example.

If a computer installation is among the alternatives presented, management must be made aware of the true costs and benefits of such a system. Assessing the true value of a computer system is a very difficult task because so many unknown factors are involved. In the early years of the computer age the machine was often justified on the basis of a direct reduction of the clerical staff. This is no longer a valid approach since the staff of the computer complex usually matches or exceeds the cost of the clerical workers who are replaced. Also, as mentioned in the early part of this text, the actual hardware cost is only part of the total cost.

The benefits of a computer system are equally difficult to list. As various management reports indicate, direct labor reduction from automating mundane accounting operations is not sufficient cost justification. The true benefits of a computer system come from:

1. Using the computer as a tool for managing the business.
2. Doing jobs that were impractical or impossible prior to the advent of the computer.

It is, of course, almost impossible to place a dollar value on such benefits, and yet they are crucial in the presentation of alternative solutions. Note that at this point the study group is not choosing equipment or listing the details of the proposed alternatives. It has outlined broad, practical solutions and is presenting them to management for its consideration. It is only after management makes a choice that we enter the third phase: systems design.

Although there have been cases where management has rejected all proposed solutions, normally it will make a choice based on the best interest of the total organization. Consequently, the choice might be based on information that is not available to either the employees as a whole or to the study group itself.

SYSTEMS DESIGN AND DEVELOPMENT

The design of a new computer system is an immensely complicated piece of work that is accomplished by teams of people spending vast amounts of time and effort. Management, of course, is quite eager for results. It has already paid for and waited through the study phase of the operation. It is precisely at this point that management needs to be aware of the value of patience because good DP systems take time to develop. A good rule of thumb is to think in terms of at least one year between the time a medium-size computer system is decided upon and the date on which it goes into operation.

Throughout the various stages of systems design we constantly keep going back to the objectives that management wishes to achieve. We keep asking the question, "Are these objectives best met by a real-time system, by an on-line communications based system, by a decentralized set of subsystems, by timesharing, etc.?" The choices become more clear as the requirements of the proposed system are more plainly identified. Sometimes the choice is limited to copying systems that have proved successful for other users in a similar situation. One common method of systems design is to start with the outputs required by the system, i.e., management reports, accounting forms, legal documents, and the like. Once the outputs are known, the designers work backward to draw up a list of necessary inputs. The business system is then designed to provide this raw data that becomes the life stream of the organization. It is at this point that forms design helps to make the collection, retention, and dissemination of information easier.

Hardware Selection. Fairly early in the design process the time will come when the actual computer hardware must be chosen. (Remember that a time lag of 1 year or more exists between the order and delivery dates.) By now the design team has outlined the broad technical specifications for a system to meet the company needs. Hardware selection is also time-consuming because it usually involves a shopping process. The basic steps in this process are outlined as follows:

1. Specifications are drawn up for the computer, allied peripheral equipment, required software, and vendor support services.
2. Requests for bids are sent to all manufacturers who have any reasonable chance of meeting the specifications.
3. Bids are received from the manufacturers.
4. Bids are evaluated and those that truly meet the specifications are then evaluated further.
5. Finally, a choice of supplier(s) is made on the basis of the ability to satisfy systems requirements, not on the basis of cost alone.

The five steps listed here are basic to the selection process, but certainly they do not tell the whole story. For example, the software requirements may well be every bit as important as the hardware itself. Often, bids will be requested with the knowledge that the manufacturer cannot meet all the requirements. In the case of software, it is then a matter of systems designers knowing other sources of compatible software. Also, it is not necessary for all the hardware to be of the same brand. Often it is more convenient to deal with a single supplier, but a great many modern systems are a true smorgasbord of hardware units. The key to selection is, "Does the system perform?" This question is answered by conducting *benchmark tests* of competing systems. Test programs and data are devised to ascertain the actual effectiveness of a system (as opposed to the claims of the manufacturer). These programs are designed to test both the equipment and the available software, and the results are noted as plus or minus factors in the selection of a vendor.

Personnel and Equipment Considerations. Although small computer systems usually can be delivered within 6 to 8 months, larger systems generally take 18 to 24 months from the date of lease/purchase. Newcomers to data processing are often amazed at this two-year time schedule. The important point to realize is that complex computer systems are not purchased on an off-the-shelf basis like items in a grocery store. Most of the components exist, but they must be shipped to a central point, assembled, and tested before delivery to the customer. In addition, the customer usually selects a few optional items that lengthen the assembly and testing time (Figure 18.6).

This waiting period is actually a blessing for the business firm, since every bit of this time is needed to refine the many facets in the new

FIGURE 18.6
Computer system in assembly and checkout.

system. It is very likely that new departments must be created, new responsibilities delegated, forms designed, and attitudes changed. The single task of drawing up new job specifications is extremely time-consuming by itself. Throughout this whole development process, the designers will lean heavily on all types of flowcharting techniques. Ultimately, the system becomes a stack of flow charts, diagrams, reports, and specifications that emerge from countless meetings and work sessions.

The system designers should look for help wherever possible. Some suggested sources include:

1. *Vendor assistance.* Most vendors have had years of experience in systems design, and their aid is really part of the price paid for the hardware. This assistance can come in a variety of forms, including appropriate manuals, films, filmstrips, and technical advice.
2. *Professional publications.* Magazines such as *Datamation, Info-systems,* and *Computerworld* offer news on current DP activities. Other good sources of information are magazines such as those published by IBM and NCR Corporation. These sources are par-

ticularly valuable, as they feature actual applications of computer systems.

3. *Other users.* Every firm that has installed a computer system has gone through the agonies inherent in such a change. Most firms (unless they are in direct competition) are quite willing to share their experience with others, perhaps because they received help from others in a similar situation.

Except in unusual circumstances, the waiting period is beneficial in that it allows the company to train programmers, operators, and systems personnel. In the early days of data processing the training of programmers was particularly necessary, as there were no standardized languages. Today, however, FORTRAN and COBOL are standardized so that rapid transition from one computer to another is facilitated. Assembly-type languages, on the other hand, may differ significantly, and time is needed to learn and perfect their use in the new system. Most vendors have training facilities to accommodate the users, but lately we have seen considerably more in-house training taking place. If the firm is totally new to data processing, it is usually wise to hire some experienced people to act as a nucleus in the formation of the DP department.

IMPLEMENTATION AND FOLLOW-UP

The last step in the system process is the one in which we finally get to some tangible evidence of the past two or more years of labor. Hopefully, the physical planning has been done well enough that the computer system can be installed quickly on the site. After testing by the vendor (usually a matter of a few days to perhaps two weeks) the system will be released to the firm. Management is now at a critical point: they have been planning (and paying) for the system for two years and now wish to reap the rewards of those expenditures.

Unfortunately, it is exactly at this time that they should not expect any rewards. Instead, they must be willing to continue paying for the system—without visible reward—for six months to a year longer. During this period, both the old and new system should be run in parallel until all the bugs in the new system are eliminated. How long this will take is unknown, but *parallel operation* should be long enough to include periods such as end-of-month billing, quarterly statements, etc.

The additional expenditure of time and money for parallel operation is a difficult idea for management to embrace. However, the horror stories of what happened to those firms that cut over or converted from one system to another without sufficient parallel operation are too numerous to mention. Management's shock can be lessened if this point is well made during the design stage.

Another way to implement the new system, called *pilot method,* is to phase it in gradually in small parts. First, a relatively simple part of the system is tried out in an area that will not harm company operations should it fail. As the system proves successful, more parts can be implemented. If modifications are needed, they usually can be made at this time with the least amount of disruption of the overall operations.

After the system has been running for a while, it is time for a critical evaluation of the entire operation. The original goals of the system should be compared with the actual results. If the goals are not being met, then it is obvious that something has gone wrong in the design process. However, computer systems are fairly flexible and it is very possible that significant adjustments can be made to the system. This, of course, points to the need for constant evaluation to make sure that the system is continuing to meet the needs of the business operation. As the needs of the business change, so should the system.

SUMMARY OF IMPORTANT POINTS

☐ The corporation itself is very similar to a computer system in that it inputs data, manipulates data, and outputs answers.

☐ Most businesses do not try to automate all the nine key operations of business, but tend to concentrate on those that will show the best return for the dollars spent.

☐ Systems analysis and design is a long-term, complex task that passes through four distinct phases.

☐ The overall systems study is a review process that attempts to ascertain how the system is operating now.

☐ Often a feasibility study is made first to determine whether a full systems study is warranted.

☐ The systems study usually makes use of four information-gathering techniques: interviews, questionnaires, analysis of corporate records, and a forms and records survey.

☐ Systems flow chart was illustrated as a tool used by the study team to depict, in graphic form, the action of the area being studied.

☐ The study team analyzes the information it has collected to isolate the strengths and weaknesses of the present system. Alternative plans of action are then presented to management along with projected costs and a realistic timetable for implementation of the plans.

☐ Hardware selection and the training of programming and operating personnel are part of the design and development phase, which may take up to a year or even longer.

☐ Implementation of the new system generally involves a period of parallel operations in which both the new and the old system are functioning. Ultimately, there is a cutover process in which the old system is abandoned in favor of the new system.

GLOSSARY OF TERMS

Benchmark testing—the process of actually testing one computer system against another in terms of time, ease of operation, ability to perform the job as described, etc.

Conversion—changing from one business system to another. The change may be in any form: from a manual to a computer system, from one computer system to another system, etc.

Cut over—see conversion.

Feasibility study—a short-term study of limited scope that is conducted to determine whether a full system study is warranted.

Parallel operation—a time during which two systems are used to do the same job.

Pilot method—the act of trying a new computer system in a single company operation rather than on a wider range of activities.

THOUGHT QUESTIONS

1. What area within a business do you think is most likely to show a relatively high payoff in terms of the dollars spent on computing? Explain your answer.

2. What are some of the problems that might occur if the new system is cut over too soon?

3. The text listed some questions that might be asked during the systems study phase. Add another six questions that you feel would be important to ask.

4. What might be some of the alternatives that are presented to management by the systems study team? Think in terms of a large corporation when answering this question.

APPENDIX A. DATA REPRESENTATION AND NUMBERING SYSTEMS

Chapters 5 and 6 introduced you to the makeup of memory and the general way in which the components of the central processing unit function. The key point was that incoming decimal data had to be converted to a more acceptable form in order to be handled effeciently by the computer's internal circuitry. As you saw then, the representation that was chosen was binary because this format exactly matched the two states of a very simple electrical switch, ON (1) and OFF (0). However, before discussing some of the more common data representation formats, we should first take a quick look at how the decimal system works, as this is how all rational numbering systems operate.

THE DECIMAL SYSTEM (BASE 10)

The decimal is based on the idea of *place value*. By the term place value we mean that a particular digit has value because of its place within the framework of a series of digits. The number 745, for example, is recognized as "seven hundred forty-five" because of place value. Specifically we recognize that the 5 is in the "units" position and represents 5 times a place value of 1. The 4 represents 4 times 10, and the seven represents 7 times the place value of 100. These place values are not arbitrarily chosen, but are determined by the base of the system (10), which increases by a power as we move toward the left. Thus, our rightmost place value is 1 (10 to the zeroth power is 1 since, by mathematical definition, any number raised to the zero power is 1). The next position to the left has a place value of 10 and is derived from 10^1. This pattern continues to the left in the sequence 10^0, 10^1, 10^2, 10^3, etc., as shown in Figure A.1.

A second major point to remember about numbering systems is that the base (10 in our case) determines the number of characters or symbols used in that system. Thus, the decimal system (base 10) has ten digits, 0 through 9, that can appear in any of the number positions. Although you understand the decimal system completely, it is a rather complex system, especially when compared to binary.

THE BINARY SYSTEM (BASE 2)

Binary, or the base 2 system, uses place value in exactly the same way as does the decimal system. The difference is, of course, that there are only 2 characters or digits in the system, 0 and 1. In decimal, the place value is 10 times larger for each position to the left. In binary the place value is two times larger for each position we move to the left. Thus, the rightmost position has a place value of 1 (since 2 to the zeroth power is 1), while the next position to the left has a place value of 2, which is derived from 2 to the first power (2^1). As with the decimal system, this format continues to the left by an increasing power of the base (2).

Figure A.2 shows the binary numbering system, and it should be apparent that it follows the same format as the decimal system. Note that the sample binary number contains only 1's and 0's because those are the only valid digits in the binary system. In this illustration the binary number 10110011 has no meaning to most of us because we are not used to this system.

The problem we now have is that of converting the binary number to its decimal equivalent so that some meaning can be attached to the value. One way to do this is to consider the place value of each binary digit in that number. As shown in Figure A.3, we can add the place value of those positions that were ON, that is, represented by ones.

Converting values from one numbering system to another can be done in several ways. We just finished a binary-to-decimal conversion by using a place-value chart to tell us the relative value of each binary

Decimal format				
Thousands	Hundreds	Tens	Units	Position
10^3	10^2	10^1	10^0	Powers
1000	100	10	1	Value
				Numeric entries (0–9)

Example: 5236 in the Decimal System (Base 10)

Thousands position or 10^3 or 1000	Hundreds position or 10^2 or 100	Tens position or 10^1 or 10	Units position or 10^0 or 1
5	2	3	6

or

6 times the place value of 1 =	6
3 times the place value of 10 =	30
2 times the place value of 100 =	200
5 times the place value of 1000 =	5000
	5236

FIGURE A.1
The decimal system.

FIGURE A.2
Binary format.

Binary format					
Sixteens	Eights	Fours	Twos	Units	Position
2^4	2^3	2^2	2^1	2^0	Powers
16	8	4	2	1	Value
					Numeric entries (0, 1)

2^7 or 128	2^6 or 64	2^5 or 32	2^4 or 16	2^3 or 8	2^2 or 4	2^1 or 2	2^0 or 1	Sample binary number
1	0	1	1	0	0	1	1	

Decimal equivalent	2^7 or 128	2^6 or 64	2^5 or 32	2^4 or 16	2^3 or 8	2^2 or 4	2^1 or 2	2^0 or 1
	1	0	1	1	0	0	1	1

or   1 times the place value of 2^0 = 1
     1 times the place value of 2^1 = 2
     1 times the place value of 2^4 = 16
     1 times the place value of 2^5 = 32
     1 times the place value of 2^7 = 128

equals 179
in the decimal system.

FIGURE A.3
Converting from binary to decimal.

digit. We can convert the opposite way, that is, from decimal to binary, using the same method. For example, suppose we have the decimal number 209 and wish to convert it to binary. We can start the process by analyzing the number to determine the largest power of 2 contained in that number. Observation shows that 2 to the seventh power (2^7), or 128, would be the largest of 2 contained in 209. Next, we subtract 128 from 209 and find the largest power of 2 contained in the remainder. This process is repeated until zero is reached (Figure A. 4).

FIGURE A.4
Decimal-to-binary conversion: Method 1.

Example: converting $209_{base\ 10}$ to Binary

```
      209
   - 128  ($2^7$)   Subtract the largest power of
                    two contained in the number.
   _____
       81
    - 64  ($2^6$)
   _____
       17
    - 16  ($2^4$)
   _____
        1
     - 1  ($2^0$)
   _____
        0
```

2^7	2^6	2^5	2^4	2^3	2^2	2^1	2^0	
128	64	32	16	8	4	2	1	= 209 in decimal
1	1	0	1	0	0	0	1	

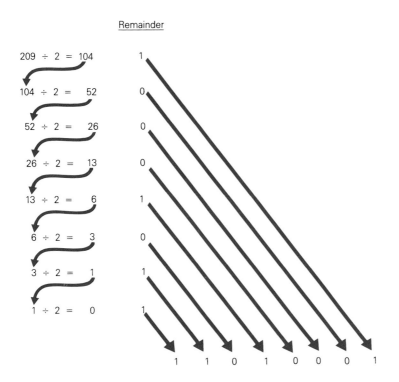

Remainder

209 ÷ 2 = 104   1

104 ÷ 2 =   52   0

52 ÷ 2 =   26   0

26 ÷ 2 =   13   0

13 ÷ 2 =   6   1

6 ÷ 2 =   3   0

3 ÷ 2 =   1   1

1 ÷ 2 =   0   1

1   1   0   1   0   0   0   1

FIGURE A.5
Decimal-to-binary conversion: Method 2.

A second method of converting from decimal involves dividing by two and keeping track of the remainder. Figure A.5 uses the same decimal value of 209 and the conversion process by dividing by two (the base of the binary system).

BINARY ADDITION AND SUBTRACTION

All the regular arithmetic functions with which you are familiar in the decimal system, such as adding, subtracting, etc., can be performed on binary values. The principles are the same, but the process may seem awkward. Fortunately, you are not likely to have to do much binary arithmetic, but the following discussion should give you an idea of how it works.

The rules of binary addition are the same as they are for decimal values. In decimal, ading a 9 and a 1 results in what we call a 10, but is more accurately described as a zero with a one carry to the left. The carry is required because the value "ten" actually exceeds the largest permissable single digit value in the decimal system. In binary the same condition occurs when 1 and 1 are added—the result is a zero with a 1 carry to the left. The rules of binary addition and some examples are shown below.

RULES OF BINARY ADDITION
1. ZERO plus ZERO equals ZERO.
2. ZERO plus ONE equals ONE.
3. ONE plus ONE equals ZERO with a ONE carry to the left.

BINARY	DECIMAL	BINARY	DECIMAL
0101	5	0111	7
+1001	9	0011	3
1110	14	1010	10

Binary subtraction is more complicated because it involves a "negative" form of adding by means of 2's complement addition. Taking the 2's complement of a number is done by reversing the ones and zeros.

Example:

Binary value of 6 is	0110
2's complement of 6 is	1001

When binary values are subtracted, the subtrahend is converted to 2's complement, but the minuend remains the same. To subtract 3 from 7, we would do the following.

	BINARY	DECIMAL
	0111	7 minuend
Regular binary format	0011	3 subtrahend
	BINARY	DECIMAL
Subtrahend	0111	7
to 2's complement	+1100	−3
	10011	4

The result of the addition is not what you would expect, but this is remedied by a carry-back operation in which the leftmost 1 is moved over to the units position and added to the previous result.

BINARY
0111
+1100
0011
11
0100 = 4

If the binary system that you have seen so far seems strange, don't feel badly. After all, most of us have had many years of experience with the decimal system so that by now it feels comfortable, and we can't imagine any other way of doing arithmetic. Today's schoolchildren, however, are very likely to encounter the binary system early in the educational process, since it is an important part of becoming "computer" literate.

Out of all this discussion you should be aware of two points. First, that binary is ideally suited to electronic machines, but, second, binary is not that easy for humans to work with. Small numbers are fairly easy to understand, but a really large decimal number would be awkward for us to handle in binary format. To get around this latter difficulty, and yet still keep the on-off or switching advantages of binary, computer designers resorted to a special form of binary called binary coded decimal (BCD).

BINARY CODED DECIMAL (BCD)

Binary coded decimal is precisely what the term indicates, as each digit of a decimal number is *individually* coded into binary form by the computer. In one of the previous examples we used the decimal value 179 and coded it into binary as follows:

10110011

This number was difficult for us to read, but the BCD code has the advantage of using small groups of binary elements. As a matter of fact, the largest *single* decimal digit—9—can be represented by four binary positions. The decimal number 179, therefore, can be coded into BCD by using three *groups* of four binary digits, as shown in Figure A.6. The same illustration shows the equivalent BCD format of all 10 decimal digits.

THE EBCDIC CODE

As you now know, the BCD numeric bit structure of 8-4-2-1 allows us to represent any of the 10 decimal digits. Alphabetic data, however, presents a problem in that alphabetic characters cannot possibly be represented by any combination of these 4 bits. To get around this problem, the BCD code was expanded by the addition of two extra switches (bits) called B and A bits, which were used extensively in second-generation equipment. These additional bits were used to record the zone portion of alphabetic data as coded in the standard (Hollerith) punched card (Figure A.7).

With the coming of third-generation computers, the 6-bit BCD code was discarded in favor of an 8-bit code that could accommodate

Example: 179 in the Decimal System would become

Place Value 2^3 2^2 2^1 2^0 or or or or 8 4 2 1	Place Value 2^3 2^2 2^1 2^0 or or or or 8 4 2 1	Place Value 2^3 2^2 2^1 2^0 or or or or 8 4 2 1	
0 0 0 1	0 1 1 1	1 0 0 1	in the BCD system.
1	7	9	

Decimal digit	BCD code 8 4 2 1
0	0 0 0 0
1	0 0 0 1
2	0 0 1 0
3	0 0 1 1
4	0 1 0 0
5	0 1 0 1
6	0 1 1 0
7	0 1 1 1
8	1 0 0 0
9	1 0 0 1

FIGURE A.6
BCD numeric coding structure.

more bit combinations. For example, this allowed systems to represent both upper and lower case alphabetic characters in addition to a greater variety of special symbols. Two versions of 8-bit codes were devised: EBCDIC (Extended Binary Coded Decimal Interchange Code: pronounced, ebb-sa-dick) and ASCII (American Standard Code for Information Interchange: pronounced, ask-key).

The EBCDIC or *byte* structure was adopted by IBM and used on their larger computer systems. Most of the rest of the industry switched to the ASCII format. As shown in Figure A.8, the 8-bit structure is divided into two groups of 4 bits. Each set of 4 bits is coded according to the 8-4-2-1 BCD structure with which you are familiar.

The illustration also shows that alphabetic characters follow much the same format as they did with the old 6-bit code. Now the leftmost 4 bits represent zone information, with the letters A through I having a zone representation of 1100, J through R having 1101, and S through Z using 1110. Note the following example of the word "binary" as coded in EBCDIC format.

6-bit BCD Coding Structure

B bit ⎫
           ⎬   Zone bits
A bit ⎭

8 bit ⎫
4 bit ⎬
2 bit ⎬   Numeric bits
1 bit ⎭

Hollerith Alphabetic Characters	BCD Zone Bits	
	B	A
A through I (12 Zone)	ON	ON
J through R (11 Zone)	ON	OFF
S through Z (0 Zone)	OFF	ON

Example: The letter C (12 and a 3 in card code form) becomes

B ON
A ON
8 OFF
4 OFF
2 ON
1 ON

in the BCD coding structure

FIGURE A.7
The 6-bit BCD coding structure.

Zone Digit	Zone Digit	Zone Digit	Zone Digit	Zone Digit	Zone Digit
1100 0010	1100 1001	1101 0101	1100 0001	1101 1001	1110 1000
B	I	N	A	R	Y

This 8-bit coding structure is known technically as a *byte* and has become the accepted term when discussing computer storage. When *alphabetic* data is being processed, the zone part of the byte contains the configuration of bits shown above. However, a large amount of the data that is processed is numeric and, as shown in Figure A.9, the sign code of "ones" is repeated for each digit value within the field. In effect, the sign part of the storage area is wasted, or is certainly not being used efficiently. This is where the byte format offers the programmer the advantage of making efficient use of storage. Because a

Numeric Character	EBCDIC 8-Bit Coding	
	Sign	Digit
0	1111	0000
1	1111	0001
2	1111	0010
3	1111	0011
4	1111	0100
5	1111	0101
6	1111	0110
7	1111	0111
8	1111	1000
9	1111	1001

Alphabetic Character	EBCDIC 8-Bit Coding	
	Zone	Digit
A	1100	0001
B	1100	0010
C	1100	0011
D	1100	0100
E	1100	0101
F	1100	0110
G	1100	0111
H	1100	1000
I	1100	1001
J	1101	0001
K	1101	0010
L	1101	0011
M	1101	0100
N	1101	0101
O	1101	0110
P	1101	0111
Q	1101	1000
R	1101	1001
S	1110	0010
T	1110	0011
U	1110	0100
V	1110	0101
W	1110	0110
X	1110	0111
Y	1110	1000
Z	1110	1001

FIGURE A.8
EBCDIC coding structure.

byte is composed of two identical 4-bit parts (often called *nibbles*), it is possible for the programmer to condense *numeric* data into fewer bytes of storage. For example, the value 73594 is represented in five EBCDIC bytes.

byte	byte	byte	byte	byte
Sign Digit	Sign Digit	Sign Digit	Sign Digit	Sign Digit
1111 0111	1111 0011	1111 0101	1111 1001	1111 0100
7	3	5	9	4

An instruction to PACK the data causes the following action to take place.

	byte	byte	byte	byte	byte
	Sign Digit	Sign Digit	Sign Digit	Sign Digit	Sign Digit
Before packing	1111 0111	1111 0011	1111 0101	1111 1001	1111 0100
	7	3	5	9	4
After	0111	0011	0101	1001	0100 1111
packing	7	3	5	9	4 sign

Note that the sign of the data field is represented in one nibble. Thereafter, two digits can be held in a single byte of storage. Consequently, 5 bytes of data have been compressed or packed down to 3.

Within certain limits the programmer determines the format the data will take. When data enters into or exits from the computer, via card reading or printing, it must be in *zoned* or EBCDIC format wherein each character takes up 1 byte of storage. Unfortunately, on most machines, no calculations can be performed on data in this form. The programmer then has two choices:

1. Pack the data (as shown earlier) and use special pack-type arithmetic instructions.
2. Convert the data to binary form and use special binary-type arithmetic instructions.

If relatively little arithmetic processing is needed, the work will probably be done with the data in packed format. If extensive arithmetic processing is required, it will be more economical for the programmer to convert the data to binary as shown in Figure A.9.

THE HEXADECIMAL SYSTEM (BASE 16)

As long as we humans are working with decimal values, we are relatively accurate and efficient. We are even fairly good at working with BCD (binary coded decimal) because the maximum size of each BCD group is four bits in the familiar 8-4-2-1 configuration. When working

Incoming Value: 3682

a Zoned Byte Format	1111 0011	1111 0110	1111 1000	1111 0010
(32) bits of storage)	3	6	8	2

b Packed Byte Format	0000 0011	0110 1000	0010 1111
(24 bits of storage)	0 3	6 8	2 sign

c Binary format	0011100	11000010
(16 bits of storage)	Sign bit position	

FIGURE A.9
Storage format: Numeric data.

with numbers expressed in pure binary form, particularly if the number is large, we are likely to become both inaccurate and inefficient. And yet, programmers have to deal with this situation all the time. When a program fails, the programmer often needs to make use of a memory "dump," which is the printed contents of memory. By now you know that memory is nothing more than 1's and 0's, and if it is a byte-oriented machine, we will get eight 1's and 0's printed out for *every* byte of memory. If we have a 100,000-byte . emory, the printer will output 800,000 ones and zeros. Imagine trying to figure out the decimal equivalent of the following string of bits taken from part of a dump:

1111 0010 1111 0011 1111 1001 0000 0001 0011 1000 1111

The BCD system shown earlier was fine for decimal values up to 9 because the 8-4-2-1 configuration could represent this easily. By looking at the configuration of 1's and 0's shown above you can see that the BCD system cannot represent a configuration of 1111 or, for that matter, any 4-bit configuration that is larger than nine. There are up to 16 possible combinations that can be made from the 8-4-2-1 configuration, and this is where the hexadecimal (base 16) system comes into use.

The hexadecimal numbering system uses 16 as its base rather than 10 for decimal or 2 for binary. Of course, this means that the system has 16 characters, or symbols. The decimal system, with which we are familiar, has only 10 digits (0 through 9); and we simply have no single digit that can represent a value beyond nine. The hexadecimal system, however, requires 6 additional characters A, B, C, D, E, and F to serve this purpose. Their relationship to decimal is shown in Figure A.10. Conversion from decimal to hexadecimal can be accomplished by several mathematical methods; but the important point is that hexadecimal, itself being a power of 2 (binary), is easily converted to and from binary coded decimal.

The table shown earlier can now be expanded to include the binary coding of hexadecimal.

Decimal	Hexadecimal	Binary 8421
0	0	0000
1	1	0001
2	2	0010
3	3	0011
4	4	0100
5	5	0101
6	6	0110
7	7	0111
8	8	1000
9	9	1001
10	A	1010
11	B	1011
12	C	1100
13	D	1101
14	E	1110
15	F	1111

FIGURE A.10
Hexadecimal representation.

Decimal	Hexadecimal
0	0
1	1
2	2
3	3
4	4
5	5
6	6
7	7
8	8
9	9
10	A
11	B
12	C
13	D
14	E
15	F

Four thousand ninety sixes	Two hundred fifty sixes	Sixteens	Units	Position
16^3 4096	16^2 256	16^1 16	16^0 1	Powers Value
				Numeric entries (0-9, A-F)

Place value in the hexadecimal system follows the same rules as in all other numbering systems.

Example: A4C8 in the Hexadecimal System

	Place Value		
16^3 or 4096	16^2 or 256	16^1 or 16	16^0 or 1
A	4	C	8

8 times the place value of 16^0 = 8

C (or 12) times the place value of 16^1. Twelve times sixteen = 192

4 times 256 = 1024

A (or 10) times 4096 = 40960

42,184

or $A4C8_{16}$ = $42,184_{10}$

```
FP REG   41DF6D87  00000000  4EC00000  0000000D    BE871000  00000000  4F000B6B
002800   00E2E8E2  F0F1F340  00E2E3E4  C4C5D5E3    60C4C1E3  C1404040  40404040
002830   40404040  00000000  0000F0F0  F0F0FCF0    F0C4D6E2  61E3D6E2  61F3F6FC
002860   00002850  0000FFFF  00002800  0000FF84    FFFFFF7C  00002850  C0002798
002890   000047F8  00000440  00000000  00000050    00000000  00000000  00000000
0028C0   00000000  00000000  0000C000  00C028FB    00002902  58C0F0C6  5BECC000
0028F0   47F0F0AC  98CEF03A  90ECD00C  185D989F    F0BA9110  D0480719  07FF0700
002920   0000388C  00003D3E  C3D6C2C6  F0F0F0F1    D7D9D6C2  F0F54040  F1F128F9
002950   40404040  40404040  40404040  40404040    40404040  40404040  40404040
002980   E2404040  40404040  40404040  40404040    40404040  40404040  40404040
0029B0   40404040  40404040  40404040  40404040    40404040  40404040  40404040
0029E0   40404040  40404040  40404040  40404040    40404040  40404040  40404040
002A10   4040D8E4  C1D5E3C9  E3E840D6  D540D6D9    C4C5D940  40404040  40404040
002A40   242E5810  25BC58F1  001045EF  000C9240    22C6D276  22C722C6  581025C0
002A70   001045EF  00185810  25C458F1  001045EF    000495F1  22944770  20A8D202
002AA0   20C0D206  230D24AC  47F020C6  D206230D    24H3D215  22D72276  404040D7
002AD0   40404040  40404040  40404040  40404040    40404040  40404040  40404040
         --SAME--
002B30   400029F8  0A020AF3  F0F0F0F0  F0F0F3F3    F3002174  00002890  00002988
002B60   103C4340  10404144  0001424C  10500501    1052F1C8  C8D6D9D5  40404C40
002B90   C9D5C740  40404040  D5E4E3E2  40404040    40404040  E6C1E2C8  C5D9E240
0028C0   C540C1E2  D4C2D3E8  C8C1D5C4  D3C540C2    C1D9E240  D3C9C7C8  E3404040
0028F0   40404040  40404040  40404040  40404040    40404040  40404040  40404040
```

FIGURE A.11
Memory dump in hexadecimal format.

Our binary memory dump (all 1's and 0's) can now be printed in hexadecimal form (Figure A.11), with each hexadecimal character representing *half* a byte.

1101	0010	1100	0011	1111	1001	0000	0001	0011	1000
D	2	C	3	F	9	0	1	3	8

THE ASCII CODE

The 8-bit EBCDIC code was first used by IBM in their System 360 series of computers that were brought out in the mid-1960s and has been continued through most of their current computer systems. However, a second standard, the American Standard Code for Information Interchange (ASCII: pronounced, ask-key, exists. (Figure A.12).

It was developed to provide a standardized code for the communication of information from one machine to another, including machines built by different firms. Today it is used on most microcomputers and the larger, non-IBM computers.

Character	Code
A	01000001
B	01000010
C	01000011
D	01000100
E	01000101
F	01000110
G	01000111
H	01000100
I	01001001
J	01001010
K	01001011
L	01001100
M	01001101
N	01001110
O	01001111
P	01010000
Q	01010001
R	01010010
S	01010011
T	01010100
U	01010101
V	01010110
W	01010111
X	01011000
Y	01011001
Z	01011010
0	00110000
1	00110001
2	00110010
3	00110011
4	00110100
5	00110101
6	00110110
7	00110111
8	00111000
9	00111001

FIGURE A.12
ASCII coding structure.

APPENDIX B. BUYING A MICROCOMPUTER

TANDY/RADIO SHACK
IBM PERSONAL COMPUTER
APPLE COMPUTERS

One of the most commonly asked questions these days is, "What brand of microprocessor should I buy?" Other variations of the question include, "Which do you recommend: Radio Shack or an Apple computer?" or "Is an Atari better than a Commodore computer?" The answer, of course, is that there is no clear-cut response to any of these or similar questions.

Even if you know relatively little about computers, you can go a long way toward answering your own question by doing a little bit of "detective work." You may have to do some digging, but the time and effort will be very much worth it. We can start with perhaps the most important question of all.

1. What do you intend to do with the computer?

    This question is not as foolish as it may seem because a great many potential buyers really have no idea of what they would do with a computer. Are you interested mainly in playing games? If so, then you don't need to buy a programmable machine, nor do you need to buy a video screen, since most devices of this type plug into a standard television set. If your response is that you not only wish to play games but would also like to be able to write programs, then other questions must be asked that will help to pinpoint your needs.

    What kind of programs do you want to run? If the only program you can think of running is one to balance your checkbook, you may want to reconsider whether the expenditure of perhaps a thousand dollars is worth it to do something that you have been doing manually for years. If your answer is in terms of multiple uses involving checkbook balancing, lists of recipes, lists of addresses and telephone numbers, stocks and bonds or general investment listings, letter writing, school reports, investment analysis, amortization schedules, computer-assisted instruction, income tax preparation, and so forth, then it appears that you really could use a personal computer.

An interesting phenomenon seems to apply to new owners or users of home computers. Either the computer is treated much like a Christmas toy that is used less and less as its newness wears off, or almost the exact reverse occurs. Each application the latter sees, hears about, or programs, seems to suggest two or three more ways in which the computer can be used. After a short while, these people can't imagine how they survived without a machine before. So, assuming that you got by the first question successfully, the next question concerns the software your unnamed machine will use.

2.   What about software?

This is a general catchall question that needs to be broken down a little further. Do you intend to write your own programs? If so, fine, because virtually all microcomputers above the game level are programmable. What language do you intend to use? BASIC is the most commonly used language, but if you want an unusual language your choice of machines may be limited. If you choose not to do the programming, then you have to consider whether "canned" software to do these tasks is available. If the software you want is not available now, is it likely that it will be available shortly? If the software is available, is it any good? Occasionally, data processing magazines attempt to rate various software packages, but the best way to find out is to talk to someone who has used that particular program.

Has the software been on the market long? How many others are using it? Is there only one source for the software you have in mind?

3.   What about service?

Is service available locally for the machine you're thinking of buying? If so, what are the arrangements? How much does it cost? Do they guarantee a repair time? Does the vendor provide carry-in, over-the-counter service? Do they sell maintenance contracts? Most vendors offer several types of service agreements and the general rate seems to be about 10% of the original purchase price per year.

Are you considering a mixed system, that is, made up of components from competing manufacturers? (For example, a brand X central processing unit, a brand Y printer, and a brand Z disk.) If so, will one vendor service all these devices? The classic problem in a mixed system is that the manufacturer of each device feels that its own device is not to blame for the problem—the problem is always in another piece of equipment.

Service is an extremely important point to be considered in your purchase of a computer system: Do not take it lightly! All you need is one experience to convince you of its importance. For example, a broken printer may have the net effect of rendering the whole system useless until that device is fixed. Now, imagine calling the vendor from whom you purchased the printer and being told that repair is not done locally and that it must be boxed and shipped to a distant city. A phone call to a service center may produce an answer stating that normal repairs will be done within *three* weeks. (Oh yes, for an extra fee, perhaps $50, the time can be cut down to three to five days.) One lesson to be learned from all this is to save the boxes in which the equipment was originally packed. Doing so can save a lot of grief and misery later.

So far we have only considered hardware maintenance, but software support and maintenance is even more important. Unfortunately, it is an item that is often overlooked by the first-time buyer.

Can the local vendor answer your questions concerning the operation (or nonoperation) of the software? If the local vendor can't do this, can you contact the company that produced the program? Does the company have a "hot-line" service that enables you to get a quick response to a particularly nagging problem? Is there some organized way in which you can be informed of or have access to software updates or patches (along with an intelligible explanation of the changes)?

Does the vendor offer classes to teach you BASIC programming or operation of the system? Are the manuals understandable? Some microcomputer manufacturers have training guides with audio cassettes to help you through the starting-up phase.

4. What hardware will your applications require?

Is a small amount of memory sufficient for your needs or do you need raw "number crunching" power? Will your applications generate large data files? Most personal computers today are sold with at least one diskette with the provision for one or more additional diskette drives. Will this be enough for your needs? If not, you may need hard disk storage.

What about the video screen—is it wide enough for your needs? How many lines can be displayed on a full screen? What about the quality of the characters displayed on the screen? Do you need color capability?

Do you have need for printed output? If so, you have to consider the quality, the quantity, and speed of the output. Will a regular matrix printer give you the print quality you need? Do your applications require letter-quality output? If so, then you will need a daisy wheel printer or some other device that gives near-letter-quality output? Are you going to print graphic material? Is black print sufficient or do you need color output?

You should also consider the speed of the output device. Generally, the faster the device, the higher the cost. The answer to how much data you intend to print will determine whether or not you need a heavy-duty or light-duty output device. Beyond that you can consider the cost of paper (plain paper is cheap, thermal or special papers are expensive), ribbon expense, and the amount of noise generated by the printer.

5. Can the system be expanded or upgraded?

The chances are fairly great that, at the moment, you cannot envision all the future uses of your computer. Therefore, you should choose a machine that has the capability of being expanded or upgraded. For example, to what extent can memory be expanded. Early microprocessors had memory limits of 32K or 64K, but many of today's machines can go to 128K or 256K or even 512K. How many disk drives can be added? Does it have communications capability?

What about software expansion—can other programming languages or application packages be added to the system? Does the use of software *not* supported by the manufacturer negate any warranties?

6. How much do you have to spend on a computer system?

Remember that a computer system cost is more than just the equipment itself. Some of the costs you need to consider are listed below.

a. Hardware costs—system components.

b. Cables to link various system components (printers, disks, etc.).

c. Set-up or installation (you should be able to do your own setup by following the directions, much like assembling a Christmas toy).

d. Furniture to house or hold the components.

e. Paper, printer ribbons, diskettes.

f. Line filters to minimize wide electrical fluctuations. (Although it is not required, a microprocessor should be on a circuit by itself. That eliminates the problem of what might happen if someone turns on a toaster, a hair dryer, and an electric heater while you are running a program!)

Along this same line of thinking, it is not wise to have the computer in a room that has wall-to-wall carpeting. A person walking across the rug can pick up a static electricity that can discharge into the system when it is touched.

g. Humidity and temperature control are usually not needed with microcomputers although there are limits within which any computer system can operate successfully.

Now, during your search for the answers to the questions posed in the last few pages, you should have learned a lot about the jargon of microcomputers, who supplies specific hardware and software, how much the components of a system cost, and who provides service and at what price. Congratulations! You have done your "homework" and you are now an informed buyer. Here are a few comments on some of the more popular microcomputers. In reading this, remember that the market is changing very rapidly, with new machines coming out every day.

TANDY/RADIO SHACK COMPUTER

Radio Shack pioneered in the production of microcomputers in the mid-1970s with its TRS-80 Model I, which was aimed at the hobbyist market. Priced at $599, the unit was an immediate success and by 1979, more than 100,000 had been sold, an amount that was greater than the entire world total of large computer systems. It used an 8-bit processor, had 16K bytes of memory, and a floppy disk. Today, the Model I is no longer manufactured, but virtually all of these systems are functioning in the hands of die-hard hobbyists who were the pioneers of the microcomputer revolution.

The Model III has superceded the Model I and was targeted as a low-cost personal computer for the home market. It also uses an 8-bit processor, but memory can be expanded to up to 64K bytes and a variety of printers and additional diskette drives can be added. Depending upon the model and peripherals chosen, the price can range from $700 to over $3000. Model III's can be arranged in a network configuration and, because of this and other features, have become extremely popular in educational institutions. A large amount of software for the Model III is available from Tandy and from independent suppliers.

Tandy's TRS-80 Model II was designed for the small business market and was the "flagship" of the line until the introduction of the Model 16 at the end of 1981. A wide range of printers can be attached, but the most apparent difference between the Model III and Model II is the high-resolution screen and the 8-inch (rather than 5¼-inch) disk drives that permit increased file storage space. Hard disk for the Model II was announced in 1981 by Tandy, but many independent suppliers can supply this capability also. Prices range from $3500 to over $8000, depending upon the peripheral equipment and software. Few games are available since it is a business system, but it can be programmed in several popular languages.

As of this writing, the latest Tandy announcement is the TRS-80 Model 16. It uses both a 16-bit and an 8-bit microprocessor and memory can be expanded to up to 512K. Although it was introduced as a stand-alone product, its ability to handle several "dumb" terminals makes it appear to be in the minicomputer class. As with the Model II, it can handle a wide range of printers, hard disks, and soft disks. Perhaps most important, however, is that Tandy provided for upward compatibility for those who have Model II's. This means that programs written for the Model II will run on the Model 16 with little or no modification. In addition, an add-on kit allows the Model II to be upgraded to a slightly less than full Model 16. As one industry observer puts it, "The Model 16 is ideal for the small business with big plans." Sales are made through 250 Radio Shack Computer Centers and nearly 500 Radio Shack stores with computer departments.

IBM
PERSONAL COMPUTER

The August 1981 announcement by IBM of their long-awaited entry into the world of microcomputers was a media event of noteworthy proportions. Almost every report spoke of the machine in glowing terms. *Popular Computing* said that IBM's Personal Computer (PC) was "the standard"—"the definitive personal computer." *Creative Computing* said "It appears that IBM has done just about everything right." However, see and test it for yourself at IBM Product Centers, some 150 Computerland stores, or at Sears Business Systems Centers.

On a point-for-point basis, IBM's Personal Computer does not offer significantly more than other microprocessor systems. However, the general consensus is that these components have been integrated efficiently. The heart of the system is an Intel 8088 16-bit microprocessor that, depending upon the mix, can handle up to 700,000 instructions per second. Memory can be expanded to up to 256K bytes, although technically the system can address up to 1 million bytes. The movable keyboard has been designed with a tactile response and an adjustable typing angle. Auxiliary storage is provided by 5¼-inch soft disks capable of storing 160,000 bytes. Hard disk capability was not announced at the machine's "grand opening," but is available from other sources. The basic system comes with 16K of memory and 5 expansion slots for additional memory or plug-in accessories. The system manuals provide design specifications and information that is planned to encourage private software and hardware vendors to support the system. In effect, IBM has taken an a la carte approach to marketing the Personal Computer by making it easy to design plug-in options. Indeed, within a few months after the announcement of the system, plug-in options were being advertised.

IBM's choice of the Intel 8088 processor chip gives the PC access to a large amount of existing software that was written for that chip. As a matter of fact, PC users have a choice of three operating systems: IBM's DOS (Disk Operating System), the industry-standard CP/M-86, and p-System. To further augment the amount of available software, IBM has chosen not to write the programs themselves. Instead, they are soliciting software from private vendors and accepting for distribution those programs that meet their standards. This approach breaks with the traditional way of handling the software for an IBM product.

One important selling point of the PC is an expanded version of BASIC that features the ability to create complex graphics with simple statements, such as DRAW, CIRCLE, LINE, and PAINT. To business users this means that business charts and diagrams can be created (in color) fairly easily. In addition, the system supports a hi-fi speaker for sound amplification.

Each time the system is turned on, the Personal Computer automatically runs a series of self-tests. Beyond that, walk-in service is provided at any of the outlets mentioned earlier. An annual maintenance contract runs 10% to 15% of the purchase price. The basic starter system (CPU with 16K memory and detachable keyboard and color monitor interface-TV hookup) costs about $1700. A 64K business system with two disk drives and a matrix printer costs about $4500 without any special software.

IBM has long been noted for making extensive additions and changes to their product line. Therefore, if you are seriously considering an IBM personal computer, keep checking with your potential sources of supply right up to the moment of purchase.

APPLE COMPUTERS

Apple Computer, along with Tandy/Radio Shack and Commodore (PET, VIC-20) has long been one of the "big three" in microprocessors. In that grouping, Tandy has been number one in sales, but followed very closely by Apple. Today, IBM has jumped into the middle of the battle, easily displacing Commodore, and may already be number one.

One of the earlier, and successful, entries in the Apple line was the Apple II system, which relied on cassette storage of programs. Today's Apple II Plus is an entirely different machine that can handle up to 64K bytes of memory, multiple diskette units, and assorted peripheral gear. An Interface Card allows the Apple to exchange data with other computers, printers, and accessories in serial format. The standard video monitor features a 40-character, 24-line screen, although larger screen units can be used. As with virtually every microcomputer, it comes with built-in BASIC language capability.

As near as anyone can guess, nearly 400,000 Apple computers have been sold, not only to individuals but to schools and businesses as well. Why is Apple so popular? One writer guessed that its success came from the fact that it didn't look like a computer. Although it may look "cute", it is an enormously popular machine. One important reason is that it has eight expansion slots that allow it to be far more versatile than most people can imagine. As with the IBM Personal Computer, private vendors have designed a wide range of options for the system. The second reason for Apple's popularity is the extensive and innovative software that is available from independent software vendors. Even a cursory examination of any of the popular microcomputing magazines will convince you of this fact. The third major reason for Apple's popularity lies in the extensive documentation that is available. It is not perfect, but certainly better than much of the documentation that is available today. The fourth reason is its reputation for powerful color graphics capability.

All of the above, combined with an impressive array of business software, communications capability, and word processing have made Apple extremely popular. Perhaps its greatest drawback is that there are too many options of hardware and software from which to choose.

Apple Computer has also brought out a newer model called the Apple III. Unfortunately, the initial systems that were delivered did not live up to either the user's or Apple's expectations. The III was, in essence, taken off the market and later reintroduced.

APPENDIX C GLOSSARY OF TERMS

Access time—the time it takes to retrieve data from a storage device or to move it from memory to the control unit. (Chapter 5)

Accumulator—a register used to hold sums during arithmetic operations. (Chapter 6)

Acoustic coupler—a special form of modulator that connects terminals (usually portable) with regular telephone equipment. (Chapter 15)

Addressability—the characteristic of certain storage devices in which each storage area or location has a unique address. This address is then usable by the programmer to access the information stored at that location. (Chapter 5)

Algorithm—a strategy or plan or series of steps for the solution of a problem. (Chapter 11)

Analog computer—a specialized computer that handles data coming from sensing devices rather than data in digital form. It is usually used in special scientific applications or as a process-control device. (Chapter 3)

Analog signal—the signal is proportional to the electrical equivalent of the original communication. (Chapter 15)

Analytical engine—the name given to a theoretical computer envisioned by Charles Babbage in the early 1800s. (Chapter 2)

Application generator—a software program that generates an application program in response to user requests. (Chapter 10)

Applications software—programs written to perform particular business functions, such as inventory, payroll, or accounts payable, as opposed to system software. (Chapter 10)

Arithmetic/logic unit—a part of the central processing unit in which calculations and logical decision-making are performed. (Chapter 3)

ASCII—an international binary code used for interchange or communication of information between machines. (Chapter 5)

Assembly language—a programming language that is similar to machine language, but at a level high enough to free the programmer from working directly in machine codes. (Chapter 10)

Asynchronous transmission—as opposed to synchronous transmission, individual characters or messages are sent at random intervals. (Chapter 15)

Atanasoff, John V.—a computer pioneer who first conceived the idea of an electronic computer. (Chapter 2)

Auxiliary storage—a place for the long-term storage of data. Storage of this type usually is on magnetic media, such as magnetic tape or disk, and has the capability of storing millions or even billions of characters. (Also known as secondary storage.) (Chapters 3 and 8)

Babbage, Charles—an English mathematician, sometimes called the "Father of the Computer" because of his pioneering work with his difference engine and analytical engine. (Chapter 2)

Backend processor—a specialized computer that takes over, or off-loads, the data base processing from the main computer. (Chapter 16)

BASIC—(Beginner All-purpose Instruction Code)—a popular language used on timesharing, microcomputer, and minicomputer systems. (Chapter 10)

Benchmark testing—the process of actually testing one computer system against another in terms of time, ease of operation, ability to perform the job as described, etc. (Chapter 18)

Binary search—a method of searching an index in which the system first goes to the middle of the index to see which half of the index could contain the item wanted. Each succeeding test goes to the midpoint of the remaining part of the index that is being searched. The net effect is that a large index can be searched very quickly. (Chapter 9)

Bit—(Binary Digit)—a single binary position that can exist in only one of two states: ON (1) or OFF (0). (Chapter 5)

Blocking—on either disk or tape, it is the act of placing together several data records in order to save storage space and to speed up data transfer. (Chapter 8)

Branch—the act of causing control to be shifted to another part of the program. The GO TO and IF-THEN statements are branch-type statements. (Chapter 12)

Bubble memory—a memory method that uses areas of negative charges in postive strata to represent binary 1 and 0. (Chapter 5)

Buffer—a small amount of memory in some terminals where data is held temporarily for editing, formatting, or similar functions. (Chapter 4)

Byte—the term applied to one storage position in many modern computers. A byte is actually comprised of a string of eight binary digits and is common to most IBM systems. (Chapter 5)

CAD/CAM—the acronym for Computer Aided Design/Computer Aided Manufacturing, which is the integration of computers into the production process. (Chapter 7)

Cathode Ray Tube—an output device very similar to television on which the computer system can display numbers, alphabetic characters, and/or lines. (Chapter 7)

Central Processing Unit (CPU)—the electronic device that controls all other parts of the computer system. (Chapter 3)

Chain printer—those printers that use a type chain or print chain as their printing mechanism. (Chapter 7)

Channel—parallel rows of bits running along the length of magnetic tape. Modern computers use nine-channel tape, although earlier computers used seven-channel tape. (Chapter 8)

Check bit—see Parity bit. (Chapter 6)

Coaxial cable—a special type of communications cable that permits the transmission of data at high speed. (Chapter 15)

COBOL (Common Business-Oriented Language)—the most commonly used language in the world today and a language that is particularly applicable to business processing. (Chapter 10)

COM (Computer Output to Microfilmer)—a CRT device that takes computer output and writes it onto microfilm. (Chapter 8)

Common carrier—a company that offers data and/or voice communication facilities for public use. (Chapter 15)

Communications channels—paths over which data is moved. These paths or links are usually described in terms of their speed and capacity to carry information. (Chapter 15)

Compiler—a software program that translates procedure-oriented or problem-oriented instructions into machine language. (Chapter 10)

Constant—a value that does not change during the execution of the program. (Chapter 12)

Control unit—the electronic part of the central processing unit that, under program direction, coordinates the action of the system hardware. (Chapter 3)

Controlled loop—as opposed to an uncontrolled loop, a controlled program loop executes a specific section of code in accordance with programmed instructions. (Chapter 12)

Conversion—changing from one business system to another. The change may be in any form: from a manual to a computer system; from one computer system to another system; etc. (Chapter 18)

Core memory—a form of storage in which information is represented by the magnetization of small iron cores. (Chapter 5)

Core plane—a grid of wires upon which small iron cores are strung. A series of core planes are stacked to make up main memory. (Chapter 5)

Counter—a programming device used to control the number of times a program loop is executed. (Chapter 11)

Cut over—see Conversion. (Chapter 18)

Cylinder—a group of disk tracks that are accessed at one time by a single set of read/write heads. A disk pack having 200 tracks on each disk surface would have 200 cylinders. (Chapter 8)

Data base—an integrated source of data that is accessed by many users, and that is controlled by a data base management system. (Chapter 16)

Data Base Administrator (DBA)—the person or group responsible for control of the data base system. (Chapter 16)

Data Base Management System (DBMS)—a package of programs designed to operate internally with a collection of computer-stored files. (Chapter 16)

Data conversion—the act of changing data from one form to another. For example, source data often has to be converted to machine-readable format before computer processing can take place. (Chapter 3)

Data entry—an ordered collection of related data items (similar to a record) as defined by a listing in the schema. (Chapter 22)

Data field—the column or consecutive columns used to store a particular piece of information. (Chapter 4)

Data file—a collection of data records usually organized on a logical basis. For example, all the data records that are created during fall enrollment at a school would comprise the Fall Student Enrollment File. (Chapters 8 and 16)

Data item—the smallest accessible element in a data base. It corresponds roughly to a data field in traditional data files. (Chapter 16)

Data record—a collection of data fields pertaining to a particular subject. A punched-card containing payroll information on a particular employee would be a record of data. (Chapter 8)

Data set—a device that performs modulation/demodulation and control functions to provide compatibility between business machines and communications lines. (Chapter 15)

Data set (in a data base)—a collection of data entries that share a common definition as defined in the schema. (Chapter 16)

Debugging—the act of removing errors or "bugs" from a computer program. (Chapters 10 and 11)

Dedicated lines—telephone-grade lines that are used by a single firm on a leased basis. (Chapter 15)

Detail file (also called transaction file)—as opposed to a master file, a detail file contains information that may be used only once. In addition, the detail records are not likely to contain extensive data fields because much of this information is already available in the master file records. (Chapter 9)

Difference engine—the name given to an advanced calculator designed by Charles Babbage. (Chapter 2)

Digit punch—any of the punches made in the 0 or 1 through 9 rows of the Hollerith card. The 1 through 9 digit punches are combined with the zone punches to make alphabetic characters. (Chapter 4)

Digital computer—a general-purpose computer that handles data in numerical or digital form. (Chapter 3)

Digital signal—a binary process restricted to either the presence or absence of a signal. (Chapter 15)

Direct-access device—see Random access. (Chapter 6)

Disk storage—a magnetic storage device that very closely resembles a stack of phonograph records. (Chapter 8)

Diskettes—small, plastic disk platters used as auxiliary storage on many small computer systems. (Chapter 8)

Documentation—the sum total of the forms, flow charts, program listings, etc., associated with a computer program. (Chapter 11)

DOUNTIL structure—a second form of the repitition or controlled loop structure that permits repetition of a section of code, depending upon the result of a test. In the DOUNTIL format the section of code is always executed at least once. (Chapter 11)

DOWHILE structure—another name for the repetition or controlled loop structure that permits repetition of a section of code, depending upon the result of a test. In the DOWHILE format the section of code may not be executed at all. (Chapter 11)

Duplex channel—a communications path that

can carry messages in both directions at the same time. (Chapter 15)

E notation—also known as scientific notation. E notation is a format for the representation of numbers that are larger than six digits. The notation consists of two parts: a mantissa and an exponent. (Chapter 13)

E time (execution time)—the time during which the instruction is actually executed by the central processing unit. (Chapter 6)

EBCDIC (Extended Binary Coded Decimal Interchange Code)—see byte. (Chapter 5)

Eckert, J.P., Jr.—a codeveloper of the ENIAC computer at the University of Pennsylvania. (Chapter 2)

Editing—as used by the programmer, editing instructions allow the programmer to place a dollar sign, decimal point, debit and credit symbols, etc., in printed output. (Chapter 6)

EDVAC (Electronic Discrete Variable Automatic Computer)—an advanced computer that followed ENIAC; built at the University of Pennsylvania.(Chapter 2)

Electronic Message/Mail Service (EMS)—a means of transmission in which data is sent and deposited in electronic mailboxes assigned to specific parties. (Chapter 17)

Emulation—the act of executing a program written for one computer on a different computer. Frequently, this is accomplished by read-only circuits. (Chapter 6)

ENIAC (Electronic Numerical Integrator and Calculator)—the world's first electronic computer.

Exception reports—reports to management that are generated automatically when a certain condition has been reached. (Chapter 16)

Exponent—the rightmost part of a number that has been converted into E notation. This position tells the power of 10 to which the original number had to be raised in order to generate a correct mantissa. (Chapter 13)

Facsimile transmission (FAX)—a system of telecommunication for the transmission of images for reproduction on a permanent form. (Chapter 15)

Feasibility study—a short-term study of limited scope that is conducted to determine if a full system study is warranted. (Chapter 18)

Firmware—special software that can be loaded into a computer system in order to emulate a specific task. (Chapter 6)

Fixed-point arithmetic—operations on numbers without decimal points. (Chapter 6)

Floppy disks—see Diskettes. (Chapter 8)

Flowcharting—a representation of a DP activity by the use of special graphic symbols. (Chapter 11)

Font—a full assortment of one size and style of printing type. (Chapter 4)

Function—in programming, a function is a prebuilt series of instructions that can be used or called by means of a single word or term. Typical functions are SQR, to do square root, and INT, to find the integer value of a variable. (Chapter 13)

Generation—a differentiation of the ages to which computer equipment belongs. Considerable controversy exists as to what generation we are currently in. Depending upon your definition we are at least into fourth generation and possibly into fifth generation. (Chapter 2)

GIGO—the term standing for garbage in–garbage out. It simply means that if incorrect data is fed into the system, incorrect answers will result. (Chapter 3)

Half-duplex—a communications path that can carry a message in either direction, but only one way at a time. (Chapter 15)

Hardware—the physical parts of a computer system such as printer, videoscreen devices, circuit chips, etc. (Chapter 1)

Hardwired—the physical connection of two pieces of electronic equipment by means of a cable. Usually the maximum distance for hardwiring is about one quarter of a mile. (Chapter 15)

Hashing routine—a mathematical formula that is applied to a key field to determine where the record is stored. (Chapter 16)

Hollerith card—the name given to the punched-card developed by Dr. Herman Hollerith. It is also commonly known as an IBM card. (Chapter 4)

Hollerith, Dr. Herman—a famous statistician and developer of the first punched-card equipment. His name is still associated with various aspects of modern DP. (Chapter 2)

I-time (Instruction time)—the time during which the instruction is analyzed by the control unit. (Chapter 6)

IFTHENELSE structure—another name for the selection or testing structure that uses an IF statement in a simple true/false condition. (Chapter 11)

Impact printer—any printing mechanism that employs some hitting or striking mechanism, such as hammers. (Chapter 7)

Index—a listing of the data records and the disk areas on which they are stored. (Chapter 9)

Indexed Sequential Access Method (ISAM)—a file access system that employs a key field and an index to provide access to the data record in auxiliary storage. (Chapter 16)

Indicators—internal switches that are turned on or off, depending upon the results of arithmetical or logical comparisons. (Chapter 6)

Information—data that is of use to management, as opposed to raw data that has not been worked upon (manipulated). (Chapter 1)

Information Resource Management (IRM)—the way in which a company manages and handles its information. Today, more and more firms are thinking of their data as a corporate asset and are managing it accordingly. (Chapter 16)

Initialize—a programming term that refers to the act of establishing fixed values in certain areas of memory. Generally, the term applies to all the housekeeping that must be completed before the main part of the program can be executed. (Chapter 11)

Input—the general term used to describe the act of entering data into a DP system, or the data being entered. (Chapter 1)

Intelligent terminal—any input/output device that is programmable. To be "intelligent", a terminal must have some type of central processing unit in addition to memory or storage capability. (Chapter 4)

Interactive graphics—the general term applied to any graphic system where the user and the computer are in active communication. (Chapter 7)

Interface—a connecting point between two systems. (Chapter 15)

IRG or IBG—interrecord gap or interblock gap. A machine-generated space on magnetic tape or disk that appears after each data record or data block. Generally, the gap is ½ inch in length. (Chapter 8)

Iteration—the act of repeating a section of code. The term was used in reference to a program counter that keeps track of the number of times a section of code has been processed. (Chapters 12 and 13)

Key—the field or fields on which the index is based and which is used to identify a unique record of data. Common key fields would be social security number, part number, or customer name. (Chapters 9 and 16)

Keypunch—a machine, much like a typewriter, for punching holes in cards. (Chapter 2)

Keypunching—in data processing, the manual act of reading information from a source document and punching it into a card by means of keystrokes. (Chapter 4)

Leased lines—see Dedicated lines. (Chapter 15)

Light pen—a penlike device used in interactive graphic units to communicate between the computer and the user. (Chapter 7)

Logic elements—various forms of electrical switches within the computer. The term is used interchangeably with switching elements. (Chapter 6)

Machine cycle—a set period of time in which the computer can perform a specific machine operation. (Chapter 6)

Machine language—the lowest level in a hierarchy of programming languages. At this level, instructions are usually in the form of a string of digits that have particular meaning to the internal circuitry of the computer. (Chapter 10)

Macro instructions—those instructions that are so complex that a single command generates several machine-language instructions. (Chapter 10)

Magnetic disk storage—storage units using a flat circular plate with a magnetic surface on which data can be stored. (Chapter 3)

Magnetic Ink Character Recording (MICR) —the term applied to the specially devised, magnetically readable characters used in the banking industry. (Chapter 7)

Magnetic tape—a plastic storage medium that has a thin coating of iron oxide (or a similar material) that is easily magnetized. (Chapter 8)

Magnetic tape storage—storage units using thin, plastic tape on which data is stored magnetically. (Chapter 3)

Management Information Systems (MIS)—an information storage and retrieval system that provides management with the information it requires in the performance of its function. (Chapter 16)

Manipulating (data)—the act of working on data to put it into a form that has greater meaning to the user. (Chapter 3)

Mantissa—the leftmost part of a number that has been put into E notation. In the mantissa portion, all numbers are reduced to single-digit whole number plus a decimal fraction. (Chapter 13)

Master file—usually an extensive file that contains relatively unchanging information. For example, a master payroll file would contain many fields that would not be needed in a payroll detail file (date of birth, telephone number, address). (Chapter 9)

Matrix printer—an output device that prints each character by means of a specially placed series of dots. Usually the dots are made by small wires that press against a ribbon and paper. (Chapter 7)

Mauchly, Dr. John—a codeveloper of the ENIAC computer at the University of Pennsylvania. (Chapter 2)

Memory—that part of the central processing unit that is used to temporarily hold the program that is being executed and the data upon which the program works. (Chapter 3)

Menu—in word processing applications, a list of alternative actions that the system can take, depending upon the choice of the operator. (Chapter 17)

Microcode—see Firmware. (Chapter 6)

Microcomputer—a functional computer, usually on a single board or on a single chip. (Chapter 14)

Micrographics—the general term applied to the storage of data on microfilm. (Chapter 16)

Microprocessor—a complete, functioning CPU on a single integrated circuit chip. (Chapter 14)

Microsecond—one-millionth of a second. (Chapter 2)

Millisecond—one-thousandth of a second. (Chapter 2)

Minicomputer—no standard definition exists today because of the rapid change of the industry. Generally, however, the term "minicomputer" refers to a physically small computer that is relatively inexpensive ($20,000 to $100,000). (Chapter 14)

Mnemonic—literally, a memory aid. Used in programming in reference to assembly language operation codes. (Chapter 10)

Modems–see Modulators/demodulators. (Chapter 15)

Modularity—the concept of designing computers in "building-block" format to promote efficient and economical upgrading of the equipment. (Chapter 2)

Modulators/demodulators – communications terminal equipment that changes signals from one form to another because of the incompatibility of computer and communications signals. (Chapter 15)

Multiplexor—an electronic device that takes data streams from many slow-speed devices and combines them into a single, high-speed output stream. (Chapter 15)

Nanosecond—one-billionth of a second. (Chapter 2)

Native language—see Machine language. (Chapter 10)

96-column card—a smaller punched-card designed for use with the IBM System 3 computer. (Chapter 4)

Node—a terminal or connection point in a network. (Chapter 15)

Object program—the machine language program that was derived from the translation of a source program into the native language of the machine. (Chapter 10)

O.E.M. (Original Equipment Manufacturer)—a manufacturer that buys microprocessors or microcomputers in large quantities for incorporation into the items they market. (Chapter 14)

Op code (Operation code)—that part of a computer instruction that specifies exactly what operation is to take place, such as ADD or SUBTRACT. (Chapter 6)

Operand—that part of a computer instruction that refers to data in storage. (Chapter 6)

Operating system—a collection of programs for operating a computer. (Chapter 10)

Optical data recognition—the general term to describe any form of optical recognition of data. Included in the ODR are optical mark readers (such as are used in test scoring), document readers, and specialized readers for specific industry usage. (Chapter 4)

Optical mark reader—an optical recognition device that is limited to the reading of marks instead of characters. (Chapter 4)

Output—the general term describing data or information leaving a DP system. Output data may be sent to the printer, to auxiliary storage, or to other devices. (Chapter 1)

Parallel arithmetic operations—a method by which the computer handles entire arithmetic fields at one time. Computers of this type are usually word-type machines. (Chapter 6)

Parallel operation—a time during which two systems are used to do the same job. (Chapter 18)

Parity bit or parity checking—the built-in feature of the machine that allows it to check itself to see whether the bit structure in the storage of data is correct. Odd or even parity refers to whether the system requires an odd or an even number of bits turned on to represent a data character. (Chapter 6 and 8)

PASCAL—a modern, structured programming language developed in the mid-1970s by Niklaus Wirth of Switzerland. (Chapter 10)

Picosecond—one-trillionth of a second. (Chapter 2)

Pilot method—the act of trying a new computer system in a single company operation rather than on a wider range of activities. (Chapter 18)

Plotter—a graphic output device that draws digits, alphabetic characters, symbols, and lines on paper. (Chapter 7)

Pointer—a data value that points to the next record of data that contains the same key field. (Chapter 16)

Pooler—a device for consolidating and/or converting key entry data into a form acceptable to the main computer. Typically, cassette tapes are converted to standard tape form. (Chapter 4)

Problem-oriented language—a high-level language designed to cover specific programming applications. (Chapter 10)

Procedure-oriented language—a machine-independent, high-level language designed to cover a wide range of applications. (Chapter 10)

Processing Cycle—seven steps (Chapter 3)

1. Collecting the data.
2. Converting the data to machine-acceptable form.
3. Verifying the data.
4. Transmitting the data.
5. Manipulating the data.
6. Storing the data.
7. Outputting the data.

Program—a set of statements or instructions to be used directly or indirectly in a computer in order to bring about a certain result. (Chapter 3)

Program loop—a series of instructions that may be executed repeatedly in accordance with the logic of the program. (Chapter 11)

PROM (Programmable Read-only Memory)—memory chips that normally can only be read, not written upon. However, the application of ultraviolet light can erase the contents of PROM so that it can be rewritten. (Chapter 5)

Protocols—interface control procedures for data transmission. (Chapter 15)

Pseudocode—in structured programming it makes reference to English sentence-type descriptions of the processing function to be performed in a logic module. (Chapter 11)

RAM (Random-access Memory)—memory whose contents can be read and/or written upon. (Chapter 5)

ROM (Read-only Memory)—memory circuitry that can only be read and which cannot be written upon. (Chapter 5)

RPG (Report Program Generator)—a problem-oriented language designed for specific applications in the preparation of business reports. (Chapter 10)

Random access—a storage retrieval method by which the programmer can, through the use of an index, access separate data records without having to sequentially search through the whole file. (Chapter 9)

Read/write head—a magnetic coil device that is capable of magnetizing or detecting magnetism on a tiny spot on the surface of a magnetic storage device. (Chapter 8)

Real-time processing—the term used to describe a computer system in which there is very rapid response to a question, communication, or situation. The term quick-response system is sometimes substituted for real-time. (Chapter 15)

Recording density—the closeness with which data is stored on magnetic tape. The most common densities are 800, 1600, and 6250 characters per inch. (Chapter 8)

Registers—memory elements that function as temporary storage for the computer system. (Chapter 6)

Relational data base—a data base system that operates with a high-level language that allows the user to access data without knowledge of how the data items are stored. (Chapter 16)

Schema—A high-level computer language used by the data base administrator to define the structure of the data base. (Chapter 16)

Scientific notation—see E notation. (Chapter 13)

Semiconductor—memory devices that store information by means of conducting or not conducting electricity. (Chapter 6)

Sequential access—a storage retrieval method that requires a record-by-record reading through the file to find a specific record. (Chapter 9)

Serial arithmetic operations—a method by which the computer handles arithmetic fields one digit at a time, usually from right to left. (Chapter 6)

Serial printers—devices that print one character at a time (typewriter). (Chapter 7)

Simplex channel—a communications channel that can carry messages in only one direction at a time. (Chapter 15)

Speech synthesis—a technique in which human voice is reproduced electronically with enough of the original characteristics to be understood by the listener. (Chapter 7)

Software—the general term applied to all programming support applied to a computer system. Specifically, operating system programs supplied by the manufacturer. (Chapter 6)

Software—in a narrow definition, software is the computer program that causes a computer to perform a particular task. If a broad definition is used, software can include almost all tasks and operations that are not specifically hardware related. (Chapter 1)

Sorter—machine used for placing punched cards into predetermined groupings. (Chapter 2)

Source program—the original program submitted to the computer operating system for translation or compiling. Also see Object program. (Chapter 10)

Structured programming—a disciplined programming technique that ensures a single entry point and a single exit point from every processing module. (Chapter 11)

Structured walkthrough—a formal review process in which the programmer explains the design and/or logic that he or she used in the preparation of the program. (Chapter 11)

Subroutine—a block of code that may have to be executed repeatedly by the main program or routine. (Chapter 13)

Synchronous transmission—a transmission arrangement in which data is sent through the channel at regular intervals. (Chapter 15)

System software—programs that control the internal operations of the computer system. Included would be the language-translator programs that translate program statements into a language that the machine can execute. (Chapter 10)

Tabulating machine—a punched-card machine capable of adding numbers from cards and printing a total. (Chapter 2)

Text editing—the general term that covers any

additions, changes, or deletions made to electronically stored material. (Chapter 17)

Timesharing—a computer system in which a great many users have access to the central processing unit on a timed, rotating basis. (Chapter 15)

Top-down design—the term applied to the theory that program design should begin at the top with the largest module and proceed downward to sublevels. (Chapter 11)

Track—in reference to magnetic disk, the term track refers to the concentric rings on the disk surface on which data are recorded. (Chapter 8)

Transaction file—see Detail file. (Chapter 9)

Transfer rate—in reference to magnetic tape or disk, it indicates how much data can be moved from auxiliary storage to memory per second. (Chapter 8)

Translator—see Compiler. (Chapter 10)

Turn-around document—a machine-readable document produced by the computer and used in a billing process. The form is sent to the customer for completion and then becomes a direct input document to the system. (Chapter 4)

Turnkey system—a operational computer system that comes complete with both the hardware and software for a particular application. The user only has to "turn the key" to make the system work. (Chapters 10 and 14)

Typeball—a typewriter striking element whose form resembles a golf ball. It contains all the usable characters and cannot possibly jam "keys," since only one character at a time can be printed. (Chapter 17)

Uncontrolled loop—a program loop that does not reach a logical end. (Chapter 12)

Unit record—the term applied to punched-card equipment because it uses a card that is a complete record itself. (Chapter 4)

UNIVAC—a division of the Sperry-Rand Corporation (formerly Remington-Rand) and also the name given to the first commercially produced computer. (Chapter 2)

Variable—as opposed to a constant, a variable is a value that does change during the execution of the program. (Chapter 12)

Verifying—the act of checking the original keyed data to see whether it is correct. (Chapter 4)

Virtual storage—a hardware/software technique that allows the programmer to write programs that are larger than main memory. The system automatically breaks the program into pages and brings the pages into memory when required. (Chapter 5)

Voice-grade channels—telephone-grade communications channels that provide for medium-speed transmission of data. (Chapter 15)

Volitality—the term used in reference to whether a memory chip loses its contents when power is turned off. (Chapter 5)

von Neumann, Dr. John—the famous mathematician who formulated the "von Neumann" concept that the program to direct the action of the computer could be stored internally within the computer. (Chapter 2)

Word processing (WP)—a system comprised of people, procedures, and automated electronic equipment to more effectively produce written communication. (Chapter 17)

Zone punch—a punch in the 12, 11, or 0 row of the Hollerith card. The zone punches are usually combined with the digit punches to make alphabetic characters. (Chapter 4)

//FOOTNOTES

CHAPTER 1
[1]*Computer Decision*, January 1977.
[2]*Modern Office Procedures*, May 1979.
[3]*Systems User*, April 1982.
[4]*Computerworld*, April 5, 1982.
[5]*Infosystems*, December 8, 1981.
[6]*Computerworld*, January 21, 1980.
[7]*U.S. News and World Report*, April 10, 1978.

CHAPTER 3
[1]*Computerworld*, April 5, 1982, p. 35.

CHAPTER 16
[1]*Computer World*, February 9, 1981, p. 15.
[2]Robert Goodell Brown, "Toward a Corporate Information System," *Data Management*, February 1972.
[3]James Martin, "An End User's Guide to Data Base," *Computerworld*, May 4, 1981.
[4]McKinsey and Company Inc., New York, *Unlocking the Computer's Profit Potential*, 1968.

CHAPTER 18
[1]L. N. Killough, "The Management System Viewed in Perspective," *Cost and Management*, May–June 1971.

CREDITS

CHAPTER 1

Page 3: *Infosystems*, April 1981, Copyright, Hitchcock Publishing Company. Figure 1.1: Courtesy of Eastman Kodak Company. Figure 1.2: Courtesy of General Motors Corporation. Figure 1.3: Courtesy of Eastman Kodak Company. Figure 1.4: Courtesy of Radio Shack, a Division of Tandy Corporation. Pages 8–9: Copyright 1981 by CW Communications/Inc. Framingham, MA 01701. Reprinted from *Computerworld*. Page 11: *Infosystems*, April 1981, Copyright, Hitchcock Publishing Company. Figure 1.5: Courtesy of Radio Shack, a Division of Tandy Corporation. Page 14: *U.S. News & World Report*, April 10, 1978, Copyright, U.S. News & World Report, Inc. Page 16: Courtesy of *Datamation*, 4/81, p. 222.

CHAPTER 2

Figures 2.1, 2.2, 2.3, 2.4, 2.5 and 2.6: Courtesy of International Business Machines Corporation. Figure 2.7: Courtesy of University of Pennsylvania. Figure 2.8: Courtesy of Sperry Univac Division, Sperry Corporation. Figures 2.9, 2.10, 2.11 and 2.12: Courtesy of International Business Machines. Page 37: Copyright 1981 by CW Communications/Inc. Framingham, MA 01701. Reprinted from *Computerworld*.

CHAPTER 3

Figure 3.1: Components of a computer system—Keith Carver's own drawing—all future references to his material will be shown as DKC. Figure 3.2: Courtesy of Sperry Univac Division, Sperry Corporation. Figure 3.3: Courtesy of International Business Machines Corporation. Page 8: *Infosystems*, April 1981, Copyright, Hitchcock Publishing Company. Figures 3.4, 3.5, 3.6, 3.7: Courtesy of DKC. Figure 3.8: Courtesy of International Business Machines Corporation. Figure 3.9: Courtesy of Honeywell, Inc. Figure 3.10: Courtesy of Radio Shack, a Division of Tandy Corp. Page 57: Reprinted from *Computer Decisions*, April 1981, p. 16A, Hayden Publishing Co.

CHAPTER 4

Figures 4.1, 4.2 and 4.3: Courtesy of DKC. Page 67: Cartoon by Sandy Dean. Figures 4.4 and 4.5: Courtesy of International Business Machines. Figures 4.6 and 4.7: Courtesy of Hewlett-Packard Corporation. Figure 4.8: Courtesy of NCR Corporation. Figure 4.9: Courtesy of DKC. Figure 4.10: Courtesy of MSI Data Corporation. Figure 4.11: Courtesy of International Business Machines Corporation. Figure 4.13: Courtesy of DKC. Figure 4.14: Courtesy of Burroughs Corporation. Figure 4.15 and 4.16: Courtesy of DKC. Figure 4.17: Courtesy of Key Tronic Corporation. Pages 82–83: Courtesy of *The Washington Post* and Art Buchwald. Figure 4.18: Courtesy of Wang Laboratories.

CHAPTER 5

Figure 5.1: Courtesy of DKC. Figure 5.2: Courtesy of Western Electric Company. Figure 5.3: Courtesy of DKC. Figure 5.4: Courtesy of Rockwell International Corporation. Figure 5.5: Courtesy of DKC. Figure 5.6: Courtesy of Cray Research, Inc. Figure 5.7: Courtesy of Bell Laboratories. Figure 5.8: Courtesy of Honeywell, Inc. Figures 5.9, 5.10 and 5.11: Courtesy of DKC.

CHAPTER 6

Figure 6.1: Courtesy of NCR Corporation. Pages 110–111: Copyright 1982 by CW Communications/Inc. Framingham, MA 01701. Reprinted from *Computerworld*. Figure 6.2: Courtesy of International Business Machines Corporation. Figure 6.3: Courtesy of Honeywell, Inc. Figures 6.4 and 6.5: Courtesy of DKC.

CHAPTER 7

Figures 7.1 and 7.2: Courtesy of DKC. Figures 7.3 and 7.4: Courtesy of International Business Machines Corporation. Figure 7.5: Courtesy of Mannesmann Tally. Figure 7.6: Courtesy of Diablo Systems Incorporated, a Xerox Company. Figure 7.7: Courtesy of Mannesman Tally. Figure 7.8: Courtesy of DKC. Page 132: Cartoon by Leland Carver. Figures 7.9 and 7.10: Courtesy of International Business Machines Corporation. Figures 7.11 and 7.12: Courtesy of DKC. Figure 7.13: Courtesy of Houston Instruments. Figure 7.14: Courtesy of California Computer Products, Inc. Figure 7.15: Courtesy of Houston Instruments. Page 137: Reprinted from *Computer Decisions*, May 1981, p. 26, copyright Hayden Publishing Company. Figures 7.16 and 7.17: Courtesy of Hewlett-Packard Corporation. Figure 7.18: Courtesy of International Business Machines Corporation. Figure 7.19: Courtesy of Interaction Systems, Inc. Figure 7.20: Courtesy of DKC. Figure 7.21: Courtesy of Burroughs Corporation. Figure 7.22: Courtesy of Texas Instruments Incorporated. Figure 7.23: Courtesy of Tri-Digital Systems, Inc. Figure 7.24: Courtesy of General Motors Corporation. Figures 7.25 and 7.26: Copyright 1982 by Cahners Publishing Company, Division of Reed Holdings Inc. Reprinted with permission from Mini-Micro Systems, April 1982.

CHAPTER 8

Figures 8.1, 8.2, 8.3 and 8.4: Courtesy of DKC. Figure 8.5: Courtesy of Honeywell, Inc. Figures 8.6 and 8.7: Courtesy of International Business Machines Corporation. Figure 8.8: Courtesy of DKC. Figure 8.9: Courtesy of Braegen Inc., ATL Division. Figure 8.10: Courtesy of DKC. Figure 8.11: Courtesy of Honeywell, Inc. Figure 8.12: Courtesy of DKC. Figure 8.13: Courtesy of International Business Machines Corporation. Figures 8.14 and 8.15: Courtesy of DKC. Page 165: Reprinted from *Infosystems*, April 1981, Copyright, Hitchcock Publishing Company. Figure 8.16: Courtesy of Quantum Corporation. Figure 8.17: Courtesy of Irwin International, Inc. Pages 168–169: Copyright 1981 by CW Communications/Inc. Framingham, MA 01701. Reprinted from *Computerworld*. Figure 8.18: Courtesy of Shugart Associated. Figure 8.19: Courtesy of International Business Machines Corporation. Figure 8.20: Courtesy of DKC. Figures 8.21 and 8.22: Courtesy of Eastman Kodak Company

CHAPTER 9

Figures 9.1, 9.2, 9.3 and 9.4: Courtesy of DKC. Page 187: Cartoon by Leland Carver. Figure 9.5: Courtesy of International Business Machines Corporation.

CHAPTER 10

Figures 10.1, 10.2, 10.3, 10.4, 10.5, 10.6, 10.7, 10.8, 10.9, 10.10, 10.11 and 10.12: Courtesy of DKC. Figure 10.13: Reprinted from the September 1, 1980 issue of *Business Week* by special permission, © 1980 by McGraw-Hill, Inc., New York, 10020. All rights reserved. Figure 10.4: Courtesy of DKC.

CHAPTER 11

Figure 11.1: Courtesy of DKC. Figure 11.2: Courtesy of International Business Machines Corporation. Figure 11.3: Courtesy of DKC. Page 235: Courtesy of DKC. Figures 11.5, 11.6 and 11.7: Courtesy of DKC. Figure 11.8: Courtesy of International Business Machines Corporation. Figures 11.9, 11.10, 11.11, 11.12: Courtesy of DKC. Page 248: Cartoon by Sandy Dean. Figures 11.13, 11.14, 11.15 and 11.16: Courtesy of DKC.

CHAPTER 13
Page 318: Cartoon by Leland Carver.

CHAPTER 14
Figure 14.1: Courtesy of Texas Instruments Incorporated. Figures 14.2 and 14.3: Courtesy of Intel Corporation. Figure 14.4: Courtesy of Bell Laboratories. Figure 14.5: Courtesy of DKC. Figure 14.6: Courtesy of Sharp Electronics Corp. Page 360: Courtesy of Bell Laboratories. Page 361: Courtesy of *Infosystems*. Figure 14.7: Courtesy of Hewlett-Packard Corporation. Figure 14.8: Courtesy of Honeywell, Inc. Page 365: Cartoon by Tom Niemann. Figure 14.9: Courtesy of Radio Shack, a Division of Tandy Corp. Figure 14.10: Courtesy of Hewlett-Packard Corporation. Figure 14.11: Courtesy of DKC. Figure 14.12: Courtesy of Digital Equipment Corporation. Figure 14.13: ATARI is a registered trademark of Atari, Inc. 800 and Caverns of Mars are trademarks of Atari, Inc., Reprinted by permission. Page 369: Courtesy of DKC. Figure 14.14: Courtesy of Apple Computer Inc. Figure 14.15: Courtesy of Xerox Corporation. Figure 14.16: Courtesy of Sharp Electronics Corporation. Figure 14.17: Courtesy of Panasonic Corporation.

CHAPTER 15
Figure 15.1: Used with permission of Anderson Jacobson, Inc. Figure 15.2: Courtesy of DKC. Figure 15.3: Courtesy of Wang Laboratories, Inc. Figures 15.4 and 15.5: Courtesy of DKC. Figure 15.6: Courtesy of Columbia Data Products. Figures 15.7, 15.8 and 15.9: Courtesy of DKC. Page 392: Reprinted from *Infosystems*, April 1981, Copyright, Hitchcock Publishing Company. Figure 15.10: Courtesy of DKC. Figure 15.11: Courtesy of Mini-Micro Systems, Cahners Publishing Co., March 1978. Page 396: Cartoon by Mr. Henry R. Martin. Figures 15.12 and 15.13: Courtesy of DKC. Page 400: Reprinted from *Computer Decisions*, March 1981, p. 27, copyright 1981, Hayden Publishing Company.

CHAPTER 16
Figure 16.1: Courtesy of Tektronix, Inc. Page 423: Cartoon by Sidney Harris.

CHAPTER 17
Figure 17.1: Courtesy of Dictaphone Corporation. Figures 17.2 and 17.3: Courtesy of International Business Machines Corporation. Figure 17.4: Courtesy of DKC. Figure 17.5: Courtesy of AM Jacquard Systems. Page 442: Copyright 1982 by CW Communications/Inc. Framingham, MA 01701. Reprinted from *Computerworld*. Figures 17.6, 17.7, 17.8, 17.9a, 17.9b and 17.9c: Courtesy of International Business Machines Corporation. Figure 17.10: Courtesy of International Business Machines Corporation. Figure 17.11: Courtesy of Wang Laboratories, Inc. Figure 17.12: Courtesy of Radio Shack, a Division of Tandy Corp. Figure 17.13: Courtesy of Wang Laboratories, Inc. Figures 17.14 and 17.15: Courtesy of International Business Machines Corporation. Figures 17.16 and 17.17: Courtesy of Xerox Corporation. Figure 17.18: Courtesy of Hewlett-Packard Corporation.

CHAPTER 18
Figures 18.1, 18.2, 18.3, 18.4 and 18.5: Courtesy of DKC. Figure 18.6: Courtesy of Honeywell, Inc.

CREDITS—
COLOR INSERT

INDEX